70936

Andrew Jackson

&

John C. Calhoun

BY DAVID LINDSEY

Professor of History

California State University at Los Angeles

Shapers of History Series

Kenneth C. Colegrove, Editor

Barron's Educational Series, Inc.

WOODBURY, NEW YORK

All inquiries should be addressed to:
Barron's Educational Series, Inc.
113 Crossways Park Drive
Woodbury, New York 11797

Library of Congress Catalog Card No. 73-2452

Paper Edition
International Standard Book No. 0-8120-0460-4

PRINTED IN THE UNITED STATES OF AMERICA

For my wife,

Suzanne

Contents

Editor's Foreword

THE DUAL BIOGRAPHY presented in the following pages conforms with the Shapers of History Series format in presenting the lives of two men who did much to mold the course of America's development in the nineteenth century. In the "Verdict of History" discussion offered in Chapter X the author traces the changing images of Andrew Jackson and John C. Calhoun. Over the years the images have undergone major modifications varying according to the biographer's generation, the biographer's own individual view of history and the climate of opinion of his own era. The Jackson of Arthur M. Schlesinger, Jr., looms as a far different figure from the Jackson of James Parton almost a century earlier. What Margaret Coit sees as the essential Calhoun stands in sharp contrast to what Herman Von Holst saw three generations before.

While the primary focus of David Lindsey's dual biography is on the public careers of Jackson and Calhoun, this volume also features other aspects of the men and their lives. Attention is turned to their personalities and private lives as these factors played upon their developing careers. Especially sharp is the closeup of the confrontations of the two men from the days when Secretary of War Calhoun supervised General Jackson through Senator Jackson's swearing in Calhoun as Vice-President to President Jackson's showdown with Calhoun in the eyeball to eyeball clash that erupted in the nullification crisis of 1832–33. Stress is further given to the constructive labors of these men in contributing to the mainstream of America's growth as a vibrant, dynamic young country and to the rising tensions that would in time tear the nation apart. Documents, letters, speeches and writings of Jackson and Calhoun, included in the Appendix, allow the reader to taste the flavor of these men's minds and to make his own assessment of the worth of their words and the value of their actions.

The author, Dr. David Lindsey, born in New Jersey, schooled at Amherst, Cornell, and the University of Chicago, has over the years been employed in a variety of jobs—as truck driver, tractor operator, forest fire fighter, brick layer, carpenter, and blueberry farmer. For the past twenty-five years he has been a professor of history—for ten years at Baldwin-Wallace College and Oberlin College and since 1956 at California State University at Los Angeles, where he also served as History Department Chairman from 1964 to 1966. Twice he was selected for appointment overseas as Fulbright Professor of American Civilization—at the University of Athens 1962–63 and at the University of Madrid 1968–69. His numerous articles have appeared widely in many newspapers and historical journals. His published books include *An Outline History of Ohio* (1953), *Ohio's Western Reserve* (1955), *"Sunset" Cox: Irrepressible Democrat* (1959), *Abraham Lincoln and Jefferson Davis* (1960), and *Andrew Jackson and Henry Clay* (1963). Forthcoming shortly will be two additional books—one dealing with the American Civil War and Reconstruction and the other exploring the origins of place names in Los Angeles County.

Preface and Acknowledgments

IN FASHIONING THIS BOOK I have aimed to tell the story of Andrew Jackson and John C. Calhoun in clear, understandable, and hopefully pleasing style. While some background of the historical stage on which they acted is offered, I have chosen to concentrate attention on the men themselves, their personalities and characters, their lives and careers, what they said and did, their confrontations and clashes, their impact upon the America of their time and the heritage they left to Americans of succeeding generations. Throughout the book, but particularly in the Appendix, I have allowed the two men to speak their own parts so that the reader may judge for himself and draw his own conclusions from their words.

The gathering of material for and the writing of this book began while I was living in Spain and lecturing on American civilization at the University of Madrid. American historical materials in Spain are not numerous, but the English Department Library at the University and the USIS Library on the Catellana proved helpful. To the staff of the latter and to my colleagues at the University I hereby give my thanks. Fortunately a summer journey to London made available the magnificent collection of the British Museum Library; to the Library staff there I am grateful beyond measure for their unstinted assistance. I have written this volume from published materials; there is no pretense of working in manuscript collections, nor was there any necessity to do so. I have at many points leaned heavily on the works of other historians. I acknowledge with gratitude my heavy debt to them both here and in the footnotes and bibliography. Any misstatements of fact or misjudgments remain my responsibility. My writing was often interrupted with time out for trips to various provinces in Spain which may account for any rubbing off of the flavor of Santillana del Mar, Bayona, Palos de la Frontera, and Estepona in the writing. Two extended journeys took me to Africa, one to Morocco and the other to Senegal, Liberia, Ghana, Nigeria, and beyond and gave me a new understanding of the origins of Afro-Americans who were fully established in the America of Jackson and Calhoun.

For their good labors in typing the manuscript for publication I hereby express my gratefulness to good friend and Madrid neighbor Raymonde Sol who performed far beyond the call of neighborly duty, to Norma Bailey of Middlebury College and to Verdel Lacour, my student assistant in Los Angeles. To my wife, Suzanne G. Lindsey, for her full assistance at every step of the way and her patient, affectionate help during the writing I give my continuing gratitude.

San Clemente, California   DAVID LINDSEY
May 1971

I Jackson: "Hero of New Orleans" in the Making, 1767-1815

ON MARCH 4, 1829 the city of Washington teemed with "a monstrous crowd of people." Ohio farmers, Pennsylvania mechanics, Baltimore teamsters, Virginia tobacco men, Tennessee backwoodsmen shouldered through the muddy streets bumping against politicians, judges, businessmen, planters, and assorted adventurers. "Persons have come from five hundred miles," recorded one observer, to see Andrew Jackson sworn in as President, "and they really seem to think the country is rescued from some dreadful danger." Most came to see for themselves whether Jackson was the "savage barbarian" or "gracious gentleman," as billed in the 1828 campaign. Surely he must be a giant of heroic proportions.

Many truly believed that the Old Hero was saving the country from the triple danger of corruption, privilege, and bloated aristocracy, as he had earlier saved it from the British and Indians. A new departure was at hand. For the first time in the Republic's 30-year history a non-Easterner, a self-made man risen by his own strength from backwoods obscurity, a non-college graduate, a non-professional politician would be President. This new Messiah would lead the people out of the wilderness of corruption and intrigue into the Promised Land of moral virtue and political integrity. It was rightly the People's day. Democracy was about to come into its own.

As thousands clustered on the steps of the Capitol's east portico and spilled across the grounds, inside the newly remodeled Senate chamber, the tall, angular form of John C. Calhoun strode to the dais, gavelled for order and took the oath as Vice President of the United States. At his left sat the diplomatic corps in colorful dress, on the right John Marshall and his fellow, black-robed Supreme Court justices. Scattered through the chamber were House members, new cabinet officials, uniformed army and navy officers, and visiting notables. At 11:30 A.M. Andrew Jackson, grave, dignified, straight, of weathered face under a shock of bristling white hair, was escorted to the front of the chamber where Vice President Calhoun gave formal greeting. A few moments later they walked together out on to the east portico for the inauguration ceremony.

These two men—Jackson and Calhoun—had come far from their obscure beginnings in the Carolina upcountry. In the preceding twenty years they had helped advance the nation's destiny. Clearly they deserved the popular acclaim of their fellow citizens. Now they stood, facing the roaring crowd—Jackson at the pinnacle of political success, Calhoun just a rung below. Doubtless through their minds raced images of the paths they had traveled to reach this moment of triumph.

The pages that follow in this book survey the lives, careers, thoughts, words, and actions of Jackson and Calhoun. The points at which their lives touched, where their paths crossed, where they supported and aided each other, where they came into collision and clashed will be examined. Attention will also focus on their major ideas, their stands on the chief questions and issues of their day. Policies that they advocated, steps they took to implement their policies will be explored. A close look will be taken at what impact they had on the growth of the United States, how their lives, careers, ideas, and actions affected the course of the nation's history. Fascinating men in their own right, Jackson and Calhoun deserve the attention of Americans not only for the color and force of their own personalities and careers, but because they came to personify in varying degrees those larger forces—nationalism, sectionalism, democracy, and expansion—that shaped the development of nineteenth century America.

During the lifetimes of Jackson and Calhoun the United States experienced a phenomenal growth by all measures. Territory, which touched only the Mississippi River when Jackson first entered politics, stretched westward to the Rockies in 1803 with the purchase of Louisiana. Florida was added in 1819, Texas in 1845, Oregon a year later, and the Mexican cession in 1848 pushed the nation to the Pacific shore. The American people, numbering 7 million in 1810, grew to over 12 million by 1830 and jumped to 23 million by mid-century, when European immigrants poured in at an annual rate of over 200,000. National wealth rose from $2.5 billion in 1810 to $3.8 billion twenty years later and then doubled by 1850.

The growth of wealth reflected swift economic changes in the nation. While most Americans continued to make their living as farmers during the first half of the nineteenth century, the proportion declined from ¾ in 1820 to less than ⅔ in 1850. Commerce, shipping, mining, manufacturing, transportation gained in proportionate numbers. Indeed, a revolution in transportation was the era's most spectacular feature. Oxcart and stage coach yielded to steam locomotive; flatboat and scow gave way to river steamboat. Farm production grew dramatically by 1850, with cotton and wheat surpluses dominating American exports and producing much needed foreign exchange. Manufacturing of textiles was well established in New England and the Middle States by the 1830's. Iron making grew increasingly productive in Pennsylvania, Ohio, and Kentucky. Banking and finance centered in Philadelphia, New York, and Boston. Most businesses were relatively small, capitalized at less than $100,000 and run by an individual entrepreneur. In the congenial climate of *laissez faire* that the Jackson era did much to buttress, with its unrestrained, individual economic enterprise, men vigorously exploited whatever economic opportunities they found. Promoters discovered that the business corporation offered large advantages for generating capital and limiting personal risk. Under government-issued charters of incorporation, business firms could raise large sums of capital, limit owners' liability, hire professional managers, and make profits in such varied operations as insurance, banking, road and canal building, mercantile and manufacturing operations. The United States pushed far along the road to becoming an industrial, business-oriented society in the Jackson era.

Political change, too, was strongly in the wind. The former dominance by the aristocracy over political affairs was giving way during these years. A greater acknowledgment of popular participation in voting and office holding advanced substantially under the impact of "Jacksonian democracy." The role of popular participation came to be recognized in the emergence of the political party and the party convention that came to displace the professional-politician-dominated caucus and clique. Political campaigns that had formerly been gentlemen's affairs became brawling, bare-fisted battles to win the favor of the sovereign people or "King Numbers" as some cynics scoffed. And a growing concern emerged for political and social reform to convert the democratic ideals of liberty, equality, and justice from hollow phrases into social realities.

With these questions and developments Jackson and Calhoun would have a close connection, and about them each would have much to say. Their acts and words offer a key to understanding the dynamic America of their era. Each man has considerable relevance for twentieth century Americans, too. Jackson provided the model of strong Presidential leadership that has become the hallmark of twentieth century Chief Executives; and Calhoun offered the philosophical framework for the defense of the rights of a numerical minority in a democratic society.

Jackson: Backwoods Orphan Moves West

Andrew Jackson began life as he would live it—in controversy and conflict. Even the site of his birth bred dispute—North and South Carolina both claiming him as a native son. In 1765 his Scotch-Irish immigrant parents settled in the raw frontier Waxhaws area some 150 miles northeast of Charleston. It was a rough, primitive backwoods. For the pioneer settler life was a ceaseless round of heavy toil. The struggle to hack home and livelihood from the harsh wilderness killed the father at age 29. Three weeks after his death, on March 15, 1767, widow Elizabeth Jackson gave birth to Andrew Jackson in the rough log house of an aunt. Whether the house stood on the North or South Carolina side of a disputed border line was long argued. Jackson himself later asserted he was a native of South Carolina.

Jackson grew up in his uncle James Crawford's house, along with his two brothers and eight Crawford youngsters. To run, jump, wrestle, frolic, play practical jokes made growing up a fun time. His mother, insisting that he aim to be a Presbyterian minister, sent him for a time to a neighborhood school. Jackson's resistance to the idea plus his early skill at swearing a blue streak made his mother relent. As a pupil he proved bright. By age nine he read sufficiently well to be designated "public reader" for the community. In this capacity in July 1776 he read publicly a copy of the American Declaration of Independence to neighbors gathered in his uncle's yard.[1]

The Carolina upcountry divided bitterly over independence—Loyalists for England, Patriots for liberty and independence. Four years later when Colonel Tarleton's British cavalry invaded the Waxhaws, the 13-year-old Jackson witnessed the brutalities of neighbor battling neighbor, as local Tories and Patriots viciously attacked each other in a bushwacking, guerrilla warfare. The bloody fighting ended Jackson's playful days of childhood, changed the course of his life, and ushered him early into young manhood amidst a wave of blood-letting. The imprint left on his young mind, facing the raw violence and naked tragedy, was decisive and lasting.

His mother, recalling her younger days in the old country, passed on to him the Scotch hatred of the British. At age 14 he fell in with William R. Davie's local militia irregulars, and at uncle Thomas Crawford's house Jackson and a brother were captured by a British scouting party. The officer in charge ordered Jackson to clean his mud-spattered boots. The boy refused point blank, saying defiantly, "Sir, I am a prisoner of war and claim to be treated as such." The officer's sabre flashed in the air; Jackson threw up his arm but only partially parried the blow. The blade cut his arm and scalp. Thereafter he would carry a scar on his head and a fixed hatred in his heart for the British, whom he would meet again on the battlefield at New Orleans 34 years later.[2]

After being held in prison under wretched conditions for a time, food scarce and a smallpox epidemic raging, the Jackson boys were at length released and hurried home in a driving rain storm. Within 48 hours brother Robert was dead, and Jackson himself feverish in bed, a "raving maniac", fighting for his life. His mother's constant care pulled him through. Shortly he learned that his second brother had died in a campaign nearby. And a few weeks later, news came from Charleston that his mother, who had gone there to nurse war prisoners, was dead of cholera and buried in an unmarked grave.

Orphaned by the American Revolutionary war at age 15, Jackson's hatred for the British whom he blamed for the loss of his family would last his lifetime. By his early teens, then, the war had taught him that survival in a harsh world required not only courage but resourcefulness and tough determination. These qualities he would develop in time, along with tenacious devotion to friends, of whom he had many, and unforgiving hostility to his enemies, of whom he also had many.[3]

For the present the war left him alone and at loose ends. To fill his loneliness, he plunged into a wild spree—drinking, gambling, carousing, cock fighting, and horse racing. Going to Charleston to claim his £300 inheritance from his Scotch-Irish grandfather, he blew it in a royal blast. Finding himself $200 in debt in a dice game, he bet his horse against $200, won, paid his debt, and left Charleston forever.

At 16 he sought to reform his habits and took a job teaching school for a few months to earn some money. At age 17, in 1784, he abandoned the Waxhaws and rode off to Salisbury, North Carolina where he began studying law in the office of Spruce Macay. But his ebullient spirit was irrepressible. Regularly, in the company of young sports, he painted the town red. One companion later recalled, "Jackson was the most roaring, rollicking, game-cocking, horse-racing, card-sharking, mischievous fellow that ever lived in Salisbury." Another commented, "He did not trouble with the law books much; he was more in the stable than in the office." One girl found "His manners most captivating. . . . We all knew that he was wild . . . that he gambled some and was by no means a Christian young man. When he was calm, he talked slowly and with good selected language. But . . . animated . . . he would talk fast with a very marked North-Irish brogue. . . . Either calm or animated there was something about him I cannot describe except to say that it was *presence*." As manager of the town's Christmas ball, sponsored by the leading local matrons, Jackson playfully invited two known strumpets, whose appearance on the scene broke up the party. After another six months of study, he was examined by two judges on September 26, 1787, and declared fit to practice law in North Carolina.[4] At age 20 he had become an attorney, but he would have to wait until his next birthday before beginning to practice.

By this time Jackson had developed a commanding presence that would be a lifelong trademark—ramrod straight at six feet-one inch, he commanded attention in any group of people. His thin, long face with sharp nose and jaw, topped by reddish hair, his unforgettable, piercing, blue eyes made Jackson a figure to remember—and respect. His single-minded determination, his aggressive vigor drove him forward in the face of any odds. His outbursts of anger, much to the bewilderment of associates, often brought surprising results, much to his own delight. One friend noted: "No man knew better than Andrew Jackson when to get into a passion and when not." He developed over the years the knack of pretending fierce fits of rage, which often gained what he wanted by intimidating opponents.

When his friend John McNairy became judge for the western district of North Carolina he appointed Jackson as public prosecutor. On the way west from Salisbury, he stopped for a few months in Jonesborough, where in trying a case he fancied himself insulted by the older opposing attorney, Waightstill Avery, to whom Jackson sent a challenging note in the court room: "My charector you have injured; and further you have insulted me in the presence of a court and a large audiance. I therefore call upon you as a gentleman to give me satisfaction for the Same; . . . for it is consistent with the charector of a gentlemen when he injures a man to make speedy reparation; Therefore I hope you will not fail in meeting me this day." Although Avery did not approve

of dueling, the western country's code of honor required that
he meet Jackson. Just outside town they met, the distance was
paced off, the duelists fired and both missed. His honor restored, Jackson shook hands and walked away.[5]

Frontier Lawyer, Judge and Man on the Make

Riding westward, Jackson and his companions barely
missed being attacked by a band of Indians, a grim reminder
that western North Carolina was still raw frontier with white
settlers few and towns small and scattered. Nashville, where
Jackson arrived in late October 1788, had been founded only
a few years earlier but now boasted several hundred residents,
a court house, two stores, two taverns, a distillery. Tents and
rough cabins were still visible, scattered among the more
permanent houses. To this town, some years earlier, Colonel
John Donelson had brought a party of 120 people including
his own eleven children, among whom was his 13-year-old
daughter Rachel. After a few years Donelson died; and
daughter Rachel grew into a dark-eyed, vivacious beauty and
married Lewis Robards of Kentucky. When marital troubles
developed she returned home to live with her widowed
mother, who took in boarders to help support her family.
Robards followed, there was a reunion, and the couple was
living in the Donelson house, when Jackson moved in as a
boarder and as extra male insurance against Indian attack.
The situation was potentially inflammable since Jackson was
high-spirited and fun-loving and the vivacious Rachel enjoyed dancing and horses as much as Jackson did. Jackson
was courteous and attentive, rousing Robards to resent Jackson's attentions to his wife.[6]

Jackson tackled his law duties as public prosecutor with
characteristic vigor. Since the Tennessee economy of the time
revolved about land and farming, together with land specula-

tion, understandably much of Jackson's work involved suits against delinquent debtors. Jackson's reputation as a stern collector of debts grew as he forced seventy payments in one month, brooked no nonsense and naturally attracted more creditors to him with their law business.

For the next ten years Jackson practiced law, and legal records in Nashville show that in his early years there he handled one-forth to one-half of all cases in the courts, mostly involving land titles, debts, sales, and assault and battery disputes. Since money was scarce and land plentiful in the frontier community, he was frequently paid in land and within a few years became one of the largest landholders in the area. He assumed the position of attorney general of the Mero District of the Southwest Territory, created by Congress in 1790, and in 1792 became judge advocate of Davidson County (Nashville) militia. The latter appointment came from territorial governor William Blount; thus Jackson moved into Tennessee politics in alliance with the Blount faction opposed to rival John Sevier's group.[7]

Jackson's personal life, meanwhile, had become ensnarled. In the Donelson household, Robards grew increasingly resentful of Jackson's presence. In one exchange between the two men, harsh words were shouted. Whether Robards blustered that he would horsewhip Jackson and Jackson threatened to cut off Robards' ears cannot be determined accurately. At any rate, Jackson was persuaded by his friend John Overton to move out of the house. But the Robardses again failed to get along and shortly separated, Robards returning to Kentucky.[8] Unhappy there, Robards again entreated his wife to rejoin him. She did but found life intolerable. She wrote to her family asking them to send someone to get her and escort her home again. That Jackson was asked and that he consented to go under the circumstances seems almost beyond belief. As one commentator has said, it was "absolute folly or absolute calculation" since Jackson's appearance could only infuriate Robards and injure both Rachel's and Jackson's reputations. By this time Jackson was clearly in love with Rachel and welcomed the possibility of a marriage with the daughter of a prominent, well-to-do family of the community. Whether Jackson suggested that Rachel leave her husband is not known. But Rachel's actions in the years in Nashville when Jackson knew her as Mrs. Robards, her dancing, flirting, laughing, were the actions of a woman "being courted, not those of a properly married woman." [9]

In late 1790 when word arrived that Robards was about to descend on Nashville to retrieve his wife, Rachel became frightened and pleaded to accompany an expedition under elderly Colonel John Stark that was heading down the Cumberland for the lower Mississippi. Stark was reluctant to take her on a hazardous 2,000 miles journey through difficult, Indian-infested country unless she were accompanied by someone responsible for her safety. Jackson, who had incidental business in Natchez where he had already established a trading post, agreed eagerly to go along, delivered Rachel to her friends in Natchez, and then returned over the Natchez Trace to Nashville.

Now another oral report reached Nashville that Robards had won a divorce granted by the Virginia legislature. (Kentucky was still part of Virginia at the time). Jackson was overjoyed with the report and blinded by love to legal reality. The legal reality—which Jackson did not know at the time, although as an attorney he could easily have checked it—was that the Virginia legislature had granted Robards' petition by authorizing him to sue for divorce in a court of the state of Kentucky, which the legislature created just fourteen days later. In fact, the Virginia legislature's action said: "It shall be lawful for Lewis Robards to sue. . . . and if the jury shall find in substance that the defendant hath deserted the plaintiff, and that she hath lived in adultery with another man since such desertion," the marriage would be "totally dissolved." [10] Clearly on a matter as critical and delicate as this, attorney Jackson might have been expected to take simple precautions. Instead:

Jackson Elopes with Another Man's Wife

Impetuously he asked Mrs. Donelson for "permission to offer his hand and heart to her daughter." "Mr. Jackson," the lady replied, "would you sacrifice your life to save my poor child's good name?" "Ten thousand lives, madam, if I had them." [11] Jackson's irrational actions are accountable only by his being madly in love. He rushed off immediately to Natchez, broke the news of the divorce to Rachel, who is reported to have said, "I expected him to kill me but this is worse." [12] Jackson reassured her and in late August 1791 they exchanged marriage vows in the parlor of a stately mansion near Natchez and honeymooned in a log house at Jackson's establishment at Pierre Bayou on a bluff overlooking the broad Mississippi.

Not until more than two years later did reality break. The Jacksons' were stunned by the news that only on September 17, 1793, did Robards receive the divorce decree in Mercer County court, Kentucky. Doubtless both Jackson and Rachel genuinely believed themselves married legally at Natchez. And now to discover that it was illegal was almost too much. Friend and sometime Jackson partner John Overton advised them to remarry at once. Jackson at first refused, saying that everybody knew they were married. But shortly he became convinced, and on January 17, 1794, he and Rachel recited the vows for a second time.

The importance of the marriage cannot be over emphasized for it colored all of Jackson's career, in many aspects. For one, Jackson could not tolerate any reference, however slight, to the irregularity of the whole affair. He would explode with rage against anyone who spoke or even hinted in that direction and during his next 20 years would fight scores of duels on this account. Even when he ran for President 33 years later, his political opponents printed the whole sorry mess in their papers, much to Jackson's disgust and fury and to Rachel's heart-rending chagrin.

The marriage had practical advantages. Jackson was now linked with one of Tennessee's first families, providing him with social standing he could not have achieved on his own. Shortly he was elected a trustee of Davidson Academy. Further, Rachel brought shrewd and skillful management to his household and domestic affairs. When Jackson was away from home, as he was much of the time during ensuing years, he could count on Rachel's steady, wise direction of the affairs on his estate. Writing years later to his ward, Jackson advised: "seek a wife who will aid you in your exertions to make a competency and will take care of it when made, for you will find it easier to spend two thousand dollars than to make five hundred."

Jackson's fortunes, both private and public, began to expand during the 1790's. He and Rachel moved into a small plantation named Poplar Grove at a bend on the Cumberland River. As his law practice flourished, they moved to a larger place called Hunter's Hill. Since he often received in payment of law fees not money, but land or other tangible items of value, Jackson acquired title to large tracts of land, amounting altogether to many thousands of acres, virtually all unimproved wilderness. He also bought, speculated, and sold land with a frequency not uncommon in frontier communities. At this time he acquired for $800 and 850-acre tract which became the basis for his Hermitage estate just a short distance outside Nashville.

In public life, Jackson served in the 1796 constitutional convention, which framed Tennessee's constitution in preparation for being admitted as a state in the Union. Jackson's part appears small, although tradition credits him with having suggested the name for the state—from a Cherokee Indian chief named Tinnasee. When Tennessee became a state, Jackson was nominated by the William Blount faction and won election as the state's single member in the national House of Representatives. And off he went to the capital in Philadelphia for his first House session. His made scarcely any dent on the record of Congress; in December 1796, he heard President Washington's Farewell Address, of which he was critical (although he himself later would give a Presidential farewell of his own); and he secured passage of a $20,000 appropriation to reimburse Tennessee for John Sevier's 1793 expedition against the Cherokees. Dressed in "black coat and breeches," Jackson appeared in the House chamber where fellow Congressman Albert Gallatin observed him as a "tall, lanky, uncouth-looking personage . . . queue down his back tied with an eelskin; . . . dress singular, . . . manners those of a backwoodsman." [13]

A year earlier Jackson had gone to Philadelphia on his own business. He had then sold 50,000 acres of land that he held jointly with friend John Overton and 18,000 for a Joel Rice to a Philadelphia businessman David Allison, who gave his own notes to cover the price. Jackson endorsed these notes and used the proceeds to buy goods to stock a trading post that he had established on the Cumberland River. Two years later Allison went into bankruptcy, and the merchants holding the Allison notes endorsed by Jackson called upon Jackson to cover the notes. Jackson had to sell much of his land, his store, and Hunter's Hill plantation and borrowed on his other land holdings in order to get the liquid funds to satisfy his Philadelphia creditors. Thereafter, Jackson distrusted paper notes, paper money, and money lenders and took a consistent hard money position. And with good reason, since it took him almost twenty years to free himself from the burden of debt encumbrance on his Hermitage, brought on by this commercial venture.

When William Blount was expelled from the United States Senate, Jackson was chosen by the Tennessee legislature to fill the Senate seat. He did little in the Senate, leading Thomas Jefferson, who presided over the Senate at the time, to note that on each of several occasions that Jackson arose to address that assemblage he became so choked with rage as to be voiceless or incoherent.

Distracted by the Allison affair and concerned over his financial obligations, Jackson resigned from the Senate in the Spring of 1798 and returned to Tennessee to try to unsnarl his tangled finances. Very soon the state legislature elected him a judge on the Tennessee Supreme Court. In appearance Jackson looked like a judge, but his mode of operation was unconventional, certainly by modern standards. His judicial opinions were characterized by a contemporary as "short, untechnical, unlearned, sometimes ungrammatical, and generally right." [14] No written judicial decision by Judge Jackson is known to exist since that practice started only with Jackson's successor, John Overton. But his frequent charge to juries, "Do what is *right* between these parties. That is what the law always *means*," is preserved in tradition. He remained on the Court for six years until his resignation in 1804.

Ever since the days of the Revolution Jackson had fancied himself a military man for which his pugnacious nature and will of iron clearly fitted him. His opportunity came in 1802 when Governor John Sevier was succeeded by Jackson's friend Archibald Roane, who arranged to get Jackson elected as major general of the Tennessee state militia at the age of thirty-five. Sevier, a Revolutionary war veteran who wanted the job, was furious and it was only a matter of time until a clash between the two headstrong men erupted.

Trouble had been brewing for some years between Jackson and Sevier since Jackson in the late 1790's and turned up evidence of Sevier's fraudulent activities to gain titles to land covering about one-fourth of the state. In October 1803 when Jackson was holding court in Knoxville, the two men encountered each other on the steps of the county courthouse. Jackson made a reference to his own services to the state, to which Sevier snorted: "Services? I know of no great service you have rendered the country except taking a trip to Natchez with another man's wife!" Jackson's blue eyes narrowed in fury: "Great God!" he cried, "Do you mention *her* sacred name?" He lunged forward swinging his walking stick at Sevier. The crowd that gathered moved in and carried the combatants off in different directions.

Immediately Jackson sent his written challenge to the Governor. Two days later the Governor replied evasively, pointing to Tennessee's statute forbidding dueling. Jackson answered at once charging Sevier with "subterfuge" and offering to fight in Georgia, Virginia, North Carolina, or in Indian territory "if it will obviate your squeamish fears . . . You must meet me . . . or I will publish you as a coward." Mutual friends attempted to patch up the quarrel. Respect for his judicial robes was pressed on Jackson—a high consideration, Jackson allowed, but Rachel's honor was higher.

After a week Jackson's patience ran out. He wrote Sevier what he said would be his last communication: "In the public street of Knoxville you appeared to pant for combat. You ransacked the vocabulary of vulgarity. . . . You took the sacred name of a lady in your polluted lips. . . . I have spoken for a place in the paper for the following advertisement: 'To all who shall see these presents Greetings. Know ye that I Andrew Jackson, do pronounce, publish and declare to the world, that his excellency John Sevier . . . is a base coward and poltroon. He will basely insult, but has not the courage to repair. ANDREW JACKSON.' You may prevent the insertion of the above by meeting me in two hours after the receipt of this."

When no reply came, Jackson gave his letter to the *Gazette* where it was printed the following day at the usual advertising rates. With one companion Jackson set out for the Cherokee country at Southwest Point believing that the ultimate insult of "publishing" would compel Sevier to follow. For five days they camped at the Point. Sevier finally appeared accompanied by several armed men. He dismounted and began "with pistols in his hands advancing" on Jackson. About twenty yards apart, they stopped and began shouting at each other, "the Governor damning him to fire away." After some haranguing, they put away their pistols, but after more words Jackson rushed toward Sevier exclaiming he was going to cane him. Sevier in reaching for his sword "frightened his horse" which "ran away with the Governor's pistols." Jackson raised his own pistol. The Governor "went behind a tree and damned Jackson, did he want to fire on a naked man." George Washington Sevier, the Governor's son, aimed his pistol at Jackson; and Jackson's companion covered the son. Finally after much fiery talk the Governor was persuaded to leave the field. But he and Jackson cursed each other loudly until both were out of earshot. Not all Jackson's quarrels would end so peacefully.[15]

A few years later Jackson, who loved betting on game cock fights and horse races, developed a stable of his own, of which "Truxton," a Virginia stallion, was his pride. In a dispute arising from one of Truxton's races and an alleged remark disparaging to Rachel, Jackson challenged a young Nashville lawyer, Charles Dickinson, twenty-seven and reputedly one of Tennessee's best marksmen. Since the encounter could not be held in Tennessee, Jackson and his second, Judge John Overton, traveled across the Kentucky border where on the banks of the Red River he met Dickinson early one dawn in May 1806. The rules:

"Distance twenty-four feet; the parties to stand facing each other, with their pistols down perpendicularly. When they are READY, the single word FIRE! to be given; at which they are to fire as soon as they please. Should either fire before the word is given, we (the seconds) pledge ourselves to shoot him down instantly." Jackson was not a quick shot, nor an especially good one for the western country. He expected Dickinson to him him on the first fire. But he was convinced that his own will power would sustain him, after he was hit, until he could aim accurately and shoot to kill if it were the last act of his life.

The two parties met. Jackson's pistols were to be used, Dickinson taking his choice. The nine-inch barrels were charged with ounce balls of 70 caliber. The principals took their places. Judge Overton called: "Gentlemen, are you ready?" Both nodded, Overton cried, "Fire!" In a flash Dickinson fired. A fleck of dust rose from Jackson's coat; his body shuddered as his left hand clutched at his chest. Battling to regain self-control, Jackson raised his pistol. Dickinson stepped back in horror, "My God, have I missed him?" "Back to the mark, sir," shouted Overton, raising his own pistol. Dickinson folded his arms. Jackson's slim figure straightened. He sighted, fired. Dickinson dropped to the ground. Within hours he was dead. Jackson was seriously wounded with a ball in his chest. His surgeon found that Dickinson's aim was perfectly good, but he had judged the location of Jackson's heart by the set of his coat, not allowing for the fact that Jackson wore his dark blue frock coat extremely loosely because of his very slender frame. "But I should have hit him," he exclaimed during the weeks of recuperating, "if he had shot me through the brain." [16] Men learned that Jackson was not a man to be trifled with, and in the course of his years he fought scores of duels chiefly to defend Rachel's reputation.

Meanwhile, his economic activities intensified. He opened another store, again with supplies shipped from Philadelphia, on the Cumberland River, but it proved only slightly more successful than his earlier venture. At his new estate, the Hermitage, he expanded his holdings of slaves (ultimately he owned 150 slaves), increased his cotton acreage, began operating a whiskey distillery and installed one of Eli Whitney's new cotton gins to boost his production. In addition, the farm produced grain, hay, fruits of all kinds, and vegetables for home comsumption. Horses and game cocks were necessary for the encounters on the track and in the ring that Jackson loved so well.

Jackson's earlier hope for appointment by President Jefferson as Governor of the new Louisiana Territory had been disappointed. Now, another disappointed office holder, Aaron Burr, appeared in the western country, visited, and was entertained at the Hermitage by Jackson, who held Burr in high esteem. When rumor suggested that Burr's activities in the western country were less than honorable, Jackson wrote and received what he considered a satisfactory explanation from Burr. Indeed, Jackson may well have hoped that Burr would eliminate Spanish influence along the southern border of the country.

To the Hermitage, visitors came in a constant stream. Rachel had countless brothers, sisters, cousins, neices, and nephews who frequented the Hermitage. Two nephews of Rachel, John and Andrew Jackson Donelson, were raised by the Jacksons' after their father had died. In 1810 the Jacksons legally adopted one of the twin sons of brother Severn Donelson, rechristening him Andrew Jackson, Jr. Jackson loved children, frequently played games with them, rolled on the floor, ran races with them, and generally had fun. Tradition has it that he never raised his voice or lost his temper where children were concerned; but it may be that the children could read the severity in his eyes and knew better than to cross him.

"Old Hickory" Becomes an Instant "Hero of New Orleans"

At the outbreak of the war of 1812 Jackson offered his services and as commander of the Tennessee militia led 2,000 troops southward, writing at the time to the Secretary of War that "if the government orders, [we] will rejoice at the opportunity of placing the American eagle on the ramparts of Mobile, Pensacola and Fort St. Augustine, effectually banishing from the southern coasts all British influence." His hopes for conquest were crushed when after arriving at Natchez, he was ordered to dismiss his troops and return home. Furious with the "idiots" in Washington, he managed with much difficulty and at the utmost strain on his endurance to get his troops back to their homes. During this march his soldiers, admiring his stamina and will power, began calling him "Old Hickory," for the strength he exhibited.

Back in Tennessee Jackson became embroiled in a dispute with Thomas Hart Benton, who had been one of Jackson's colonels during the march to Natchez, and with Benton's brother Jesse. The dispute arose from a horse race and a duel involving Jesse. Thomas Benton wrote Jackson that he thought it was bad business for Jackson to assist in a duel between two young men who had no reason to fight. When later it was reported to Jackson that Tom Benton was circulating insulting stories about Jackson, the latter declared he would "horsewhip Tom Benton the next time I see him." What followed could happen only in a frontier atmosphere like Nashville's.

On September 4, 1813, the Benton brothers rode into Nashville and checked in at the City Hotel, each carrying a pair of pistols. At noon Jackson and his friends John Coffee and Stockley Hays arrived at Nashville Inn, diagonally across the Court House Square from the Bentons' hotel. Jackson, carrying a riding whip and accompanied by Coffee, walked to the post office and returning, passed directly in front of City Hotel. When Jackson saw Tom Benton standing in the doorway, he rushed at him brandishing his horsewhip: "Now, defend yourself, you damned rascal." Benton reached for his pistol, but before he could draw Jackson's gun was at his chest. He backed slowly through the door, Jackson following step by step. Glancing beyond Jackson, Benton saw his brother Jesse glide through a doorway behind Jackson, raise his pistol and shoot. Jackson fell forward, firing. His powder burned Tom Benton's sleeve. Tom Benton fired twice at the falling Jackson, and when Jesse aimed to fire again, a bystander threw himself in between to shield Jackson, whose leftside was gushing blood.

Massive John Coffee came charging through the smoke firing at Tom Benton. He missed but pushed forward with clubbed pistol. Benton slipped and fell down a flight of stairs, and his brother Jesse escaped knifing when the large metal buckle on his coat broke a thrusting knife blade.

Jackson's wounds soaked the mattress with blood at the Nashville Inn. He was nearly dead—his left shoulder shattered by a slug, and a ball from Benton's pistol embedded against the upper bone. The attending physicians announced amputation of the arm was necessary. Jackson, barely conscious, roused. "I'll keep my arm," he ruled. Jackson's friends vowed to even the score. "I'm literally in hell here," wrote Benton as he left town.[17]

The feud faded as news came that Creek Indians had massacred 250 whites at Fort Mims in Alabama. Facing Indian warfare, a committee of public safety hastened to the Hermitage. "By the Eternal, these people must be saved," cried Old Hickory, too sick to leave his bed but strong enough to make war. Within days, militia men were forming regiments. "The health of your general is restored," penned Jackson, propped against a pillow, "he will command in person." A 2,500-man expedition was authorized by the Governor; in less than two weeks Jackson was ready to march—arm in a sling, face pallid, body shaky from loss of blood. But his determination and iron will never showed stronger.[18]

He planned his campaign astutely, executed it with swift, driving precision. Twice his army met the Creeks and inflicted crushing defeats. After victory at Horseshoe Bend on the Tallapoosa River, Jackson summoned the Creek chiefs to parley in the spring of 1814. At Fort Jackson he compelled them to accept a treaty ceding to the United States 23 million acres, comprising $\frac{3}{5}$ of present Alabama and $\frac{1}{5}$ of present Georgia and opening the way south to Florida. In triumph the General could be as magananimous as he was relentless in battle. One Indian chief, whose "manliness of sentiment, . . . heroism of soul, . . . comprehension of intellect, . . . modesty and yet firmness" impressed Jackson, confessed frankly: "I am come to give myself up. I can oppose you no longer. I have done you much injury. I should have done you more . . . [but] my warriors are killed. . . . I am in your power. Dispose of me as you please." Jackson ordered brandy for his foe and insisted that Indian women and children be provided rations of food. In fact, one Indian baby found separated from his dead mother Jackson took home to the Hermitage, named him Lincoyer and raised him as a son.[19]

During the campaign Jackson was commissioned as a major general in the United States army in command of the Southern Department. Receiving reports that a British military expedition of 10,000 men, under General Pakenham, having recently defeated Napoleon's crack forces in the Spanish Peninsular campaign, were about to land on the Gulf coast, Jackson moved swiftly into Spanish Florida seizing Pensacola and strengthening its defenses. Then, leaving a small garrison at Mobile, he led his main force to New Orleans, expected target of the coming British invasion.

In December 1814 he began preparing that city's defenses with characteristic energy and thoroughness, brooking no excuses, delays, or hindrance. He found in the city a home guard of 600 men ill-prepared for the city's defense. In his own command he had some regular army units and companies of militiamen from Tennessee and Kentucky (soon to be celebrated in song as "The Hunters of Kentucky"), totaling about 5,000 effectives. He issued an appeal for volunteers among blacks as well as whites: "Our country has been invaded and threatened with destruction. She wants soldiers to fight her battles. The free men of color in [the] city are inured to the Southern climate and . . . make excellent soldiers." Some 600 Negroes responded as volunteers. Jackson also accepted the services of notorious Jean LaFitte and his fellow pirates of Barataria Bay who operated under the protection of Edward Livingston, a local business man, a former Congressman and former mayor of New York, and later to be a member of Jackson's Presidential cabinet.[20] (See *Appendix* Docs. No. 1-A and 1-B on defense of New Orleans.)

In making preparations, Jackson gripped the city with an iron hand. He instituted martial law to prevent any disorders or internal subversion. When the city's French residents now claimed French citizenship and went to the French consul to get official papers, Jackson ordered them to remove 100 miles from the city. This order applied to one member of the Louisiana Legislature who obtained from the federal court a writ of habeas corpus for release from arrest. Thereupon Jackson ordered the arrest and detention of the federal judge, Dominick Hall, and had him detained by military guard.

After the city was secured and martial law lifted, Judge Hall held Jackson in contempt of court, imposed a $1,000 fine, which the general paid saying that respect for law was required of all, even of the man who had saved the city.

Anticipating the British approach, Jackson constructed along the line of the Rodriquez Canal five miles below the city—a five-foot high rampart running from the Mississippi River on his right flank about 1½ miles to a large swamp on his left. Two miles closer to the city another rampart was thrown up, and still another on the city's rim. Along the first set of ramparts the general mounted his cannon in commanding positions, with supporting troops arranged behind the defenses. The British forces, during the first week of January, 1815, were observed moving slowly forward. Their full scale assault came early in the morning of January 8. Heavy river fog, delay by some British units, and confusion among British officers blunted the attack. In a strange maneuver a large body of British troops attempted to cross from the left to right flank directly in front of the American lines and were literally mowed down by American cannon fire. Later tales of deadeye sharp-shooting by the "Hunters of Kentucky," although pure invention, added glamour to the legend of New Orleans. Out of 10,000 British soldiers over 2,000 lay dead, including Pakenham, and thousands were wounded. The American loss ran to 24 killed, 150 wounded. Ten days later the British forces withdrew to their ships.[20]

Jackson had saved the city—and won the only genuine American military victory of the War of 1812. He had also won the notice and eternal thanks of his fellow Americans, who hailed him as the "Hero of New Orleans." Locally a triumphal arch greeted the victor and his troops as they returned to the city. The city's center, formerly Place d'Armes when New Orleans was French, was now renamed Jackson Square, where the "Hero's" bronze statue would be erected in time. As the news of the victory flashed across the country, Jackson emerged not simply as a great military figure but would shortly became a legendary hero.[21]

Jackson's stunning victory over the British at New Orleans reverberated through the land, changing despair to elation. Americans, who had plunged bouyantly into war in 1812, had seen their armies repulsed in Canada, British forces invade at will, American soldiers flee in terror before advancing redcoats at Bladensburg, President Madison and officials hastily evacuate Washington only hours before the British moved in and burned the city. The young nation's pride sagged badly. Optimism yielded to despair by the dark winter of 1814–15. New England's doomcrying protestors gathered at the Hartford Convention to discuss possible breakup of the Union—just as British forces approached New Orleans. The city's fall appeared certain. Americans sank into a mood of gloomy pessimism as the end of the Republic loomed ahead. Then—the news of Andrew Jackson's crushing triumph boomed "like a clap of thunder" across the land. Newspaper headlines screamed: "INCREDIBLE VICTORY!!" "GLORIOUS NEWS," "UNPARALLELED VICTORY," "RISING GLORY OF THE AMERICAN REPUBLIC." Overnight despair turned into elation. Jackson's "brilliant victory" all Americans agreed lifted "the nation . . . above disgrace" and "placed America on the very pinnacle of fame." [22] (See *Appendix* Docs. No. 1-C and 1-D for Jackson's views of the battle.)

Andrew Jackson purged the nation of shame and despair. Threats of New England's secession evaporated. Andrew Jackson restored Americans' self confidence and belief in the nation's strength and destiny. In Washington a Georgia Congressman proclaimed that the victory of "General Jackson and the troops" he commanded "is a fit subject for the genius of Homer." ". . . the yeomanry of the country marching to

the defense of the City of Orleans . . . triumphantly victori-
ous over the conquerors of the Conquerors of Europe. . . .
The God of Battles and of Righteousness" stood "with the
defenders of their country," as God and Nature . . . bounti-
fully placed at our disposal" the means to be "invincible."

Overnight, Andrew Jackson himself became the instant
"Hero of New Orleans." Not only did he become personally
famous throughout the country, as his name flashed across
the pages of all newspapers and was spoken by all lips. Not
only did the day of victory, January 8, become Jackson Day
to be celebrated by all patriots. These were perhaps the least
of it. But over and above becoming a national hero, he came
to be viewed as the personal embodiment "of the true spirit
of the nation." He came to symbolize, as John Ward has
perceptively noted, those large ideas that all Americans sub-
scribed to—"Nature" in the embattled yeomanry defending
liberty, "Providence" in the "God of Battles" standing on the
side of His chosen people, and "will" in exerting almost
superhuman drive and determination to capture victory.[23]
Much of Americans' thinking revolved about these broad
ideas for the first half of the nineteenth century. Certainly,
the man who personified them must inevitably be a national
hero. The Jackson legend was in the making.

II Calhoun: "Young Hercules" Emerges, 1782-1815

LIKE JACKSON, John Caldwell Calhoun also came out of the South Carolina upcountry. His father, Patrick Calhoun, had arrived with other Scotch-Irish immigrants in Pennsylvania about 1730. He migrated southward through Virginia and finally settled in the Abbeville district of South Carolina's piedmont. Here in the raw wilderness, Partrick Calhoun fought successively against Cherokee raiders who killed his mother, uncle, and two neices, against low country aristocrats who blocked upcountry legislative representation and suffrage, against Tory and British forces in the area during the American Revolution. A land surveyor, he acquired many acres, held as many as 30 slaves, built the first frame, two-storey house in the neighborhood and was considered a leading citizen, entitled to be addressed as "Squire." Politically active, he battled for legislative representation for the Carolina interior. After the battle was won in 1769, he was elected the first upcountry representative in South Carolina's Assemby and served continuously until his death 30 years later. A man of eminence and affluence, he served as local justice of the peace, county judge, and state senator.

From Carolina's Piedmont to Yankee Law School

Before the Revolution Patrick had married Martha Caldwell, who bore him four sons and a daughter. The third son,

John Caldwell Calhoun, was born at Abbeville on March 17, 1782. In his early years formal schooling was scanty, and John learned from his mother the rudiments of reading, writing, and cyphering. When he gave signs of mental precocity at age 13, he was sent to a formal school run by Reverend Moses Waddel. Here he read avidly all the books he could get, including Locke and Voltaire. But formal instruction lasted less than four months, and he was soon back home working the fields and helping his widowed mother run the family farm. "Many's the times," recalled Negro Sawney, "in the brilin' sun me and Marse John has plowed together." [1] His living and working on the farm developed in him a love for land and home area of the piedmont.

Urged by his older brother James to pursue an education leading to a profession, John agreed, but only on condition that James would "so manage his property to keep him in funds for seven years of study preparatory to entering his profession." In 1800 John resumed his studies at Waddel's Academy (which would also graduate such famed Southern leaders as William H. Crawford, George McDuffie, and James L. Pettigru). At the Academy, Calhoun experienced a rigorous existence as well as sturdy academic preparation. Students lived in log cabin dormitories, ate corn bread and salt pork at the common table, at night studied by the light of pine torches. In the two-room log school house, where chairs were few, students stood while reciting and studying in Latin, moral philosophy, mathematics, and rhetoric at the weekly debating sessions.

At the age of twenty Calhoun, emerging from rural Carolina, traveled north to enter Yale as a junior and face his first encounter with the Yankee environment of New Haven. Arriving in October 1802 at Yale, he quickly discovered that his own mental powers fitted him admirably to meet the challenge of intellectual competition. "I went to Yale," he wrote later, "fresh from the backwoods. My opportunities for learning had been very limited. I had a high opinion of the New England system of education. My first recitation was in mathematics, and we had been told to fetch our slates into the classroom. On taking our seats the professor proceeded to propound certain arithmetical questions to us. I found no difficulty in working out the first, and on looking about me was surprised to find the others busy with their slates. The professor, noticing my movement, asked me if I had got the answer, and I handed him my slate. The answer proved to be correct. The same thing occurred every time. On returning to my apartment I felt gratified." [2]

Clearly the Carolinian found the Yale intellectual atmosphere stimulating. Studies included the traditional classics, mathematics, philosophy, but Yale had recently added history, politics, and science with Benjamin Silliman assuming the chair in chemistry in the month Calhoun arrived. Overall presided the guiding genius of Timothy Dwight, tough, intolerant, determined to provide quality education but also to indoctrinate his students with his Puritan views in religion and his Federalist attitudes in politics. Dwight was convinced that the election of Jefferson to power in 1800 was a major catastrophe for the country, introducing dangerous leveling "democratical" ideas that threatened to undermine the old Federalist, aristocratic framework of politics and government.

Calhoun, inheriting his father's hostility to aristocracy and adopting the Jeffersonian Republican philosophy, argued regularly with fellow students of Federalist persuasion. As a member of Phi Beta Kappa, he enjoyed the weekly "disputations" where students debated political questions, with Dwight and Silliman acting as judges. On one such occasion, so runs the story, Dwight, much impressed with Calhoun's forceful logic, questioned him on the source of political power. When Calhoun replied that the people themselves were the only legitimate source, Dr. Dwight shot back: "Young man, your talents are of a high order . . . but I deeply regret that you do not love sound principles better than sophistry—you . . . possess an unfortunate bias for error." A later version of the story (written when Calhoun was actively seeking the Presidency) had Calhoun defending Republican (Jeffersonian) principles against Dwight's vigorous attack for a full hour, after which Dwight reportedly remarked that "the young man had talent enough to be President of the United States" and added the prediction "that he would one day reach that station." [1]

Whether Dwight ever made this exact prediction is of little concern. What is important is that by the time he graduated from Yale in September 1804, Calhoun clearly demonstrated qualities that drew him along the path to political leadership. His high intelligence was beyond question; his self-discipline, and industriousness, initiative, drive, and determination to rise above the ordinary were shown by his leaving Carolina and successfully pursuing the best formal education available. The Yale experience reinforced his already strong self-confidence and convinced him that he could overpower all obstacles to worldly success and prominence by dint of his own tireless industry and by the compelling power of his logic and reason. Aware of his exceptional abilities, he would push himself into public notice.

While the backwoods Carolina boy had made good scholastically at Yale, his social life remained limited. He mixed little with fellow students perhaps because of his drive to excel in his studies, perhaps because of the solitary nature of his own withdrawn personality. At any rate he was no more embraced by society in New Haven than he had been by the aristocratic society of South Carolina's tidewater. At this point luck broke for him.

A serious illness (probably yellow fever) prevented his delivering an oration on "The Qualifications Necessary for a Perfect Statesman" at the Yale graduation exercises in the fall of 1804. But he recieved an invitation from Mrs. Floride Bonneau Calhoun, wealthy widow of his first cousin, the late Senator John Ewing Colhoun (sic) (the widow changed the spelling from Colhoun to Calhoun shortly after her husband's death). Mrs. Calhoun invited him to convalesce at her summer estate in Newport, Rhode Island.

During three months at Newport, Calhoun not only recovered his health but developed a close attachment for Mrs. Calhoun, who became his confidante and substitute mother (his own mother having died four years earlier). The attachment became a lasting one, running until Mrs. Calhoun's death decades later. At the same time Calhoun became acquainted with the 12-year-old daughter, also named Floride, whom he would marry seven years later. Mrs. Calhoun insisted that Calhoun travel with her family on the sea voyage south to Charleston, where she introduced him to influential friends. Among the latter, her attorney, William H. De Saussure (later Chancellor of South Carolina) took Calhoun into his law office for the winter, allowing him to study Blackstone and develop contacts among the city's leading men. Calhoun was well on his way to becoming accepted as a gentleman in Carolina society.

The following Spring (1805) Calhoun headed north again, Mrs. Calhoun taking him personally in her carriage driven by a liveried coachman. Legend has it that en route they stopped at Monticello for a brief visit with Jefferson who reportedly spoke highly of Calhoun's abilities. After a few weeks at Newport, Calhoun went on to Litchfield, Connecticut, where he enrolled in Judge Tapping Reeve's Law School. Here for the next year he pursued his studies with characteristic single-minded concentration—the "dry and solitary journey through the exterior fields of the law," as he called it. "I take little amusement," he wrote Mrs. Calhoun, "and live a very studious life." His roommate and only friend for the year was John M. Felder, Fellow Yale alumnus and Carolinian. The townspeople, solidly Federalist, were so anti-Jefferson (who the Yankees believed was subverting American society) that Calhoun found it "prudent to form few connections in town. . . . This is a rather solitary place, and . . . we rarely see anyone from our end of the Union. . . . [consoling] ourselves that . . . we shall acquire a pretty thorough knowledge of our profession" to qualify as lawyers.

The Law School, one of the few in America at the time, had one small building, two instructors, and forty students. Its program included lectures, reading Blackstone and English common law cases, and a weekly moot court. In the last Calhoun got his best training. Fashioning arguments under instructor James Gould's tutelage, he developed the skill in lucid analysis and logical reasoning that later made him formidable in extemporaneous debate in Congress. Judge Reeve, denouncing Jefferson's centralizing tendencies, especially after the Louisiana Purchase, devised the full blown theory of state sovereignty, nullification, and even secession—indeed openly advocated New England's secession to preserve its rights. At the time these doctrines had a reverse effect on Calhoun, who deplored "the working of the odious party machinery" of New England that he feared "in the end . . . would supersede the authority of law and the Constitution." Calhoun's concern over possible disunion and disruption of the American experiment (which in 1805 seemed imminent in Connecticut) led Calhoun to reject state-rightism and advocate nationalist doctrines. These he retained for a generation; but 25 years later, when his home state's interests seemed threatened, his mind revived Reeve's theory and elaborated even more fully into the state rights position.[4]

Partly his own frustration and partly the Litchfield atmosphere turned Calhoun sour on the law. His own inquiring mind rejected the notion that Blackstone and English common law comprised the sum and acme of human reason. "I am not so much in love with law," he confided to a friend; "many things I study for the love of study, but not so with the law." His Scotch-Irish, Calvinist-bred tenacity drove him to complete his studies: "It must be done, and the sooner the better is my logic." [5] Rigorous endeavors enabled him to finish in one year the law course which normally took 14 to 18 months.

Calhoun Gains a Wife and Wealth

After a brief stop in Newport, he rode south to visit his family at Abbeville and then resumed his duties in De Saussure's busy law office in Charleston, one of America's leading sea ports in the fall of 1806. Here he boarded with the family of the French Protestant minister, Mr. Deyarguey, but stayed pretty much to himself, viewing the Charleston social swirl as "intemperate and debauched." [6] The Calvinist, dogmatic spirit in which he had been raised at home remained with him in essence long after he had abandoned concern over the Calvinist creed (he never officially joined the Presbyterian Church but much later attended Unitarian meetings). After six months in Charleston, Calhoun moved to Abbeville continuing his study in attorney George Bowie's office. By early 1808 he was admitted to the bar, an event he celebrated by visiting the Bonneau's Ferry plantation of his cousin, Mrs. Calhoun. Floride, now about 17, had blossomed into a sparkling belle in the year and a half since he had last seen her. John fell as deeply in love as he was capable of and shortly asked Mrs. Calhoun's advice on how to present his undeclared suit to her daughter.

In his law practice Calhoun won practically instant success. His industry and personal integrity, plus the prestige of Litchfield training and prominent Charleston connections, brought him within a year and a half as much business as he could handle. But he did not enjoy the profession. "I feel myself almost as a slave chained down to a particular place and course in life," he complained to Mrs. Calhoun. His "strong aversion to the law" made him determined "to foresake it as soon as I can make a decent independence; for I am not ambitious of great wealth." [8] He would give up the law for the life of a Carolina country gentleman-planter as soon as he could find suitable estate.

Three developments conspired to remove him from law and thrust him into a political career, which he combined successfully with that of planter, a common combination in the ante-bellum South. On June 22, 1807, the British frigate *Leopard* fired upon the USS *Chesapeake*, which had rejected the British demand to board and search for deserters. Since the attack occurred just off the Virginia capes, Americans were outraged.

Public protest meetings sprouted instantly throughout the land. In Abbeville indignant citizens formed a public committee, including young attorney John C. Calhoun, who proceeded to draft the resolutions denouncing the British action and demanding amends. These he presented forcefully at a public gathering that drew aroused residents from miles around Abbeville. What Calhoun said on this occasion was not recorded. But the sequel shows that his maiden public speech brought him instant notice. In less than a year he was elected Abbeville's representative in the state legislature. In another year he became engaged to marry Floride Calhoun. A political career, financial independence, and social acceptance were now all within his grasp.

Calhoun conducted his courtship of Floride as if preparing

a legal case or running a political campaign to win election as bridegroom in this case. His over-serious, reticent, reflective temperament scarcely fitted him for the role of romantic lover. Of the correspondence between him and Floride only one letter survives which suggests some emotion on his part expressed in overly rigid, stilted terms (even for an age which engaged in conventional formalities). In lining up allies in his campaign to win the girl, he appeared to woo the mother more ardently than the daughter. "You exceed all my friends," he wrote Mrs. Calhoun. "Never shall I be able to make you suitable return . . . Let me add . . . that to be so nearly related to you is a fruitful source of happiness. I know not why, from my first acquaintance with you at Newport, I have loved you as a mother. . . . Such is the warmth of my affection, which I feel towards you, that I can scarcely refrain from addressing you by the endearing epithet of mother. I hope that the time now may not be long when I may with propriety use it." To his sweetheart he attempted a poem, each line of which began with "whereas." [9]

In the face of such a campaign, Floride understandably held back, wondering no doubt what kind of man was this; especially for a young woman who loved dancing, gaiety, and fun. But as he contemplated Floride, even the "cast-iron man" began to thaw, and his pulse quickened as the intensity of his feelings surprised even himself. "This language does not correspond with my former opinion on the subject," he wrote, analyzing lawyerlike his own emotions; "I formerly thought it would be impossible for me to be strongly agitated in an affair of this kind; but that opinion now to me seems wholly unfounded, since. . . . it can produce such effects." As "such effects" increased Calhoun's warmth, Floride's reluctance weakened, no doubt with an assist from her mother. Shortly, the engagement was announced. Some complication arose over arranging the property settlement. Mrs.

Calhoun consulted Judge De Saussure to arrange the details regarding the property to be conferred on her daughter. Calhoun objected that the proposed property arrangement, with Floride retaining title, reflected lack of confidence in him. His view was accepted, and the settlement gave Calhoun full control of extensive land holdings in southeastern South Carolina and in the Pendleton area of the state's Piedmont.

For the wedding on January 8, 1811, hundreds of relatives and friends from all over the state came to the Bonneau's Ferry estate. The petite, black haired, 18-year-old bride, her dark eyes dancing with excitement, looked entrancing standing beside the tall, lanky 28-year-old Calhoun, with deep-set, luminous, dark eyes and somber face, as they recited their vows. After the wedding the couple made their home at "Bath," a plantation Calhoun had bought between the Savannah and Little Rivers. Marriage brought financial independence and release from the law for more appealing pursuits.

Even before marriage Calhoun's political career was well launched. In 1808 he had won election as Abbeville's representative in the state Assembly, where members following ancient British practice sat with their hats on, removing them only when speaking, and settled most questions by acclamation. One of the first issues demanding the legislature's attention was an amendment to the state constitution dealing with representation in the legislature. This was the climax of a 50-year-old battle, dating back to pre-Revolutionary days, between the wealthy, powerful, politically over-represented Carolina low country planters and the less prosperous, hardy, politically under-represented upcountry farmers. By a compromise in 1790, which Calhoun's father Patrick Calhoun helped to shape, the upland Scotch-Irish had won increased representation but still not proportionate to their numbers.

The two sections of the state remained suspicious and hostile toward each other. Finally, the 1808 compromise, embodied in the constitutional amendment, recognized the interests of both sections of the state, by providing that half the legislature's members be chosen on the basis of population (what the upcountry had long demanded) and half on the basis of property as indicated by taxes paid (as the lowcountry had long insisted). Thus as a 26-year-old new member, Calhoun in his first legislative session voted for final ratification of this sectional compromise—an exposure to sectional conflict and adjustment of majority-minority conflict that would recur to him a quarter century later as he strove to develop protective devices for the numerical minority on the national stage.[10]

Calhoun Leads Congress to War with England

Shortly Calhoun attracted attention as a coming, aggressive politician with a speech attacking President Jefferson's "restrictive" embargo, which hurt Carolina's export and Charleston's trade and asserting that war with England was inevitable. As the upcountry's indignation against England grew over British interference with American shipping during the Napoleonic wars and over rumors that British agents were inciting Indians on the Florida and Canadian borders to attack American settlements, Abbeville voters responded in 1810 by electing John C. Calhoun, anti-British spokesman, to represent them in Congress.

So in October 1811, shortly after the birth of their first child, named Andrew Pickens in honor of the family's Revolutionary hero. Calhoun left his bride of ten months and set out for Washington and the national political arena he would occupy for the next four decades.

When Calhoun arrived at the capital, he joined other new Congressmen—young, in their first term and elected by constituents angry with Great Britain. The grievances against England were British practices, during the Napoleonic wars of the past decade, of interfering with American ships on the seas, confiscating contraband cargoes, impressing sailors from American vessels into the British navy. But the aggravation that rasped Americans most, especially western tempers, was the alleged British inciting of Indians to attack American settlements in the Great Lakes region and along the southern border.

Recently, in the fall of 1811, General William Henry Harrison's troops at Tippecanoe battled northwestern Indians, suspected of confederating under British guidance to repel American occupation of lands in the old Northwest. Such British aggression could not be tolerated, cried the young Congressmen labeled "War Hawks," who shouted that English influence and presence on the North American continent must be eradicated. Jefferson's policy of an embargo on all foreign trade to force Britain to revoke its restrictions on American shipping was in effect being continued by his successor President James Madison. This namby-pamby policy War Hawks denounced as dishonorable and beneath contempt.

In Washington Calhoun took quarters in the strongest war "mess" (i.e., boarding house), which also housed Henry Clay of Kentucky, newly elected Speaker of the House and War Hawk spokesman, Felix Grundy of Tennessee, and fellow South Carolinians William Lowndes and Langdon Cheves. Calhoun's mental powers, skill in logic, adeptness at debate soon impressed his colleagues. Speaker Clay relied on Calhoun as a trusted lieutenant, appointing him to the crucial Foreign Relations Committee (of which Calhoun soon became acting chairman) and assigning him the exasperating task of checking the vitriolic attacks of iconoclastic John Randolph, that boyish looking Virginia representative whose high-pitched voice deceptively shot venomous criticism at both administration and War Hawks. All agreed that Calhoun at 29 made an impressive figure—well over six feet tall, rangey, large head, shock of dark hair, prominent cheek bones, dignified bearing (some saw a likeness to Andrew Jackson, certainly accurate in the common Scotch-Irish grit), but most of all, his eyes drew attention—large, deepset, dark (although their exact color was in dispute), but luminous and piercing and burning with "timeless fires." As Harriet Martineau commented on Calhoun, "the cast-iron man . . . looks as if he had never been born and never could be extinguished." [11]

As the session of Congress opened, the chauvinistic spirit of the House soon erupted. The new generation of Americans, born at the close of the Revolution, viewed the world as its oyster, abided no insults to American honor, would tackle all comers for the glory of the nation. With immense confidence, Speaker Clay denounced the "insolence of British cannon" and urged fellow Americans to march northward; indeed, he blustered, "a thousand Kentucky riflemen" could seize Canada and throw the British into the sea.

Calhoun, bursting with national pride and self confidence, delivered his first national speech replying to Randolph's sneer that the country was unprepared for war. Said Calhoun:

> let us remedy that evil as soon as possible. . . . But it may be that the nation will not pay taxes because the rights violated are not worth defending or that the defense will cost more than the profits. Sir, I here enter my most solemn protest against this low and 'calculating avarice' entering this hall of legislation. It is fit only for shops and counting houses . . . [and should not] disgrace [us] by its squalid and vile appearance. . . . I only know of one principle to make a nation great, to produce in this country not the form but real spirit of Union, and that is to protect every citizen. . . . He will then feel that he is backed by his Government; that its arm is his arm. . . . Protection and patriotism are reciprocal. . . . I am

not versed in this calculating policy, and will not, there-fore, pretend to estimate in dollars and cents the value of national independence or national affection. . . . the honor of a nation is its life. Deliberately to abandon it, is to commit an act of political suicide.[12]

While President Madison held back, War Hawks led by Clay and Calhoun, pressed for military preparedness and war. In rapid succession they forced through Congress bills increasing the army, raising taxes, authorizing government loans. By the spring of 1812, Calhoun complained that the "greatest impediment" was the President himself, who "reluctantly gives up his system of peace," meaning the policy of commercial coercion pursued since the days of Jefferson's 1807 embargo.

But the War Hawks refused to wait, hotly forced the President's hand and in June 1812 pushed through Congress a declaration of war (ironically, only days before Britain announced removal of the restrictions on American shipping, the alleged cause of war—but the news did not reach America for a month). In whipping up war enthusiasm, Calhoun cried in the last days of debate, "In four weeks . . . from a declaration of war, the whole of Upper Canada and a part of Lower Canada will be in our possession." And it was Calhoun who finally submitted the war resolution in the House. In his first session in Congress Calhoun had made a deep impression on his colleagues; little wonder that the Richmond *Enquirer* hailed "this young South Carolinian as one of those master spirits, who stamp their name upon the age in which they live."[13]

During the war Calhoun spoke often and cogently for vigorous Congressional support to provide the military hardware for success. His main concern was to see that the administration received the men, money, and materials needed

to prosecute the war successfully. At the outset of the war
he did differ with the administration on one point and argued
strenuously for repeal of embargo legislation on the grounds
that "We are at war. It is wisdom to make it [war] efficient."
Since the embargo was restrictive class legislation that deprived northeastern merchants of their livelihood, it thereby
bred disaffection, opposition, and even disunion sentiment in
New England, which weakened the war effort. He missed by
one vote winning repeal but gained the respect of New England Federalists and emerged a figure of commanding national prominence. At home, too, he won reelection to Congress without opposition; a former Congressman declined to
run against him saying: "You can meet [John] Randolph
in debate—I cannot." [14] Calhoun's unrelenting labors to
strengthen the nation's fighting machine led Secretary of the
Treasury Alexander J. Dallas to praise him as the "young
Hercules who carried the war on his shoulders." [15]

Calhoun demonstrated a moderate, level-headed, temperate stance (even while demanding war with England), seeking
to persuade by the compelling force of his intellectual argument, rather than attempting to thrust his opinion down the
throats of other men. Surprising was his sudden, senseless
fracas with New York Representative Thomas P. Grosvenor,
in which hot words flew, leading to a duel challenge being
issued and accepted. Only the last minute intervention of
persuasive attorney Francis Scott Key got the affair canceled
without mishap or loss of honor. In sharp contrast to Jackson's duel-happy exploits, this is the only instance of Calhoun's being involved in an affair of honor requiring a duel;
it was an exception since Calhoun seldom permitted his own
emotions to break through his shatter-proof self-restraint.

The War of 1812 made Calhoun into a major national
figure—a young man still (only 33 at war's end) with a highly
promising future, already influential in the nation's high

councils, trusted, admitted by executive and legislative leaders alike for his clear vision, sharp forensic skill, firm determination, broad national views coupled with tolerant concern for all sections and classes. As John Quincy Adams noted, Calhoun was "a man of fair and candid mind, of honorable principles, of clear and quick understanding, of cool self possession, of enlarged philosophical views, and of ardent patriotism. He is above all sectional and factional prejudices more than any other statesman in this Union. . . ." [16] That Calhoun possessed exceptional talents was conceded by all, including Calhoun whose ample ego suffered little from modesty.

While Calhoun appeared as the "young Hercules" carrying the war on his shoulders, Jackson emerged from the war as the "Hero of New Orleans," [17] the only genuine national hero of an otherwise drab war. By 1815 both South Carolina natives, Jackson and Calhoun, had moved far from their obscure frontier beginnings. Calhoun had gained a formal education by dint of his own industry, acquired social position and wealth by a fortuitous marriage, won fame in politics as spokesman for a strong nation. Jackson, with virtually no formal schooling, had married on impetuous impulse, acquired a plantation and land holdings by dint of his wits, captured fame on the battlefield through exercise of iron will. Calhoun's was a fame won by words as a politician, Jackson's by deeds as a warrior. That nineteenth century Americans preferred action to talk would become clearer in the next two decades.

III Jackson: Military Chieftain to President, 1815-1828

The Border Captain Triggers an International Incident

SOON AFTER the close of the War of 1812, the United States Army was reorganized into northern and southern divisions. Andrew Jackson was placed in command of the southern division with his headquarters at the Hermitage. By the fall of 1815 this convenient arrangement gave him time for a leisurely trip to receive the thanks of a grateful populace as he journeyed through Tennessee and Virginia to Washington. Everywhere along his route he was greeted with crowds of people cheering the "Hero of New Orleans," with parades, parties, and banquets to do him honor. To his natural courtesy and dignity, he now joined an added skill in gracefully receiving the universal plaudits and graciously returning appropriate compliments to prominent local hosts who arranged the welcoming affairs. Whether he was consciously aware of it, his future political career was clearly in the making.[1]

At Lynchburg, Virginia, Thomas Jefferson, former President and founder of the now dominant Republican party, attended with 300 other diners the banquet in Jackson's honor. Jefferson and Jackson had not seen each other since 1798 when the former as Vice President had observed unimpressed the performance of the latter as freshman Senator from Tennessee; a bit later as President, Jefferson had fumed over Jackson's association with Aaron Burr and defense of Burr at Richmond, joined with an uncalled-for denunciation by Jackson of the feebleness of Jefferson's leadership. Now, with the old irritations muted, at the Lynchburg banquet Jefferson raised his glass in toast: "Honor and gratitude to those who have filled the measure of their country's honor." The General responded: "James Monroe, late Secretary of War," thereby praising Jefferson's long time protegee.[2]

In Washington greetings for Jackson were as enthusiastic as those received en route. Congress ordered a medal struck in his honor for the victory at New Orleans. The General was wined and dined. President Madison, soon to retire from office, and Monroe, soon to succeed Madison in the White House, were warm in their praises. Whether Jackson met John Calhoun during this visit to Wahington is not clear from contemporary records, but the probability is strong that they did have their first meeting at this time, since Calhoun returned from South Carolina to Washington in early December and Jackson did not leave the capital until January 1816.

Back in Tennessee the General refocused on military problems. As southern division commander, he was responsible for the security of the nation's southern border, a duty he took with utmost earnestness and driving attention. In 1817 the Florida border flared into violence as Seminoles raided into southern Georgia and Alabama, killing settlers, burning cabins, and abducting hostages. As military commander, Jackson would not stand idly by. Besides, he had something of a personal interest in the area of what is today western Florida where his close friends John Donelson and John Eaton were already speculating in lands near Pensacola that they expected soon to become American territory.

What happened next became a matter of angry controversy

and years later caused a sharp break between Jackson and Calhoun, who after 1831 refused to speak to each other because of what happened during the Seminole campaign of 1817. As the Seminole border raids intensified, Jackson was ordered to take personal command in the field by John C. Calhoun, only recently installed as Monroe's Secretary of War. Already engaged in a caustic dispute with his War Department superiors (antedating Calhoun's assuming office) over War Department practice of sending military orders directly to officers under Jackson's command without notifying him, Jackson was threatening to resign unless all orders cleared through him. That dispute had been practically resolved when Calhoun's orders to proceed in person to the Georgia-Florida border arrived. Jackson noted the instructions were very broad: "Adopt the necessary measures to terminate . . . [the] conflict."[3] He also inherited orders of an earlier date to General Edmund Gaines, in active command on the border, directing full-scale operations against the Seminoles with authorization to pursue them across the border, if necessary, and to attack them within Florida "unless they should shelter themselves under a Spanish post. In the last event, you will notify this [War] Department." These orders to Gaines, intentionally vague and conferring wide latitude, Jackson now inherited.

Rereading the Gaines' orders, Jackson dashed off a letter directly to Monroe (bypassing Secretary of War Calhoun) urging even stronger action. "Suppose," he wrote, "the Indians . . . take refuge in either Pensacola or St. Augustine. . . . [our commander] has to halt before the . . . [fort and] communicate with his Government; in the meantime the militia grows restless, and he has to defend himself with regulars. The enemy, with the aid of Spanish . . . and British, partisans . . . attacks him, what may not be the result? —defeat and massacre." Rather than run such risk, the General specifically proposed that "The whole of East Florida [be] seized and . . . this can be done without implicating the Government. Let it be signified to me through any channel, say Mr. J. Rhea [Tennessee Congressman-friend of Jackson], that the possession of Florida would be desirable . . . and in sixty days it will be accomplished." [4]

Shortly after sending this letter (but before President Monroe had time to receive it), Jackson received from Monroe a dispatch saying: "The movement against the Seminoles . . . will bring you on a theatre where you may possibly have other services to perform. . . . Great interests are at issue. . . . This is no time for repose . . . untill our cause is carried triumphantly thro'." [5] What "other services," what "great interests," what was "our cause?" The letter was vague, purposely so, Jackson surmised. In Jackson's mind there was no doubt that the President was telling him to drive ahead and seize Florida. Certainly that thought dominated Jackson's mind, still thinking of the "Rhea letter."

In actual fact, in January 1818, Jackson's "Rhea letter" was delivered to Monroe. The President, too ill at the time to read it, passed the letter on to Secretary of War Calhoun, who read and returned it, indicating it required the President's decision. But Monroe appears not to have read the letter then. Whether Jackson actually received a letter from Congressman Rhea bearing Presidential approval of Jackson's proposed Florida invasion (as Jackson later asserted positively) is highly doubtful. But the administration, especially Monroe and Calhoun, must have understood the General's intentions. In the absence of any restraining sign from Washington, Jackson assumed consent (later he appears to have come genuinely to believe he had received official sanction for the course he pursued). Indeed, after Jackson occupied St. Marks in Florida, Calhoun notified Alabama's Governor, "General Jackson is vested with full power to conduct the war as he may think best." Surely, Calhoun must have known what Jackson thought "best" for Florida, having already read Jackson's clear, unambiguous letter to Monroe.

No restraining order having been received, General Jackson took command at Fort Scott near the Florida border of 800 regulars and 900 Georgia militiamen at dawn, March 9, 1818. Quickly Jackson marched his force across the border into Spanish Florida, seized the Spanish fort at St. Marks, where the Indians had been reported earlier, lowered the Spanish flag and raised the Stars and Stripes. Scouts now reported hostile Indians on the Suwanee River 100 miles away. Jackson rushed there only to miss the Indians again. In the course of operations, however, he discovered and arrested two Englishmen, Robert Ambrister and Alexander Arbuthnot, both known Indian traders, whom Jackson now court-martialed on charges of inciting and supplying Indians with weapons. The court sentenced the former to be hanged, the latter to receive 50 lashes. Jackson overrode the verdict and had both men executed.

Moving on, Jackson crushed several small bands of Indians and then turned on the Spanish in Florida, whom he suspected of supplying the Indians. He captured without contest the Spanish post at Pensacola, informing the Spanish Governor he was assuming control until the American and Spanish governments worked out details of the transfer—and sending the Governor and his garrison packing to Havana. Leaving a garrison at St. Marks and Pensacola, Old Hickory then returned to the Hermitage, well satisfied that he had effected what Washington expected of him. His home town greeted him ecstatically.

But word came from Washington that Monroe faced a crisis over the impetuous general's invasion of Florida, expulsion of the Spanish forces there, and execution of two British subjects. When the Spanish minister, Luis de Onis, lodged a formal protest, Monroe gathered his cabinet into council. In secret session (details of which were not revealed until years later) most cabinet members favored disavowing the Florida invasion as unauthorized, restoring the forts to Spain, and initiating a reprimand, censure, or at least investigation of Jackson's conduct. Calhoun, miffed that Jackson had gone over his head directly to the President for authority regarding Florida, sided with the majority, along with Treasury Secretary William H. Crawford. But tough, shrewd, brilliant Secretary of State, John Quincy Adams, argued sturdily for hours that Jackson's course was not only proper but was required by his principal duty of subduing the Seminoles. Adams at length prevailed; Monroe adopted the course Adams proposed, although he could not publicly say he had authorized Jack's actions. Actually Jackson had been a long time friend and supporter of Monroe who, as Secretary of War for a time, had been Jackson's superior in the War of 1812. Jackson had supported Monroe's bid for the presidency as early as 1808. On the basis of friendship Monroe tactfully explained to Jackson the need to return the Spanish forts.

Secretary Adams accomplished the equally delicate task of mollifying the Spanish government. He justified Jackson's invasion as necessary self defense against Indian attacks, contending that since Spain had not kept the peace along the border the United States had to and finally suggesting that Spain might wish to consider selling her troubled Florida province. The suggested solution led in 1819 to the Adams-Onis Treaty transferring Florida to the United States in return for American surrender of claims to Texas and a fixed western boundary between American and Spanish territories from Texas and beyond to the Pacific.

In Tennessee, Old Hickory, incensed over reports of the Monroe administration dilemma, suspected Crawford as the chief villain (earlier Jackson had stormed over Crawford's action as Secretary of War in returning four million acres to the Creeks which Jackson had wrested from them by conquest and treaty.) Now he was convinced that Crawford was seeking to discredit Jackson's reputation. Somehow Jackson conceived at this time the erroneous impression that Calhoun had been his staunch defender in the cabinet debate, writing of Calhoun as "my friend," who "approves my conduct and that of the President." And Calhoun kept quiet about his disapproval in cabinet of Jackson's actions (which was only proper since cabinet sessions are secret). But the secret would leak out a dozen years later, to Calhoun's regret and chagrin. At the time, however, Calhoun's part remained unknown to Jackson, who charged out of Tennessee and swept into Washington in late January 1819 to observe how Congress and the administration would handle the matter. En route, Jackson, entertained at a public dinner in Winchester, Va., had offered the toast: "John C. Calhoun: an honest man is the noblest work of God." [6]

In Congress, Henry Clay, smarting under imagined slights by Monroe, led the assault on the President and General Jackson. Calling for Congressional denunciation, Clay charged Jackson with violating international law and with seeking selfishly to put his military authority above civilian control. Clearly, Clay argued, Jackson's unauthorized invasion of Florida and execution of two British subjects and Indian leaders required that the general be disavowed by the government and dismissed from the service. While Congress deliberated, Jackson exploded furiously over "the hypocracy and baseness of Clay in . . . endeavoring to crush the executive through me . . . [his efforts] make me despise the Villain." [7] But Jackson's supporters easily defeated the Clay resolutions of censure in the House of Representatives. Jackson was cleared and praised in Congress and out. Leaving Washington, he set forth on a triumphal tour northward to

Baltimore, Philadelphia, and New York. Hailed as a hero everywhere he stopped, he was feted with parades, banquets, toasts, and celebrations of popular gratitude. During this jaunt Jackson perfected his skill at greeting people warmly, extending personal compliments and responding graciously to the outpouring of laudatory toasts. As his taste for and skill at politicking grew, so did his political ambitions.

After his vindication in Washington, Jackson returned to the more peaceful haunts of the Hermitage. He had developed an affection for James Monroe, and when the President toured as far south as Georgia later in the year, Jackson joined him there and accompanied him across the mountains to Knoxville and Nashville, to the tune of continuous ovations along the route. A little later Jackson, still a Major General, wrote the President: "I am wearied with public life . . . I have been accused of acts I never committed, or crimes I never thought of, and . . . charged . . . in the Senate . . . of doing acts in my official capacity to promote my private interest." This had wounded him deeply since "I have labored through life to establish an honest Charactor." If only "our affairs with Spain would have been finally settled by her ratifying the treaty [to transfer Florida]," Jackson would "tender my resignation." [8]

But Spain had not ratified the Florida treaty. As the weeks of delay stretched into months, Secretary Adams grew increasingly impatient. When Jackson received confidential notice to prepare a military movement to awe the Spanish, he sprang instantly into action and fired back to Secretary of War Calhoun a full plan, complete with estimates of manpower, guns and supplies needed, to seize all of Florida. With this communication he enclosed a private note to the Secretary. Would it embarrass the government if he should seize Cuba also? Calhoun, staggered by the General's impetuous scheme, replied that although he, too, favored acquisition of

Cuba, "we ought at present limit our operations to Florida." [9]

At this point Monroe may have wished that he had earlier acted on his inclination to send his aggressive commander abroad. The embassy at St. Petersburg fell vacant. Its remoteness appealed to the President. How about sending Jackson on a mission to Russia? When Monroe consulted his venerated advisor, Thomas Jefferson, the Sage of Monticello exploded, "Great God, he would breed you a quarrel before he had been there a month. [10]

Tennessee Planter Tosses his Hat in the Ring

So when the Florida treaty was at length ratified, Jackson accepted Monroe's offer to be Governor of Florida where a quarrel arose in a month. Florida's formal transfer to the United States he received at Pensacola in July 1821. Old Hickory, supervising the details of the transfer, became so irritated with the annoying delays of the former Spanish Governor that he jailed him for a time. After seeing to the establishment of counties and courts, Old Hickory wearied of the task, quietly resigned, and returned to the Hermitage, announcing his permanent retirement from public life. Mrs. Jackson, relieved and happy that her husband was, now at home, looked forward to enjoying their country estate together, writing to her sister: "I do hope they will now leave Mr. Jackson alone. He is not a well man. . . . In the thirty years of our wedded life . . . he has not spent one-fourth of his days under his own roof. The rest of the time away, travelling, holding court, or at the capital of his country, or in camp, or fighting its battles, or treating with the Indians; mercy knows what not. . . . Through all such trials I have not said aye, yes or no. It was his work to do, he seemed called to it, and I watched, waited and prayed most of the time alone. Now I hope this is at an end." [11] But Rachel would hope in vain that "they will now leave Mr. Jackson alone."

Now in his mid-fifties, Jackson did perhaps genuinely desire a chance to enjoy the peaceful tranquility of country life at the Hermitage, whose graceful brick mansion had been built just two years before. But friends would not "leave Mr. Jackson alone." Some years earlier he had explosively rejected as fantasy the notion of his becoming President, saying, "I know what I am fit for. I can command a body of men in a rough way; but I am not fit to be President." [12] When in 1822, old friend George W. Campbell stopped by the Hermitage and dropped a hint that Jackson would be President, Old Hickory shouted, "You don't think, George, that I'm damned fool enough to believe that! . . . . I'm not vain enough for that." [13] When some newspapers suggested Jackson's name, he said nothing publicly but privately his answer was a resounding no.

But his friends were not listening. A group of Tennessee cohorts recognizing Presidential timber when they saw it, began in 1822 a muted, subtle drive to prepare Jackson and the country for his Presidency. Long-time friend and neighbor John Overton, planter, judge, and local bank president; William B. Lewis, tall, powerful, energetic, also a neighbor, who had served as Jackson's commisary major in the Indian campaigns and who would soon become his most trusted political adviser; Senator John H. Eaton, wealthy lawyer-planter from Franklin, Tennessee, who had earlier published a biography extolling the General's military prowess and defended him against censure in the Senate—formed the inner circle of the "Nashville Junto," as the newspapers called them. Associates included rough and tumble Congressman Felix Grundy, familiar with political ways in both Tennessee and Washington; George W. Campbell, former Congressman and Secretary of the Treasury; and up-and-coming Nashville attorney Sam Houston.

Their shrewd plan, conceived in the spring of 1822, refrained from pressuring the Old Hero himself, which they recognized as next to impossible. He would not have to do anything except to say, as he did on repeated occasions: "I have never been an applicant for office. I never will. . . . I have no desire nor do I ever expect to be called to fill the Presidential chair, but should this be the case . . . it will be without exertion on my part." [14] Rather they would ignore party machinery, alliances with big wig politicians. Quietly they would generate a large groundswell of popular, grass roots support. It would not be easy to present Jackson as champion of the poor, unprivileged mass of the people, since in the wake of the 1819 panic he had opposed legislative enactment of stay laws to postpone collection of debts and the easy money panacaeas debtors demanded. But this aside, Jackson could appear as the "Old Hero" of New Orleans, the scourge of redcoats, red men, Spaniards, and assorted other enemies of the republic.

To stir Jackson's own interest, his managers were counting on his hostility, bordering on hatred, of two professional politicians already running hard for President. As to William H. Crawford, who as Secretary of War had returned some lands which Jackson had pried from the Creek Indians by war and treaty and had later condemned Jackson's Seminole war in Florida—"I would support the Devil first," Jackson fumed.[15] He would not waste his breath on "that base hypocrite" from Kentucky, Henry Clay, who had led the Congressional attack on Jackson's Florida invasion. John Quincy Adams, in Jackson's opinion, stood as "a man of as first rate mind as any in America as a civilian and a scholar," and "I will," Old Hickory had written at the end of 1821, "support Mr. Adams unless Mr. Calhoun should be brought forward." [16] As long as Jackson could be kept from publicly expressing a preference and not giving any firm commitment of support, his managers felt safe.

To build the groundswell of popular support, Lewis, Grundy, Houston, and Eaton took frequent journeys, talking with friends, relatives and in-laws, both in Tennessee and neighboring states. Correspondence developed with old Jackson friends in more distant states like Pennsylvania, where in Pittsburgh Jackson was still remembered favorably from his earlier visits there to buy supplies for his Tennessee store. These distant contacts, cultivated carefully by the Jackson managers, would ultimately pay off.

But the first task was to nail down Tennessee. When the Tennessee legislature met in July 1822, Jackson's managers were on hand, notably Sam Houston who from his six-foot-six height watched closely to see that members voted right on the resolution "that the name of Andrew Jackson be submitted to the consideration of the people of the United States . . . to fill the presidential chair." [17] The vote was unanimous, although "one or two gentlemen quit the house" rather than vote aye. Jackson gave no outward hint of acknowledgment, writing to his nephew only that "I mean to be silent—and let the people do as seemeth good unto them." [18] Silence was not, of course, refusal. The Nashville Junto privately congratulated themselves.

Some months later Senator John Eaton summoned to the White House, where President Monroe reviewed the state of our relations with Mexico and raised the question of the advisability of sending Jackson as our minister to Mexico City. Eaton left the President with the impression that Jackson would accept the appointment. Whereupon the nomination was sent to the Senate and quickly confirmed. The commission went to the Hermitage, accompanied by a Presidential note expressing "confidence in your integrity and patriotism." The die was now cast, as Eaton fully realized. Jackson could readily take himself out of the Presidential contest by accepting; but if he refused, clearly he was giving his consent to stand as a candidate.

Some evidence suggests that Jackson's decision sprang from a report by a Massachusetts Congressman to this effect: with 132 votes needed to win the Presidency, Crawford at the moment appeared to have 114 sure, Adams 48, Clay 41, Calhoun 39 (South Carolina and Pennsylvania) and Jackson 19 (Tennessee, Mississippi, Alabama, Louisiana). On this calculation, as Jackson speedily observed, his own withdrawal would likely throw southwestern votes to Crawford, putting him dangerously close to the winning number. Pondering that prospect ("I would support the Devil first") and Eaton's report from Washington that Jackson's acceptance of the Mexican mission was favored by Adams and opposed by Calhoun, Jackson consulted Mrs. Jackson and Joel R. Poinsett, well informed on Mexican affairs. On February 19, 1823, Jackson sent his regrets to Monroe.

The signal was clear—Old Hickory would not seek but neither would he reject the Presidency. Four days later, responding to an inquiry from a committee in Pennsylvania, where a Jackson boomlet was mushrooming, he made it explicit: "My undeviating rule . . . has been neither to seek or decline public invitations to office. . . . As the office of Chief Magistrate . . . should not be sought, . . . so it cannot with propriety be declined." [19] Less than two weeks later the Pennsylvania state convention, which had previously been considered in Calhoun's pocket, met in Harrisburg and declined to endorse a Presidential candidate, confining its labors to a state ticket.

A "Corrupt Bargain" Thwarts the "People's Will"

While the Calhoun drive lost steam, Crawford still appeared far in front, almost uncatchable. The Treasury Secretary was the "regular" candidate of the Republican party, enjoying the blessing of both Jefferson and Madison. A native Virginian, though reared in Georgia, he would continue the

"Virginia Dynasty," in alliance with New York where Martin Van Buren's resourceful efforts bolstered Crawford's cause. A state rights advocate, he had performed adequately in the Senate, War and Treasury Secretaryships, while his large size, physical strength, mental vitality, and hearty personality won him many adherents. John Quincy Adams, with the best qualifications of all for the Presidency, stood for a strong, active national government, but his cold manner and refusal to use the patronage to further his cause turned off potential supporters. Calhoun, suffering the disadvantage of youth, had won support in New England and Pennsylvania by advocating internal improvements and a protective tariff. Henry Clay, Speaker of the House, found his greatest strength in the West, where his stand for federal internal improvements and tariff to stimulate industry won support; while his natural affability and charm made him personally irresistible to a host of followers.

None of the four aspirants, not even Clay, could match the charisma of the Old Hero. Shortly, Jackson's name was added to the foursome. In 1823, he aided his own cause in acknowledging a hat of "domestic manufacture" sent by a Pennsylvania admirer: "Mrs. Jackson will wear with pride a hat made by American hands, . . . its workmanship will be . . . evidence of the perfection which our domestic manufactures may hereafter acquire, if properly fostered and protected. Upon the success of our manufactures, as the handmaiden of agriculture and commerce, depends in great measure the independence of our country." [20] Surely tariff-conscious Pennsylvanians could go for a candidate who saw the economic light as clearly as he revealed his political shrewdness.

As the Calhoun political machine sputtered, Crawford's drive encountered disaster when Crawford himself suffered a devastating stroke, that left him for the time being speechless, nearly blind, and paralyzed from the neck down. His managers kept him in seclusion and the public in the dark as to his actual condition. But public suspicions that something was amiss grew, and although Crawford made a partial recovery, his active candidacy was at an end by late 1823.

At the same time Jackson managers encountered rough weather—and that in their own state. Senator John Williams, pro-Crawford and long a Jackson foe, was up for re-election. Jackson managers John Eaton and Major Lewis hastened to the state capital to bolster the faltering campaign of Congressman John Rhea, who was running as Williams's opponent. Their best efforts at arm-twisting lifted Rhea's total to a point three votes shy of victory. "It has now become necessary to play a bold game." "Desperate" would have been more accurate. For a Jackson man to lose in his own state would have punctured the Jackson candidacy before it got off the ground. Lewis played his ace: he entered Jackson's name for Senator, then sent a message to the Hermitage asking consent. Jackson refused; but a second messenger wrung from him the concession that he would serve if elected. That was all Lewis needed. On the legislative roll-call, seven men switched; the vote—Jackson 35, Williams 25. "I have been elected senator," Old Hickory wrote resignedly to friend John Coffee, "a circumstance I regret more than any other in my life." [21]

In early December Jackson took up lodging in Washington at Major William O'Neale's boarding house, where he noted that his fellow boarder Senator John Eaton appeared to be much taken with the vivacious Peggy, 27-year-old daughter of the proprietor. Jackson wrote home to Rachel, "nothing doing here but *vissiting* and *carding*. You know how much I was disgusted with Those scenes when you and I were here [in 1815]." But Eaton gave a different slant to Mrs. Jackson: "The general is constantly in motion to some Dinner party or other, and tonight stands engaged at a large Dancing party at General [Jacob] Browns." [22] In the Senate chamber itself Jackson discovered that his seat adjoined that of Thomas Hart Benton, now Missouri's senator. This was the first time the two men had seen each other since the tavern brawl in Nashville in 1813 when two bullets from the Benton brothers' pistols almost cost the General his life (one he still carried in his left shoulder). Benton bowed in deference, Jackson extended his hand. Old Hickory seemed "resolved upon a general amnesty," even extending an invitation to old foe Henry Clay to a large dinner along with two other competitors for the presidency, Adams and Calhoun. Cordially Adams returned the compliment. The Secretary of State fittingly set January 8, 1824 (9th anniversary of New Orleans) for a huge reception for the General. Mrs. Adams spent a week preparing—decorations of colored tissue paper and evergreens, large eagles, flags, and a giant wall motto screaming "Welcome to the Hero of New Orleans." Hundreds of guests crowded the mansion and watched as "Mrs. Adams gracefully took his [Jackson's] arm and walked" through the room. A short time later Adams let it be known that he believed Old Hickory's character would lend lustre to the Vice Presidential office which would "afford an easy and dignified retirement for his old age." Besides, Adams noted wryly in his diary, "The Vice Presidency . . . [is] a station in which the General could hang no one." A campaign jingle urged voters to support "John Quincy Adams who can write, Andrew Jackson who can fight." [23] However, Old Hickory gave no outward indication of interest in such a combination.

At O'Neale's inn Jackson was pleased with his "comfortable quarters" thanks to "the kind attention of my friend Eaton." He, too, was charmed by the proprietor's married daughter, Peggy O'Neale Timberlake "who plays the piano delightfully, and every Sunday evening entertains her pious mother with sacred music." She also poured after-dinner coffee for Eaton, Jackson, and other guests whom she coquettishly amused with her lively conversation. A suspicion that she "would dispense her favors wherever she took a fancy" was held by some, including Mrs. Monroe, who made it clear that Peggy was not wanted at presidential receptions, which as a naval officer's wife, she was entitled to attend.[24]

Despite his physical condition, Crawford still retained the lead in the big race. In February his managers pushed his name before a Congressional caucus. Although boycotted and scoffed at as "undemocratic" by other candidates' handlers, the caucus endorsed Crawford by 65 votes (150 members stayed away in protest). A few days later the crucial Pennsylvania state convention in Harrisburg nominated by acclamation Andrew Jackson for President and John C. Calhoun for Vice-President.

This unexpected action, the result of the grass-roots ground-swell generated by the Jackson managers, killed off Calhoun, who readily acknowledged he now had no chance. Jackson, whose dignity, grace, and good manners in the Senate had caused many in Washington to revise their original estimates of him as an untutored wild man (even Daniel Webster conceded that Jackson was the most presidential-looking of the candidates) now forged forward as the Calhoun organizations shifted to his support. Crawford leaders found it difficult to hold adherents in line. Even New England felt the surge for Jackson. "I have no doubt if I was to travel to Boston where I have been invited," the General wrote Lewis, "that would insure my election. But this I cannot do—I would feel degraded the balance of my life." [25]

But Jackson could not avoid taking a stand on at least one issue when a protective tariff bill came before the Senate. He voted for it, explaining that "the design of fostering, protecting . . . within ourselves the means of national defense" was

crucial, that "lead, iron, and copper, . . . being the grand
materials of our national defense" ought to have "protection,
that manufacturers and laborers may produce within our own
borders a supply . . . essential to war." Then, sounding very
much like Henry Clay defending the "American System," the
General explained that American farmers would gain by
"this judicious Tariff . . . a home market for your breadstuffs." [26] (See *Appendix*, Doc. No. 2 for fuller text.) The
Nashville Junto managers, alarmed that their man might
alienate voters by expressing such views, could only console
themselves by emphasizing "the judicious Tariff" phrase and
by continuing to urge voters to support Jackson as the champion of virtue, the "Old Hero," the "People's Friend." Jackson's cause gained steadily, especially as word of Crawford's
incapacity spread.

In 1824 state elections to choose presidential electors were
held as each state prescribed, on a day falling between October 27 and December 1. Since communications, as well as
ballot counting, were extremely slow, the final outcome was
not known until December when Congress reassembled in
Washington. The returns gave Jackson 99 electoral votes,
Adams 84, Crawford 41, Clay 37. The popular vote, not
entirely complete nor accurate since at least one state did not
use such an arrangement, gave Jackson 152,901 (42%),
Adams 114,023 (32%), Crawford 46,979 (13%), Clay 47,217
(13%). Since no candidate had a majority, the next President
would be chosen, as the Constitution directed, from the top
three contenders by the House of Representatives, each state
delegation there having a single vote. Hence, of the 24 states,
the votes of 13 would determine the winner. As Jackson had
carried 11 states to Adams's 7, the General needed only two
more to prevail (assuming that House delegations would vote
as their home states did in the fall balloting).

Out of contention by finishing only fourth in the electoral

college count, Henry Clay held the key to determining the final choice because of his powerful influence as Speaker of the House. Through the winter of 1824–25, all eyes focused on the Kentuckian. Clay kept his own counsel, giving no outward sign of his preference. Clay's friends, however, eager to boost his ambitions for prominent place, were busy putting out feelers. When it was hinted to Jackson that a promise to make Clay Secretary of State "would put an end to the presidential contest in one hour," Jackson exploded: "Say to Mr. Clay and his friends that before I would reach the presidential chair by such means . . . I would see the earth open and swallow both Mr. Clay and his friends and myself with them. If they had not the confidence . . . that I would call to the cabinet men of the first virtue, talent, and integrity, [tell them] not to vote for me." [27]

After much maneuvering and endless comings and goings, Speaker Clay at length gave a public endorsement of Adams. Whatever his motives—conviction that the New Englander was far and away the best qualified man, "fear" (as Clay himself put it) "that the election of General Jackson would give to the Military spirit a stimulus that might lead to most pernicious results," concern that electing Jackson, a Westerner, would undermine Kentuckian Clay's chances for the Presidency for years, belief that he could get the best deal from Adams, Clay decided for the latter. He may possibly have heard Daniel Webster's report of his visit to Monticello where Jefferson declared, "I feel much alarmed at the prospect of seeing General Jackson President. He is one of the most unfit men I know of for such a place . . . His passions are terrible." [28] With which sentiment Clay doubtless concurred.

Throughout all the jockeying, gossiping, and wheeling-dealing, Old Hickory in the seething capital remained calm, above the battle, writing a friend: "There are various ru-

mours . . . but I do not join in any conversation on the
subject of the presidential election. . . . Mrs. Jackson and
myself goes to no parties . . . [instead] Mrs. Jackson and
myself [remain] at home smoking our pipe." [29]

When the House proceeded on February 9, 1825 with the
ballotting for President, Clay's influence became clear as
many western state delegations announced their votes for
Adams, whose total moved closer to the magic number 13.
The critical decision rested with New York, whose 34-man
delegation was split 17 for Adams and 17 under control of
Martin Van Buren, a staunch Crawford supporter. Among
the latter 17 was elderly, absent-minded Stephen Van Rensselaer, who having promised to stick by Van Buren was pres-
sured by Clay and Webster to consider the national chaos
impending from failure to choose a president. As state delegations were directed to poll their members, Van Rensselaer sat
with head down on his desk as though in silent appeal to his
Maker. Upon raising his head he saw at his feet a discarded
Adams ballot. Accepting it as Providence's answer, he
swooped up the ticket and dropped it quickly into the ballot
box, thereby giving Adams a majority of one in New York's
delegation, the vote of that state, and with it the Presidency.[30]
House tellers tallied the results: Adams 13 states, Jackson
7, Crawford 4. Speaker Henry Clay arose: "John Quincy
Adams, having a majority of the votes of these United States,
is duly elected President."

That evening Monroe gave his last Presidential levee. The
White House glowed with the brilliance of the social elite,
the politically prominent, friends, and hangers on. Lafayette,
President-elect Adams, Calhoun, and Clay were there along
with many guests, including artist Samuel F. B. Morse of
New York and Edward Stanley, an English visitor. Adams
"seemed" to Morse "to shake off his habitual reserve, and

although he endeavored to suppress his feeling of gratification at his success," it was easy to see "he felt in high spirits." But from Stanley's vantage point, "I never saw a more sinister expression of countenance than that of Mr. Adams—his figure is short & thick, and his air is that of low cunning & dissimulation, which I believe has been much belied by the course of his political career." [31]

Erect, dignified and unaffected, Jackson, with a lady on his right arm, approached the short, round-faced Adams, and "reaching out his long arm said—'How do you do, Mr. Adams? I give you my left hand for my right as you see is devoted to the fair; I hope you are very well, sir.' " At this "Mr. Adams took the General's hand and said, 'Very well, sir; I hope Gen. Jackson is well.' as he thanked Jackson for his congratulations." [32] Standing nearby, President Monroe, seeking as always to avoid unpleasantness, offered no congratulations lest it be construed as showing favoritism, treated both men with calm impartiality and steered the conversation to less touchy topics.

On March 4, 1825, Adams took the oath of office as President as General Jackson watched. A few moments earlier Jackson, as the oldest Senator, had administered the oath of office to young J. C. Calhoun as Vice-President. Clay duly accepted the Adams offer of Secretary of State. Immediately the political arena resounded to Jacksonians' cries of "corrupt bargain" between "the Puritan and the black leg." Jackson partisans and press ballooned the issue to gigantic proportions. Acid-tongued John Randolph scourged "black leg" Clay in the Senate. General Jackson maintained a public silence on the question but privately snarled: "So you see the Judas of the West has closed the contract and will receive the thirty pieces of silver. His end will be the same. Was there ever witnessed such bare faced corruption?" [33]

Old Hickory Fights for and Wins the Presidency

Andrew Jackson, his Scotch-Irish dander up, was fighting mad. That "gambler, black leg and traitor" from Kentucky must be taught a lesson. Returning home, the old General now approached the Hermitage not as a permanent refuge from the trials of the world but as a military winter quarters to regroup, recruit, refurbish his forces, and then sally forth to destroy Henry Clay. In a private letter he served notice: "I became a soldier for the good of my country. . . . If this makes me so, I am a 'Military Chieftain.' . . . To him [Clay] I am in no wise responsible. There is a purer tribunal to which in preference I would refer myself—to the Judgment of an enlightened patriotic and uncorrupted electorate." [34] The "Military Chieftain" would even the score with the "base hipocrite" from Kentucky. He would win the Presidency in 1828 over Clay or Adams or any rival. He would redeem the "People's Will."

Now he was no reluctant citizen backing away from a slugfest for the Executive Office. Rather, he cooperated fully with his political associates in pushing his own cause as vigorously as possible. His first step was to resign from the Senate to be free to direct the campaign and avoid intrigues in Washington that might alienate potential support. Although his close counselors, Lewis and Sam Houston, warned him against John Calhoun as a scheming, self-seeking, untrustworthy politician, Jackson was not deterred from making overtures in view of Calhoun's demonstrated political strength in capturing the Vice Presidency by such an overwhelming margin in the 1824 race. Calhoun, whose own position as Vice President in the Adams administration left him uncomfortable, facing the prospect of Clay's succession to Adams, was himself casting about for political allies and moved into a working alliance with the Jackson forces. A new

Washington newspaper, the *United States Telegraph*, was established in Washington, with Calhoun's supporter fiery Duff Green brought on from St. Louis and installed as editor.

A Jackson-for-President central committee, with headquarters in Washington, moved into action before the Adams administration was a year old and broadcast feelers for support in all directions. The responses were gratifyingly cordial. Thomas Hart Benton, disturbed over the Clay performance of 1825, readily signified his allegiance to Jackson. Another former Clay booster, Amos Kendall, editor of a Kentucky newspaper, also joined the General's crusade. In New York Martin Van Buren, "the Red Fox of Kinderhook" as opponents called him, contemplating the devastation left in his own tattered ranks by his clinging to the sinking Crawford ship too long, came into alliance, bringing all the political moxey for which the "Little Magician" was already noted. A new political combination was in the making—Benton, Van Buren, Kendall would form the solid basis of the new Jacksonian party that would before long take the name of the Democratic Party. Before 1825 was out, the Tennessee legislature placed Jackson's name in nomination for President, and Old Hickory responded in person at the state capitol making perhaps the longest political speech of his career, lasting 15 minutes.

The Jackson political machine largely under John Eaton's supervision in Washington continued to attract vigorous supporters, notably Edward Livingston of Louisiana, George McDuffie of South Carolina, and redoubtable maverick John Randolph whose flailing of the Adams-Clay "coalition of Blifil and Black George—the Puritan and the Blackleg" sparked a duel. In what Benton called the last "high-toned duel," Randolph, one of the best marksmen in Virginia, threw away his fire while Clay's bullet plowed through his coat-tail. In consequent generosity, the Secretary of State sent his adversary a brand new coat. Jackson committees sprang into operation in every state and kept up a high pitch of enthusiasm for the Old Hero, while the Jacksonians in Washington stalemated the incumbent administration at every turn.

To Calhoun's offer of an alliance of Calhoun forces with Jackson men in 1826, looking toward the 1828 election, the Old Hero replied: "I trust that my name will always be found on the side of the people, and as their confidence in your talents and virtue has placed you in the second office of government, that we shall march hand in hand in their cause." [35]

The making of public policy gave way to making political capital, as all eyes focused on the coming 1828 presidential sweepstakes. Eaton regularly advised Jackson on developments in Washington, while urging "All that is necessary for you is to be still and quiet," to "say nothing and plant cotton." But the Cincinnatus of the Hermitage had to forego hours behind the plow in order to acknowledge meticulously the tidal wave of mail flowing in from well-wishers throughout the land. He begged off speaking at public meetings because "having lost many of my teeth it is with difficulty I can articulate." A set of teeth, made by a Nashville dentist, remedied the handicap, but Jackson still steered clear of public appearances.

When the opposition press revived in full detail the irregularities of Jackson's marriage and gave nation-wide play to the story of Rachel's pre-1791 relations with Robards and Jackson, broadcasting charges of adultery, Jackson raged and fumed, scarcely able to restrain himself from challenging assorted editors to duels. He finally agreed to allow a committee of partisans, ably directed by John Overton, to prepare a carefully documented defense, which put his case in the most favorable light possible.

The campaign built to a crescendo of raucous rancor and vicious slander. In desperate efforts to put Jackson down as unfit for the Presidency, the administration press charged him not only with seduction and adultery but pictured him as a lawless ruffian and pitiless murderer, trotting out lengthy accounts of his duels, land speculation, cursing, sabbath breaking, cock fighting, horse racing, betting, "treasonable" associating with Aaron Burr. The nadir of character assassination came in 1828. The publication of the "Coffin Handbill," printed with a black border, depicting six black coffins with the accompanying account of Jackson's execution of mutinous Tennessee militiamen during the Creek campaign make him appear as a cold-blooded murderer. Produced with the appearance of a government document and bearing the legend "Ordered to be printed by the Congress," thousands of copies of the "Handbill" were mailed under franks of Adams Congressmen to all parts of the country.[36]

But the Jackson band-wagon rolled on irresistibly. A giant celebration was arranged at New Orleans to commemorate the thirteenth anniversary of the battle. The General, accompanied by Mrs. Jackson and a host of friends, was persuaded to attend the affair, which lasted longer than the battle itself. An effort was made at the time to dump Calhoun as Vice-Presidential candidate, when Sam Houston showed his chief an 1818 letter written by Monroe to Calhoun which threw some light on the cabinet's secret deliberations concerning Jackson and the Florida campaign. "My hair stood on end for an hour," exclaimed Jackson after reading the letter.[37] But conciliators soothed Jackson's feelings, and Calhoun remained in the General's good graces.

Jacksonian campaigners did their work so well that when the election returns of 1828 were in, their man swept to a smashing victory. Jackson carried the West, South, and most Middle Atlantic states. Only New England, New Jersey, and

Delaware voted against him. Heavy Adams majorities in those areas kept Jackson's popular vote to 56% (647,276) of the total. But the triumph in the electoral college was stunning—Jackson 178, Adams 83. The country had repudiated, said Jacksonians, the Northeast, "corrupt" politicians, and aristocracy in favor of a new spirit from the West reflecting democratic virtue and the "Man of the People" (leaving out of account shrewd political management and tight organization).

The victory redressed the wrong done by "corrupt" schemers four years earlier. A wave of elation swept the Jackson camp, as all members of the entourage at the Hermitage savored the sweet flavor of success. All, that is, except Rachel Jackson. For her the closing weeks of the campaign had turned into a nightmare. Despite efforts to shield her, she had learned of the vile slanders and outrageous language circulated about her. At the news of the victory, she confessed to Lewis: "For Mr. Jackson's sake I am glad. For my own part, I never wished it." [38] The thought of moving to Washington and facing again the political gossiping and widespread slanders there was more than she could endure. "I had rather be a doorkeeper in the house of God," she said contemplating the White House, "than to live in that palace in Washington." [39] In late November 1828 she grew ill and weak. Three weeks later a heart seizure ended her life. Jackson sat motionless, numb and speechless for a full day by the lifeless body of "the woman he had made his own thirty-seven years before and from that hour to this defended against . . . all men." On December 24, as 10,000 visitors gathered for the funeral, Rachel was buried in her rose garden 150 paces from the east door of the Hermitage.

In the weeks that followed Andrew Jackson remained frozen in a state of shocked stupor. Some associates feared his powerful will might crack. His grief-chilled mind convinced him that "those vile wretches who have slandered her" had killed his Rachel. "May Almighty God forgive her murderers as I know she forgives them. I never can." To make preparations to leave for Washington in January 1829, he had to rally all the resources of his will: "My heart is nearly broke. I try to summon up my usual fortitude but in vain." At the capital he would crush the enemies who had destroyed his wife.[40]

IV Calhoun: From Congress to Vice President, 1815–1828

Congressman Calhoun: Building a Strong Nation, 1815–1817

WITH THE END of the War of 1812, the United States turned its face away from Europe and began to crawl, in John Randolph's phrase, like a giant land monster toward the setting sun. Internal affairs would command Americans' attention for the next half century—clearing the wilderness, planting crops, erecting settlements, pushing over plains, mountains, and deserts to the Pacific shore, seeking out the hidden wealth of the earth. Too long Americans had felt themselves simply an appendage of Europe, subject to its fits of rivalry and controversy. While one American eye remained still half-cocked on Europe, the main focus lay on the North American continent itself. A new spirit prevailed—confidence, optimism, assurance that no task was too big, no obstacle too great to be conquered by native American energy and ingenuity. It was a heady vision—leveling the forests, prodding the land into production, building factories to satisfy American demands, thrusting roads, canals, and railroads to tie the interior to the older settled areas, striding toward a self-sufficiency that would be the envy of Europe. If it did nothing else, the War of 1812 gave America its chance to concentrate on continental expansion and internal development.

In the post-war years John Calhoun played a large part in pushing for rapid internal development and in boosting national strength and self-respect. The war taught many lessons. None was clearer than the lack of adequate defensive strength, as the British capture of Washington during the conflict so dramatically demonstrated. First as Congressman, then Secretary of War for seven years, and finally Vice President, he labored for national economic growth and for national defensive security.

After an 8-month stint looking after home affairs at his plantation at Bath, Calhoun returned to Washington in December 1815, when Congress assembled in a hastily erected temporary building replacing the old Capitol burned by the British. With Clay again Speaker, Calhoun became chairman of a select Committee on the National Currency. His committee would propose legislation over which national controversy would swirl for the next quarter century. Concern over offsetting national weakness in the recent war with future strength led Calhoun early in the session to speak in favor of a proposal to establish three more academies for training military officers.

In the course of his speech, he argued that the nation must be made secure and flourishing in all its parts, nationwide, not by sections or classes. A military academy was needed to train officers, but equal opportunity for all must be assured. Thus a single academy would be filled by the sons of the rich. But talent and ability came not alone from that class. Indeed, they were more likely to develop in the ranks of the lesser rank of society, not because "these classes actually contain a greater portion of talent, but . . . they have stronger stimulants to its exertion. Rich men, being already at the top of the ladder have no further motive to climb. It is that class of the community who find it necessary to strive for elevation, that furnishes you with officers. . . ." [1] Since life was a struggle in which all competed for place and eminence, only those of ability and determination would rise to the top, and upon these society must rely for its leaders. More than one academy should be established. Hence, a body of military officers trained in advance would serve as leaders for training citizen sodiers in time of war.

Shortly afterward Calhoun supported a measure for retaining direct federal taxes, contending that a system of revenue could not be created after war began but must be operating in advance. Taxes, he asserted, were not oppressive if necessary and what was more necessary, as the late war showed, than to provide adequately for the national defense. The United States must be ready for future conflicts. England remained "the most formidable power in the world . . . We, on the other hand, are the most growing nation on earth: most rapidly improving in those very particulars in which she excels. . . . Will Great Britain permit us to go on in an uninterrupted march to the height of national greatness and prosperity? I fear not." We will "encounter British . . . hostility in every shape; not immediately manifested by open force . . . but by indirect attempts to check your growth and prosperity." We must, therefore, develop a policy designed to repel future British aggression and maintain American security. A sizable navy, a standing army, including a trained officer corps, sufficient to garrison an expanded chain of border forts, and an adequate militia would provide the bare necessities of defense. If war should come, a military draft from the whole citizenry would supply the needed forces—a revolutionary proposal, Calhoun conceded, but necessary, since those who would enjoy liberty must be willing to work for it. Further, development of basic manufactures, even at the price of federal subsidies, to render the country independent of foreign sources and an expanded system of roads and canals to improve communications and transportation rounded out the Calhoun defense proposals.[2]

To objections raised by John Randolph that such projects would consolidate the central government at the expense of the states Calhoun paid little heed at the time, unaware that sixteen years later he would be voicing the same protest on the same grounds as the Virginian.

As part of his plan for strengthening the nation, Calhoun offered a bill early in 1816 to charter for twenty years as a semiprivate corporation a Bank of the United States. The provisions were very similar to those of Alexander Hamilton's 1791 First Bank of the United States, the demise of which in 1811 had created serious government financial problems in the war. The Bank's capital was to be $35 million, one-fifth of the stock to be held by the government, private investors to hold the other four-fifths. The 25-man board of directors was similarly apportioned, five chosen by the government, the other twenty by private stockholders. The Bank's notes were to be legal tender; and in return for its privileges the Bank would serve as exclusive depository for government funds, fiscal agent, and floater of government bond issues. Over the first four years of operation it would pay the Treasury $1,500,000 in three installments. The Bank would have headquarters in Philadelphia but might establish branches in other cities.

Such a Bank, Calhoun argued, was not only constitutional but necessary. The Constitution specifically empowered Congress to regulate the nation's currency and prohibited states from issuing bills of credit. But the states had chartered state banks, some 260 of them with $80 million in capital in the last 25 years. Since the state banks issued notes which formed the nation's currency and which fluctuated widely in value, not only were the states in effect doing something which the

Constitution forbade but the financial ills, foisted on the American economy as inflation spread, could lead to disaster.

Since the currency problem in the nation was growing progressively worse, Congress should exercise its constitutional power to regulate the currency. The most efficient means—a Bank of the United States itself making payments in specie and refusing notes of state-chartered banks that failed to redeem such notes in specie—would soon compel all banks to return to a solid base for their notes and thereby stabilize the nation's currency, providing a firm ground for economic growth.[1]

During the House debate opposition arguments came from John Randolph and Daniel Webster (later to become a Bank attorney). Calhoun adroitly beat off all counter arguments. The Bank bill moved speedily through Congress. In the Spring of 1816 the second Bank of the United States went into operation.

At the same time the Bank bill passed, Secretary of the Treasury Alexander J. Dallas submitted to the House proposals for a protective tariff, designed to encourage domestic manufactures by levying customs duties high enough to reduce or exclude entirely foreign manufactured goods. The arguments in favor had already all been set forth ably in Hamilton's 1791 Report on Manufactures: since a balanced American economy was desirable, domestic manufactures should be encouraged; the government should set tariff rates in order to encourage and protect domestic manufacturing; although prices of domestic manufactured goods would initially be higher, the rise of internal competition and better transportation would ultimately reduce such prices until they were lower than prices of similar imported manufactures. The logic of the protective position was unassailable so long as one conceded the desirability of manufacturing and the use of government subsidy as a stimulant.

By 1816, with the reopening of war-strangled foreign trade, a deluge of British manufactured goods swamped the American market, drastically lowering prices and threatening pigmy-sized American manufacturing firms. Demands for a protective tariff flooded Congress from all sides—from producers of wool and cotton textiles, iron and steel, rope, glass, hats, and dozens of other articles.

The Dallas report of 1816 reiterated Hamilton's reasoning, divided manufactures into three classes, and called for prohibitive duties on goods where domestic manufacturers produced a sufficient supply to meet domestic demand, intermediate rates on recently established manufactures not yet capable of supplying domestic needs, and no duties at all on products Americans could not manufacture. A tariff bill in the House incorporated the Dallas recommendations, immediately modified by amendment to reset the rate on cottons and woolens at 25% *ad valorem*. Opposition came from such members as Daniel Webster, still representing the mercantile interests of Portsmouth, New Hampshire, and John Randolph, who attacked the entire principle of tariff protection as an "immense tax on one portion of the community to put money into the pockets of another."

During several weeks of debate Calhoun took little part. Approached by Representative Samuel D. Ingham of Pennsylvania who believed Calhoun's influence in the House would help give the bill a needed boost, the Carolinian agreed to speak. Without preparation or previous meditation, Calhoun addressed the House. Pointing out that he represented an agricultural constituency and disavowing therefore any personal interest, he proceeded to elaborate his continuing concern for the nation's defense. Development of manufacturing was necessary to make the United States self sufficient and independent of foreign manufactured goods. Since he considered another war with England a distinct probability, the country must develop a prosperous, balanced economy. Government encouragement of manufacturing was needed to accomplish this. "Neither agriculture, manufacture, nor commerce, taken separately, is the cause of wealth; it flows from the three combined and cannot exist without each."

Calhoun then proceeded to refute objections against the protective tariff. The country was clearly equipped to start manufacturing: raw materials readily available; capital at hand accumulated mainly from commerce—"What channel can it take but . . . manufactures?" Shipping interests would not be materially injured since an increase in coastal trade would offset the decline in foreign commerce. Nor, contrary to the old Jeffersonian notion, would manufacturing weaken the moral fiber of the people, although he conceded that "manufacturing produced a greater dependence on the part of the employed" factory workers. But such objection was more than outweighed by the gains in strengthening the nation through mutual dependence of its parts and building better transportation facilities.[4] (See *Appendix,* Doc. No. 11 for fuller text.)

The day after the tariff bill of 1816 passed (though not known to Calhoun and his fellow Americans), a British minister told Parliament it was "well worth while to incur a loss on the first exportation in order by the glut to stifle in the cradle rising manufactures in the United States." If American manufacturing was to survive, surely the protective tariff had been adopted none too soon. Later in 1833, Calhoun would deny that the 1816 tariff was a protective measure—but his denial is utter nonsense since the 1816 bill was presented, debated, and passed with intention to protect American manufacturers against British competition. And beyond that, as early as 1813, Calhoun had spoken in favor of protection.

Calhoun won reelection to the House in 1816, but not until he beat back four opposing candidates who denounced his voting for the act by which Congress raised its own pay from $6 per working day to $1,500 per year. Because of the public outcry against this "salary grab," two-thirds of the House lost their seats. Calhoun refused to be swayed. Just because a law proved unpopular, he saw no reason for Congressmen to repeal it when reason and conscience told them they were right and the people wrong. "Have the people snatched the power of deliberation from this body? Are we . . . a body of . . . agents, . . . without the power" of legislating? Public opinion should be taken into account, but each Congressman should show "that erectness of mind which in all cases is disposed to embrace what is . . . just and wise." [5]

At length Congress turned to consider ways improving transportation. If national economic self-sufficiency was to be achieved, clearly roads, canals, and deepened river channels were needed to facilitate the flow of raw materials from West and South to feed the rising industry of the Northeast, from which manufactured goods would return via the same routes. None doubted the value of better transportation. The main argument revolved about who had power to build. Was it the states or federal government? This argument had long raged: earlier Federalists leaning toward active federal stimulating of the economy; Jeffersonians opposed, although Jefferson himself had approved using federal funds for the National Road west from Cumberland, Maryland. President Madison called Congress's attention to "the great importance of establishing . . . the roads and canals which can be best executed under national authority," while at the same time he suggested "that any defect of Constitutional authority" be remedied by amendment.

Shortly Calhoun proposed a bill to apply the bonus to be paid by the Bank of the United States to the building of internal improvements. On February 4, 1817 he delivered a lengthy supporting speech. All sectors of the economy,

agriculture, industry, and commerce, would benefit from better transportation. But military necessity, as the recent war
testified, cried out for a government-built system of roads and
canals to speed military forces to threatened points of attack
—especially needed in a country of such vast extent as the
United States.

Appealing for means to unify into a strong nation the
diverse and scattered sections and states, Calhoun declaimed:

"We are great, and rapidly—I was about to say fearfully—
growing. This is our pride and our danger; our weakness and
our strength. . . . We are under the most imperious of obligations to counteract every tendency to disunion. . . . [The
measure we] are now deliberating. . . . deserves the most
serious consideration. Whatever impedes the intercourse of
the extremes with this, the centre of the republic, weakens
the union. The more enlarged the sphere of commercial circulation . . . the more strongly are we bound together. . . .
Those who understand the human heart best know how powerfully distance tends to break the sympathies of our nature.
. . . Let us, then, bind the republic together with a perfect
system of roads and canals. Let us conquer space."

Having established the economic, military, and emotional
necessity of good transportation, Calhoun moved on to meet
the constitutional objections. First, that Congress had no
power to build a road through any state without the state's
consent, he believed, was no obstacle since a state would
certainly give consent to a project so clearly in its own interest. Second, that the enumerated powers in the Constitution
did not grant Congress the power to build roads Calhoun
considered a quibbling form of argument. Being "no advocate
for refined arguments on the constitution," he asserted, in a
statement that later would rise to haunt him, "The instrument was not intended as a thesis for the logician to exercise
his ingenuity on. It ought to be construed with plain, good

sense." And it was "plain, good sense" that building roads and canals lay within Congress's constitutional power to provide for the common defense and promote the general welfare. Here Calhoun reached his peak as an advocate of nationalism. He offered a scheme of transportation arteries running from Atlantic coast cities into the Mississippi Valley, from the Hudson to the Great Lakes and a crucial highway running north-south through coastal and piedmont regions to link Maine with Louisiana at the extremities of the Union.[6] (See *Appendix,* Doc. 12-A, for fuller text.)

Beating down opposition attacks by forceful logic and tenacious persistence, Calhoun drove the bill through to House passage by 86–84 vote; the Senate approved a few days later. Calling upon President Madison just two days before Madison would leave office, Calhoun expressed good wishes and was about to depart when Madison called him back to his desk. He had before him, the President said, Calhoun's internal improvements bill. When Madison explained he must veto the bill on constitutional grounds, Calhoun froze, stunned by an unexpected blow, seeing his past month's labor pulverized and his dream of a national transportation system demolished in a single paralyzing moment.

In view of Calhoun's later development of the state sovereignty theory, that has become indelibly associated with his name, his nationalist views of this period are especially intriguing. By 1817 he had pushed vigorously a broad nationalistic program, closely resembling Alexander Hamilton's earlier and Henry Clay's later proposal for an economically self-contained "American System," rendering the United States fully independent of Europe and staunchly self-reliant. The United States must be made into a strong nation or run the risk of being "sunk into insignificance through inbecility and apathy," a danger, "to which the people of this country are peculiarly liable."[7] To avert this danger, an adequate defense establishment should be buttressed by a sound, growing economy, resting upon domestic manufacturing nurtured by a protective tariff and relying on a stable financial system firmed up by the Bank of the United States. And to offset the centrifugal pull of distance and sectional selfishness a national transportation network had to be constructed.

In sharp contrast to his later sectionalist views stand his words of 1816: "To legislate for our country requires not only the most enlarged views. . . . In a country so extensive and so various in its interests what is necessary for the common good may apparently be opposed to the interests of particular sections. It must be submitted to as a condition of our greatness." [8] This view arose from Calhoun's belief that the United States as a nation had a special mission in world history: "We are charged by Providence, not only with the happiness of this great rising people, but, in a considerable degree, with that of the human race. We have a government of a new order, perfectly distinct from all others which have preceded it—a government founded on the rights of man; resting, not on authority, not on prejudice, not on superstition, but reason. If it shall succeed . . . it will be the commencement of a new era in human affairs. All civilized governments must, in the course of time, conform to its principles." [9]

The great objective was liberty for men. In America liberty could be maintained only with a strong Union, secure against foreign dangers and sectional disruption. As Calhoun put it in 1816 (in words almost identical with those Webster would employ fourteen years later in his celebrated debate with Hayne): ". . . . the liberty and union of this country were inseparably united. . . . [as] destruction of the latter would certainly involve the former, so its maintenance will, with equal certainty, preserve it." Calhoun "did not speak lightly" for "he had often and long revolved it in his mind, and . . .

examined into the causes that destroyed liberty in other states. . . . The basis of our republic is too broad, and its structure too strong, to be shaken by them [causes that destroy liberty]. Its extension and organization will . . . afford effectual security against their operation; but let it be deeply impressed on the heart of this . . . country, that . . . they exposed us to a new and terrible danger, Disunion. This single word comprehended almost the sum of out political dangers, and against it we ought to be perpetually guarded." [10]

Secretary of War: "System out of Chaos," 1817–1825

After Monroe assumed the Presidency in 1817, Calhoun joined the administration as Secretary of War—belatedly in December, the post having been turned down by Jackson and at least three others, before Calhoun accepted.[11] Although advised by friends to decline, Calhoun ultimately took the place largely out of long-range ambition to become President. After six years in Congress he had already proven his skill as a legislative leader, as a master of abstract reasoning, and as an intense and persuasive if not spectacular speaker. One contemporary commented that Calhoun "had so carefully cultivated his naturally poor voice as to make his utterance clear, full and distinct in speaking and while not at all musical it yet fell pleasantly on the ear." [12] But no man had held the Presidency without administrative experience. Clearly Calhoun wanted to remedy this lack as well as prove to himself and the public his administrative capacity.[13]

His decision proved a crucial milestone in his political career. The Monroe years, deceptively labeled the "Era of Good Feelings," shortly disintegrated into a selfish scramble for the presidential succession, and Calhoun was drawn into the swirling vortex of conflicting ambitions. The expectations of John Quincy Adams, as Secretary of State, to succeed

Monroe in keeping with an unspoken, long-standing practice ran counter to Crawford's plans to rectify his near-miss of 1816, while Henry Clay barked his resentment over not being made Secretary of State by attacking Monroe's administration mercilessly. During the next eight years Calhoun found himself the object of attacks and intrigue by all three of these aspirants.[14]

Monroe's cabinet, gathered as much by accident as design, was stronger and abler than that of any preceding President. A diverse lot in appearance and style, the cabinet members pooled an immense supply of governmental experience and political savvy. Adams had been in or close to government service since his teens when he served as secretary to his father in Europe. Short, round and bald Harvard graduate, scholar, Senator, diplomat with years of experience in the Netherlands, Berlin, and Russia, negotiator of the Treaty of Ghent ending the war of 1812, he was shrewd, caustic, eloquently convincing in speech, careless in dress, but withal a man who tirelessly pursued the nation's interest without neglecting his own. In contrast, Crawford, built on a massive physical scale with a bluff, hearty nature, sharp mind, attractive personality, brought to the Treasury experience as Senator, envoy to France, and War Secretary. Attorney General William Wirt, also large in size, genial in manner, had won dual fame as a trial attorney in Virginia and author of several popular works (he would hold his office for the next 12 years). Calhoun, the youngest of the group, tall, angular, flashing black eyes, sporting a mass of dark hair, made up in self-confidence what he lacked in age. Not viewed as a political rival and considered a possible useful ally by Adams and Crawford, Calhoun also developed a close, confidential relationship with Monroe, who had known him since 1811 and now frequently invited Calhoun to accompany the President on journeys to various parts of the country.

In 1817 the War Department's jurisdiction covered not only the army and coastal forts but also Indian affairs, pensions, and land warrants issued to military veterans. Supply services were provided by private contractors, whose unsettled accounts surpassed $40,000,000 when Calhoun took office. The army's strength, including engineers, stood on paper at 12,000, but in reality only 8,000 men were in service. There was no central unity of command. Major Generals Andrew Jackson and Jacob Brown, commanding respectively the Southern and Northern Departments, operated independently of each other though each was responsible through the Secretary to the President. The program of constructing coastal forts urged by Calhoun earlier in Congress had not yet started. An ineffective, fuzzy Indian policy was already under attack by settlers and fur traders alike.

In December 1817 Calhoun, as Secretary of War, with characteristic energy plunged into dealing with these problems. The recent war had left the Department in a disorganized, chaotic condition. Calhoun started from scratch Applying himself fourteen to fifteen hours a day, delving through reports and records to enlarge and pinpoint his general knowledge acquired in Congress, prodding military and civilian associates for advice and suggestions, he shortly developed an overall appreciation of the size and complexity of the problems needing resolution. Quickly he demonstrated a knack for administration. Recognizing that "minute and constant attention to details" was "indispensable to a perfect administration," he took a large view, meeting the immediate day-to-day problems but also ranging ahead to anticipate future challenges. His colleagues were impressed by his incisive mind, decisiveness, self confidence, and energy; Wirt saw him as a "most captivating man . . . ardent, generous, high minded, brave, with a genius full fire, energy and light."

Seeking to clear away the ragged clutter of inefficiency in

the Department, Calhoun insisted on authority at the center, clear responsibility and accountability in all branches, and eminently qualified men as his assistants. A loose Army General Staff emerged from the war, including the adjutant general, inspector general, quartermaster general, commissary general of ordnance, paymaster, assistant topographical engineer. "No part of our military organization," Calhoun informed Congress, "requires more attention in peace than the general staff. . . . it should receive a perfect organization. . . . With a defective staff, we must carry on our military operations under great disadvantages, and be exposed . . . [in war] to great disasters." Congress adopted Calhoun's proposals for a permanent, centralized General Staff which incorporated all the housekeeping management functions of the army. In the form Calhoun set it up in 1818 (not signifying a central strategic planning body), the General Staff operated effectively throughout the nineteenth century (Mexican War, Civil War, Spanish American War) until finally replaced in 1903 by a revised General Staff as a military planning agency. Under Calhoun's direction a Surgeon General and Judge Advocate General were added to the Staff. Each Staff officer was placed in charge of a bureau with authority to deal with a particular function (marking the first appearance in the federal government of the bureau type of organization). The advantages of this arrangement were soon extended by creating a Land Warrant Bureau and Pension Bureau, the latter carrying a heavy load by passing upon some 30,000 veterans' applications in its first year.

Calhoun succeeded in picking able men for top positions and persuading them to stay on as permanent public servants. In appointing the first surgeon general, for example, he chose Dr. Joseph Lovell, Harvard medical graduate with six years experience as an army surgeon. Lovell, in office from 1818 till his death in 1836, made a skillful analysis of the problem of feeding the army to maintain good health. In seeking a correlation between weather and army diseases, he required daily weather reports from army doctors scattered throughout the country, thereby laying the foundation of the present United States Weather Service.[15]

In managing department affairs, the Secretary insisted upon strict accountability and rigid acceptance of responsibility. The office of inspector general he viewed as the eyes and ears of the Secretary for concentrating authority in the military establishment. "On the skill, the industry, firmness and impartiality of the Inspector General," he wrote, "the discipline and condition of the troops . . . must depend. If he . . . [possesses] the requisite qualifications, very few officers would venture to neglect their duty." [16] He also incorporated into the army regulations of 1818 "a minute and rigid responsibility into every branch of the military disbursements. . . . one principle pervades the whole organization—to hold the head of each subordinate department responsible for the disbursements of his department." [17]

Clarification of the chain of Army command demanded Calhoun's attention. At the end of the war of 1812, no single supreme military commander existed; as already noted, the two geographic divisions, northern and southern, were under the respective commands of Generals Jacob Brown and Andrew Jackson. Since units of the regular army were scattered widely, especially in the west, the War Department in the interest of speed often sent orders directly to a given officer, sometimes neglecting to forward a copy of his commanding general. Early in 1817 Jackson discovered that one of his subordinates, Major Stephen Long, had been ordered and had already reported to Washington. Jackson immediately wrote the War Department protesting violation of the proper channels. When Monroe assumed office, Jackson laid the issue squarely before him in a sharp note objecting to War

Department's orders to subordinate officers "without the knowledge of the commanding General. . . . Such a doctrine is a violation of . . . every principle of subordination." To admit this practice, "you destroy all subordination, deprive at the pleasure of the Secretary the Commanding General . . . of the services of his best Officers," thereby "establishing in the person of the Secretary of War a Tyrant superior to the law, whose will is the constitution, his caprice the law." From now on, Jackson lectured the President, "Every military order must pass through regular channels." [18]

Within six weeks Jackson followed through by issuing an order to all officers within his division prohibiting them from obeying a direct War Department order "unless coming through him [Jackson] as the proper organ of communication" in command of the division.

Monroe retorted crisply: "The principle is clear, that every order from the Department of War, to whomever directed, must be obeyed. I cannot think that you are of a different opinion." General Jackson noted on the back of Monroe's letter: "This is to be filed, and the further explanation awaited for." To Monroe he responded, hinting at resignation if the direct chain of military command was disregarded. Monroe, not about to yield to his ruffled General, reasserted the principle that "no officer of the army can rightfully disobey an order from the President," having already asserted that the War Department was merely an extension of the President. He continued: "Whatever may be said of the right of a commander of a . . . division, to command within his . . . division, applies with full force to the President as Commander in chief of the army." Seeking to mollify Jackson he added, "As to the policy . . . of giving orders . . . to officers in any division, without passing them thro' the commander of the division, I am far from advocating it. . . . I think the practice should be otherwise and be deviated from in cases of urgency only. . . . in all cases, when departed from, the commander . . . should be promptly advised . . . and a copy of the order sent to him." [19]

Jackson was appeased to the extent of revoking his earlier divisional order, advising Monroe that he did not object to any order being issued in cases of necessity, when "I was immediately advised thereof" and that he would await the issuance of new war department regulations. Drafting new regulations fell to Calhoun, who coming into office at this juncture in Monroe-Jackson controversy, stipulated: "As a general rule, all orders will issue, in the first instance, to the commanders of the division. In cases where the nature of the duty to be performed, and the public interest may require it, orders will issue directly to officers commanding departments, posts or detachments, and to any officer attached to the division; but in such cases, a copy of the order will be transmitted to the General of division, for his information." [20]

Calhoun's sensible arrangement closed off a year-long dispute allowing Jackson to assert, not entirely accurately, that it adopted "the principles I contended for." But the outcome is significant beyond the specific issue. Calhoun confirmed civilian supremacy over the army, reinforced the control of central staff departments over staff officers, while simultaneously accepting the necessary normal channel of communication through the line. The relationship of staff officers to the department and to the army again became spotlighted in 1819. Post surgeons, who were required by general order to report directly to the surgeon general, had neglected to report promptly. The delay having stemmed from Jackson's order that all southern division post surgeons report to the assistant surgeon general of Jackson's division. Calhoun wrote an informal but firm letter to Jackson asking him to modify his order and pointing out that surgeons were staff, not line officers standing therefore in a different relation to the commanding general: "It would certainly be perfectly agreeable to me to order all reports to pass through the Headquarters of the Divisions, were it not for the delay . . . which is inconsistent with the proper management of the department. . . . The Commanding General would be kept promptly informed . . . but this can be effected consistently with the correctest principles, by ordering a duplicate of such reports . . . to his headquarters." Calhoun made clear his insistence on prompt, efficient management by concluding with the hope that he would not have to "determine whether I shall permit the orders of the Government to be habitually neglected, or resort to the proper means of enforcing them. Should the alternative be presented I will not hesitate to do my duty." [21] Strong words indeed to send to Andrew Jackson, already a national figure with a sizable political following, who had fought off administration and Congressional critics of his Florida invasion and come off unscathed.

The United States Military Academy at West Point had struggled along feebly for years until the War of 1812 gave it a boost. Calhoun took particular interest in the Academy, convinced that a well trained officer corps was crucial to defense. He passed upon applications for admission as cadets, including among others those of young Robert E. Lee and Jefferson Davis. He sought to strengthen the Academy's academic program, cooperated closely with Major Sylvanus Thayer who became superintendent in 1817, and reported to the House in 1820: ". . . military science, in the present state of the world, cannot be neglected with impunity. It has become so complicated and extensive as to require for its acquisition extensive means, and much time. . . . It can flourish only under the patronage of the Government." [22] He put General Winfield Scott to work on a manual of infantry tactics, adopted in 1818. He urged in vain the establishing of a second government military academy. Failing that, he moved to create a "school of practice" to provide practical training at a post-graduate level—out of which grew the artillery school at Fortress Monroe and in time the Army War College.

The Army Corps of Engineers performed invaluable service under Calhoun's administration. Under an 1816 appropriation a survey of the entire coast was begun, and construction of coastal fortifications occupied the corps for the following six years with major works rising from Boston and New York to Savannah and New Orleans. Legislation in 1824 gave the engineers further impetus in providing funds for surveys of potential internal improvements of national importance. Calhoun praised the integrity and competence of the engineers operating under the regularity of system he had imposed.

Indian affairs also were managed under War Department supervision. These involved three aspects: 1) treaty making for acquisition of lands occupied by Indians and for removal of such occupants;   2) trading with the Indians;   3) civilizing the Indians. All three of these activities, begun many years before, were continued during the Calhoun era by the War Department, with varying degrees of opposition and success. These topics will be treated later in Chapter VII.

Calhoun proved an exceptionally effective administrator, entitling him to top rank among War Secretaries in our history. The list of his achievements is overwhelmingly impressive: a working General Staff; good organization for the army that lasted through the Civil War; improved officer training through revitalizing West Point and a new artillery school at Fortress Monroe; the first systematic, rational plan for coastal defense; maintenance of civilian control over the army and fair handling of such temperamental generals as Jackson and Winfield Scott; perfecting the supply system, while reducing the annual cost of maintaining a soldier from $451

to $287 at a saving of $1,300,000 yearly; liquidating $45,-
000,000 of unsettled accounts and eliminating an annual em-
bezzlement loss of 3 per cent of disbursements; pushing army
posts to the Rockies; and introducing steamboats for army
transport.

By the time he left office in 1825 he had implemented his
belief that "the utility of a military establishment depended
much more on organization and science than on numbers,"
directed his labors "to give ours the best possible organization
and the highest degree of science." After eight years his claim
that "I left it [the War Department] in the most perfect
condition" was no idle boast, as the General Staff testified,
"The degree of perfection to which you have carried the
several branches of this department is . . . without parallel."
Niles Weekly Register agreed: "The order and harmony,
regularity and promptitude, punctuality and responsibility,
introduced by Mr. Calhoun in every branch of the service,
has never been rivaled, and perhaps cannot be excelled . . .
he brought this system out of chaos." The best modern historian of American public administration concludes that
"Calhoun had transformed an administrative wreck to a well-
managed, smooth-working . . . organization. . . . His administrative record was outstanding." [21]

Political Infighting: Calhoun Seeks the Presidency

In his eight years of administering the War Department,
a determined Calhoun encountered resistance to his proposals and clashed with his strong-willed associates. Two personality clashes had long-range effects upon his political career,
especially his ambition to be President. One conflict pitted
him against Andrew Jackson in the secrecy of Monroe's cabinet discussions over the General's impetuous actions in the

Florida-Seminole affair, as noted above. The immediate outcome of this affair was peaceful, but a dozen years later it would rise again, and change the whole course of Calhoun's thinking and career.

The other conflict, within Monroe's cabinet, threw Calhoun into an unsought clash with his colleague Secretary of the Treasury Crawford. A lesser discord also arose between Calhoun and Adams toward the end of Monroe's second term.

Calhoun's nationalism, born in the *Chesapeake-Leopard* affair of 1807 and nurtured in the anti-British atmosphere of the war of 1812, burst into full bloom in the post war years. Convinced that another war with England was inevitable, he proposed regularly that Congress should authorize increases in coastal defenses, size of the army, and military appropriations of all kinds. While England posed the principal threat to the nation's security, Spain and the Indians also constituted a possible danger. Calhoun, therefore, called for strong fortifications along the Great Lakes and Atlantic seaboard and Gulf coast. These would be manned by relatively small garrisons, who would operate in conjunction with the navy. In the trans-Mississippi west the Indian menace would be checked by a chain of forts along the frontier. For efficient, fast movement of troops a good network of roads must be provided along east-west and north-south channels.

Since war with England might arise in the West where the British working from Canada and Oregon might incite Indians to join British plans to block American expansion westward, Indian policy was therefore essential to American security. What Calhoun proposed in an exhaustive 1818 report to Congress was to protect western settlers from the Indians and vice versa. Semi-civilized tribes east of the Mississippi should be induced to move to the western plains. A string of forts from Minnesota to Arkansas would protect the trans-Mississippi Indians from white invasion and white settlers from Indian attacks.

Calhoun's program won general approval at first—Monroe pushing the coastal fortification scheme and Congress accepting the recommendations of his Report on Indian Affairs so far as extending the government factor system of trading with the Indians. But shortly forces converged to stall Calhoun's program. The supposed menace of Spain was removed by the 1819 treaty which transferred Florida to the United States and set a firm western boundary and by Mexico's achieving independence in the 1820's. Anglo-American tensions were lessened by agreements for Great Lakes demilitarization and joint occupation of Oregon, plus the British 1822 proposal for a joint Anglo-American declaration regarding potential European interference by force in the Western Hemisphere, especially in regard to Spain's revolted colonies. American post-war nationalism, so far as it rested on British and Spanish threats, was subsiding.

At this juncture, the Panic of 1819 threw the country into a severe economic depression. Government revenues declined drastically. Pressures for government retrenchment grew. Treasury Secretary Crawford demanded cutting federal expenses to keep the budget in balance. What easier and more logical place to cut than in costly military expenditures? Crawford supporters in Congress, joined by Clay men, chopped Calhoun's $1,500,000 request for fortifications by almost half in 1820, and pared it to $202,000 in 1821. Further, Congress reduced the regular army from 12,000 to 6,000 officers and men.

These moves stemmed partly from genuine desire for economy, but they were also partly dictated by political ambitions. Crawford, with his eye on the Presidency, saw Calhoun as a very real rival, especially as War Department operations grew, putting in Calhoun's hands the power to distribute profitable construction contracts and to make appointments. Reductions in manpower would force Calhoun into the politically unpopular task of dismissing or demoting army officers. For example, the law called for only one commanding general. Calhoun was saved from the unenviable chore of choosing between Generals Jackson and Jacob Brown by Jackson's timely decision to resign his commission and accept appointment as Governor of Florida Territory. Curtailment of fortification construction meant that Calhoun could not use government contracts to build a political following among local contractors and suppliers.

Hence Calhoun's military program, launched so hopefully during Monroe's first administration, floundered in the shoals of political rivalries during the second administration. Personally, Calhoun had won much respect for his character, administrative talent, and nationalist policies. President Monroe found him a reliable counselor, frequently called Calhoun to the White House for counsel, and sought him out as a traveling companion. Even normally critical John Quincy Adams, with whom Calhoun associated more closely than any other cabinet member, had high praise: "Calhoun thinks for himself independently of all the rest, with sound judgment, quick discrimination and keen observation. He supports his opinions, too, with powerful eloquence." [24]

For his part, Calhoun admired and respected Adams, whom he considered the best qualified man to succeed Monroe. As to his own views, Calhoun wrote a friend: "The importance which you attach to the good and harmonious conduct of myself, and a few other individuals, . . . is over estimated. The prosperity of our country never has . . . depended much on the conduct of any single individual. Those rise whose principles and conduct are congenial to a majority of the people. . . . My politics . . . has been founded on certain fixed principles; and to carry them into effect has been my highest ambition. I would despise myself if I were to change this noble object for the mean one of personal aggrandizement. Provided our country be free, . . . I care not whether I have the principal say or not." [25] But personal ambition has a way of growing, and Calhoun, once nipped by the Presidential bug, found the lure irresistible.

The Missouri Compromise legislation, passed by Congress, admitted Missouri to the Union as a slave state, Maine as a free state, and prohibited slavery from entering the remaining region of the Louisiana Purchase area lying north of the 36°30′ parallel, a westward extension of Missouri's southern boundary line.

Even when in 1820 the Missouri Compromise debates raised tempers in Congress and out to the exploding point, Calhoun remained calm, taking the broad nationalist view, as an aspirant to the Presidency should. President Monroe was sufficiently disturbed by the compromise legislation to ask his cabinet's views. When a conflict of opinion arose between Adams and the Southern members, Calhoun persuaded Monroe to rephrase the question to simply whether the act was constitutional. All could then say yes, and Southerners could later claim they understood the prohibition of slavery to apply only to north of the Compromise's dividing line and not to *states*. Monroe followed Calhoun's suggestion and eased his own constitutional qualms. Later discussing privately the whole issue with Adams, as they walked home together, Calhoun conceded frankly as "just and noble" Adams's view that slavery was contrary to the Declaration of Independence and an abuse of the rights of the governed. But Calhoun went on to argue the social necessity of slavery in the South, given the existing prejudice against Negroes and the present social structure. [26] On the other side, Calhoun tried to cool Southern tempers. "We of the South," he wrote a friend, "ought not to assent easily to the belief that there is a conspiracy either against our property or just weight in the Union. . . . If we, from such a belief, systematically oppose the north, they must from necessity resort to a similar opposition to us. Our true system is to look to the country; and to support such measures and such men, without a regard to sections, as are best calculated to advance the general interest. . . . Should emancipation be attempted," he reassured Southerners, "it must and will be resisted at all costs, but let us be certain first that it is the real object, not by a few, but by a large portion of the non-slave holding states." [27]

When Calhoun joined the cabinet in 1817, Floride and his family (he sired seven children before 1825, two of whom died as infants) joined him in Washington. After renting for a few years, they moved into the Georgetown Heights mansion "Oakly" (now Dumbarton Oaks) with its 30 acres of spacious lawns, gardens and woods, which Floride's mother had bought.[28] She lived with the Calhouns for a time, zealously seeking converts for the Presbyterian church during the 1822 cholera epidemic. While Floride attended the Episcopal church, John helped establish the first Unitarian group in Washington.[29]

Although the Calhouns in these years entertained with frequent dinners and levees and appeared at the center of the capital's social swirl, Calhoun himself developed few close friendships. With Lowndes he was intimate, and for a time also with Adams, but most associates found his conversation, while brilliant, often became a monologue. He never played cards, smoked, read books for pleasure, or drank anything but a little wine. His nature remained unbending and essentially humorless. "I never heard him utter a jest," observed a family friend; "There was unvarying dignity and gravity in his manner; and yet the playful child regarded him fearlessly and lovingly." [10] Work and attention to "duty" became his all-absorbing obsession, with 15–hour gobs of it a day.

After Northern tours through Pennsylvania, New York, and New England, ostensibly to inspect military fortifications, which Calhoun used to sound out opinion, in December 1821 he gave a delegation of Pennsylvania Congressmen permission to regard him as a serious candidate for the Presidency. Calhoun's decision to stand for President stemmed from the mixed sources of personal ambition and belief that he could win. The Missouri debates of 1820–21 revealed the frightening face of sectional hostility and potential disunion, which Calhoun abhorred. Among Presidential aspirants, already nominated by their respective state legislatures, Crawford, Adams, and Clay, the conviction grew in Calhoun's mind that Crawford was the most dangerous candidate—particularly in the light of the Georgian's extreme sectionalism and state rights position in the Missouri controversy. Further, Crawford had inspired the opposition to Calhoun's military defense program, encouraged Congressional investigations of War Department operations and reduction of its appropriations. Moreover, Crawford's personal hostility toward Calhoun, originating in the 1816 caucus that passed over Crawford for Monroe, now erupted in insinuations of irregularities and corruption in some War Department contract awards. Infuriated, Calhoun struck back by inspiring a series of newspaper articles charging dishonesty in the Treasury, Crawford's own department. Crawford must be blocked from the Presidency, not so much, in Calhoun's view, for his unscrupulous tactics but because of the threat he posed to the national security program and national harmony.

But the other candidates Calhoun found less than ideal. Clay, although earlier a friend, had joined the assault in Congress on Calhoun's defense program and on Monroe's administration generally, and was therefore untrustworthy. Adams, with whom Calhoun was on close terms and whose ability he respected, appeared the best bet. Not only had Adams consistently supported Calhoun's strong military policy, but the two men saw eye to eye on Bank, internal improvements, and money questions. Indeed, the two men resembled each other in Calvinistic attitudes, temperament, mode of rational thinking, personal manner, besides developing great mutual respect. To Adams, Calhoun confided many of his thoughts and to Adams for President he had implied earlier his tacit if not open support.[11]

His Northern journeys of 1820 and 1821 changed Calhoun's mind. Up until then his analysis of the contest to succeed Monroe ran in this fashion: Crawford would carry the South, Clay the West, Adams New England, leaving the outcome essentially in the hands of Pennsylvania and New York, with their large electoral votes. (Jackson at this point insisted that he would not consider running.) During his Northern journeys, Calhoun learned that Adams was much weaker in his home section than previously appeared, that Martin Van Buren who had just secured political ascendancy in New York would probably join the Crawford camp. He also discovered that he himself had a sizable following in the North. In New England Webster declared his support for Calhoun thinking him the only leader with a chance of defeating Crawford, while Justice Joseph Story, though believing Calhoun too young (only 39 in 1821), pronounced him "superior to most, if not to all of the candidates." In Pennsylvania, where his partisans controlled the powerful *Franklin Gazette* and most of the state offices, he was assured by Samuel Ingham and other political leaders that he could carry the state against either Crawford or Adams.[12]

Upon reevaluating the lineup of contestants, Calhoun now concluded that Adams simply did not have the strength in

New York and Pennsylvania (and possibly not even in New England) to defeat Crawford. Therefore, to beat Crawford Calhoun would have to enter the race. He calculated he could fight Crawford even in the South, might pick up some votes in the West where his advocacy of internal improvements and his military measures had won friends, and with Pennsylvania in his column, the outcome would be close. If he himself did not succeed, at least Crawford would not win a majority, and the contest would go to the House. With these considerations in mind, Calhoun became a candidate at the close of 1821.

Calhoun first approached his friend William Lowndes, who a few months earlier had been nominated for President by the South Carolina legislature. Lowndes assured Calhoun that he did not seek the presidency and that at a "favorable" time would throw his support to Calhoun. In South Carolina it was said: "Mr. Lowndes had most of the State, but Mr. Calhoun had Pendleton District and Mr. Lowndes." [13] But Lowndes, already in failing health, resigned from his Congressional seat in May, 1822, and died less than six months later. Calhoun's spokesmen, George McDuffie and Joel Poinsett, carried the fight in Congress. Outside, a laudatory biography of Calhoun, probably written by George M. Dallas, was published in the *Franklin Gazette,* and a year later *Measures Not Men* praising Calhoun's ability and programs appeared in New York (some critics said it was inspired if not written by its subject). In Washington a new newspaper, the *Republican,* under the editorship of Thomas L. McKenney, a former assistant in the War Department, appeared as Calhoun's official organ, and launched a withering barrage of criticism against Crawford. New cabinet appointments of Calhoun supporters to Navy and Post Office increased Calhoun's prestige and prospects. [14]

Calhoun's candidacy suffered from external obstacles and

personal limitations. Adams, at first incredulous since he had considered Calhoun a loyal adherent, became antagonized and bitter in his caustic diary comments, although he gave no immediate outward sign to Calhoun. Other men were less discreet. One Senator spoke of him as "the most presuming man in the Nation"; Albert Gallatin put him down as merely "a smart fellow, one of the first among second-rate men, but of lax political principles and a disordinate ambition not over-delicate in the means of satisfying itself." Fellow South Carolinian Thomas Cooper thought him "too pretending, too fond of the brilliant, the magnificent, too calculating, how all his sayings and doings will work with respect to his own honor and glory." Henry A. Wise saw Calhoun as "a giant of intellect, who was a child in party politics." [35] Certainly, Calhoun paid too little attention to human nature and human foibles and vanities to make a master politician. His own ego and self-righteousness often led him into self delusion.

But Calhoun's determination was fixed. He would have the Presidency by beating down all obstacles. His age (39 in 1821) was no obstacle; and he brushed aside Adams's very sensible objection that all the older men of ability would refuse to serve under so young a man. When a friendly editor, pointing out he would still be in his forties "at the end of your second term," asked, "What would you do?" Calhoun replied calmly, "I would retire and write my memoirs." Supremely confident, Calhoun pushed ahead, and so did his rivals. All of them shrugged off the threat of Andrew Jackson, accepting at face value his alleged declaration, "Do they think that I am . . . damned fool enough to think myself fit for President? No. Sir?" [36]

But the Jackson boom zoomed phenomenally, while the partisan press slugged it out. Stories were planted, rumors fabricated, slanders invented. Calhoun was sneered at as "the Army candidate" with "loose principles," Clay as the "gam-

bling candidate" with "loose morals," Adams was reported
to have been disinherited for private and public indiscretions.
Jackson was called "a slave speculator," "conspirator with
the notorious Aaron Burr," a swindler, and a murderer who
had tried to kill Benton and who "deliberately shot down
Charles Dickinson and then exultingly wrote, I left the d---d
scoundrel weltering in his blood!" Crawford was charged
with cowardice and stealing public funds. Adams coolly
watching the slugfest confided to his diary that Calhoun and
Crawford were nothing but "two famished wolves grappling
for the carcass of a sheep" and that the campaign was a battle
of "mining and countermining between Crawford and Calhoun to blow up each other, and a continued underhand
working of both, jointly against me. . . . At this game Crawford is much superior . . . to Calhoun, whose hurried ambition will probably ruin himself and secure the triumph of
Crawford." [37]

But the campaign was shaken by startling surprises towards its close. In September 1823 Crawford's stroke left him
semi-paralyzed and virtually speechless for many months. He
made only a partial recovery by February 1824 when the
Congressional caucus met, which gave Crawford the nomination on the basis of 65 members voting for him. Some 150
members boycotted what they considered an unfair undemocratic system of nominating for the Presidency. Shortly Calhoun's hopes, buoyed by Crawford's misfortune, received
their death blow. The Pennsylvania party convention at Harrisburg proceeded to nominate by acclamation Andrew Jackson for President, John Calhoun for Vice President. Calhoun,
having banked on Pennsylvania, knew he could not now
win—accepted his fate sadly, withdrew from the Presidential
contest, and settled for the Vice Presidency. He had suffered
his first defeat in sixteen years in politics.

The four-way struggle that resulted in placing Adams in the White House has been treated in Chapter II above.

Calhoun Becomes Vice President, 1824–25

In the 1824 election, while the four candidates for President balloted to a divided vote, Calhoun floated smoothly through, capturing 182 (out of a possible 261) electoral votes from all corners of the land. In only four states did he fail to win a single vote. In the ensuing power struggle in the House for selection of the President, Calhoun, as Vice-President-elect, steered a public course of uneasy neutrality between Jackson and Adams, although he was reported to have expressed a private preference for the latter. In the maneuverings for support among Congressmen in the winter of 1824–25, Calhoun did remain impartial, even though Adams fumed in his diary that he was working in Jackson's interest. At first, Calhoun refused to take it seriously but as rumors intensified that Clay would become Adams' Secretary of State, South Carolina's Congressional delegation, doubtless with Calhoun's knowledge and approval, made Adams an offer to support his administration on condition that Clay be excluded from the cabinet. The offer was rejected. Quickly it dawned on Calhoun that the presidential succession would now move to Clay, thereby blocking Calhoun's path to the White House. He would now have to look elsewhere to fulfill his Presidential aspirations.

On March 4, 1825, the United States Senate met in special session and immediately adopted a motion that the oath of office should be administered to the new Vice President by Andrew Jackson, the oldest Senator present. Standing tall and straight, Calhoun faced the erect, lean Jackson—two sons of South Carolina, "young Hercules" and the "Old

Hero." Calhoun, his dark, magnetic eyes fixed on the flashing, blue eyes of the General, raised his right hand and pronounced the oath in clear, solemn tones. Following a tap of
the gavel, he briefly addressed the Senators reminding them
"that a successful discharge of the duties" of the Senate
"must depend . . . on the patriotism and wisdom of its members." [18]

The Adams administration had barely begun when Calhoun began moving toward the ranks of the opposition. As
he phrased it in a personal letter: "I see in the fact that Mr.
Clay has made the Prs't. against the voice of his constituents,
and that he has been rewarded by the man elevated by him
to the first office . . . a most dangerous stab which the liberty
of this country has ever received. I will not be on that side.
I am with the people, and shall remain so." [19] To be "with
the people," he would soon discern, meant to board the band-
wagon of Andrew Jackson. In that direction Calhoun moved
with ready agility.

Calhoun, in switching to the Jackson bandwagon, had well
judged the temper of the times and of the country. In the 1828
election, he stood virtually unopposed and swept into the
Vice Presidency handily a second time. In the light of Jackson's repeated assertion that he would serve only one term
in the White House, Calhoun appeared to be a sure bet as
successor to the Presidential chair in 1832 when it was fully
expected Old Hickory would retire to his beloved Hermitage.
In 1828 Calhoun stood as close to the Presidency as he would
ever get. Events of the next few years would change dramatically not only the country's course but John Calhoun's career.

John Quincy Adams wrote about Calhoun early in 1828:
"Calhoun is a man of considerable talent and burning ambition; stimulated to frenzy by success, flattery, and premature
advancement; governed by no steady principle, but sagacious

to seize upon every prevailing popular breeze to swell his own sails; showering favors with lavish hands to make partisans, without discernment in the choice of his instruments, and the dupe and tool of every knave cunning enough to drop the oil of fools in his ear." This was a harsh judgment for a President to render on his Vice President, but not entirely unjustified, and perfectly understandable in the light of Calhoun's having abandoned Adams' sinking ship and having hitched his wagon to the swiftly rising star of Andrew Jackson.

V Jackson and Calhoun in Collision, 1829-1832

Jackson Takes Command

As Jackson was leaving the Hermitage in January 1829, Daniel Webster in Washington wrote: "Nobody knows what he will do [after he arrives]. . . . My own opinion is that when he comes he will bring a breeze with him." [1] Little did Webster suspect that the "breeze" would become a gale, then a tornado creating a whirlwind that would drive the American ship of state on a new course and spin furiously the national political windmill for decades to come. As Webster said, no one in Washington knew what to expect.

Everybody knew the General by his military accomplishments, but impressions of his character and personality varied widely. "Of his habitual [lack of] self control," recorded Van Buren at an earlier date, "many of his warmest supporters were not without lively apprehensions—a portion anxiously distrustful." [2] Political opponents like Adams called him "a barbarian who could not write a sentence of grammar and hardly . . . spell his own name." [3] To Clay he was "ignorant, passionate, hypocritical, corrupt and easily swayed by the base men who surround him." [4]

Jackson himself was aware of this picture of himself as of "savage disposition, who allways carried a scalping knife in one hand and a tomahawk in the other, allways ready to knock down and scalp any and every person who differed with me." [5] But Jackson knew how to regulate his temper, often shrewdly used outbursts of seeming rage to intimidate others and get his own way. Indeed, when he chose, he could not only control his temper, but his charm of manner, social grace, courtesy, and urbanity were impressive; to Webster in 1824 he appeared "more presidential" than any candidate being "grave, mild and reserved." [6]

Whether he was savage barbarian or gracious gentleman, the people wanted to see for themselves the new President in person, who was after all (the campaign posters said so) "the People's Friend." "A monstrous crowd of people" streamed into Washington. Tennessee backwoodsmen, Baltimore stevedores, Pennsylvania draymen, Ohio mechanics, soldier veterans, Virginia shopkeepers, Carolina dirt farmers jostled in Washington's muddy streets against politicians, judges, gentlemen, and assorted adventurers. "I never saw anything like it before," wrote Webster. "Persons have come from five hundred miles to see General Jackson, and they really seem to think the country is rescued from some dreadful danger." [7] And they did truly believe the Hero was saving the country from the triple danger of corruption, privilege, and aristocracy. A new departure seemed at hand. For the first time in more than thirty years of the Republic, a non-Eastern aristocrat, a Western self-made man risen by his own energy, virtue and strength from backwoods obscurity, a non-college graduate, a non-professional politician would fill the Presidency; a new Messiah would lead the people out of the wilderness of corruption and intrigue back to the Promised Land of moral virtue and political integrity of the Republic's early years. [8]

On March 4, 1829, in the newly remodeled semi-circular gallery of the Senate chamber in the Capitol, distinguished guests watched closely as the floor filled with Senators. The tall, angular form of John C. Calhoun entered and strode to the presiding officer's chair on the dais. At 11 o'clock (as Jackson was leaving the Indian Queen Tavern for the Capitol) Calhoun, Vice-President of the United States and Vice-President-elect, called the Senate to order, took the oath from Senator Samuel Smith before administering the oath to a dozen new Senators, including Robert Y. Hayne, a Calhoun cohort from South Carolina.[9]

At 11:30 Andrew Jackson, grave, dignified, of straight frame, weathered face, shock of bristling white hair, was escorted to a front seat in the chamber. At the left sat the diplomatic corps showy in the formal attire, on the right John Marshall and his fellow black-robed justices. House members, new Cabinet officers (except Martin Van Buren) sat scattered through the chamber along with military and naval officers and visiting notables. Only retiring President John Quincy Adams, who had vowed not to "go near," was absent, sulking at the suburban house of a friend. At noon Calhoun adjourned the Senate, and the entire procession walked through the rotunda to the east portico to face the crowd of thousands jammed on the steps and spread across the grounds.

A tremendous roar that seemed "to shake the very ground" burst from the crowd as the Old Hero emerged. Jackson, moved with feeling, bowed before "the majesty of the people." He delivered in inaudible tones his brief (10 minute) inaugural address. Stepping forward, Chief Justice John Marshall administered the oath; Jackson raised to his lips a Bible. Francis Scott Key, standing nearby, marveled at the scene: 'It is beautiful, it is sublime." [10] The cannon boomed over the cheering of the crowd as the new Executive, mobbed by admirers, struggled his way to his carriage. Rolling slowly up Pennsylvania Avenue, Jackson stood waving to the cheering mass of "countrymen, farmers, gentlemen, . . . boys, women, children, black and white." [11]

Upon reaching the White House, the mob flooded through the doors, invited and uninvited, for the President's reception —"statesmen and stableboys, fine ladies and washerwomen." To watching Supreme Court Justice Joseph Story "King Mob seemed triumphant" and "I was glad to escape as soon as possible." In the stately East Room where tables spread with cakes, ice cream, and orange punch shivered under the press of humanity as eager, screaming partisans pushed, shoved, clawed to get a glimpse of the Hero. One Georgia Representative shuddering at seeing the mob wolf down food, smash glasses and plates, tear clothing, pocket silverware, "$150 official chairs profaned by the feet of clodhoppers," felt lucky to leap to safety through a side window. "A regular Saturnalia," remarked one guest. The President himself in a crush of well-wishers appeared helpless, "sinking into a listless state of exhaustion." Only a cordon of husky men, locking arms, were able to cleave a path that enabled Jackson to flee by the back door and make it to the security of Gadsby's Tavern. In the White House the revelers remained until the tubs of punch were at length placed outside on the lawn, drawing the mob outside. Many individuals, acting on their belief that the people's government belonged literally to the people, carried away White House china, plates, goblets, silverware, and cups as souvenirs of the day the "Man of the People" assumed the Presidency.

That evening a grand inaugural ball was held at Carusi's hall. Cabinet members and wives greeted Congressmen, assorted politicians, newspaper editors, and guests elegantly dressed and decorous in manner. Since Jackson himself remained at Gadsby's exhausted from the afternoon's ordeal at the White House, the place of honor at the evening's ball was occupied by Vice President John Calhoun and his vivacious, brunette wife Floride, to whom deference was shown by all guests, including the much talked-of Mrs. Peggy Timberlake Eaton, bride of the new Secretary of War.

A new day in American politics was clearly dawning. New faces and new men filled the Washington scene. Even before his inauguration Jackson was seeking advice and counsel from a coterie of intimates—John Eaton and William B. Lewis of "Nashville Junto" days, former Congressman Richard K. Call of Tennessee, Amos Kendall, a wizened but incisive editor who brought one of the most skillful pens in America to Jackson's service, and James A. Hamilton (son of Alexander) who served as emissary for Governor Martin Van Buren of New York. From suggestions offered by these men and others including Vice President Calhoun, Jackson chose his official cabinet in an effort to satisfy all factions of the political coalition that raised him to the White House.

As Secretary of State Jackson chose Martin Van Buren partly as a reward for having turned New York from Adams to Jackson and partly because of Van Buren's political acumen. The Treasury office went to Samuel D. Ingham, Pennsylvania Congressman, in recognition of that state's importance to the Jackson victory. John Branch of North Carolina for the Navy Department, John M. Berrien of Georgia for Attorney-General, William T. Barry of Kentucky for Postmaster-General to replace John McLean who was elevated to the Supreme Court, and old crony John Eaton for the War Department rounded out the cabinet.

The Ingham, Branch, and Berrien appointments acknowledged support of the Calhoun wing of the coalition. Altogether the cabinet was not impressive—a "millenium of minnows," one hostile observer called it. Besides, Old Hickory did not intend to use the cabinet very much as a consulting council; rather he preferred talking things over with close intimates, like Major Lewis, who lived at the White House, along with Jackson's personal secretary and nephew Andrew Jackson Donelson. Also living at the White House were Donelson's wife Emily and a portrait painter, Ralph E. W. Earl of Nashville, whom Rachel Jackson had been very fond of. Martin Van Buren came to be included along with Eaton and Kendall in the inner circle, dubbed the "Kitchen Cabinet" by the opposing press. So too were Isaac Hill, staunch Jacksonian editor from New Hampshire; and later Francis P. Blair, brought to Washington in 1830 as editor of the administration paper, the *Globe;* and Roger B. Taney of Maryland, who would become Attorney General and Secretary of the Treasury later on.

In his inaugural remarks, Jackson spoke of "the task of *reform*" as high "on the list of executive duties." Translated to ordinary language "reform" meant "turn the rascals out," remove the hold-over office holders from the Adams-Clay regime. Since a major theme of the Jackson 1828 campaign had been to root out corruption in the administrative branch, many office seekers had come to Washington fully expecting the new President to sweep the "Augean stables" clean, and Jackson found himself bombarded with requests for political appointments.

Back in 1798 Jackson had denounced President John Adams for "removing all those from office who differ with him in politics." Again in 1824, he observed, "the very moment I proscribe an individual from office, on account of his political opinion, I become myself a despot."

A dozen years earlier Jackson had advised President-elect Monroe "to eradicate the *monster* called party spirit. By selecting characters most conspicuous for their probity, virtue, capacity and firmness, without regard to party, you will go far" to eradicate party hostility in the public service. But Jackson's views had now changed. "It is certain," he wrote after assuming the Presidency, "that whichever party makes the President, must give direction to his administration. . . . No one can carry on this Government without support, and the Head of it must rely for support on the party by whose suffrages he is elected;" to which he added his celebrated declaration, "It is as true in politics as in morals, that those who are not with us are against us." [12]

Upon assuming office in 1829, he proceeded to dismiss many federal office holders, some for reasons of malfeasance or inattention to duty, but many were fired simply to make way for good Jackson partisans. The insistent clamor for office forced upon him, he said, "the most disagreeable duty I have to perform" in making "removals and appointments to office." Noting "great distress here" in Washington, he remarked, "it appears that all who possess office depend upon the emolument for support" while "thousands who are pressing for office do it on the ground that they are starving. . . . Those hungry expectants, as well as those who enjoy office, are dangerous contestants over the public purse . . . and when any and every man can get recommendations of the strongest kind, it requires great circumspection to avoid imposition and select honest men." [13]

Because removals were numerous, Jackson was charged with introducing the "spoils system" in the national government—a charge much distorted by his critics, both contemporary and subsequent. It is obvious that Jackson did not invent the spoils system since firing for political reasons had long been practiced in many states and cities. He did not engage in wholesale dismissals simply for political reasons. But it is also true that he approved removals on a sizable scale. In his first year and a half in office, removals totaled 919 out of 10,093 federal offices. Less than 10%, this was far from the clean sweep his opponents charged. For his two administrations, dismissals for political reasons ran somewhat over 10%, and considerably above that figure within the President's office itself. [14]

When complaints arose over removals, Old Hickory noted in his private journal in June 1829: "There has been a great noise made about removals. This to be brought before Congress . . . with the propriety of passing a law vacating all offices periodically—then the good can be reappointed, and the bad . . . left out without murmurs. Now, every man who has been in office a few years believes he has a life estate in it . . . and if it has been held twenty years or upwards . . . that it ought to descend to his children, and if no children then the next of kin. This is not the principle of our government. It is rotation of office that will perpetuate our liberty."

Jackson defended his practice of replacing old office holders with new men loyal to his party on two grounds—one democratic, the other pragmatic. On democratic grounds, he argued: "In a country where offices are created solely for the benefit of the people no one man has any more intrinsic right to official station than another. Offices were not established" to support "particular men at the public expense. No individual wrong is, therefore, done by removal," since office holding is not "a matter of right. The incumbent became an officer with a view to public benefits, and when these require his removal, they are not to be sacrificed to private interests. . . . He who is removed has the same means of obtaining a living that are enjoyed by the millions who never held office." Here, then, is an assertion of the democratic principle of equality of opportunity. No special privilege in office holding! Since government in a democracy must respond to the will of the people, "it becomes" the President's duty "to . . . dismiss all officers who were appointed against the manifest will of the people." [15] Further, the duties of most public offices at the time were so plain and simple that any man of ordinary intelligence could perform them; hence all should have the chance at office. The foremost modern student of public administration concludes that "Jackson sincerely believed he was about to introduce reform, and he could make a case for it; but he did not foresee the subsequent consequences" with attendant abuses and weakening of the efficiency of the public service. (See *Appendix*, Doc. No. 3B for fuller text.)

The other line of defense rested on practical grounds. Political parties, having become necessary to the successful functioning of government, could maintain themselves and attract loyal, energetic activists only by astute dispensing of the patronage. Men would enter politics and work loyally for a party only if they could foresee some practical reward in the form of political office. The old Federalist view that had prevailed from the days of Washington to John Q. Adams that no office holder should be fired for his political opinions (John Q. Adams indeed, refusing to fire, had reappointed friend and foe alike to office)—now gave way to the practical demands of political party organization and support. Those who worked for the party should be rewarded. A Van Buren associate in 1829 put it: "All who do not support the present administration you will not consider your friends, and of course will lose your confidence" (read, their offices). Senator William L. Marcy of New York gave the doctrine its bluntest expression: "politicians are not so fastidious as to disclosing the principles on which they act. . . . When . . . contending for victory, they avow their intention of enjoying the fruits of it. . . . If they are successful, they claim, as a matter of right, the advantages of success. They see nothing wrong in the rule, that to the victor belong the spoils of the enemy." By the time he left the White House, Jackson himself fully embraced this view, writing to Lewis: "ours in a Government based upon public opinion, and that opinion is for . . . rotation in office." [16]

In retrospect, it is clear that Jackson did much to establish the rotation principle, which later successors pushed to a wholesale "spoils system." The advantage of the arrangement was to strengthen political party organization, making it an effective instrument whereby public opinion could express itself. The disadvantages of rotation—decline of efficiency and continuity and intrusion of party obligations in the civil service—were partially offset in the Jackson years by insistence upon competence and honesty in public office, although here, the Jacksonians sometimes tripped badly, as in the notorious case of Samuel Swartwout, who as New York Customs Collector and Jackson's worst appointment, embezzled over a million dollars.

At the outset of Jackson's Presidency, John C. Calhoun appeared in an unassailable political position. As Vice President, he stood close to the administration and was thought to be held in high esteem by the President himself. His longtime, faithful supporter, Duff Green, continued to edit the administration organ, the *United States Telegraph,* and as the government's public printer remained privy to the administration and received inside dope and administration handouts for public dissemination. Jackson's announced intention of serving only one term put Calhoun in the favored spot as the General's probable successor in the Presidency, and clearly Calhoun believed as much himself. Indeed, to strengthen his cause he had given a dinner in March 1829 in honor of the press, including not only Duff Green, but Amos Kendall, Isaac Hill along with editors from Boston, New York, and Philadelphia. But within a year's time, Calhoun's influence in the administration would be severely undermined; within two years Jackson would cut him off as a friend; and three years later President and Vice President would declare open war on each other. An incredible turn of events that shattered Calhoun's hopes to be President.

For more than a dozen years prior to inauguration, Jackson and Calhoun had known each other in varying relationships—General to Secretary of War, ardent co-advocates of national defense measures, fellow participants in the Senate, co-candidates for high office in 1828. Invariably they had professed a cordial, if formal, regard for each other. In 1821 Calhoun told Jackson: "I would rather have your good opinion . . . than all the popularity which a pretended love of the people and a course of popularity hunting can excite;" and again in 1823: "I find few men with whom I accord so fully in relation to political affairs than yourself." The General, too, had reciprocated at various times, as in 1821 when he wrote Calhoun: "my breast will always cherish . . . that friendly feeling . . . your honorable conduct towards me ever since you have been placed in the Department of War was well calculated to inspire. This feeling for you will never cease during life." [17] The "friendly feeling" would soon dissipate as fickle Fortune spun the wheel of political roulette.

"The Petticoat War!" Peggy Eaton Scuttles Jackson's Cabinet

In the first year of his administration Jackson's "friendly feeling" toward Calhoun began to undergo a subtle change. Three factors contributed: personality differences, the "Eaton malaria," and a major political difference. With his cold, tense, intellectual Vice President Jackson found himself unable to relax in easy natural fashion. On the other hand, he found himself much more comfortable with his Secretary of State, affable, relaxed, witty Martin Van Buren. More and more he spent time with the red-faced New Yorker, who even brushed up his long-abandoned horseback riding and began taking frequent rides with his chief during which Jackson became much enchanted by Van Buren's charm and political horse sense.

Even more crucial in moving Old Hickory closer to the "Little Magician" was the "Eaton malaria," as Van Buren termed it. Eaton, Jackson's old Tennessee friend and biographer, had married pretty, saucy Peggy O'Neale, who had often served as barmaid in her father's tavern, where many Washington politicos had fancied her pert manner and vivacious conversation. Senator Eaton who had boarded at O'Neal's tavern, was captivated by Peggy. Her first husband, John B. Timberlake, a Navy purser, whose deficient accounts Eaton had settled, had died at sea. The ship's log listed cause of death as "pulmonary disease"; crew members said he had cut his throat in a fit of drunken melancholy, which Washington gossips claimed was brought on by his knowledge that he had been cuckolded by Eaton. Peggy's salacious reputation had long been ventilated in Washington's circles, one Virginia Congressman commenting, "Mrs. Timberlake was considered as a lady who would dispense her favors wherever she took a fancy. . . . Eaton's connection with [her] was notorious."

When news of Timberlake's death reached the United States, Eaton, "anxious and distressed" in mind decided to consult Jackson about his desire to marry Peggy. "Why, yes, Major," replied the General, "if you love the woman and she will have you, marry her by all means." When the Major remarked that Peggy's reputation in Washington was not above reproach, Jackson shot back, "Major, if you love Margaret Timberlake, marry her and shut their [gossipers'] mouths." When Eaton hesitantly remarked he would do so "at a proper time" Jackson dispatched a pointed message from the Hermitage that Eaton in Washington should marry Peggy "forthwith" or leave O'Neale's boarding house at once.[19]

So, on January 1, 1829, seven weeks after Jackson's election, Senator Eaton and Peggy exchanged their vows in the presence of the Senate chaplain. Official Washington was incredulous. Politicians were convinced that Eaton was mad. Said one, "The General's enemies laugh and divert themselves." Many crude jokes and remarks circulated. New York Congressman Churchill C. Cambreleng reported the news to his preceptor Van Buren: "Poor Eaton is to be married tonight to Mrs. T_____! There is a certain vulgar saying of some vulgar man, I believe Swift, on such unions—about using a certain household _____ [sic] and then putting it on one's head." [20] Mrs. Margaret Bayard Smith, a leader of Washington society, observed: "Eaton, the bosom friend and almost adopted son of General Jackson, is to be married to a lady, whose reputation, her previous connection with him both before and after her husband's death, has totally destroyed. . . . She has never before been admitted to good society, is very handsome and of not an inspiring character and a violent temper. She is . . . irresistible and carries whatever point she sets her mind on." [21]

But whether Peggy's determination was strong enough to crack the haut monde of Washington remained to be seen. Washington society from the days of Mrs. Monroe refused to accept Mrs. Timberlake; and Washington society now in the days of Jackson raised its barriers to Mrs. Eaton. Friends tried to dissuade Jackson from naming Eaton to his cabinet and thereby causing needless embarrassment. But Jackson was not to be deterred.

In early December 1828, when Congress opened, Senator Eaton had made the customary courtesy call on the Vice President. Calhoun returned the call—alone, in January while the Eatons were honeymooning in Philadelphia. After their return Senator and Mrs. Eaton called on the Calhouns. As it happened the Vice President was not at home, and Mrs. Calhoun, recognizing Eaton, received the couple graciously, although she had never seen Peggy before. Even though she had not been in Washington since 1826, Floride Calhoun had naturally heard the gossip and was doubtless glad to satisfy her curiosity by getting a close look at the most-talked-about woman in town. The Eatons chatted for a time and then departed. When Calhoun returned, he and his wife discussed the question of Peggy and her standing in society withou reaching any conclusion, although they viewed the Eatons' call as something of a challenge.

In the absence of a First Lady, the Vice President's wife occupied the highest social position in Washington; her acceptance of Peggy Eaton would be the key to opening Washington society. Floride Calhoun found herself in the awkward position of having been in the city only a month and intending to stay only until the inauguration two months later (and this after an absence of three years). Next morning she told her husband that she would not return the call because being "a stranger in the place . . . she knew nothing of the truth or falsehood of the imputations on" Peggy's character and "she conceived it the duty of Mrs. Eaton" to initiate social relations "with the ladies who resided in the place" who could better form "a correct opinion of her conduct" in contrast to Mrs. Calhoun, "who . . . had no means of forming a correct judgment." [22] So Floride, according to Calhoun's account, deferred to the judgment of more experienced Washington hands, whose thumbs were turned down on Peggy Eaton.

When Jackson offered Eaton the War Department, he hesitated. But when friends suggested the Senator might be more useful in a foreign capital, Peggy pushed her husband to accept the War portfolio, saying she would remain in Washington "in the presence of my enemies" and conquer there. (Shades of Old Hickory's spirit!) So as bride of the Secretary of War, Peggy became the vortex of a social storm that hung embarrassingly over the new regime, destined eventually to blast the cabinet apart and refashion the political careers of two principal members, John Calhoun and Martin Van Buren. Peggy Eaton was thirtyish, small but with a well-rounded, voluptuous figure, a peach-pink complexion; her large, active, dark eyes could communicate much even with a glance; full, sensuous lips ready to break into an engaging smile and with a toss of the head the generous mouth opening wide in immoderate laughing exhibited the prettiest teeth in Washington. One observer noted, "she talked away about anything and every thing—jumbling great and small subjects together. . . . She loves admiration and bedaubs every one . . . with flattery. The gentlemen . . . knowing this, pay her considerable attention." [23] Mrs. Calhoun remained in Washington until March 18 when she returned with her husband to South Carolina, pregnant, and gave birth to a baby boy on August 13, 1829. Martin Van Buren appeared in Washington March 25, 1829, one week after the Calhouns departed. Calhoun remained in South Carolina until early December 1829 when he returned to Washington alone. The Calhouns' home near Pendleton, South Carolina, on a hill in the piedmont overlooking Seneca River, was known as Clergy Hall till 1830, when it was renamed Fort Hill.

So at the start of his term Jackson found his administration enmeshed in intramural social squabbling that spelled at least personal turmoil and at most political trouble. At the inaugural celebrations Mrs. Eaton was cut socially by cabinet wives Ingham, Berrien, Calhoun, and by the daughters of Branch (a widower), who would have nothing to do with her. Neither would Emily Donelson, petite, auburn-haired wife of Jackson's nephew-secretary, or Emily's cousin Mary Eastin, who also lived at the White House. Postmaster General William Barry, whose wife did not come to Washington, actually lodged with the Eatons in their fine house across from the British Embassy and actively took Peggy's part. To him, Peggy was "an artless, sincere, friendly woman," who might have been imprudent; but he dismissed the rumors with the comment, "If rumours were to be credited, but few handsome ladies in . . . this city would be free from blemish." [24] In Peggy's defense Barry was joined by Van Buren, who as a widower, without daughters, felt none of the domestic pressures applied to his colleagues. Clearly conscious of where the President's sympathies lay, Van Buren proceeded to treat all cabinet ladies, including Mrs. Eaton, with equal deference and courtesy. Of all cabinet advisers Jackson relied most heavily on John Eaton, as a trusted friend and an old Washington hand, well versed in national politics. As one observer disturbingly wrote to Calhoun, "The U.S. are governed by the President. The President by the Secretary of War and the latter by his W[ife]." [25]

Jackson, who saw Peggy as "a helpless and virtuous female" used every effort to get her accepted. But at state functions he noted the hostile feelings toward Peggy. He convinced himself readily that Peggy was the object of malicious, false slanders and that in taking up her defense he was in effect resuming his lifelong campaign of the defense of his beloved Rachel, whose saintly life he believed had been cut short by scandal mongers. In time the "Eaton Malaria" affair became an obsession with Jackson, determined to defeat the evil schemes of his "enemies."

Close friends urged Jackson to avoid needless difficulties for his administration by sending Eaton abroad. But Jackson refused to budge, telling John Randolph that if cabinet officers could not treat Peggy decently, then they should resign. Even the clergy interceded. Reverend J. N. Campbell, of the Presbyterian church which Jackson and Rachel had earlier attended in Washington, with Reverend S. Ely of Philadelphia, remonstrated with Jackson. Jackson responded in a sharp note, dismissing charges against Peggy as gross slanders and asserting that "Mrs. Jackson to the last moment of her life believed Mrs. Eaton to be an innocent and much injured woman"; furthermore, that since both Timberlake

and Eaton were Masons neither could "have criminal intercourse with another mason's wife, without being one of the
most abandoned of men. . . . Female virtue is like a tender
and delicate flower; let the breath of suspicion rest upon it,
and it withers and perhaps perishes forever. When it shall be
assailed by envy and malice, the good and the pious will
maintain its purity and innocence until guilt is made manifest—not by rumors . . . but by facts . . . sustained by . . .
fearless witnesses in the face of day."

After sending Lewis to check out rumors, Jackson held a
cabinet meeting September 10, 1829, to hear "facts" from the
Reverends Ely and Campbell. Eaton was not present. Jackson
opened with a statement about the meanness of calumny,
then denied a charge by Campbell that Peggy had a miscar-
riage during one of Timberlake's more-than-a-year-long ab-
sences from home. Under Jackson's questioning Ely
conceded no evidence indicated improper conduct on Eaton's
part. "Nor, Mrs. Eaton either." Jackson interjected fiercely.
"On that point," Ely responded, somewhat cowed, "I would
rather not give an opinion." "She is chaste a virgin!" roared
the President, giving short shrift to her two marriages. Campbell, insisting that his only concern was to save the administration from reproach, was cut short by Jackson's explosive
command, "Give evidence!" Both Campbell and Ely gathered their papers and hastily left the room, whereupon Jackson closed the meeting, with the air of a man who had completely vindicated Mrs. Eaton's reputation.[26]

But the vindication would not stick. Even though the President succeeded in getting all cabinet members and wives to
attend his first state dinner at the White House on November
26, 1829, it turned out to be a "hollow affair," leaving Old
Hickory "mortified and resentful." Jackson was rapidly moving to the conviction that the prestige of his administration
depended on his fight to defend Margaret Eaton. Rumor

insinuated that somehow Calhoun was the inspirer of the anti-Eaton faction, even though the South Carolinian had been absent from Washington since March 18 and would not return until mid-December 1829. As John Q. Adams saw it, "Calhoun leads the moral party" of purity and "Van Buren that of the frail sisterhood." [27]

Actually, Calhoun was totally blameless himself. Though Jackson had developed mental doubts about Calhoun, he gave no outward sign of connecting the Vice President with the Eaton imbroglio until almost a year later.

Following the President's dinner, Secretary of State Van Buren entertained at dinner, all cabinet members except Branch attending, but no wives present. In quick succession followed parties by Ingham, Branch, and Berrien, to none of which was Mrs. Eaton invited. When she was mercilessly snubbed again at the Jackson Day ball of January 8, 1830, the "Eaton malaria" reached crisis stage. Eaton threatened to challenge to a duel any traducer of his wife's reputation. Reported to be raging "like a roaring lion," the President in late January summoned Ingham, Branch, and Berrien to the White House and laid down the law: "I do not claim the right to interfere in the domestic relations of personal intercourse of any member of my Cabinet. . . . [But continued efforts] to avoid Mrs. Eaton and thereby to exclude her from society and degrade him [Eaton] must [cease]. . . . I will not part with Major Eaton, and those of my cabinet who cannot harmonize with him had better withdraw; for harmony I must and will have." The trio denied any design to injure either Eaton or Jackson, disclaimed either the ability or desire to compel their wives to socialize with Mrs. Eaton and emphatically denied the right of the President to ask it.

The trio did not resign nor were they dismissed at this point. Senator Hugh L. White of Tennessee and Edward Livingston of Louisiana (both firm Jackson friends) dissuaded Jackson from making the removals that would alienate other Senators, friends of the Cabinet trio, who would join the opposition in voting down Jackson's appointment list just then before the Senate for confirmation. Van Buren, too, during his morning horseback rides with the President urged prudence and delay.

But the "petticoat war" continued, striking Jackson in the White House itself. Emily Donelson, White House hostess through her husband, Andrew Jackson Donelson, the President's nephew and private secretary, notified the President that henceforth she would receive Mrs. Eaton at the White House, as her duty required, but would not call on her. Jackson, stunned by this household mutiny, gave his niece and nephew the choice of befriending Peggy or banishment to Tennessee, explaining that he "was willing to yield to my family everything but the government of my House and the abandonment of my friend without cause." Off to Tennessee went Emily and her husband, who expressed his sadness over parting from the man "to whom I have stood from my infancy in the relation of son to Father." [28]

Their banishment would last for six months until friends effected a reconciliation—after Eaton's departure from the cabinet. "For once in his life, Andrew Jackson was defeated. Creek and Spaniards and Redcoats he could conquer, but the ladies of Washington never surrendered, and Peggy Eaton, though her affairs became a national question, never got into Washington society." [29]

The first year of Jackson's administration unfortunately had been paralyzed by the miasma of the "Eaton malaria." The winter and spring of 1830 would open contention on another front that would drive a further wedge into the opening rift between President Andrew Jackson and Vice President John Calhoun.

Nation or Confederation? "Liberty and Union"

To many close observers, a backstage struggle for preference in the Jackson regime had been visible for some months.
Many observed Martin Van Buren subtly maneuvering to
replace Vice President John Calhoun as crown prince in the
Jackson realm of power. The "Little Magician's" frequent
rides with General Jackson generated a close feeling of
mutual respect and affection. The whole Eaton affair raised
the New Yorker in the President's esteem since Van Buren
had proven especially courteous and receptive to the Eatons,
while Calhoun appeared as an obstacle in the path of Peggy's
acceptance. A correspondent reported to Clay in December,
1829, "Van Buren is making rapid strides. . . . Calhoun is
going down," while another wrote, "The Secretary of State
by his address and attentions to *Madame* [Eaton] . . . and
the President will undoubtedly give Calhoun . . . much trouble." [10] Further, the "Red Fox" of Kinderhook, as Calhoun
called Van Buren, had succeeded in quietly gaining control
over much of the federal patronage, from which a future
political machine could be built.

When Jackson's first message went to Congress, many professed to see Van Buren's hand in it, especially in the cautious
tone with which it handled touchy issues. On the tariff of
abominations of 1828, for example, Jackson pursuing a "middle course" asserted that it had neither injured agriculture
or commerce nor benefited manufacturing so much as had
been predicted but suggesting "some modifications." This
was a shrewdly phrased and timed passage in view of South
Carolina's "Exposition and Protest" (See Chapter VI) against
the tariff of a year earlier. Further, Jackson showed his sensitivity to state rightists' feelings when he attributed "the
success of the constitution . . . to the watchful and auxiliary

operation of the State authorities. This is . . . one of the most deeply rooted convictions of my mind. I can not, therefore, too strongly or too earnestly . . . warn you against all encroachments upon the legitimate sphere of State sovereignty." [1]

Although the reference to State sovereignty was pleasing, Calhoun was disturbed over Jackson's failure to come out strongly for tariff reduction. Calhoun's authorship of the South Carolina "Exposition and Protest" of 1828 was not publicly known; indeed it remained a well guarded secret among Calhoun's associates. But he had succeeded in 1828 in restraining South Carolina extremists from taking the drastic action of nullifying the 1828 tariff (an action for which Calhoun's "Exposition" advanced a constitutional justification) only by persuading their leaders to hold off until Jackson could bring about tariff reduction. But now Jackson, far from taking a strong stand against a protective tariff, had given only a slight nod toward "reform," and even that he pushed not at all.

The Vice President was pondering what might be done to nudge the President into action on the tariff. In January 1830, as the Senate's presiding officer, he listened closely to an exchange between his young friend Senator Robert Y. Hayne of South Carolina and his long time adversary Senator Webster. The debate had nothing to do with the tariff but sprang rather from a dispute over government land policy. It soon mushroomed into a general examination of the constitutional nature of the Union and federal-state relations. During six days of Senate sessions Hayne and Webster sparred and punched at each other. In refuting imputations of New England's selfishness, Webster defended his section's loyalty to the nation for while New England earlier opposed the tariff of 1816, it later had raised no complaint. Then looking directly at Calhoun on the dais, he clearly alluded to South

Carolina's recent outcry over the 1828 tariff: "I know there are some persons in that part of the country from which the honorable gentleman comes who habitually speak of the Union in terms of indifference, or even of disparagement. . . . They significantly declare that it is time to calculate the value of the Union."

In a reply, which Hayne prepared doubtless in consultation with Calhoun (legend has it that the latter sent Hayne notes of encouragement and supporting arguments from the chair), the young, handsome South Carolinian bitterly attacked New England's opposition to the War of 1812, Webster's association with the party that called the near treasonous Hartford Convention of 1814. He then developed in full the "true" constitutional doctrine that the United States was not intended to be a consolidated government determining the limits of its own power but rather it was a government of limited powers, the extent of which only the states could properly judge, and the states retained the right to set aside oppressive, unconstitutional federal legislation. Here was the nullification doctrine in sharp outline.

In calm, good nature, with a sure sense of mastery flowing through his rich, deep voice, "Black Daniel" assailed Hayne's proposals of nullification as impossible in practical application, ruinous to the welfare of all and clearly unconstitutional. "The Constitution is not the creature of the State governments. The very chief end . . . for which [it] . . . was framed and adopted was to establish government that should not depend on State opinon and State direction." For two days Webster held Senators and packed galleries enthralled with the most powerful plea yet heard in the Senate for perpetuating the nation, for rejecting as "folly" the notion of "liberty first and Union afterwards," for wholeheartedly supporting "Liberty and Union, now and forever, one and inseparable!" As the galleries exploded in thunderous applause,

few heard Calhoun's gavel and petulant cry, "Order! Order!"
That evening, Major Lewis, whom the President sent regu-
larly to observe the sessions on Capitol Hill, reported to
Jackson that Webster had demolished Hayne.[12]

After rephrasing and editing, both the Webster and Hayne
speeches were printed, and tens of thousands of copies bobbed
up across the country. Men discussed nationalism and nullification at crossroads taverns, in shops, in fine drawing rooms.
Did the President stand with Hayne or with Webster? Re-
perusal of the inaugural address and first message to Congress
gave little clue other than a general sense of his being a state
rights advocate. One report said that after Hayne's first
speech, Jackson had sent him a note of congratulation. It was
known that Webster entered the White House only on formal
occasions, while Hayne was a frequent social visitor. Hayne's
brother had been with the General at New Orleans and his
wife accompanied Emily Donelson on a New York journey.

While the President gave no outward sign of his position,
opponents of state sovereignty recalled his professions of belief in Jeffersonian principles as "an admirer of State authorities" in favor of "banishing the dangerous doctrine of implication" for enlarging federal power, his opposition to the
Alien and Sedition Acts of 1798 which had elicited the Jefferson-Madison broad enunciation of state interposition against
overexpanding federal power to the destruction of liberty
within the states. Indeed, it was the Jefferson-Madison doctrines of 1798 that the pro-nullification group now in 1830
were advancing as the correct interpretation of the Constitution and the nature of the Union.

But the question was neither simple nor clear cut. In framing the Constitution in 1787, the Founding Fathers of the
Republic proclaimed that "We the people of the United
States . . . do ordain and establish this Constitution." Had
the framers, by this, intended to create a consolidated nation

or a federation of sovereign distinct states brought together in formal compact by the Constitution? They failed to specify what "people"; whether it was the "people" of each of the states acting in a separate, sovereign capacity or whether it was the "people" of the entire country en masse acting as a sovereign whole was not made clear. The obscurity of meaning, perhaps intentional, led equally honest men into ceaseless argument over what was meant.

All agreed that sovereignty rested with the people, but again the nagging question continued as to which "people"? Further, though all agreed that the "sovereign" "people" had endowed the federal government with certain limited powers, precisely what were the limits of those powers? Who was entitled to determine the limits of those powers? And if the federal government exceeded the granted powers, who had the authority and power to prevent such an unconstitutional extension of federal powers? These questions had been vigorously debated since the Republic's founding.

On the question of the extent of federal powers, the Tenth Amendment to the Constitution, adopted in 1791, seemed to provide an answer in stating that "the powers not delegated to the United States by the Constitution, nor prohibited by it to the States, are reserved to the States respectively, or to the people." Offering seeming clarification, this amendment, however, did not resolve the still open question of the extent to which the federal government could adopt "laws . . . necessary and proper for carrying into execution" the delegated powers.

On the question of who should restrain the federal government from exercising power not granted in the Constitution or determining the extent of what was "necessary and proper," two conflicting views had grown up over the years. The nationalist view, as expounded by Chief Justice John Marshall in a series of Supreme Court decisions maintained that the federal Supreme Court was the proper referee of the extent of federal power. An opposing doctrine asserted that the people of each of the states, acting in their sovereign capacity, were the appropriate judges to call a halt to federal exercise of power not delegated to the federal government. In the Kentucky and Virginia Resolutions of 1798–99 Jefferson and Madison had given full expression to this view, which had come to be termed the state sovereignty or state rights view. Calhoun asserted with some justice that the nullification doctrine, derived directly from the Jefferson-Madison principles of 1798, was the correct interpretation of what the Constitution meant. In this position Calhoun was joined by others. Jackson had years earlier stated that "My opinion is so firmly invested in the sovereignty of the State" as to be unshakeable. And again his 1829 message warned against encroaching upon "State sovereignty." [11]

Jefferson Dinner: Jackson Cuts Calhoun

Hopefully acting on the assumption that Jackson's expressed views placed him on their side in the nationalist-state sovereignty controversy, state rights advocates concocted a plan to bring the President's views more clearly into the open. A dinner was arranged for April 13, 1830, birthday of Thomas Jefferson (who had died only four years earlier). Jefferson stood as the political giant of the era just ended, not only framer of the Declaration of Independence but founder of the political party in which Jackson, Calhoun, and Van Buren were allied. Jefferson was also the champion of state sovereignty and the originator of the state interposition (nullification) doctrine. The sponsors of the proposed dinner hoped to make clear the revered Jefferson's connection with the views South Carolina was now advocating and subtly to bring Jackson closer to their position.

The grand dinner for April 13 was to be both distinguished and democratic. On a subscription list at the bar of Brown's Indian Queen Hotel even the humblest follower of the great Virginian could subscribe his name, pay for, and receive his ticket to dine with the political celebrities of the day. The program of speeches and toasts was ingeniously contrived to begin with broad appreciation of Jeffersonian ideals, move to Kentucky Resolutions' state interposition doctrine, and finally focus on the supposedly analogous case of South Carolina's resistance to the 1828 tariff.

Since the President accepted an invitation, he would, after the scheduled speeches and twenty-four arranged toasts, offer the first "volunteer" toast of the evening. From information gathered by lieutenants Lewis and Donelson, Jackson sniffed the intended tenor of the affair, which he feared "might menace the stability of the Union." His own views of state sovereignty fell short of approving the notion that any state, like South Carolina, could pick and choose which federal laws, tariff or otherwise, it would obey, especially so long as he was Chief Magistrate. Beforehand, Jackson, consulting Van Buren, composed what he considered a compact, expressive toast; then with the Secretary he set out for the dinner "as animated as if he were preparing to defend the Union on a field of battle."

The Indian Queen dining room was crowded with "a full assemblage" of great, near-great, and hangers-on. The banquet over, Hayne delivered a flowery speech, following which came the scheduled toasts, twenty-four in number, building gradually expanding support for the South Carolina position. Then, the toastmaster intoned: "The President of the United States." Jackson stood waiting for the cheers to subside. So many guests were on their feet that the diminutive Van Buren climbed on his chair in order to see the President.[14]

Old Hickory fixed his steel blue eyes upon John C. Cal-

houn. Glass in hand, his voice boomed: "Our Federal Union: it must be preserved."

Nullificationists froze in stunned silence. "An order to arrest Calhoun where he sat could not have come with more
blinding, staggering force," observed eyewitness Isaac Hill.
"The President lifted his glass as a signal that the toast was
to be quaffed standing. Calhoun rose with the rest. His glass
so trembled in his hand that a little of the amber fluid trickled
down the side. Jackson stood silent and impassive" as all
drank. Calhoun waited a moment, then "slowly and with
hesitating accent offered the second volunteer toast: 'The
Union! Next to our liberty, most dear!' "

After a moment's hesitation, and in a way that left hearers
in doubt as to whether he was continuing the toast or beginning a speech, he added, "May we all remember that it can
only be preserved by respecting the rights of the States and
by distributing equally the benefits and burdens of the Union." [35]

Calhoun's verbose statement came out flaccid and waver-
ing in the face of the punch in Jackson's seven-word cruncher.
Clearly the President had swept the honors of the evening,
as the diners scurried from the room to spread the word
through Washington: Old Hickory had chopped the Vice
President and would-be nullifiers down to size. Some even
speculated that Jackson's toast was the opening gun in a
personal war to shoot down the Vice President. Events would
prove them correct.

Calhoun clearly labored under a strain. Van Buren had
again scored in the rivalry to ride the chief's coattails into
the Presidency. A Senate visitor noted that the Vice President
appeared "more wrinkled and careworn than I had expected
from his . . . age [48]. His voice is shrill and . . . disagreeable. . . . His manners have . . . an uneasiness, a hurried,
incoherent air." Indeed, Calhoun was in a state of agitated

uneasiness as he looked about him: "The times are perilous beyond any that I have ever witnessed." [16] How "perilous" they were for his own career would soon become evident.

Jackson may already have determined to strip Calhoun of any influence in the administration and any expectation of the succession. Clearly some Jackson advisers like Lewis, who had already grown antagonistic toward Calhoun, hoped the President would move. Indeed in the years between 1823 and 1828 Lewis and Sam Houston had gathered and given Jackson information showing that Calhoun had urged in Monroe's cabinet meeting a censure of Jackson during the Seminole controversy of 1818–19. Whether Jackson was not convinced or whether he was simply not paying attention is not clear. At any rate, he did nothing, said nothing, perhaps because he did not want to lose the support of the Calhoun followers in the 1828 election.

Early in 1828 James A. Hamilton, a Van Burenite of New York, had secured a letter from Governor John Forsyth of Georgia quoting William Crawford's assertion that in Monroe's cabinet discussions of the Seminole affair "Mr. Calhoun, the Secretary of War, submitted to and urged upon the President the propriety of arresting and trying Gen. Jackson." Lewis, to whom Hamilton showed the Forsyth letter in the spring of 1828, thought the letter too weak to bring to Jackson's attention and besides did not want to disturb the already launched presidential campaign.

When the Peggy Eaton furore was at its peak in the winter of 1820–30, a visit of ex-President Monroe to the White House reminded Lewis of the Forsyth letter, which he now mentioned to Jackson, who demanded to see it. Now a Georgia Senator in Washington, Forsyth was approached directly and on April 16, 1830, just three days after the Jefferson dinner, communicated with Crawford, now a Georgia Judge, with partially restored health and bitter memories of how close he had once come to the scepter of national power. Crawford replied that his earlier letter to Forsyth was substantially correct except that he denied saying that Calhoun favored "arresting and trying" but instead had urged "reprimanding" Jackson.

The Crawford letter was a nasty, vindictive stroke by which Crawford sought to cover his own former hatred of Jackson by throwing the full onus on Calhoun. A more reasonable man than Jackson would have let sleeping dogs lie and avoided rekindling old animosities that would do nothing to strengthen his already strife-torn administration. But not a man to let real or fancied injury pass unnoticed, Jackson followed his belligerent instincts, despite the counsel of trusted friend John Overton, who dismissed the Crawford letter as "A poor tale this, scarcely fit to deceive a sensible school boy." Overton added that it was perfectly legitimate for Calhoun to aspire to the Presidency and he would undoubtedly make a good President, that Calhoun differed from his Monroe cabinet colleagues only in being more honest, that Jackson should drop the whole matter to avoid further embarrassment.[17]

But Jackson forwarded Crawford's letter to Calhoun on May 13, asking if the account of Calhoun's stance in Monroe's cabinet was correct. The Vice President, upset at the reappearance of the Seminole affair which he had twice before repelled, immediately acknowledged the communication, promising a full answer as soon as he had time. "Time to explain," commented Jackson, "is due him. . . . He shall have it, but I am afraid he is in a dilemma." In a dilemma for sure! The following weekend Calhoun consulted with Monroe, now in retirement near Washington, and also with William Wirt, who as Attorney General in Monroe's cabinet had been its most impartial observer. Calhoun labored two weeks scratching out in his nervous scrawl an astonishing

52-page reply, delivered to Jackson on May 29, 1830. He began by challenging the old General's right to question any part of his own conduct as head of the War Department. He would have done well to let it go at that. He might also with perfect propriety have asserted the inviolability of the secrecy of cabinet discussions and ended his reply. But unfortunately Calhoun never learned the virtue of brevity. So, followed an intricate, tortuous rehash of the numerous communications of 1818–19 between Monroe, Calhoun and General Jackson regarding the Florida invasion, all to the general effect that Jackson had in fact exceeded his orders. To which he added in a not unsubtle reference to Van Buren, "I should be blind not to see that [the revival of] this whole affair is a political manoevre, in which the design is that you should be the instrument, and myself the victim" of scheming, ambitious "actors." [38]

Old Hickory's curt reply clearly showed his belief that Calhoun was a two-faced deceiver: "In all your [previous] letters to me [you have] professed to approve . . . entirely my conduct in relation to the Seminole campaign. . . . Your letter now before me is the first intimation that *you* ever entertained any other opinion. . . . Understanding you now, no further communication with you on this subject is necessary." [39]

Calhoun Fights Back

Incensed, Jackson turned sharply away from his Vice President. In the months that followed he grew increasingly bitter and was soon irrationally blaming Calhoun for all the troubles of his administration, privately denouncing him as an "ambitious Demagogue" who would sacrifice friends and country . . . to gratify his unholy ambition." Reviewing in his mind past tribulations, Jackson now convinced himself that Calhoun was behind the "persecution" of Peggy Eaton as a scheme to "coerce me to abandon Eaton and thereby weaken me in the affections of the nation, and open the way to his preferment on my ruin."

After the virus of Calhoun's "duplicity" infected Jackson's thinking, Jackson came in another year and a half to believe that Calhoun's "plot" to ruin Andrew Jackson was broadening into a "plot" against the Union itself. In a private letter the Old Hero referred to the Vice President as the "great Political magician," reversing the phrase so often applied to Van Buren.[40]

For his part, Calhoun, at home in South Carolina during the summer and fall of 1830, contemplated the stormy political horizon. Not wishing to break openly with Jackson he nonetheless could see clearly that his political future on the Jackson bandwagon was now futile. But he said he would not "yield the hundredth part of an inch." [41] Rather, he would shore up his political foundations at home, where the pressures for tariff nullification were mounting. If he was to have a political future at all he must strengthen his home base. This he proceeded to do, as noted in the next Chapter.

Meanwhile, Jackson moved to smash any remaining Calhoun influence in Washington. First to go was Duff Green, Calhoun's ardent supporter. In early December, Francis P. Blair, a lean, thin-faced editor from Kentucky was brought to Washington to edit the *Globe* which shortly replaced the *Telegraph* as the administration organ to which all loyal office holders were required to subscribe. In another six weeks the *Globe* made it clear that should "the nation . . . call on the President to serve a second term," he "will not decline." Calhoun, echoing something of the Jackson persecution complex, labeled these moves "a conspiracy for my destruction." [42]

But he proceeded to complete his own "destruction"

within the Jackson party by having the *Telegraph* publish a full-scale attack on the administration in a 50-page pamphlet, "Correspondence between General Jackson and John C. Calhoun . . . on the subject of . . . the deliberations of the cabinet of Mr. Monroe on the occurrences of the Seminole war." After quoting in full who said what in regard to Jackson's orders of 1818–19 and in the Monroe cabinet deliberations, he followed with an involved review of the personal feuding within the Jackson cabinet of the past two years, with the clear implication that Van Buren was the scheming villain seeking to advance his own ambitions for the Presidency upon Jackson's retirement. The overall effect was to hold the administration up to public ridicule.

"A pathetic political error" on Calhoun's part, one historian has called it. He thereby exposed his own party to ridicule and forfeited any prospect of future support from the Democratic ranks. The Jacksonian press leaped hard on the Vice President, accusing him of deliberately destroying Democratic harmony and humiliating Jackson because of his own thwarted ambitions.

Jackson's response was predictable. Outraged by "the duplicity and insincerity," Jackson saw in Calhoun "a littleness and entire want of those high, dignified and honorable feelings which I once thought he possessed." [41] He composed a long reply to the Calhoun pamphlet, but second thought and advice from his confidants persuaded him not to publish it. Nor was there any need to; Calhoun had already destroyed his own position within the party. It remained only to root out Calhoun himself.

In the spring of 1831 Van Buren proposed the eventual solution. On a morning horseback ride the New Yorker suggested his own resignation to relieve the administration of further embarrassing, internal tensions. "Never!" roared Old Hickory; "Even you know little of Andrew Jackson if you suppose him capable of consenting to such a humiliation of his friend by his enemies." It took "little Van" four hours of fast talking to persuade his chief to allow his resignation. Jackson consented but only after insisting that he would appoint the personable "Matty," as Jackson liked to call him, minister to England. Van Buren and Lewis carried the news of Van Buren's impending resignation to Eaton, who after consulting Peggy agreed that he, too, should resign. So in late April, 1831, the two resignations, along with the President's acceptance "with regret" were announced in the *Globe*. Before Van Buren left Washington, he and Jackson paid a courtesy call on Mrs. Eaton. "Our reception," wrote the ex-Secretary, "was to the last degree formal and cold." Leaving the house Jackson shrugged his shoulders: "It is strange." [44]

Jackson requested and received the resignations of Ingham, Branch, and Berrien, all pro-Calhoun men. Van Buren was rewarded with appointment as minister to England, and Eaton was scheduled for a Senate seat as soon as one should become vacant. Louis McLane, returning from the London legation, took over the Treasury Department, Edward Livingston went to State, Lewis Cass and Levi Woodbury to War and Navy respectively; Roger B. Taney came in as Attorney General. Of the original cabinet only the incompetent Barry was persuaded to retain the Post Office. The cabinet reshuffle drove the three Calhounites from office. For alleged slanders on Peggy, Eaton issued an angry challenge to duel with each of the trio, who suddenly found reasons to leave Washington in haste. The Calhoun forces had been routed by the President's obstinacy and Van Buren's dexterity. A new alignment of political forces was in the making, from which the modern Democratic party under Andrew Jackson's aegis took form.

The postscript to the whole affair came months later. Van Buren had been at his post in England since the preceding

September, when in January 1832 the Senate finally got around to acting on his nomination. While the Senate stalled, Jackson fumed in a letter to Coffee: "I have no hesitation in saying that Calhoun is one of the most base hypocritical and unprincipled villains in the United States." [45] He found his opinion confirmed when the Senate vote on confirmation produced a pre-arranged tie vote, which allowed Vice President Calhoun the "exquisite pleasure" of defeating Van Buren's nomination. An observer overheard Calhoun say gloatingly, "It will kill him, sir, kill him dead. He will never kick." To which Benton retorted to a colleague: "You have broken a minister and elected a Vice President." [46] An accurate prediction. Later in 1832 the convention at Baltimore named Van Buren as Jackson's running mate for the coming Presidential contest. The vote on Van Buren in the Senate, where the Calhoun adherents joined with the Clay-Webster men in voting against, also contributed much to a new political combination that would see Calhoun and Clay working side by side to oppose the General in the White House. For a brief time the opposition considered nominating both Clay and Calhoun for President, the expectation being that Calhoun could carry Georgia, the Carolinas, and Virginia which, joined with Clay-won states in Northeast and West, would be enough to throw the election to the House. But the Virginians balked on Calhoun, and the scheme came to nought.[47] The South Carolinian turned southward seeking other means to rebuild his ruptured political fortunes.

VI Nation and State in Collision, 1832-1833

Nationalism versus State Rights

AS THE YEAR 1832 BEGAN, the Jackson-Calhoun collision rankled largely as a personal feud. By the end of the year it ballooned into a showdown fight between nation and state. For some time Calhoun had been watching apprehensively South Carolina's rising resentment againt the protective tariff. Fully conscious of the problem of nation and state relations, he had, for his own part in earlier years ranged on the nationalist side. Chauvinist advocate of the nationalist 1812 war against England, he had in post-war years supported national bank, protective tariff, and comprehensive national internal improvements. Yet he knew all the arguments and noted rising feeling among those who opposed national "consolidation" in the 1820's.

The argument flowed from the framing of the Constitution itself in 1787. Later, Jefferson as Vice President had elaborated the state rights argument (incorporated in the Kentucky and Virginia Resolutions of 1798–99) that a state had ultimate power to raise the alarm over federal legislation violating the Constitution. Other Virginians, notably John Taylor of Caroline and John Randolph, continued a running fire of argument against nationalizing tendencies. But Virginian John Marshall, speaking from the Supreme Court bench, boldly laid down the broad proposition that the United States comprised a "single nation" supreme in its area of delegated powers, that a state could not tax federal "instrumentalities" like the Bank of the United States, that a state was subject to federal jurisdiction in a legal case where a state was a party even though only a state statute was involved.

In the nineteenth century's first two decades, first Pennsylvania had resisted federal judicial jurisdiction; then New England protested the 1807 embargo and expanding federal authority in the war of 1812. In the 1820's it became the South's turn again. Virginia's chief justice Spencer Roane published a series of articles arguing that the Union was a compact among sovereign states and that Marshall's contrary rationalization was entirely fallacious. Jefferson himself heartily endorsed Roane's views. The Virginia legislature solemnly proclaimed that the courts of the states were the proper final arbiters of the Constitution's meaning. Hailing this pronouncement, Jefferson added his own denunciation of the Supreme Court's centralizing, consolidating tendency, and urged Virginia's legislature to nullify all federal internal improvement laws. Here, then, lay clear precedents for a state seeking means to block federal legislation (even though approved by a numerical majority or the federal judiciary) inimical to the protesting state's interest.

By the late 1820's Calhoun found his own state's sentiment on nation-state relations undergoing rapid change. Traditionally South Carolina had favored nationalist policies—tariff, war with England, Bank, internal improvements—and as late as 1822 elected the then nationalist Hayne over a candidate who proposed secession rather than submission to the 1820 Missouri Compromise. But feeling was shifting swiftly. Generally, South Carolinians had favored the protective tariff policy when first introduced, thinking local manufacturing would develop. Within a few years doubts arose, especially as factories did not appear.

From 1816 to 1832 Congress periodically passed new tariffs, each extending protective rates higher (the 1816 average of 20% rose to 37% in 1824) and covering more articles than its predecessor. Often the bills were far more the work of politicians than of manufacturers' lobbyists. The reason for South Carolina's shift in sentiment was not far to seek. As Frederick Jackson Turner put it, "In 1816 the average price of . . . [cotton] was nearly 30¢, and South Carolina's leaders favored the tariff; in 1820 it was 17¢ and the South saw in the protective system a grievance; in 1824 it was 14¾¢ and the South Carolinians denounced the tariff as unconstitutional." [1] In the mid-1820's a severe economic depression hit South Carolina—it was blamed on the tariff. Imports to Charleston dropped 50% between 1823 and 1828; exports from $11 million to $8 million. Costs of manufacturing articles rose. The tariff was to blame, asserted a political faction rapidly gaining strength in the state.

During these years, Calhoun, staying in Washington much of the time, retained his nationalist inclinations. While serving as Adams' Vice President, he attempted to pursue a triple course: to undercut the Adams-Clay faction that had taken over the old Calhoun nationalist program; to ally himself so closely with the Jackson faction that his claim to the Presidency in 1832 would have to be honored; to retain his popularity in South Carolina and the Southeast without alienating Northeastern supporters. Since the three courses generated difficult contradictions, Calhoun ultimately discovered that they required greater political dexterity than he could manage. But he attempted the impossible balancing act—toting water on both shoulders and on head, satisfying his three constituencies (Jacksonians, Northeast nationalists, and South Carolinians), keeping his options open as long as possible. At last, he was forced to make a clear commitment —forced not only by the Jackson quarrel but by developments in his home state. Even so, he continued his effort to straddle both the nationalist bronco and the state rights stallion and rein them into harmonious harness. A neat trick —requiring a super-dextrous hand. Whether Calhoun could swing it, his years as Jackson's Vice President would tell.

In the early 1820's Calhoun attracted the younger South Carolina politicos—Hayne, George McDuffie, James Hamilton, Jr., who at first supported his nationalist proposals. But by the mid-20's as Carolina opinion shifted, Hayne became an outspoken foe of the tariff, McDuffie and Hamilton vociferous champions of state rights. In 1824 an anti-Calhoun faction pushed through the legislature resolutions condemning both internal improvements and tariff as unconstitutional. In 1827 some South Carolina state rightists were disowning Calhoun and boldly announcing nullification as the only remedy for the hated tariff.[2]

In the same year Calhoun as Vice President was pushed into an awkward spot. A tariff bill raising duties on woolens had passed the House. In the Senate, Hayne moved to table the bill, in effect to kill it. Senator Van Buren, seeking to smoke out Calhoun, arranged for the Senate vote to result in a tie. Consequently, the Vice President as the Senate's presiding officer had to choose—withdraw from the chair and thus remain non-committal on the tariff or vote to table thereby risking loss of Northern protectionists' support. He swiftly chose to defeat the bill and showed Carolinians he was sound on the tariff issue.

This 1827 tariff squeeze shook Calhoun severely. National harmony, he wrote his brother-in-law, was being undermined by the rising tendency "of arraying the great geographical interests of the union against one another." While it was disputable whether Congress had the power to levy a protective tariff, clearly "the power itself . . . may be perverted" into a "most unjust and oppressive" instrument whereby "one section of the country may really be made tributary to another." Unscrupulous men might use it to set "great Geographical interests" against each other and "to make two of one nation." He prophesied that further protective tariff legislation, enriching the North at the South's expense, "must lead to defeat or oppression or resistance [on the South's part], or the correction of what perhaps is the greatest defect in our system." In August 1827 his mind was clearly wrestling with the problem of how to develop "a conservative solution to a problem which threatened" through sectional hostility to rupture the Union.[3]

But demands for tariff protection grew. A convention at Harrisburg, Pennsylvania, urged a comprehensive increase. Facing a presidential election in 1828, the Jackson managers sensed danger in the proposal—to support it would alienate the South, to oppose it would lose votes in Pennsylvania. Either way Jackson might be defeated in the coming election. Realizing that the issue could not be evaded, an ingenious plan was devised to propose a tariff bill "framed precisely to defeat itself." The Jackson lieutenants offered a measure raising rates generally but incorporating prohibitively high rates on raw wool. In Congress, they calculated that Northern Jackson men would vote for the bill, Southerners against, thus staying right with their constituents, while New Englanders (whose wool manufacturers would face higher prices for raw wool) would provide the votes to defeat the bill. Since Jackson could not expect to carry New England anyway, nothing would be lost; his support in South, Middle states, and Northwest would be preserved intact. Clearly, as John Randolph shrewdly observed, the object of the bill was to encourage "manufactures of no sort but the manufacture of a President." But the scheme backfired, as the "bill to rob and plunder one half of the Union, for the benefit of the residue" passed in May 1828.

Outraged by this "tariff bill of abominations," South Carolina's delegation (not including Calhoun and Senator Smith) met at Hayne's home in Washington. All agreed that the 1828 tariff violated the Constitution. What to do? Discussion focused on how South Carolina might most effectively register her opposition to the measure. Hayne, McDuffie and Hamilton, all officers in the state's militia, suggested how economic and military measures might possibly be employed in the future to prevent usurpation of power and oppression by the central government.

Calhoun was clearly distressed as he returned to South Carolina from Washington in late spring 1828. As Vice President and heir apparent to Jackson, he sensed by his political instincts the dangers of extreme agitation, especially in an election year with his own political prospects riding on the outcome. His conservative instincts also turned him away from the angry protest meetings that were sprouting weekly in his home state. But he was also convinced that the protective tariff was now such an explosive issue that it could spell dissolution of the Union. How to meet this dilemma? His mind was fully occupied, as he headed home, carrying with him from the Library of Congress Thomas Hobbes's works, a collection of political pamphlets written during the 1798–1799 controversy over state sentinelship over the Constitution, and Supreme Court Reports containing Marshall's elaborations of national power.[4]

On arriving at his Clergy Hall estate near Pendleton, he found his state seething with resentment. The newspapers carried reports of mass protest meetings and rallies, at one of which in Columbia Clay and Webster were burned in effigy, of politicians calling for defiant action by the state. To those who consulted him, Calhoun counseled restraint at least until the Presidential election was past. In a letter to General Jackson, he bluntly warned that restive South

Carolinians counted on Jackson as President to push tariff reform and bring about "an equal distribution of the benefit and burden of government . . . and the removal of oppressive duties." Calhoun seems genuinely to have pinned his hopes on Jackson to reduce the tariff: "That your administration may be the means of restoring harmony to this distracted country and of averting the alarming crisis before us is my sincere prayer." On the same day Calhoun informed ex-President Monroe of the restless discontent he saw in his home state: "I greatly fear that . . . many of the laws . . . act very unequally, and that some portion of the country may be enriched by legislation at the expense of others." Unless "a speedy and effective remedy" be applied, "a shock . . . may be expected" very soon.'

Nullification: Calhoun Supplies the Doctrine

At its preceding session the South Carolina legislature had pronounced the tariff unconstitutional and appointed a legislative committee to prepare an expositon of grievances and a protest for consideration by the next legislature. This committee's spokesman, William C. Preston, carried to Clergy Hall in the summer of 1828 a request that Calhoun draft the "Exposition and Protest." Many streams of thought doubtless coursed through Calhoun's mind as he penned the document: the volumes brought from Washington with him, the proceedings of the Constitutional Convention of 1787, the *Federalist* papers, articles in the *Southern Review* whose first two issues had appeared in the past six months, the teachings of Judge Tapping Reeve at Litchfield on state sovereignty (long buried in his mind), the writings of Thomas Cooper on political economy. Perhaps as influential as any of these was a pamphlet by fellow South Carolina lawyer and planter, Robert J. Turnbull, entitled *The Crisis* and published in October 1827. Turnbull argued cogently that the American Revolution was fought not for union but for liberty; that liberty, constantly in jeopardy, could be preserved only by force; that when the national government adopts unconstitutional acts endangering liberty, the states have the right to interpose force to protect liberty from being destroyed.

Convinced by his study that the proceedings of the Constitutional Convention, the *Federalist,* even the Constitution itself (as he now interpreted it) and the Virginia Report of 1799 sanctioned nullification of unconstitutional federal legislation, Calhoun gave systematic form to the doctrine of nullification in the *Exposition.* Calhoun laid down the doctrine that a state (or more accurately the people of a state), as one of the parties to the constitutional compact, have the undeniable right to negate federal laws made in violation of the Constitution.

Congressman James Hamilton, Jr., some weeks after visiting Calhoun, announced nullification as the "rightful remedy" for the protective tariff in a speech on October 21, 1828.ᵃ

Calhoun's *Exposition* of 1828 was generally misunderstood at the time and has often been misrepresented since. It had nothing to do with secession from the Union or rationalizing secession. Rather, it explained an allegedly constitutional method whereby a state could refuse to obey a federal law and still remain in the Union. To this extent, the device provided a means of preserving the Union from disruption. As his correspondence shows, Calhoun clearly hoped that applying the nullification remedy would never become necessary, and for four years after writing the *Exposition* he took no step to induce his state to implement nullification. Not until political self-preservation demanded it in July 1831, did he acknowledge his authorship of the *Exposition.* Only after that date did he throw his persuasive powers and energies into the drive to have South Carolina nullify the tariff.

Since the "Abominations" tariff of 1828 ignited the fire in

South Carolina, it provides the point of departure for Calhoun's *Exposition*. But it was only a particular case, from which he moved quickly to generalization. As he had opposed the restrictive commercial legislation of 1812 because it imposed an unequal burden on one class (shippers) and one section (New England), he now opposed the tariff for the same reason. It imposed an unequal economic handicap on one class (farmers) and one section (the South).

The *Exposition* consists of three major parts. The first presents the argument that the protective tariff is unconstitutional legislation. The second examines the economic effects of a protective tariff on the country's economy. The third elaborates the constitutional means by which a state can reject the tariff and still remain in the Union without fear of coercion by the central government.

The *Exposition's* fundamental premise is that sovereignty resides in the people of each state, each being sovereign (owing allegiance to no superior) at the time the United States was formed, each approving the Constitution as a compact among the several sovereign states acting in their corporate capacity. Since powers to govern are "delegated" and "divided between the General and the State Governments," "it would seem impossible to deny to the States the right of deciding on the infractions of their powers, and the proper remedy to be applied for their correction. The right of judging . . . is an essential attribute of sovereignty itself." To the opposing argument that a state *legislature* could not nullify a federal law, Calhoun conceded the point. But the people of a state acting in their sovereign capacity in a specially elected Convention have the right "to determine, authoritatively, whether the acts of which we complain, be unconstitutional; and if so, whether they constitute such a violation . . . as to justify the interposition of the State to protect its rights."

Regarding a tariff, Calhoun conceded that Congress had the power to levy duties on imports in order to raise revenue. But he denied categorically that they could be levied for purposes of encouraging and "rearing up the industry of one section of the country on the ruins of another." By such legislation Congress put "its burdens . . . exclusively on one side and its benefits on the other. It imposes on the agricultural interest of the South . . . and that portion engaged in commerce and navigation, the burden not only of sustaining the system itself, but that also of the government."

Further economic effects of the tariff included forcing the agricultural staple-crop producing South "to sell *low*" in the free competitive world market and at the same time "to buy *high*" in the home market protected from outside competition by the tariff. Not only would "this doube action" insure that "Our ruin must follow," but eventually the tariff's destructive effects would be felt in the manufacturing states as well. Pointing to Europe, Calhoun maintained that the tariff "operated as one of the most efficient causes of that great inequality of wealth . . . [and of] a moneyed aristocracy" tending "to make the poor poorer, and the rich richer. Heretofore, in our country, this tendency has displayed itself principally in its effects as regard the different sections,—but the time will come when it will produce the same effects in the manufacturing States. After we [the South] are exhausted, the contest will be between the capitalists and the operatives [workers]; for into these two classes it must, ultimately divide society. . . . Under the operation of the system, wages must sink more rapidly than the prices of the necessaries of life, till . . . the portion of the products of their labor left to them [the workers] will be barely sufficient to preserve existence."

When Calhoun wrote this paragraph, Karl Marx was in his eleventh year, and his theory of an inevitable class struggle in a capitalist economy was some distance in the future.

Calhoun's prophesy came close to approximation in late-nineteenth-century industrial labor struggles, although far from twentieth-century reality. This paragraph, not appreciated by the South Carolina legislature, was deleted in the final version.

Finally the *Exposition* asserted that the state should delay nullification (though indisputably a constitutional right) in the hope that the majority, by electing Jackson, would "restore the pure principles of our government" and reduce the tariff. Should this not occur, then South Carolina would pursue "her sacred duty to interpose; a duty to herself—to the Union—to the present and to future generations—and to the cause of liberty over the world." [7] (See fuller text in *Appendix*, Doc. No. 13.)

The fall election of 1828 raising Jackson to the Presidency and continuing Calhoun as Vice President lowered tempers and gave Carolinians hope of relief on the tariff. In December Preston's Special Committee reported the *Exposition* to the state legislature along with a "Protest" to the United States Senate, also written by Calhoun. The legislature adopted the latter, sent it on to the Senate, but took no formal action on the *Exposition* other than to order 5,000 copies printed. The Vice President, whose authorship remained secret, was pleased that hotheads did not push for immediate action—to state the grievance and assert the right to nullify was enough, he thought, to spur the incoming administration into action.

Calhoun's motives in developing the nullification doctrine have been a subject of lively dispute. Some scholars contend it reflected simply his relentless ambition in striving for the Presidency. Others assert he was genuinely concerned for the South's welfare and for saving the Union. Although the tariff was an immense economic burden to the South, he feared more the attack on slavery soon to come and wished to establish nullification as a defense in advance of that attack. And in his concern for the Union, he sought to undercut disaffected extremists in pushing radical action leading to dissolution or civil war. Another view suggests "It is much more plausible . . . that . . . [Calhoun's] political ambitions, the welfare of the South, and the preservation of the Union were supplementary. . . ." He convinced himself "that the best method of protecting the South and preventing disunion was the election of John C. Calhoun chief executive." He might imagine that it was a matter of principle: "I must merge my interest in the higher sense of duty; and . . . do that, which . . . may seem right, regardless of consequences;" and although not indifferent to "future advancement . . . I trust, however strong . . . my ambition, my sense of duty is still stronger." In this light, his ambition is simply merged with the best interests of the South and of the nation.[8]

In adopting the position he took in the *Exposition,* Calhoun had clearly moved away from being any longer a small "d" democrat. Clearly, the *Exposition's* argument rejected the will of the numerical majority, democracy's major premise. His later writings would contend that determining public policy by the will of the numerical majority was often neither wise nor desirable policy and must be restrained by a more effective means than simply counting votes in popular elections. Much of his later thinking and writing would revolve around this question.

From 1828 until mid-1831, publicly Calhoun remained silent on nullification and gave little encouragement to the movement in South Carolina to apply nullification in actual practice to the tariff. During 1828–31 his authorship of the *Exposition* remained generally unknown, since the document appeared officially as a legislative committee report. He was after all Vice President and appeared in 1828–30 the visible heir to Jackson. Calhoun as President would speed tariff reduction if Jackson had not done so.

But as Jackson's position on the tariff remained obscure, Calhoun grew increasingly distressed, viewing "the Tariff but as the occasion, rather than the real cause of the present [1830] unhappy state of things." Instead, the real target of attack was slavery, "the peculiar domestick institution of the Southern States." Slavery, joined with soil and climate fastened staple agriculture upon the South, which had already slid into a minority position vulnerable to legislative assault by a Congressional majority. If there was no way to defend against oppressive tariff legislation now, there would be no way to defend against abolition of slavery later. Or, in Calhoun's words, "If there be no protective power in the reserved rights of the States, they [Southerners] must in the end be forced to rebel, or submit to have their permanent interests sacrificed, their domestic institutions [read slavery] subverted by Colonization and other schemes [read abolition], and themselves and children reduced to wretchedness." [9] For the time, however, he remained outwardly cool, affirming in Washington his allegiance to the Union while at the same time professing state sovereignty views at home. The showdown could not be postponed indefinitely.

The Showdown: Union in Crisis—South Carolina Nullifies

During 1830–31 Calhoun's hopes disintegrated swiftly. His whole design came apart at the seams. The blows fell rapidly: the Webster-Hayne debate; the facedown with Jackson at the Jefferson Dinner; the Eaton imbroglio; the Crawford letter; the final break with Jackson killing all Presidential prospects; loss of all influence in Washington. James Madison, a Framer, co-author of the *Federalist* papers, promulgator of the Virginia Resolutions of 1798, on which Calhoun rested much of his state sovereignty-nullification case, was still very much alive in 1831–32. He came out with a sharp disclaimer that his 1798 doctrine in any way supported nullification. Madison declared that nullification "has the effect of putting powder under the Constitution and the Union, and match in the hand of every party to blow them up at pleasure." Calhoun's position before the nation seemed virtually annihilated.

Meanwhile in South Carolina lines between nullifiers and Unionists were sharply drawn. Both agreed that the protective tariff must go but differed over means. The latter favored working through Congress for revision; the latter urged interposing the state's sovereign authority to nullify. In 1830 both sides solidified their positions and strengthened their organizations. As McDuffie and Hayne came out strongly for nullification, Calhoun remained publicly uncommitted.

President Andrew Jackson, too, remained publicly silent after making his vigorous Union toast of April 1830. Privately he was reported to have told a South Carolina Congressman, about to leave Washington for home: "Tell them [the nullifiers] from me that they can talk and write resolutions and print threats to their hearts' content. But if one drop of blood is shed in defiance of the laws of the United States, I will hang the first man of them I can get my hands on to the first tree I can find." When Senator Hayne heard this and told Tom Benton that he doubted Jackson would go that far, Benton, who recalled his days in the Indian wars with Jackson, snorted, "I tell you, Hayne, when Jackson begins to talk about hanging, they can begin to look for the ropes." [10]

Jackson's public position appeared equivocal to South Carolinians. While he recommended that Congress consider revising the tariff, he did not actively push tariff reduction. Hope was fading for tariff reform from the Executive. On the other hand, he acted leniently in the case of Georgia versus Indian tribes within her territory. Indeed, as Georgia had asserted her authority over lands assured to the Indians by

solemn treaties with the United States, Jackson made no
protest or assertion of exclusive federal power. When the
Supreme Court rendered a judgment adverse to the state of
Georgia's action, Jackson stood aside. He was widely believed
to have remarked, "John Marshall has made his decision,
now let him enforce it." Whether he made such a comment
is doubtful, but he did write to Coffee: "The decision of the
supreme court has fell still born, and they find it cannot
coerce Georgia to yield. . . . If a colision take place between
them [the Indians] and the Georgians, the arm of government
is not sufficiently strong to preserve them from destruction." [11]

Some South Carolina nullificationists may have taken heart
from Jackson's failure to enforce a federal individual decision
against the state of Georgia. Some, indeed, saw an analogy
to their own prospective resistance to the federal tariff. But
probably few were deceived for long about what could be
expected from the President. The circumstances of the two
cases were so entirely different as to warrant drawing no
conclusions, especially in view of Jackson's known anti-
Indian attitude.

Although Jackson had in effect sustained the state of
Georgia in her refusal to carry out the Supreme Court's
decision and had even withdrawn federal troops from the
state at the Governor's request, he was preparing to take firm
action abainst any nullification move in South Carolina.
Whether he made a distinction between the Georgia and
South Carolina cases because of his quarrel with Calhoun is
not clear but it may have been a factor in determining his
course. In the summer of 1831 he took pains to prevent a legal
case, trumped up by McDuffie, to test the constitutionality
of the 1828 tariff from reaching the Supreme Court. The
defendant-importers refused to pay certain duties on the
ground that the law was invalid. At Jackson's insistence, the

case was argued and decided on the narrow, technical grounds of the legality of the bonds posted by the defendants. The nullifiers lost the case and with it any chance of getting a Supreme Court ruling on the tariff's constitutionality. Jackson became erroneously convinced that "Calhoun is at the bottom of this thing." [12] The President's action in the case was unknown to the nullifiers, but informed Unionists in South Carolina found their hand strengthened.

When his break with the President became irretrievable in late spring 1831, Calhoun returned to South Carolina, his course of action clear in his mind. He now acknowledged his authorship of the *Exposition* of three years before. On July 26, 1831, he published his "Fort Hill Address," in which he further refined his earlier arguments. [13] The use of a simple numerical majority for making decisions, Calhoun now contended, should be supplemented by the concurrent majority, whereby interest groups (read states) would have an opportunity to give or withhold concurrent approval of a proposed government policy. He developed his argument with such tight logic that, granting his premises, the conclusion was irresistible. One writer has commented: Calhoun "unconsciously started with the conclusion he wanted and reasoned back to the premises. . . . he leads you willy-nilly to his conclusions" and "the sure grip of Calhoun's logic will end by making one a nullifier or a lunatic." [14] The Constitution, Calhoun restated, was a compact between sovereign states. Each state could determine when it was violated and interpose to halt the operation of the unconstitutional law, which then became suspended. Following this, the general government could appeal to the Constitution makers, the states, and the will of three-fourths would decide the issue. Here was a kind of judicial review by the states, a process whereby ¼ of the states plus one could effectively check the will of ¾ of the states.

With the "Fort Hill Address," Calhoun of course surrendered any hope of becoming President in 1832 (a small surrender since Jackson was sure to run again). He was at the same time addressing a wider audience in the nation. As he wrote to one friend, "The rule of the majority and the right of suffrage are good things, but they alone are not sufficient to guard liberty"; and to another, "I know I am right. I have gone over the whole subject with more care than I did any other." [15] Having 3,000 copies of the "Address" printed, he distributed copies to friends throughout the state and the country.

The long-awaited showdown finally came in 1832. Early in that year Henry Clay introduced a new tariff bill, which should have been an honest attempt to eliminate 1828's "abominations." After much legislative log-rolling, the tariff act of 1832 passed by a 2–1 Congressional margin and signed by Jackson on July 14, 1832, reduced some rates, enlarged the free list but retained high duties on most articles already protected. It was still a highly protective measure, not the major slash Calhoun and other tariff opponents wanted. Upon his approval of the tariff in July 1832, Jackson said he expected "to hear a great noise from South Carolina" but believed the benefits to the South by the act's reducing of "duties upon cotton bagging, on blankets, on course woollings [sic] and on sugar will convince the people that the whole attempt at nullification is an effort of disappointed ambition" of (in a clear reference to Calhoun) "unprincipled men who would rather rule in hell, than be subordinate in heaven." [16]

By this time the Presidential campaign was already under way—Jackson, with Van Buren as his running mate, against Henry Clay standing for the major opposition and William Wirt for the maverick Anti-Mason party. On Calhoun's fury over Van Buren's nomination for Vice President after his return from England (Calhoun had defeated Van Buren's diplomatic appointment), John Randolph remarked: "Calhoun, by this time, must be in Hell. . . . He is self mutilated like the Fanatic that emasculated himself." [17]

South Carolina's reaction to the 1832 tariff was swift and angry. Senator Hayne and a majority of South Carolina's Congressional delegation issued an "Address," urging their constituents as the "sovereign power" to decide whether their liberties should be "tamely surrendered without a struggle or transmitted undiminished to your posterity." Calhoun, who agreed that "protection" was now "the settled policy of the country," found himself looked to as the leader of the nullifiers. At Governor James Hamilton's request, he produced a new "Fort Hill Letter" (August 1832) in an effort to clarify the earlier statement of nullification which many people found difficult to understand even after they had read it. In September the nullifiers swept the state elections, winning a ⅔ majority in the house and ¾ majority of the senate of the legislature. Hamilton summoned a special session of the legislature which arranged for a special election of a convention to meet at Columbia on November 19. In a whirlwind campaign, in which disheartened Unionists scarcely tried, nullifiers captured the overwhelming majority of convention seats.

At the Hermitage President Jackson at first dismissed the "distant thunder" of nullification, remarking that "Calhoun is prostrate. I heard one of his best former friends say, . . . he ought to be hung." That "friend had also volunteered to march with 10,000 volunteers against the nullifiers. These must be the sentiments of all honest men." As the news from South Carolina grew more ominous, Jackson acted instantly. Orders went to the naval squadron at Norfolk to prepare to sail. Reacting to a report that officers of Charleston harbor's forts were ready to surrender these, Old Hickory instantly ordered new garrisons of unquestioned loyalty to Charleston.

Post haste he left the Hermitage to assume command in Washington in person. General Winfield Scott was sent to command the Charleston forts with "secrete orders . . . to prevent a surprise [attack] in the night or by day. . . . *The attempt will* be made . . . by the militia and must be repelled with prompt and exemplary punishment." [18]

In November the South Carolina convention rushed to act before Congress could convene in December. Calhoun himself took no direct part in the convention proceedings, remaining at his Fort Hill estate where he was kept informed by lieutenants. After five days' deliberation an ordinance of nullification was adopted by a 136–62 vote. It declared the tariff acts of 1828 and 1832 "null, void and no law, nor binding upon this state, its officers or citizens." No tariff duties were to be permitted to be collected in South Carolina after February 1, 1833. Appeals to federal courts under the invalidated acts were forbidden. All public office holders were required to take an oath to uphold the ordinance, which further declared that the people of the sovereign state of South Carolina would not "submit to the application of force . . . [by] the federal Government to reduce this State to obedience." If force should be used, such action would be regarded as "inconsistent with the longer continuance of South Carolina in the Union" with the consequence that "the people of this State" would "thenceforth hold themselves absolved from all further obligations to maintain or preserve their political connection with the people of the other States, and will forthwith proceed to organize a separate Government," and act as "a sovereign and independent State."

The legislature reconvened and passed laws implementing the convention's nullification ordinance, which incidentally was not submitted to the sovereign people for approval. New legislation allowed citizens to sue for recovery of goods seized for non-payment of customs duties, authorized use of military

force, including volunteers to "repel invasion" and appropriated funds to purchase arms, munitions, and equipment.
At public rallies throughout the state, extremists wearing
blue cockades with a palmetto button in the center demanded
immediate secession. Medals were struck bearing the inscrip-
tion, "John C. Calhoun, First President of the Southern
Confederacy." At which Calhoun recoiled in horror. Having
set in motion a move merely to check rising tariffs, he now
found he had touched off a raging fire of secession that would
not easily be contained.

The Columbia convention, in addition to adopting the nullification ordinance, adopted an "Address to the People of
South Carolina" and an "Address to the People of the United
States." For the latter McDuffie provided the text, which
incorporating parts of an earlier draft by Calhoun assured the
American people that South Carolina acted in no unfriendly
spirit and restated the principle of nullification. A resolution
was forwarded to Congress and the other states proposing a
general convention of states to consider the question in dispute. A caucus of convention leaders mapped strategy for the
coming collision: Hayne to resign his Senate seat and take
over as Governor; Calhoun to resign as Vice President and
assume Hayne's Senate seat, where he could defend the state
from outside attacks. The move was dictated not so much to
place Calhoun in the Senate, but more by the need to have
in the Governor's chair Hayne, a man who commanded respect in state and out, who had good personal relations with
President Jackson, and who as a conservative could be relied
on to restrain any untoward belligerence.[19]

The Union Saved: Jackson Blasts Nullification

Unionists in South Carolina were far from passive. Joel R.
Poinsett, former minister to Mexico, received Jackson's as-

surance: "I repeat to the union men again, fear not, *the union will be preserved* and treason and rebellion promptly put down, when and where it may show its monster head." [20] To federal depots in neighboring North Carolina the President sent guns and munitions. To South Carolina he sent George Breathitt, brother of Kentucky's Governor, ostensibly as a postal inspector but actually to serve as liaison man with the Unionists and to keep Jackson informed of new developments.

The President had earlier written to (of all people) Senator Hayne that "For the rights of the states, no one has a higher regard and respect than myself. . . . But, how I ask, is this [maintaining the rights of states] to be effected? Certainly not by conceding to one state authority to declare an act of Congress void. . . . There is a better remedy. . . . If Congress . . . shall overleap [its powers], . . . the remedy is with the people . . . not thro open and direct resistance, but thro . . . submitting the whole matter to them at their elections, [where] . . . their free suffrage . . . will always in the end, bring about the repeal of obnoxious laws which violate the constitution. . . . This is the only course. . . . That a state has the power to nullify the Legislative enactments of the General Government I never did believe. . . . Assert that a state may declare acts . . . [of] Congress . . . void, and revolution with all its attendant evils . . . must be expected. [21]

During the fall of 1832, Jackson was still willing to give conciliation a try, believing that the carrot rather than the stick might work better in bringing balky Carolina to pull in harness. When Congress gathered in early December (Calhoun absent from the Vice President's chair for the first time in eight years), Jackson in his annual message made a brief, calm reference to the nullification drive suggesting that the laws at present were adequate to meet the problem. As to the supposed source of difficulty, the tariff, he asserted that "If upon investigation it shall be found . . . that the legislative protection is greater than indispensably requisite for these objects [national security and defense], I recommend that it be gradually diminished." The message, thought John Quincy Adams, "is a complete surrender to the nullifiers." ·

But in his private journal, Jackson had already recorded a reminder to himself, "South Carolina has passed her ordinance of nullification and secession. . . . [I will] meet it with a proclamation, [showing] the absurdity of nullification . . . the principles of our government fully set forth, as a government based on the confederation of perpetual union made more perfect by the present Constitution, which is the act of the people. . . ." ²·

Any illusions the President may have had about the nullifiers backing off in the face of conciliatory gestures vanished as Poinsett's reports arrived from Charleston. With jaw set and eyes flashing, Old Hickory roared: "Nullification means insurrection and war. . . . I will meet it at the threshold and have the leaders arrested and arraigned for treason. . . . The Union will be preserved . . . [or] I will die with the Union." He notified Poinsett, "In forty days I can have within the limits of South Carolina fifty thousand men, and in another forty days more another fifty thousand" and "I am assured . . . that I will be sustained by congress." ²⁴ (See *Appendix* Doc. No. 6-A for fuller text.)

Preparing for a showdown by force if necessary, Jackson realized that he needed the support of public opinion. He would use words as weapons, too, to repel the high-flying verbal barrage of Calhoun and the nullifiers. Closing himself in his White House study with "great steel pen" in hand he poured words onto paper so fast "he was obliged to scatter the written pages all over the table to let them dry." These pages he turned over to Secretary of State Edward Livingston saying, "I submit [these] . . . as the conclusion of the procla-

mation. Let it receive your best flight of eloquence. . . . The
Union must be preserved, without blood if this be possible,
but it must be preserved at all hazards and at any price." [25]
What the soldier had risked his life for in the Revolution and
at New Orleans, the President was not about to yield meekly
to threat of traitors. On December 10 he issued his Proclamation to the people of South Carolina, one of the greatest state
papers produced by any American President. (See *Appendix*,
No. 6-B for fuller text.)

In the Proclamation Jackson skillfully warned but entreated, demanded but sympathized, threatened but consoled,
in a masterful appeal to South Carolinians' fears, interests
and pride. Unequivocally he rejected nullification as an "im-
practical absurdity." To concede nullification as a right
would dissolve the Union: ". . . the power to annul a law
of the United States, assumed by one State, [is] incompatible
with the existence of the Union, contradicted expressly by
. . . the Constitution, unauthorized by its spirit, inconsistent
with every principle on which it was founded, and destructive
of the great object for which it was formed." Just as categorically was secession rejected: "To say that any State may at
pleasure secede from the Union is to say that the United
States is not a nation." Finally, speaking almost as father to
son, the Old Hero moved to "admonish you . . . Fellow-
citizens of my native State. . . . The laws of the United States
must be enforced. I have no [discretion] . . . ; my duty is
emphatically pronounced in the Constitution. Those who
told you that you might peaceably prevent their execution
deceived you. . . . Their object is disunion. . . . Disunion
by armed force is *treason*. Are you really ready to incur its
guilt?" [26]

Jackson's Proclamation evoked patriotic support from all
quarters. Parades, bonfires, meetings everywhere—in New
York's Central Park, in Boston's Faneuil Hall ("Cradle of

American liberty")—hailed the President's courageous defense of the Union. State legislatures adopted resolutions of support for the Chief Executive while denouncing the nullifiers. Northern Democrats rallied to their leader's side; so, too, did old foes John Quincy Adams, Daniel Webster, and even Henry Clay, whom Jackson had just a month earlier slaughtered in the Presidential election by 219–49 electoral votes with 687,000 (55%) to 530,000 (42%) popular votes. In far off Illinois an obscure New Salem village storekeeper read the Proclamation; in 1861 Abraham Lincoln would read it again and incorporate large chunks of it in his first inaugural address.[27]

Two unorthodox visitors to the capital observed Jackson during the crisis over nullification. Fanny Kemble, an English actress performing on the Washington stage, attended a White House reception, where she noted the President was "very tall and thin, but erect and dignified in his carriage"; a "fine old well-battered soldier" with "manners . . . perfectly simple and quiet, therefore very good." About the same time Sam Dale, who had served the General at New Orleans in 1815, visited with Jackson, who "grasped me warmly by the hand," and although engaged with friends in "talking over 'Nullification,' . . . the President turning to me, said, 'General Dale, if this thing goes on, our country will be like a sack of meal with both ends open. Pick it up in the middle or endwise, and it will run out. I must tie the bag and save the country.' . . . The iron man trembled with emotion . . . took two or three turns across the room, and then abruptly said, 'Dale they are trying me here; . . . but, by the God of heaven, I will uphold the laws." [28]

Few doubted that Jackson meant what he said. But South Carolina nullifiers showed no signs of weakening. On the day (December 10) of Jackson's Proclamation, the state legislature elected Hayne Governor; two days later Calhoun was chosen Senator (he would resign as Vice President December 28, 1832). Governor Hayne issued a counter blast to the Proclamation warning "the good people of this State against the attempt of the President to seduce them from their allegiance," urging all to remain firm in their resolve and loyal to their State which would defend its sovereignty or be "buried beneath its ruins." Others saw the Proclamation as calculated "to bring about another reign of terror" and determined never to yield their principles. South Carolina Presidential electors signified defiance by casting the state's vote for John Floyd of Virginia, as an anti-Jackson protest. Proffers of military service poured into Hayne's office. Plans were drafted organizing companies of "Mounted Minute Men" who would rush "2,500 of the *elite* of the whole state upon any given point in three or four days." [29]

In Washington Jackson prepared for action, "waiting," as he wrote Van Buren, for official "information" of Carolina's action of raising an army to resist . . . the laws, which will be a levying of war," at which point "I will . . . [ask] Congress . . . [for] power to call upon volunteers"; South Carolina's resisting leaders would be seized "regardless of the force that surrounds them," and hauled into court to be tried for treason. [30]

While South Carolinians roared defiance and the President prepared, forces of moderation began to work, quietly at first but with increasing pressure. The *Globe,* the administration organ, was vigorously urging tariff reduction. From New York, Vice President-elect Van Buren was urging caution on the President, pointing out that merely raising troops by South Carolina did not constitute actual treason, arguing that impetuous haste might drive other states into opposition.

To forestall the latter danger, loyal Jacksonian Unionists prodded other state legislatures to reject nullification. Mississippi, North Carolina, and Alabama denounced it as "a heresy fatal . . . to the Union," "subversive of the Constitution." Georgia and Kentucky refuted it as "neither a peaceful or constitutional remedy." Virginia denied that South Carolina's action was sanctioned by the 1798 doctrine, urged revoking its nullification ordinance, called on Congress to reduce the tariff, and sent a commissioner southward to help mediate the dispute. If South Carolina counted on outside help, it was now clear none would come from sister states. As 1832 closed, South Carolina stood as isolated among the states of the Union as Calhoun had stood isolated among the leaders of the Jackson administration in 1831.[11]

Early in January 1833 New York Representative Gulian C. Verplanck, a Van Buren partisan, offered in the House a tariff bill to reduce duties by 50% within two years, roughly returning to 1816's level. This was no new enforced concession; it was implied in Jackson's December 4 message and in his December 10 Proclamation.[12] Here was the first real crack in the showdown.

As talk droned on in Congress, President Jackson, viewing the approaching February 1 deadline set by South Carolina for the end of United States customs collection in the state, grew increasingly edgy. On January 16 he asked Congress for authority to use military force to collect customs duties. If Congress did not approve within two weeks, he would act on his own initiative to enforce the law. A week later he wrote Poinsett that he would "in ten or fifteen days . . . have in Charleston ten to fifteen thousand well organized troops" and in another 40 days 200,000 volunteers to put down insurrection—*"the union will* be preserved."[13]

Meanwhile, former Vice President and now Senator-elect John C. Calhoun left his home December 28 and began his journey northward, curious onlookers crowding streets of towns en route. He must have been tense and apprehensive, for rumor had it that among threats attributed to Jackson one

had him saying that "if one more step was taken he would
try Calhoun for treason and, if convicted, hang him as high
as Haman." If Calhoun was frightened, he gave no sign of
it. "Alone, unfaltering, with head erect and steady eyes, he
walked slowly . . . into the Senate chamber at noon on Fri-
day, January 4, 1833, and presented his credentials as Senator
from South Carolina." [14] Around him were men whose presiding officer he had been for eight years; some had served
with him in Congress back in 1812. Before jam-packed galleries, Calhoun raised his right hand and repeated the oath to
uphold and defend the Constitution of the United States.
Friends moved up the aisle to shake his hand.

When some days later the Senate received Jackson's request for authority to use military force to execute the laws,
Calhoun leaped to his feet and for a half hour poured out a
powerful defense of his own and his state's conduct in a style
which, John Tyler said, "I have never heard surpassed—his
manner was different from anything I ever heard from him
before—warm—impassioned—burning. . . . he is more than
a match for his opponents." [15] Having remained publicly silent for so long, his Scotch-Irish ire and fire as strong as
Jackson's, he now boiled over in explosive, moving self defense that won him respect if not approval from even opponents, as one reported to Van Buren.

The Force Bill, authorizing the President to use the military to suppress resistance to laws, was reported to the Senate. Calhoun denounced it as "the bloody bill" that would
create a military tyranny and sought to offset it by introducing a series of resolutions to reaffirm the federal nature of the
Union and deny any power to coerce a state—"a federal
system, uniting free and independent States in a bond of
union . . . to be preserved by the concurrent consent of the
parts" not "a government of the sword." [16]

As the Force Bill came under deliberation in the Senate

and as House discussion of the Verplanck tariff reduction bill ground on, the words seemed to flow endlessly. Obviously, Jackson's stubborn insistence on enforcing the laws was not about to change. But a softening was noted as Jacksonians in Congress spoke favorably of tariff lowering. With relief on the tariff in sight, a meeting in Charleston (perhaps under urging from the recently arrived Virginia commissioner) voted to postpone the effective date of the nullification ordinance from February 1 to March 4. The stage was set for the leaven of compromise to work in Congress.

Henry Clay, after a two-year absence from Washington, had recently resumed his seat in the Senate. As a long-time Jackson-hater, still smarting under his Presidential defeat the past November and resentful over the President's Bank recharter veto of the previous summer, he was in no mood to let Jackson win the credit for a peaceful resolution of the crisis. Mustering his own followers, Clay reached an understanding with Calhoun by the third week of January 1833: Clay agreed to a gradual reduction of tariff duties, while Calhoun pledged South Carolina's repeal of the nullification ordinance.[37]

Clay forces in Congress scuttled the Verplanck tariff bill. Then, on February 12 Clay introduced his own compromise tariff bill, which would lower rates annually until they reached in 1842 the 20% level of the 1816 tariff, all duties after 1842 to be levied only "for the purpose of raising . . . revenue" to operate the Government. When Clay was attacked by administration spokesmen, Calhoun rose to his defense, declaring fiercely that all who loved the Union must want an end of sectional conflict, that Clay's bill would restore harmony and would therefore have his support. Their common opposition to Jackson and fear of military ascendancy in the executive drew Clay and Calhoun together in a joint effort.[38]

The Clay bill rolled smoothly through the two houses to passage on March 1 by a 4–3 margin in the House and almost 2–1 in the Senate. On the same day the Force Bill was also approved but only after weeks of bitter wrangling and acrid debate. Calhoun kept up a running fire, objecting that the bill would make Jackson a military dictator and endanger liberty everywhere in the land, while Clay gave it reluctant support. When the Senate voted, Clay was purposely absent; Calhoun and his supporters in silent protest left the chamber. Only Senator John Tyler of Virginia remained to cast the lone negative against 32 votes affirming the President's power to use military force.

Jackson signed both bills into law March 2, two days before his second inauguration. The South Carolina convention reconvened on March 11, repealed its nullification ordinance of the tariff but adopted a new nullification of the Force Act—a gesture to save face that Jackson chose to ignore. Both sides now claimed victory. The President asserted that as a practical matter the Union had been preserved; the alleged constitutional principle of state interposition to block federal laws had been rejected by a majority; neither nullification nor secession could be resorted to short of revolution; that federal laws must be obeyed by the people in all the states. In administrative terms he had again strengthened the Presidency by providing energetic leadership and direction. In political terms, he had placed his own Democratic party squarely on the side of national supremacy, although not favoring an elastic interpretation of federal powers. In so doing, he had driven off some of his state rights supporters, but his appeals to patriotism had won followers in other quarters. Hindsight may declare that Jackson should have moved earlier, say, in 1828 or 1829, to make clear his views and nip nullification's threat when it first appeared in the *Exposition.* His delay doubtless intensified the crisis and made dealing with it more troublesome, but, whether intended or not, it had the advantage of providing a dramatic, spectacular setting that gave greater impact to his ringing affirmation that the Union was indestructible.

On his side, Calhoun and the nullifiers could and did claim that, in practical terms, they had achieved their objective—to get the protective tariff reduced. In constitutional theory, at least, they had not yielded the asserted right of state interposition. In political terms, they had subtracted the ardent state righters from the Jackson ranks and brought to a focus the opposition to the "military chieftain" in the White House in a kind of coalition which would last so long as Jackson's penchant for crisis politics continued.

From the standpoint of the long range development of the nation in the nineteenth century, a case can be made for the argument that Jackson allowed himself to be restrained too much. He should have carried through with the use of military force to suppress proposed disobedience to national legislation and thereby killed the state sovereignty-nullification-secessionist drive in its cradle and spared Americans of a later generation the agony of a much larger tragedy—the Civil War. But to do this, he would have had to operate outside legal, constitutional restraints of his position—perhaps too much to expect for the generation of 1832.

VII Jackson and the Bank War

In 1832 while the nullification controversy was edging toward the brink, President Andrew Jackson was fully engaged in war on another front—against the second Bank of the United States. In 1816 the Bank had been issued a 20-year charter as a corporation by Congressional legislation drafted partly by John C. Calhoun. (See Chapter IV above.) With one-fifth of its capital supplied by the national government, the rest by private stock holders, the Bank as a semi-public, semi-private corporation, was controlled chiefly by the latter who chose 20 of its 25-man board of directors, the President appointing the government directors. In effect a central bank, it functioned as sole depository for federal funds, as fiscal agent for the government. On the basis of government and private deposits, it issued bank notes that circulated as currency, made loans and investments for profits that were divided among stockholders, the government receiving one-fifth of the semi-annual dividend. With branches in major cities, it served not only as a clearing house but also exercised control of credit extension and interest rates on loans.

At the same time many other banks were functioning under special acts of state legislatures, granting corporation charters that bank promoters often obtained through dubious if not crooked means. These state banks issued bank notes circulating as currency side by side with United States Bank notes. The latter frequently put the brake on loosely run state banks by, refusing to accept their notes or by discounting them heavily. The Bank of the United States's original management proved hopelessly incompetent until 1819, when

Calhoun's close friend Langdon Cheves assumed its presidency, called in loans, tightened credit, foreclosed mortgages, and required state banks to cover their notes in gold and silver. This credit squeeze loosed the Panic of 1819, forced many banks and individuals into bankruptcy, and roused stormy resentment, especially among Westerners. In 1823 a new president took over direction of the Bank. He was urbane Nicholas Biddle, a 37-year-old Philadelphian with brains, good looks, money, family, social position, education, widely traveled in Europe, lover of the classics, fancier of the arts, brilliant in social conversation. From the Bank's Greek Temple headquarters on Philadelphia's Chestnut Street, Biddle conducted Bank affairs with efficiency, dispatch, and flair. Through its branches in 29 cities the Bank did a flourishing $70 million a year business. But big as it was, it made only 20% of the country's total loans, its notes comprised only one-fifth of the nation's paper currency, and its deposits and specie only one-third.[1]

Many debtors who paid high interest rates or suffered foreclosures on collateral property pledged for loans viewed banking as essentially a crooked operation—a kind of heartless usury working hardships on small shopkeepers, businessmen, farmers, and artisans who had to borrow funds. Others looked on banks as economic parasites sucking profits from the public through special privileges not available to all comers. Further antagonism came from state bank officers and stock holders who eyed enviously the power and prosperity of their stronger, gigantic rival—"the Monster of Chestnut Street." Intercity jealousy contributed, too—New York, Boston, and Baltimore bankers resenting Philadelphia's preeminence as the country's financial center.

Youthful financial reverses and unhappy borrowing entanglements made Andrew Jackson generally distrustful of banking practices and paper notes. But he had earlier owned

some shares in the Nashville Bank, a pioneer Tennessee institution, which may have led him to oppose a proposal to set
up a Bank of the United States branch in Nashville in 1817.
However, four years later as Florida Governor, he forwarded
a local petition calling for a Bank branch in Pensacola. In
Tennessee politics during the general financial distress following the Panic of 1819 he stood sturdily with the anti-Relief
party opposing legislation for relief of debtors who owed
banks or other creditors and objecting to permitting loosely
run, printing-press banks to operate in the state. Indeed, his
banking stand in the early 1820's ranged him with the hard-
money opponents of the small farmer, artisan, shopkeeper,
small business man, as whose champion he later presented
himself in the national political arena—in the Bank War of
1832–33. When the Bank at length did establish a Nashville
branch in 1827, Jackson was consulted but remained non-
committal, although his close friend William B. Lewis became a local director.[2]

When Jackson went to Washington in 1829, he carried
misgivings about the Bank and originally intended to speak
out against it in his first inaugural, but his advisers talked him
out of it. In an attempt to develop good relations with Jackson, Biddle offered to have the Bank pay off the balance of
the national debt (which Jackson considered a horrible burden) by January 8, 1833, which would be the eighteenth
anniversary of Jackson's great triumph at New Orleans. Jackson wrote Biddle, expressing his appreciation of the gesture,
but stating his belief that Congress had no constitutional
power to charter a bank to operate outside the District of
Columbia, adding "I do not dislike your bank more than all
banks . . . but I have been afraid of banks" ever since reading
about the financial fiasco of the British "South Sea bubble."
Preparing his first annual message to Congress, he consulted
and got mixed advice from Kendall, Grundy, and James

Alexander Hamilton. He listened most to Hamilton (son of the founder of the First Bank of the United States), whose suggestions he wove into the message's section on the Bank. It was a mild, for Jackson, passage, reminding Congress that the Bank whose charter would expire in 1836 should receive timely attention: "Both the [Bank's] constitutionality and expediency . . . are well questioned by a large portion of our fellow citizens; and it must be admitted . . . that it has failed in the great end of establishing a uniform and sound currency." [1]

To charge the Bank with failing to maintain a "sound currency" was rank distortion of fact, for the Bank had since 1819's panic stood rocklike in preventing state banks from flooding the country with paper money of uncertain, fluctuating value. If Jackson's primary concern was a stable currency, he assumed a curiously contradictory stance, particularly in view of his earlier suffering from promissory notes in the Allison affair and his fight in Tennessee against loose state banking practices, which the Bank had managed to restrain.

But his concern was more political than financial. Rumors that the Bank used financial leverage in seeking to influence the 1828 elections disturbed Jackson. Even though false, the rumors raised in Old Hickory a fear that the Bank's potential entry into politics, with its vast resources, would "destroy our republican institutions." Recognizing that the Bank had broad support, he wrote to old friend Overton in June 1829 that he was considering a plan to change "the present, incorporated Bank to . . . a National Bank—This being the only way that a recharter of the present U.S. Bank can be prevented and . . . the only thing that can prevent our liberties to be crushed by the Bank and its influence, for I [have learned] of the . . . interference of the . . . Bank . . . in our late elections which if not *curbed* must destroy the purity of the right of suffrage." [4]

"Everyone that knows me," the President commented later, "does know, that I have always been opposed to the U. States Bank, nay all Banks." ` While his opposition to the Bank was firm, as a political realist, Jackson realized that he did not have in 1829 the political strength needed to eliminate the Bank, hence his reference in the Overton letter to making it a "National Bank," presumably under direct government control, rather than allowing it to function, as it did, as a private corporation subject to practically no government restraints. In order to effect even this change, the President would have to rally public support. This he proceeded to do among groups already leaning against the Bank.

Many Western Jackson followers disliked the Bank for the controls it exercised over state banks limiting the paper money supply, which Western debtors wanted increased so their debts could be repaid in cheaper money. Second, Eastern state bankers resented the Bank as an awesome competitor. But another source of support came from Eastern working class groups. In early 1829 a Philadelphia workingmen's meeting, held in the very shadow of the Bank's sumptuous Chestnut Street headquarters, protested creating "any more new banks, blamed hard times on "too great extension of paper credit," and appointed a committee to draft a report on banking. The report, prepared by editor William M. Gouge of the *Gazette* and William J. Duane (later Jackson's Secretary of Treasury) among others, condemned the paper money system: "That banks are useful . . . [for] deposit and transfer, we readily admit; but . . . [these] benefits . . . [do not] compensate for the evils they produce in . . . laying the foundation of *artificial* inequality of wealth, and, thereby, of *artificial* inequality of power. . . . If the present system of banking and paper money be extended . . . , the great body of working people must give over all hopes of ever acquiring any property." ° Here lay additional fuel for any Jackson backfire against the Bank.

Forging an anti-Bank coalition from such disparate factions called for nimble dexterity. Western debtors wanted easy money—copious paper issues and easy credit extension; eastern workingmen plugged for hard money and tight restrictions on credit banking. Eastern state bankers generally leaned toward easier money with credit in their own hands, while doctrinaire hard money men urged both hard money and credit restraint. Such divergent groups shared one common interest—dislike of the Bank, but to get them to pull in harness required a master hand.

In order to "chain the monster" Bank, Jackson needed all the support he could muster, since backers of the Bank were numerous and influential, especially in Congress. Responding to the President's charge of the Bank's failure in money management, both Houses appointed investigating committees (the House committee chaired by Calhoun's friend, George McDuffie). In the spring of 1830 both committees returned reports acquitting the Bank.

Biddle had reprints of these reports distributed widely throughout the country, an action that irritated Jackson though he gave no outward sign at the time. Indeed, Biddle stepped up correspondence with Presidential advisers Lewis and Livingston and got the impression that he was making progress in changing the President's attitude when Lewis reported that if Congress extended the life of the Bank, the President would "not object." [7] It may be that at this point Jackson would have been willing to compromise on the question of a new Bank charter.

When Jackson returned to the subject in his December 1830 message, he suggested the Bank might be made a branch of the Treasury, receiving public and private deposits, but not operate as a corporation with private stockholders, with limited note-issuing capability but no power to make loans or buy property. This, he believed, would obviate "constitutional objections" and end its "influence" to play "on the

hopes, fears of interests of large masses of the community." [8]
In the 1831 cabinet reshuffle new appointees Livingston
(State) and McLane (Treasury) were known friends and defenders of the Bank. In fact, McLane's first annual Treasury
report to Congress argued for recharter of the Bank; while
at the same time Jackson's message told Congress that while
"still entertaining the opinions heretofore expressed" about
the Bank, he would leave the Bank question "for the present"
to the decision of "an enlightened people and their representatives." [9]

If Jackson appeared to be dropping the issue entirely, appearances were misleading. He was simply saying he stuck
to his "expressed" view that the Bank would have to be
modified but would leave to Congress the details of modification, on which he was doubtless willing to compromise substantially. But he certainly had not abandoned his position
that the Bank, as it stood, was harmful and capable of much
potential harm.

President Biddle, believing accurately that opposition to
Bank recharter was "not a cabinet measure, nor a party measure, but a personal [Jackson] measure," found the President's
attitude puzzling and exasperating.[10] Biddle preferred to keep
the Bank out of politics and in fact had meticulously done
so, despite Jackson's suspicions. True, some public men like
Webster were paid annual retainer fees as legal counsel for
the Bank and loans had been made to prominent public fig-
ures, but this had been done on a strictly business basis without regard to party or faction. And true, the Bank had also
paid large sums to newspapers and printers, but for the understandable purpose of presenting the Bank's case to the
public. Biddle had scrupulously insisted on and maintained
the Bank's political neutrality."

But as the year 1832 opened, Biddle and the Bank changed
attitude, and with some justification. Outward signs sug-

gested a softening of the President's antagonism; perhaps he would after all accept a recharter for the Bank. Further, since 1832 would bring a Presidential election in the fall, Old Hickory might be more tractable now in the face of possible defeat at the polls. Finally, Biddle was convinced that the Bank had sufficient political muscle in Congress and with the voters to win a recharter. Having hesitated and stalled long enough, Biddle got the final stiffener when the National Republican convention in December 1831 nominated Henry Clay for President and denounced Jackson's position on the Bank. Biddle hesitated no longer. In January 1832 the Bank entered the political area with petitions' for recharter submitted in each House of Congress—four years before the present Bank charter was due to expire. Clearly, here was a move calculated to drive the issue to a political showdown. Jackson so interpreted it and prepared to fight.

Already the preliminaries of the Jackson offensive in the Bank war had been set in February 1831, when sturdy Jacksonian lieutenant Thomas Hart Benton in the Senate boomed his objection "to the renewal of the charter . . . because I look upon the bank as an institution too great and powerful to be tolerated in a Government of free and equal laws. . . . Secondly, I object . . . because its tendencies are dangerous and pernicious . . . [aggravating] the inequality of fortunes; [tending] to make the rich richer and the poor poorer; to multiply the nabobs and paupers. . . . Thirdly, I object . . . on account of the exclusive privileges, and anti-republican monopoly, which it gives to the stockholders." The remedy in Benton's view: "Gold and silver is the best currency for a republic; it suits the men of middle property and the working people best; and if I was going to establish a working man's party, it should be on the basis of hard money; a hard money party against a paper party." [12]

When the petition for recharter reached the Senate in early

1832, Benton was there again to fight it with all the obstruc-
tionist weapons he could command. Delay was the strategy,
and, at Benton's instigation, delay was achieved in the House
by appointing another investigating committee. The committee, stacked by the Speaker against the Bank, accordingly
made a 4-man majority report against recharter and two
minority reports (John Quincy Adams presenting his own)
in favor of the Bank.[13]

Benton continued his anti-Bank barrage in the Senate. Indeed Benton and Jackson had moved closer in recent years,
a far cry from the 1813 tavern brawl with the Benton brothers
that left a bullet lodged in Old Hickory's left shoulder. In
January 1832, as the Bank war opened, Jackson had a visiting
Philadelphia surgeon remove the bullet. A story made the
rounds that Frank Blair got hold of the bullet and offered it
to Senator Benton. The latter declined, saying that Jackson
had "acquired clear title to it in common law by twenty years
peaceable possession." "Only nineteen years," interjected
Blair. "Oh, well," Benton replied, "in consideration of the
extra care he has taken of it—keeping it constantly about his
person . . . I'll waive the odd year."[14]

The Bank's application for recharter ignited fiery resentment in the White House. It was the final straw for Jackson—
now convinced that here was a blatant effort to pressure him
in an election year and thereby tamper with free elections.
As Attorney-General Taney saw it, "the application at the
present time . . . means in plain English this—the Bank says
to the President, your next election is at hand—if you charter
us, well—if not, beware of your power." To one intimate,
Jackson roared with fury: "I will prove to them that I will
never flinch."[15] Fighting mad, Jackson prodded Benton to
double his anti-Bank fire. Blair's *Globe* slanted the House
committee reports to magnify the Bank's evil influence in
making loans to Congressmen, editors, and other politicos.

Despite Benton's boisterous fight, the Senate, where John Calhoun presided, impassive and impartial, passed the bill for a 20-year renewed charter in mid June; a month later it rolled through the House. Biddle's strategy was working to a T; as his chief lieutenant phrased it, "Our life [the Bank's] depends on this session and getting the veto now, so that the nation may be roused by the autumnal elections." [16] The bill went to the White House.

Bank men would not have long to wait for Old Hickory's response. When the bill reached his desk, Jackson was half-sick, weary, and crochety. Van Buren, just back from England, called at the White House, found his chief stretched on a sofa looking pale, faint, almost ghostlike. Jackson reached out, warmly grasped his friend's hand and whispered, "The Bank, Mr. Van Buren, is trying to kill me, *but I will kill it,*" his voice devoid of anger or bluster but fairly screaming defiance. He was convinced that "providence" gave him with the Bank bill a chance to save "the republic from its thral-dome and corrupting influence." He would frame a veto message to "leave the Subject *open* for decision of the people at their next Election." [17]

Huddling with advisers Taney, Kendall, Donelson, and Woodbury, the Old Hero whipped into shape a thunderous veto message, sent to Congress July 10, 1832. Jackson's Bank recharter veto message reverberates down to today as one of the great statements of democratic equality. (See fuller text in *Appendix,* Doc. No. 5) "It is to be regretted," he observed, "that the rich and the powerful too often bend the acts of government to their selfish purposes. Distinctions in society will always exist under every just government. Equality of talents, of education, or of wealth cannot be produced by human institutions. In the full enjoyment of the gifts of Heaven and the fruits of superior industry, economy and virtue, every man is equally entitled to protection by law; but when the laws undertake to add to these natural and just advantages artificial distinctions . . . to make the rich richer and the potent more powerful, the humble members of society—the farmers, mechanics and laborers—who have neither the time nor the means of securing like favors to themselves, have a right to complain of the injustice of their Government." [18]

But, as Schlesinger acutely observes, "the case against the Bank could not rest simply on generalities" of democratic equality. Jackson's basic objection to the Bank, like Taney's and Benton's, stemmed from hard-money convictions. Yet, needing political support of cheap money men, "powerful hard-money arguments . . . that the paper system caused periodic depressions, and . . . built up an aristocracy—were unavailable because they" undercut "the debtor and state banking positions" as effectively as they did the Bank's.[19] Therefore, the "monster" "hydra of corruption" had to be "chained" on other grounds.

Jackson's brilliant message adroitly wove together five major indictments of the Bank—unconstitutional, unAmerican, undemocratic, corrupting in its political influence, and unjust in exercising special privilege. Condensed, the arguments run: the Bank is unconstitutional because the Constitution contains no specific provision empowering Congress to establish a stock-issuing corporation; unAmerican and dangerous because "more than a fourth . . . of the stock . . . is held by foreigners"; undemocratic in that it denied to all comers equal opportunity in banking and placed "such a concentration of power in the hands of a few men irresponsible to the people"; corrupting in that its immense financial resources could be used to determine election of the people's representatives; unjust in its effects of making rich men "richer by act of Congress" through their exercise of special privilege and monopoly over America's money system.[20]

Here, for the first time a President vetoed a Congressional act on grounds other than constitutional-legal grounds—a staggering departure for a generation geared to narrow constitutional thinking. Social and economic considerations, a political philosophy that government in a democracy should serve as an impartial referee among contending economic groups, Presidential sharing in policy determination—all these buttress the veto message. Further, advancing the claim, not made by a previous President, that a President can properly reject a bill for enacting what he considered an unwise or inexpedient policy, he complained that Congress had not consulted with the President in advance of framing the legislation. Here was a totally novel stance for a President, a vigorous assertion of an enlarged realm of Presidential power—an assertion that would later grow into accepted practice.

Reactions to the veto erupted on all sides. Many men, particularly debtors, state bank promoters, workingmen spokesmen hailed it as a stroke of admirable statesmanship. Home in the Hermitage by August, Jackson was pleased with the response commenting: "The veto works well everywhere; it has put down the Bank instead of prostrating me." [21] To Biddle, the message roaring with "all the fury of a chained panther biting the bars of his cage" rang as "a manifesto of anarchy such as Marat or Robespierre . . . issued to the mobs." [22] In the Senate, with Calhoun presiding, Clay and Webster ranted against the message for its "fearful and appalling" notion that a President can control the legislative process, force his will on Congress, thereby undermine "the genius of representative government." [23]

The fall election would decide who truly reflected the "will of the people," pitting Andrew Jackson, champion of "the humble members of society," against Henry Clay, champion of the Bank—Andrew Jackson "Tyrant" vs Henry Clay "de-

fender of representative government." When the people
spoke in November, the voice rang loud but less than clear
in meaning. As the country reeled under a deadly cholera
epidemic and threats of nullification from South Carolina,
Andrew Jackson was reelected—687,000 to the combined
opposition's 560,000-plus; but his total was down 40,000
from 1828, the percentage declining to 55%. The only President whose reelection showed a decrease in votes, his decline
may have stemmed from the Bank issue. But his leadership
won majority endorsement—a tribute to the affection he attracted and his ability to inspire the people to follow his lead.
Only South Carolina and Kentucky (Clay's home state) and
six northeast states voted against him; Jackson swept all the
rest from New York to Louisiana—and even in New England
captured Maine and New Hampshire.

Post-election analysis is risky at best, but particularly so
for 1832 when returns were incomplete (e.g., Missouri
showed the impossible result of no votes for Clay). Whether
citizens voted for the man or the issue is impossible to say.
But the Old Hero showed guts in taking the Bank question
to the people—an issue that could only do him harm. Another first in 1832, effective party organization contributed
to victory—Jacksonians, using the name Democrats, employed assorted popular appeals, parades, barbecues, hickory
pole raisings, and played the "Hero of New Orleans" tune.
One lasting effect of Jacksonian Democracy was to stimulate
public participation in politics through party organizations.
The people responded warmly; Jackson could now assert with
justice that the President was the representative and spokesman of all the people, supported by and accountable to
them.[24]

In the Bank struggle Jackson became convinced that the
"monster" was totally evil, that his veto had only crippled
it, that it must be completely destroyed before the country

could feel safe from its vicious clutch. The present charter having three more years to run, the Bank could with its control over government deposits constrict credit to sway political leaders and policy. The only remedy, Jackson now insisted, was to remove the government's deposits.

After his second inauguration on March 4, 1833 (11 days before he turned 66), Jackson postponed acting on the deposits question in order to tour New York and New England. It turned into a four-week triumphal procession. Three days of greetings, ceremonial dinners in Baltimore, topped by four days in Philadelphia. New York outdid them both, honoring the Chief with parades, banquets, toasts; everybody turned out to see the Hero triumphant over Biddle and his Bank, Calhoun and his nullification, Clay and his cronies. "I have bowed to . . . 200,000 people today," Jackson recorded.[25] To one New Yorker, Jackson appeared "the most popular man we have ever known. . . . He has a kind expression for each [person he greets], the same for all. . . . His manners are certainly good, and he makes the most of them. . . . Adams is the wisest man, the best scholar, the most accomplished statesman; but Jackson has most tact. So huzza for Jackson!" [26]

And "huzzas" echoed for Jackson journeying across Connecticut, Rhode Island, Massachusetts to an endless roar of cannon in salute, banquets, receptions, and parties. Bostonians outdid themselves with such enthusiastic outpourings that Jackson had to take a two-day respite in bed at his hotel to recover from exhaustion. His social grace, friendly and dignified manners charmed Bay Staters, his official guide pronouncing him "a knightly personage".[27] When Harvard College overseers voted to confer an honorary degree, one of them, stern John Quincy Adams, aghast and unreconciled, refused to attend "my Alma Mater's disgrace . . . in conferring her highest literary honor upon a barbarian who could hardly spell his own name." [28] Since the degree presentation was preceded by an address in Latin, a newspaper humorist reported, tongue in cheek, that after Jackson expressed his thanks, "the General was going to stop, but I says in his ear, 'You must give 'em a little Latin, Doctor! . . . 'E pluribus unum,' says he, 'my friends, sina qua non.' " [29] A few days later Jackson collapsed from exhaustion and bleeding in the lungs; under a physician's care he was rushed back to the White House.

Weak as he was, Jackson had strength enough to resume his war on the Bank. Discovering his cabinet divided over removing the government's deposits, even Van Buren opposing, he sent Livingston off to France, kicked McLane upstairs to the State Department, installed William J. Duane as Treasury Secretary. Over a mountain of letters on his desk urging caution on the deposits, Jackson barked at Blair: "Providence may change me but it is not in the power of man to do it." [30]

Relentlessly, his drive on the Bank rolled on. At a September 1833 cabinet meeting, three of five members strongly opposed removal. To Jackson's astonished dismay, new Treasury Secretary Duane refused to order removal of the deposits. Under the law the deposits could be removed only by order of the Secretary who must report his reasons to Congress. After pleas with Duane failed, Jackson suggested he resign. The Secretary refused point blank to remove the deposits or to resign. Exasperated, Jackson fired Duane and appointed Taney to the post. Taney immediately issued the "removal" order that after October 1, government funds would be deposited only in selected state banks (dubbed "pet banks" by critics) and present government deposits in the Bank would be drawn on until exhausted.

On his side, Biddle, unfazed and determined, fought back, snorting, "This worthy President thinks that because he has scalped Indians and imprisoned judges, he is to have his way

with the Bank. He is mistaken." [11] The Bank responded by
refusing to make new loans and calling in old ones. The
resulting "credit crunch" drove many businesses and individuals to the verge of bankruptcy or over the brink, Biddle
expecting the resulting outcry would compel the President
to back off. Many deputations of businessmen streamed to
the White House protesting Taney's removal order and urging its withdrawal. Jackson refused: "I have it chained, the
monster must perish." [12]

In-fighting now switched to Congress where pro-Bank,
anti-administration men resumed harrassing attacks on Jackson begun months earlier in a formal resolution "that Government deposits may, in the opinion of the House, be safely
continued in the Bank." Taney's report on removal submitted
to the House now declared: "It is a fixed principle to guard
against the unnecessary accumulation of power over persons
and property in any hands; and no hands are less worthy to
be trusted with it than those of a moneyed corporation"; if
government now accedes to demands for return of deposits
and charter renewal, "what may they not next require?"
Taney answered his own question: "we may [then] quietly
resign ourselves to the chains with which it is proposed to
bind us." [13]

In the Senate, the Bank won new support from John Calhoun, serving in his first term there. The South Carolinian
denied that it was "a question of Bank or no Bank. If it were,
if it involved the existence of our banking system, . . . I
would hesitate, long hesitate before I would be found under
the banner of the system." What was the fight about? Smarting from his recent fall from Jackson's favor and from Jackson's slashing put down of nullification, Calhoun confidently
answered: "It is a struggle between the executive and legislative departments . . . ; a struggle, not in relation to the
existence of the bank, but *which,* Congress or the President,

should have the power to create a bank, and the consequent control over the currency of the country. This is the real question." [4] Thus Calhoun switched the struggle away from real economic issues by insinuating the charge of Jackson's one-man rule which quickly became the theme of the opposition and the practical basis for a coalition between Calhoun and Clay against "executive usurpation" by "that man in the White House."

Around the political grouping, known earlier as Adams-Clay men and more recently as National Republicans, now began to cluster factions of opposition. Some former Jackson adherents, driven off by his high-handed treatment of Bank and deposit issues, moved to make common cause with avowed National Republicans, nullifiers, state rights men, tariff advocates, and other dissidents. Melding such curiously incongruous elements, the opposition party took the name Whigs (shades of patriots of 1776 fighting King George III) when its leader Henry Clay spoke of Whigs rallying to block the monarchical tyranny of "King Andrew I." For some years Calhoun, although he never really joined, operated in loose conjunction with the Clay coalition. It was clearly a marriage of convenience allowing Calhoun to recover some prestige and power lost in the 1832–33 nullification debacle, Clay to recover from his defeat by Jackson in 1832's Presidential battle.

As the economic panic stemming from the Bank's 1833–34 tightening of the credit screws spread, discontent over Jackson policies mounted. Jacksonian Democrats, alarmed by the vociferous outcry, looked for means to mute the rising protest. The new Attorney General, Benjamin F. Butler, Van Buren's law partner, suggested a new, government-owned Bank, headquartered in Washington to serve as depository and fiscal agent for the government—a plan Jackson himself seriously considered. Others proposed a "people's bank" owned jointly by state and federal governments. Many were convinced that state banks ("pet banks" to opponents) were too risky for safe-keeping of federal deposits—a fear realized all too disastrously a few years later. Moreover, said the Jackson critics, the "pet banks" were subject to the same Jackson objections as the Bank on the scores of credit extension, paper money issues, potential political influence—only more so.

Jackson remained immovable on the deposits question. A report had it that a Baltimore mob was about to camp on Capitol Hill until the deposits were restored, and a Congressional delegation scurried fearfully to the White House. "Gentlemen," Old Hickory reportedly told them, "I shall be glad to see this . . . mob on Capitol Hill. I will fix their heads on the iron palisades around the square to assist your deliberations. The leaders I will hang as high as Haman to deter forever all attempts to control . . . Congress by intimidation." [35] A group of New York businessmen suffering acute distress in the financial panic appealed to the President, sitting at his desk calmly puffing his long clay pipe. After a few minutes of listening, Jackson exploded, "Go to Nicholas Biddle. We have no money here, gentlemen. Biddle has all the money. . . . millions of specie in his vaults, lying idle, and yet you come to *me* to save you from breaking." As the group hastened from the White House, Jackson turned to an aide chuckling, "Didn't I manage them well?" [36]

When he faced an enemy, Jackson became characteristically more pugnacious. To a protesting Philadelphia delegation, he roared he "would never restore the deposites to the bank . . . would never recharter that monster of corruption" and that "sooner than live in a country where such a power prevailed, he would seek an asylum in the wilds of Arabia." [37]

On the positive side, Jackson was fully convinced that hard money—gold and silver—was the only reliable currency, that

paper notes, bills of credit, and the rest simply created an
artificial moneyed aristocracy. His fight against the Bank was
dictated by this belief; further, his removal of the deposits he
believed would move the country toward a sound, solid, equitable currency. He got Taney to prepare a bill that would
require all state banks receiving federal deposits to cease
receiving or issuing bank notes in denominations under $5,
later to be increased to $25. James K. Polk introduced the
bill in the House; Benton fought for it in the Senate, arguing
insistently that specie was the only honest money, that paper
notes should be eliminated to make sure that workingmen
received solid money as pay and to end the boom-bust financial cycle that paper money bred.[38] (See *Appendix* Doc. No.
9 for Jackson's views.)

But the bill got nowhere, just as Jackson's December 1833
message and Taney's report justifying removal had stirred
trouble in an angry Congress. (See *Appendix* Doc. No. 7 for
fuller text.) The House moved to consider whether the President had authority to remove the deposits. In the Senate,
attacks on Jackson's arbitrary action spewed daily abuse on
the Executive. Clay, leading the assault, contended with some
justice that the Secretary of Treasury stood in a position of
special responsibility to Congress and called for the President
to submit documents bearing on the removal order. When
Jackson refused, Clay pushed two resolutions: 1) an official
censure of Jackson for removing the deposits in a misuse of
Presidential power; 2) rejecting Taney's stated reasons for
removal as "unsatisfactory and insufficient." In a free-swing-
ing speech, Clay denounced Jackson's "open, palpable and
daring usurpation" of power as rushing the country into "a
revolution . . . rapidly tending . . . [to] change . . . the pure
republican character of the Government" by "concentration
of all power in the hands of one man." Unless Congress called
an immediate half to "despotism," Clay boomed, "the fatal

collapse will soon come on, and we shall die—ignobly die—base, mean, abject slaves; the scorn and contempt of mankind; unpitied, unwept, unmourned." [39]

Calhoun joined the attack on Jackson. Likening the deterioration of the American republic to that of the ancient Roman republic, he labeled Julius Caesar a virtuous statesman compared to Jackson, since Caesar simply plundered the Roman treasury openly; but "the actors in our case are . . . artful, cunning and corrupt politicians. . . . They have entered the treasury, not sword in hand as public plunderers, but with the false keys of sophistry, as pilferers under the silence of midnight. [40] (See *Appendix* Doc. No. 15 for fuller text.)

As Jackson haters railed in Congress, Old Hickory snarled back: "The storm in Congress is still raging. Clay reckless and as full of fury as a drunken man in a brothel, his abuse and coadjutors pass harmless by me. The Deposites will not be renewed nor the Bank rechartered. The mamoth of power and corruption must die. . . . I have it chained, the *Monster must perish.*" [41]

On March 21, 1834, Calhoun delivered a speech analyzing the banking and money situation. He saw the problem, not as a question of one bank or many banks or no bank at all, but essentially as a matter of government itself assuming control of the circulation medium. By law, legal money consisted of gold, silver, and copper coins. In addition, paper notes, issued by the Bank and 450 banks incorporated by 24 different states, totaled more than $70,000,000, compared to $15,000,000 in metallic currency, the bulk of which lay in Bank of United States vaults.

Calhoun objected that paper money was increasing at a rate much faster than the population, its ratio to metal exceeded safe limits and paper money was depreciating rapidly as was its corresponding purchasing power. If this process continued, banks would soon not even pretend to redeem their paper notes in gold, the notes would become worthless and business would collapse. Calhoun's remedy proposed reestablishing a safe ratio between paper and specie by decreasing the former and increasing the latter.

The best way to do this was by means of some kind of a bank, using "a bank to unbank the banks," as he put it. As to the precise nature of such a bank—national or state, new or old—Calhoun would leave the details of others better versed than he in banking. But he insisted no precipitate action (such as Jackson's killing the Bank and removing the deposits) should be taken since it caused a sudden disruption of business and undue shock to the economy. Rather, a new Bank of the United States with a 12-year charter could over that period move gradually to reestablish a safe balance between paper and specie thereby shoring the defenses against inflation only now starting a runaway spiral. Such a measure could be supported by all, he believed—state rightists, strict constructionists since the Bank-government connection would be only temporary, Whigs who liked a Bank, and Jacksonian hard money men since specie would now increase. Thus a sound currency would be restored "gradually and slowly, and to the extent that experience may show that it can be done consistently with the public interest." [42] (See *Appendix* Doc. No. 16 for fuller text.) Here was a sensible, realistic approach, that unfortunately received no careful attention at the moment but was swept aside in the fury of political bombast and recrimination.

In the same month, March 1834, the Senate responded to Clay's furious denunciation of the administration's Bank-deposits-removal policy by refusing to confirm Taney as Treasury Secretary and by adopting a resolution aimed at Jackson. The resolution censured the President for having "in the late executive proceeding in relation to the public revenue

. . . assumed upon himself authority and power not conferred by the Constitution and laws, and in derogation of both, . . . and dangerous to the liberties of the people.''

Stung by the censure, Jackson fired back a "Protest" against the Senate's action. The censure resolution, he declared, was contrary to the "spirit of the Constitution" and "the plainest dictates of humanity and justice." Defending his own course, Jackson asserted: "So glaring were the abuses and corruption of the Bank . . . so palpable its design by its money and power to control the Government . . . that I deemed it the imperative duty of the Executive . . . to check and lessen its ability to do mischief." The Senate's resolution "presupposes a right in that body to interfere with this exercise of Executive power. . . . If by a mere denunciation like this resolution the President should ever be induced to act . . . contrary to the honest convictions of his own mind in compliance with the wishes of the Senate, the constitutional independence of the executive department would be effectively destroyed and its power . . . transferred to the Senate." Finally, Jackson insisted "The President is the direct representative of the American people," responsible to them for executing the laws, while the Secretary of Treasury having "no direct responsibility to the people" must therefore act in accord with "the Chief Magistrate" who is "elected by the people and responsible to them." [43] (See fuller text in *Appendix,* Doc. No. 16B.)

Here was a vigorous assertion of the independence and prerogatives of the President. Skillfully Jackson added an appeal to the people: he wanted to protect the Presidential office from domination by the Senate and to "return to the people unimpaired the sacred trust they have confided to my charge," to protect the people from "powerful monopolies and aristocratical establishments" and preserve "a plain system of government protecting all and granting favors to none, dispensing its blessing like the dews of Heaven, unseen and unfelt." If "such a government" survives. "I shall anticipate with pleasure the place assigned me in the history of my country and die contented with the belief that I have contributed in some small degree to increase the value and prolong the duration of American liberty."

Along with the Whigs, Calhoun rejected outright Jackson's claim to be "the immediate representative of the American people!. . . What effrontery! What boldness of assertion! . . . Why, he never even received a single vote from the American people. He was elected by electors . . . and is at least as far removed from the people as members of this body [Senate], who are elected by legislatures chosen by the people." Jackson's purpose was plain, said Calhoun; he wants to "place himself near the people . . . make himself their sole representative" so that in the future he can "appeal to the people . . . to enlist them as his allies in the war which he contemplates against" the Congress.[44]

Calhoun of course exaggerated for political purposes, but many impartial contemporaries viewed Jackson's assertion that the President was the direct representative of the people as a novel doctrine, upsetting the traditional balance between legislative and executive branches. But in the long view of history, Jackson's insistence on Executive independence and on the President's serving as the spokesman of the people proved a constructive development that made future, strong presidents (along with Jackson) effective molders of public opinion and genuine leaders in policy.

Eventually, Jackson won the contest with the Senate. Benton periodically moved to expunge from the Senate's journal the offensive censure resolution. When the Democrats finally gained a majority in January 1837, six weeks before Jackson would leave office, the Senate voted to erase the stricture from its record. Old Hickory was of course elated, "gave a grand dinner to the expungers," as Benton chronicled, and "being too weak [from illness] to sit at the table, placed the 'head expunger' [Benton] in the chair, and withdrew to his sick chamber. That expurgation! it was the 'crowning glory' of his civil, as New Orleans has been of his military life!" [45]

Meanwhile, Jackson had won the immediate battle of the Bank. Weakened by his veto and crippled by losing government deposits, the Bank limped along to its end in 1836. But whether, in realistic economic terms, Jackson won the Bank war was at the time and remains a matter of dispute. Elimination of a specially privileged corporation he clearly achieved. Thereby he checked a financial institution, over which no effective public controls existed, from exercising enormous power over the economic well-being of individuals and of the nation. But in so doing he destroyed an agency that performed for no charge valuable services for the government, that could also serve as stimulator and regulator of the nation's economy. In its place the state banks proved an ineffective, irresponsible substitute, whose reckless practices fueled speculation, inflation, and panic-depression in the year Jackson left office (1837).

If Jackson's objective was simply to replace paper with hard money, his course of action defeated his objective. Removing the one agency strong enough to enforce sound money practices, he encouraged countless unreliable banks that produced the very flood of paper and speculative excess Jackson sought to prevent. True, he persuaded Congress to require "pet banks" to refuse paper notes under $5 denominations and issued the "Specie Circular" executive order in 1836 requiring payment in specie for purchases of government land by buyers who were not also occupants. The penalty paid for eliminating the Bank—the economic catastrophe of the 1837 Panic and its consequences—could have been avoided, or minimized, by retaining the Bank (or some similar institution) but instituting effective government controls over operations contrary to the public interest.

Following Jackson's term, successor Martin Van Buren attempted such a plan. In 1837 he proposed and three years later Congress enacted the Independent Treasury law, similar to the scheme proposed by Calhoun, whereby branches of the federal treasure, operating in cities throughout the country, served as custodian of government funds, fiscal agents for paying pensions and other government obligations. In a Senate speech Calhoun heartily approved the proposal for entirely divorcing government from banking. Since the economic catastrophe he had predicted in 1834 had arrived in 1837 due to a chaotic monetary system, he urged that reform go a step further, proposing that gradually over the next four years the country's currency be standardized by phasing out state bank notes and replacing them with United States treasury notes, which together with gold and silver coins would constitute a uniform currency satisfying the needs of the country.[46] Neither the Van Buren nor Calhoun proposal won Congress's approval in 1837. But in 1840, with Calhoun's vigorous support the Independent Treasury law passed Congress readily, and the old Calhoun-Van Buren breach stemming from the Eaton-Crawford mess of 1830–31 was finally healed, at least for the time being.[47]

Jackson's war on the Bank left three results of lasting significance. One, firmly established, was the principle that heads of all departments (including Treasury) were agents of the President: he appointed, gave directions to and removed them in his discretion; since 1833 no Secretary has even thought of challenging his President. Second, Jackson asserted, maintained, and defended the independence of the Executive as a co-equal branch, not subject to intimidation by Congress. He expanded the President's influence—by appeal to his position as the single nationally elected spokesman for all the people; further by exercise (or threat) of the veto, the President's influence acquired a weight equal to two-thirds of both houses of Congress in the legislative process. Finally, Jackson, through the Bank war, welded diverse factions into a functioning Democratic party capable through party discipline of proposing, adopting, and implementing national policy.[48] Three major advances in American political practice resulted.

So Andrew Jackson, fighting with the full powers of the President, destroyed a corporation he feared was becoming more powerful than the government itself. "The Monster," he wrote in a later assessment, "was likely to destroy our republican institutions, and would have entirely subverted them if it had not been arrested in its course." [49]

VIII Battles Over Issues

Indians and Land Policy

WHILE THE BANK WAR was being fought out to its destructive end, other issues crowded each other for attention. Fundamental and some ways more critical than the Bank issue in the agricultural society of the Jackson era was land. Since land was the basic element in an economy devoted primarily to raising crops and livestock, how to acquire land for farming assumed elemental significance to more Americans of that era than any other question.

The Indians as original occupiers of America's land were viewed by most early nineteenth century Americans as uncivilized savages who stood in the way of progress. Since most Eastern Indians were semi-nomadic hunters and fishers, farming played but a small part in their economic existence. To most Americans, reared in the Jeffersonian tradition, farming was the noblest pursuit of man; hence failure to work the land to produce food and fiber was wasteful if not downright sinful. The common conviction was that the Indians would have to go—nobody cared much where—and their land inevitably would pass into white hands.

Andrew Jackson shared his generation's conviction, viewing the Indians in typically Western fashion—as an obstacle to steadily advancing progress on the frontier, the tribes would have to move to make way for white farmers, who put the land to productive use. As a Tennessee pioneer, he had seen the Indians pushed relentlessly off the land they had formerly roamed and confined to narrower limits. Indeed, in his military campaigns of 1813–14, he helped hasten the process—forcing Creek Indians to cede by treaty large tracts in Alabama and Georgia to the United States. But the practice of dealing with an Indian tribe as a domestic, dependent nation, a practice followed since colonial times, Jackson considered foolish and unrealistic. In 1817 he wrote President Monroe: "I have long viewed treaties with the Indians as an absurdity. . . . The Indians are the subjects of the United States, inhabiting its territory and ackowledging its sovereignty—then is it not absurd for the sovereign to negotiate by treaty with the subject? I have always thought, that Congress had as much right to regulate . . . all Indian concerns as they had of the Territories; there is only this difference, that the inhabitans of the Territories are Citizens of the United States and . . . Indians are Subjects. . . . If they are viewed as an independent nation, possessing . . . sovereignty and domain, then negotiating with them and concluding treaties, would be right and proper. But this is not the fact; all Indians within the . . . United States . . . have only a possessory right to the soil, for the purpose of hunting and not the right of domain. . . ." The old policy should be abandoned since "Their existence and happiness now depend upon a change in their habits and customs which can only be effected by a change of policy. . . . The game being destroyed, they can no longer exist by their bows and arrows and Guns. They must lay them aside and produce by labour from the earth a subsistence; in short, they must be civilized; to effect which their territorial boundary must be curtailed. . . ." [1]

In the same year Jackson expressed these views, John Calhoun became Secretary of War and thereby assumed charge of Indian affairs. His views of the Indians resembled those of his generation, with a slight humanitarian tempering. In 1818 his lengthy report on Indian Affairs to Congress concluded with policy proposals. The government should attempt to persuade the Eastern tribes (east of the Mississippi) to migrate to new lands west of the Mississippi. Since the area was semi-arid and thought to be unfit for fixed agriculture, it was thought appropriate for Indian occupation, which the government must guarantee for all future time.

For Indians who refused to migrate, assimilation in white culture should be encouraged, and when this process was completed under direction of government agents, they should acquire full rights as citizens.

Trade with the Indians would be conducted by government factors and by private traders, who should be licensed and tightly controlled by the government.

Private traders would pay a government license fee of $100 to $500; their operations and accounts would be subject to periodic, strict inspection by the government. As to the trans-Mississippi Indians of the Great Plains, a chain of military forts along the frontier between them and white settlements to the east would forestall foreign intrigue among them and protect nearby settlers. After a 30-year transition period the government would launch civilizing efforts among these tribes, too.[2]

President Monroe and Congress approved Calhoun's Indian civilizing policy in principle—and in practice to the extent of approving an annual $10,000 appropriation to check "further decline and extinction" of the tribes. To implement the program Calhoun employed missionary groups to provide educational plans that "in addition to reading, writing and arithmetic, should . . . [for boys] extend to the practical knowledge of . . . agriculture and . . . the mechanical arts . . . ; and . . . [for girls] to spinning, weaving, and sewing." It was from this fund that Rev. Jedidiah Morse was paid for making his survey of conditions among the Indians 1820–21.[3]

But the Calhoun program ran into rough sailing. The Panic of 1819 brought retrenchment of government expenditures, and Calhoun's Indian civilizing program was the first to go. Pioneer Southern farmers who coveted nearby Indian lands pressed for rejection of the program. Added pressures came from fur trading interests, with lobbyists of John Jacob Astor's American Fur Company joining Senator Benton of Missouri (St. Louis was the center of the fur trade) in scuttling completely the government trading houses, which competed too well with private traders.

Recognizing the intensity of white pressure for Indian lands east of the Mississippi, Calhoun bowed to reality. In 1824 he got established an Office of Indian Affairs within his War Department and in consultation with Indian Chiefs who visited his Washington office worked out complete plans for the removal of 80,000 Eastern Indians and their relocation on lands in what ultimately would become Oklahoma, Kansas, Nebraska, Iowa. He insisted that the Indians must be guaranteed permanent, undisturbed possession of lands allotted to them. But his carefully designed plans became snagged when Congress failed in 1824–25 to make the necessary appropriations.

When Jackson became President in 1829, more than 50,000 Cherokees, Creeks, Choctaws, and Chickasaws still occupied some 33 million acres east of the Mississippi, mostly in Georgia, Alabama; and Mississippi. (See *Appendix* Doc. No. 3-C for Jackson's views on Indian policy.) Favoring a policy of moving the Eastern Indians, Jackson wrote a government agent: "Say to [the Creeks], where they are now, they and my white children are too near each other to live in harmony and peace. . . . Beyond the great river Mississippi . . . their father has provided a country large enough for them all, and he advises them to remove to it. There, their white brethren will not trouble them . . . and they can live . . . in peace and plenty. It will be theirs forever." [4]

While removal treaties were in the making, Jackson noted

the mounting white pressures in Georgia against the Cherokees, a very advanced tribe that had settled down, built houses, worked farms in the white manner, and intended to remain. The state of Georgia applied Georgia law to the Cherokees and prohibited unlicensed missionaries to enter the Indian area, twice defying Supreme Court judgments, which the President took no step to enforce. In the summer of 1830 Jackson on a trip south visited an assemblage of Chickasaw chiefs in Mississippi. After the ceremonial pipe was passed and smoked, the President spoke: "Friends and Brothers: . . . You have dwelt long on the soil you occupy . . . before the white man kindled his fires too near to yours. . . . [But now] there is no alternative." The tribe should accept the government offer of lands farther west and "obtain comfortable homes" there. The Indians reluctantly accepted his advice. Congress in the Indian Removal Act of 1830 provided the funds. Treaties, providing cession of Indian lands to the United States which in turn paid the cost of removal westward, granted lands in present-day Oklahoma and stipulated government annuity, were arranged—with the Creeks in 1832, Choctaws, and Chickasaws in 1833, and finally the Cherokees in 1835. Between 1829 and 1837, 90 treaties were made with Eastern Indians, and in the latter year Jackson reported to Congress that "all of the tribes on the east of the Mississippi . . . and extending from Lake Michigan to Florida, have entered into engagements which lead to their transplantation." [5]

Half-forced, half-persuaded the Eastern tribes trudged reluctantly westward to the newly established Indian territory. The Seminoles flatly refused to budge and fought a guerrilla war for decades, retreating ever farther into the swampy everglades of Florida. When some Northern tribes procrastinated, they were ejected from Illinois and Wisconsin by federal and state troops, including a 23-year-old lieutenant named Jefferson Davis and a 22-year-old captain named Abraham Lincoln. In 1834 the Indian Intercourse Act forbade whites to enter the Indian country without a special federal license; and the Army proceeded to establish a chain of forts to enforce the separation policy.

The government had long been selling former Indian lands to individual buyers. Indeed, in the nineteenth century the federal government functioned as the world's largest real estate broker. Selling land was its principal peacetime function. Originally it owned all the land west of the Appalachians from the Lakes to the Gulf, with the exception of Kentucky and a few small tracts. To this Jefferson's 1803 purchase added the vast trans-Mississippi imperial domain stretching from Louisiana to the Canadian border and west to the Continental Divide. In its first 100 years the United States government disposed of one billion acres of land; it sold about twenty per cent at a fraction of its true value and gave away free the other eighty per cent.

The federal Land Ordinance of 1785 set basic land policy by providing (1) government survey of land into one-square-mile (640 acres) tracts (called sections) and (2) sale at public auction, with a $2 per acre minimum price. Later the Land Act of 1820 stipulated an 80-acre minimum purchase and reduced the price to $1.25 per acre, payable in cash. Thus for $100 cash a buyer could acquire from the government a fair-sized farm.

When Jackson became President, public land policy was so enmeshed with tariff and fiscal issues as to be inextricable from clashing sectional, class, political, and economic antagonisms. Generally, landless men and small farmers everywhere wanted a low-price or cost-free land policy, while large land holders and speculators wanted the government to hold the price line.

In sectional terms, Northwest and Southwest wanted a

liberal land policy—cheap or free land. The Northeast opposed, manufacturers fearing a drain of labor to western
lands, thereby raising wages and production costs. Calhoun's
Southeast was torn by conflicting impulses. Desiring a low
tariff and realizing that increased land sales filled the federal
treasury and thereby minimized the need for a high tariff,
Calhoun and the Southeast often supported Western demands for lower land prices. With the West's help in return,
the Southeast hoped to win tariff reduction.

During Jackson's era various land policies were proposed: preemption, cession, graduation, distribution, and free
land. Free land or *homestead* legislation was advocated
mainly by Westerners but received some support from Eastern utopians like Thomas Skidmore and George H. Evans.[6]
Preemption would allow a squatter occupying and improving
federal land before the official survey to buy at minimum
price the occupied parcel without competitive bidding. *Cession* would grant federal lands to the state in which they lay,
for support of education or roads. *Graduation* proposed periodic reductions of the $1.25-per-acre minimum on lands re-
maining unsold after one, two, or five year periods. *Distribution* called for dividing proceeds of federal land sales among
the states, on the theory that the public domain was the
common property of all.

A large land speculator himself in earlier years, Jackson
as President pursued no settled, thought-out land policy. Although many Jacksonians proposed a land policy more generous than that of 1820, Jackson himself in 1830 threatened to
use military force to drive squatters off public land in
Alabama. In 1832 he declared for maintaining "the present
system" for the moment but added that "our true policy"
should be to sell land to actual "settlers in limited parcels at
a price barely sufficient" to cover federal costs of acquisition
and survey. Ultimately, he conceded, the government should

cede federal land to the state "in which it lies." [7] Here was modified *graduation* combined with eventual *cession*.

As to distribution, in his messages of 1829 and 1830 Jackson suggested that Congress consider, after final payment of the national debt, dividing the prospective surplus government income among the states in proportion to their representation in Congress.

For Jackson the important goal was to pay off the national debt, which he called "a curse" to be quickly removed. When in 1833, with the end of the national debt in sight, Clay pushed through Congress a bill to distribute proceeds of land sales, (not revenues from regular taxes). Jackson gave the bill a pocket veto.

But federal revenues continued to mount leaving an annual surplus in the Treasury. Proceeds from government land sales climbed steadily—from an annual average of $1,000,000 prior to 1830, to $4,000,000 in 1833, $5,000,000 in 1834, $15,000,000 in 1835, and $25,000,000 in 1836. They produced more than enough to cover the government's yearly expenses. And the tariff, even after the 1833 reduction, continued to yield substantial revenue. Total government receipts rose from $16,000,000 in 1834 to $24,000,000 by 1836. By the former year the national debt, for the only time in the nation's history, was entirely paid, and the unused surplus on deposit in the "pet banks" climbed to $30,000,000 by 1836.

With the debt eliminated, Jackson cautioned against "the unnecessary accumulation of public revenue," advising that "no political maxim is better established than that . . . an improvident expenditure of money is the parent of profligacy." Further, Jackson's constitutional scruples over distribution of the surplus had increased since 1829: ". . . the only safe rule . . . is to regard the absence of express authority [in the Constitution] . . . as equivalent to a prohibition;" therefore a constitutional amendment should be adopted before handing the surplus to the states.

As a practical matter, Jackson feared that federal gifts would lead to "prodigality" and undermine "State governments" by encouraging state legislatures to "harrass the General Government for increased supplies" in the future. The consequent danger was that "there would soon be but one taxing power . . . vested in a body of men far removed from the people" whereby the "States would gradually lose their purity" and "independence" becoming "merged in a consolidation, cemented by widespread corruption." Rather, said Jackson, let the general government "collect only revenue enough to meet" its needs and let "the people keep the balance of their property in their own hands. . . ." [8]

But despite his own misgivings, Jackson in 1836 gave approval to an act to distribute the surplus among the states in proportion to the federal ratio (i.e., the number of each state's electors in the Presidential electoral college). Jackson approved because the bill stipulated "a loan deposit" of funds to the state, rather than an outright gift. [9]

On January 1, 1837, the first installment of the distribution was paid to the states. Since the funds were withdrawn from the deposit banks, a general contraction of credit resulted. Many land speculators had borrowed heavily from state banks, which now called for payment of loans. Unable to pay, speculators defaulted, and banks, unable to collect loans, often went out of business and federal funds on deposit evaporated with them. In consequence, the Panic of 1837 hit the nation. In killing the Bank, Jackson had removed the only effective brake on credit expansion; placing federal deposits in state banks had accelerated inflation. Credit now tightened; specie evaporated; businesses failed—a full-scale economic depression gripped the country just a few months after Jackson retired from office in 1837. Clearly the country was reaping the whirlwind of unwise over-extension of credit, banking practices, monetary inflation, and land speculation, which Jackson's policies had encouraged.

In regard to land policy, Calhoun as Vice President had remained non-committal. Upon assuming a seat in the Senate in 1833, Calhoun took his first official stand opposing Clay's distribution bill. The recent compromise tariff of 1833 would reduce government revenues and therefore, he protested, distributing funds to the states now would revive pressures for raising tariff duties in violation of the compromise. In 1836 Clay revived his distribution scheme. In Senate debate Calhoun countered by proposing a constitutional amendment that would allow a temporary (until 1842) distribution to the states for the specific purpose of building internal improvements (understood to mean railroads at this time).[10] His proposed amendment made no headway in Congress. To another proposal to graduate the price of public lands Calhoun objected. After much Senate wrangling, Calhoun contributed substantially to drafting a bill that would distribute the surplus to the states according to population. But rather than an outright gift, Calhoun insisted on its being termed a "deposit" for which each state would give a promissory note payable on demand to the United States Treasury. In this form the bill finally passed both houses and received the President's approval on June 23, 1836. Calhoun, elated, saw the act as redressing the balance between federal and state governments; it would go far, he wrote, "to restore the ascendancy of the States, and effect a deep political reform."[11] What Calhoun meant was that by shifting funds out of federal and into states hands, the latter would gain relative strength, lost in the Force Act showdown of 1833.

When early in 1839 the land price graduation proposal was renewed, Calhoun again opposed it. Rather, he favored outright cession of public lands to the states in which they lay;

he was prepared to offer adequate compensation to older states which contained no public lands. But consistent with his state sovereignty convictions, he argued that in justice each state was entitled to control lands within its borders. Politically he was hoping to weld an effective combination of West and South. In his supporting speech he reasserted the state rights philosophy: "It is a *Federal Union*—an Union of Sovereign States; and can be as effectually and much more easily destroyed by *consolidation* than by *dismemberment.*"

Reviewing events of the past six years, he pictured his own actions as designed to preserve the Union from the dangers of "consolidation." He opposed excessive powers being exercised by the general government, hence opposition to the protective tariff, which nullification had destroyed. A huge general government, with vast revenues, a large public debt and immense patronage at its disposal, created a monstrous machine endangering liberty. Hence, federal revenues had to be reduced; they had been as a consequence of the Compromise tariff of 1833. With the national debt extinguished, the Distribution-Deposit Act of 1836 removed the menace of a huge surplus at the center, placing it instead in the safe hands of the states. The end of the Bank made possible a complete separation of the political and money power. The country was moving in the direction of restoring original principles he approved. Appealing to Jefferson and "the good old Virginia school," he urged that the government should continue along these lines so that "our free and happy institutions may be perpetuated for generations." [12]

With these speeches Calhoun had completed moving through the spectrum from nationalism through state sovereignty to reaction. Where he had once looked eagerly toward a bright future he now looked backward to a golden age buried in the past. He would spend his remaining years, in a reactionary grip, defending the vested interests of his minority section—slavery and agriculture.

Internal Improvements

As Indian tribes migrated to the Plains and government land passed into the hands of farmers, the need for improved transportation became readily apparent. To reach the new lands, settlers struggled their way alone or in groups along faint paths, dim trails or even blazed new trails. After settling, clearing a few acres, building a cabin, planting a few acres of corn, letting the livestock run loose, they quickly felt a desire for social contact with the outside world and the need for some means of getting their surplus crops and animals to market for sale. Pressures in the West grew steadily for roads and canals to supplement the rivers and streams that accommodated flat boats and small craft. Eastern cities, too, were eager for better connections with the interior settlements in order to tap sources of food and raw materials and to sell Eastern or imported products. In a country rapidly growing with its people swiftly filling an area stretching 1,500 miles from Maine to Florida and 1,000 miles from the Atlantic to the Mississippi the need for better transportation to bind together the widely scattered settlements was clear.

Everybody wanted roads, canals, and later railroads built close to where they lived. The only question was who should do the building—local communities, states, or the federal government. The first two had built some roads and canals by 1820, but new areas had trouble raising funds for better transportation and hence looked to Washington for help. Washington's response was mixed. In Jefferson's day the National Road, financed with federal funds, was constructed running from Cumberland, Maryland, westward into Ohio. After this initial effort older national leaders developed

doubts about constitutionality. The War of 1812 proved the
need for good roads for military defense. In 1817 Calhoun
got through Congress his comprehensive federal road-building bill, only to be shocked by President Madison's blunt veto
of the measure. A few years later as Secretary of War he
drafted elaborate plans for federal building of an extensive
network of canals and roads, as noted in Chapter IV. When
this was shelved, he moved to support a measure calling for
federal surveys of possible transportation routes for military
defense purposes, only to encounter again a Presidential veto
by Monroe. At this time Calhoun had no doubt of federal
constitutional power to construct internal improvements.
Meanwhile, many states forged ahead with transportation
projects of their own. By 1825 New York completed its Erie
Canal tying the Hudson River together with Lake Erie;
Maryland entrepreneurs started constructing the Baltimore
and Ohio Railroad on July 4, 1828, the same day that President Adams turned the first spadeful of earth for the Chesapeake and Ohio Canal.

As military commander on the southern border General
Andrew Jackson had been impressed by the army's need for
good roads to move troops quickly to trouble spots. Later,
as Senator from Tennessee, Old Hickory took the floor only
four times and altogether spoke less than twenty minutes; but
twice he strongly urged federal building of roads of military
value, and his vote was cast consistently in support of every
internal improvement proposal on the grounds of national
defense.

After becoming President in 1829, Jackson like predecessors Madison and Monroe developed some constitutional
qualms and moved more cautiously in this area. His 1829
message suggested Congress consider only "great national
works of internal improvements" that clearly met the constitutional requirement of "national defense." [13] During his first

year in office he approved Congressional measures for aiding
certain internal improvement projects that were scarcely
more than local in nature. But in 1830, when Congress
adopted a bill to invest federal funds in the stock of a company building a road in Kentucky between Maysville on the
Ohio river and Lexington 65 miles southwest, Jackson struck
down the measure with a sharp veto message. It was written
largely by Martin Van Buren, who doubtless feared competition with New York's highly successful Erie Canal.

Jackson rested his case largely on constitutional grounds,
gave a few practical objections, and appealed to his fellow
citizens' pride in their democratic experiment. In his original
notes for the Maysville Road veto message, he resisted most
strongly the creation of a Kentucky corporation in whose
stock the federal government would place federal funds (although he had approved such an arrangement in a few previous instances). No power was granted in the Constitution,
wrote the President, "to authorize the United States to
become a member of a corporation created by the states." To
follow such a practice would engender "flagitious legislation
arising from combination if you will vote with me I will vote
with you so disgraceful to our country." [14]

For Jackson the critical constitutional question in an internal improvement proposal was: "Is it national and conducive to the benefit of the whole, or local and operating only
to the advantage of a portion of the Union?" The proposed
Maysville road, as "a measure of purely local character," was
inadmissable by this test.

Further, appropriations for local projects would lead to
"abuses" that "far exceed the good" they might promote.
They "may be resorted to by artful expedients to shift upon
the Government the losses of unsuccessful private speculation, and thus . . . sap the foundations of public virtue and
taint the . . . Government with a demoralizing influence."

Underscoring the Jeffersonian view of the American experiment in democracy as "the world's best hope," Old Hickory insisted all Americans must work to insure "success of the republican principle" and "to elevate its character and extend its influence" in order that "the superior success of its operations will" win "the admiration and respect of the world." Moreover, if "expediency be made a rule of construction in interpreting the Constitution," then we may be forced to admit the skeptics' assertion of "the degrading truth that man is unfit for self-government." Instead, said Jackson, let "an honest observance of constitutional" restraints insure the virtue and superiority of republican self-government.[15] (See fuller text in *Appendix*, Doc. No. 4.)

Jackson's ringing appeal to principle here was also good politics. It enabled him to slap down his principal political opponents, Clay and Adams, who were already on record favoring federal internal improvements. If Calhoun, also an early advocate of such a program, also caught some of the sting, it was only incidental.

But Jackson did not close the door completely. "I am not hostile to internal improvements," he told Congress in his 1834 message, "and wish to see them extended to every part of the country." As a strict constructionist, he immediately added, let them be "commenced in a proper manner, confined to proper objects, and conducted under authority generally conceded to be rightful." "Proper objects" he stipulated as "Fortresses and . . . roads and canals of a character National and not local." "Proper manner" meant to Jackson that "Congress cannot exercise an exclusive jurisdiction and invade the Sovereignty of the States." To exercise powers not clearly granted by the Constitution would, he declared (sounding very much like Calhoun) "produce . . . a consolidation of the States" and introduce amongst the States anarchy, rivalry and disunion. "Therefore, if the people wished the general government to build roads, let them adopt an amendment to the Constitution, delegating the necessary power." [16]

As Vice President, Calhoun took no public stand on the Maysville Road, but Jackson's reference to "the Sovereignty of the States" must have met his approval. In a private interview early in 1831, Calhoun explained that he now favored a constitutional amendment to set aside the proceeds of public land sales in a special fund to pay for building roads, canals, and railroads, on the same routes that he had projected in his War Department reports. He did not specify whether the fund would be administered by the federal government or by the states. [17] Later, as a Senator in 1836 he pushed the distribution-deposit bill at least partly in the expectation that states would build internal improvements with the money received.

As a private citizen, Calhoun strongly encouraged a project for building a railroad to connect Charleston and Cincinnati. And when in January 1837 the Louisville, Cincinnati, and Charleston Railroad company was organized, he was elected one of its 24 directors. But he had misgivings about the proposed route, being convinced that a route farther south, swinging through northern Georgia and on to Nashville and then west to the Mississippi valley was far superior, more practical and politically advantageous in tying West and South together economically. But the Panic of 1837 intervened to make financing impossible, which when added to continued disagreement over route location led Calhoun to resign. He told Hayne he still believed a rail connection with the West vital both economically and politically, but he remained convinced "we ought to look . . . much farther to the West than Cincinnati." [18] A few years later a new South Carolina Railroad, with plans for a rail line by a more southerly route to terminate at Memphis, won Calhoun's full endorsement even though it failed to raise the needed capital.[19]

In 1845 a commerical convention at Memphis brought together delegates from Southern and Mississippi valley states to discuss means of improving transportation in the valley and to the Atlantic seaboard. Calhoun, attending as a South Carolina delegate, was elected president of the convention. Upon taking the chair he delivered a long speech outlining a massive scheme encompassing rail lines from the south Atlantic seaboard to the lower Mississippi with projections of future lines westward to the Pacific, plus improvement of the Mississippi River channel, and a ship canal to the Great Lakes.

On the long disputed question of federal aid, he contended that the steamboat had converted the Mississippi into an inland sea qualifying it for federal aid; as for railroad building the government could assist by granting alternate sections of public domain to the railroads, since such grants would enhance the value of lands retained. Again his hope, in advancing this vast scheme, was to weld South and West closer together. The Memphis proposals were hammered into shape for presentation to Congress, a task that Calhoun himself performed in the Senate on February 3, 1846. He now argued that federal power to improve Mississippi River navigation derived from the interstate commerce clause of the Constitution. He, thereupon, submitted a bill to create a 3-man board of engineers who would make surveys of the Mississippi and its major tributaries to determine how navigation might be improved. The Senate approved, sent the bill to the House, which substituted a much larger river-harbors appropriation bill, which President James K. Polk vetoed in July, 1846.[20]

In summary, federal building of internal improvements remained stymied throughout the 1830's and 1840's under the restrictive impact of Jackson's strict constitutionalism in the Maysville veto (reiterated later by Polk, a Jackson disciple). But the evasive device of federal grants (at first in the form of land, later money grants) to the states came to be adopted—the first instance being Congressional approval in 1850 of the Illinois Central Railroad project, paralleling the Mississippi from Chicago to New Orleans. Federal grants to states who supervised the building of transportation facilities has been for the most part the basis of the arrangement for road-building followed down to the present day.

The Tariff

Periodically, during the Jacksonian era national politics were convulsed by bitter wrangles over the tariff question. The chief policy point at issue was whether the Congress should levy customs duties at such a high level as to bar or discourage foreign manufactured goods from entering the American domestic market. The economic interest involved was clear: American manufacturers wanted a protective tariff to insure to so-called "infant industries" exclusive access to the domestic market. The general effect was to maintain, in the absence of foreign competition, relatively high prices for domestic manufactured products. American agricultural producers, more concerned with foreign markets for their surplus products, generally resisted protective tariff legislation that made more costly the manufactures they had to buy. One exception, among American farmers, encompassed those who produced sugar, hemp, and raw wool, who favored tariffs on those imports that would bar foreign competition in the home market. Shipping interests also opposed protection. During his nationalist years John C. Calhoun as noted above, favored a protective tariff which he believed would strengthen the American economy in the face of a hostile England and would foster manufacturing in South Carolina and the south. By the late 1820's manufacturing had not developed in the

South and economic distress from declining raw cotton prices depressed South Carolina. Calhoun moved to defend Southern economic interests. He focused his attack on the federal protective tariff as the cause of the South Atlantic area's depression. He became convinced that a protective tariff, granting special privilege to one section and one economic class (i.e., manufacturers), was unconstitutional.

The 1828 tariff of "Abominations," as noted above, aroused Calhoun in the "Exposition and Protest" to state that in imposing duties, designed not for producing revenue but for the purpose of "rearing up the industry of one section of the country on the ruins of another," Congress clearly violated the Constitution. "So partial are the effects" of a protective tariff, Calhoun protested, "that its burdens are exclusively on one side and its benefits on the other. It imposes on the agricultural interest of the South, including the Southwest, and that portion of the country particularly engaged in commerce and navigation, the burden not only of sustaining the system itself, but that also of the government." [21]

Since the major portion of the South's chief crops—cotton, tobacco, rice—was exported, the South's economic livelihood depended upon foreign markets. As a staple-producing section, the South's interest lay in selling her crops at as high a price as possible and in buying manufactured goods as cheaply as possible. The tariff, therefore, worked a devastating hardship, because protective policy forced the South "to sell *low:* and on the other hand, . . . to buy *high.* We cannot withstand this double action. Our ruin must follow. In fact, our only permanent and safe remedy is, not from the rise in the price of what we *sell,* . . . but a reduction in the price of what we buy [i.e., manufactured goods], which is prevented by the interference of the Government" in levying protective tariffs.

The tariff hit Southern agricultural producers, Calhoun

estimated, with a 44% increase in cost of tools and supplies, raising production costs proportionately. The effect lessened the South's chance to compete profitably in world markets. Further, a high tariff by making cotton growers more dependent on the home market, consequently placed them at the mercy of manufacturers who pay only such prices as "they choose to give."

Federal tariff acts, asserted the South Carolinian, compelled the South to contribute annually to the government treasury $16,650,000, taken out of "the products of our labor" and "placed . . . at the disposal of Congress," while federal disbursements in the South were less than $2,000,000. This "annual . . . uncompensated draft" of almost $15,000,-000, was patently unjust, not intended by the framers of the Constitution, unconstitutional, and should end by eliminating protective tariffs.[22] (See *Appendix* Doc. No. 13 for fuller text.)

The hope of Calhoun and Southerners that Jackson would push for reduction was pure wishful thinking since nothing in his record suggested it. If anything, Jackson's vague views on the tariff leaned toward protection. His banal, innocuous statement on the tariff as a Senator in 1824 declared, "I am in favor of a judicious examination and revision of it." Later he emphasized using the tariff "for fostering, protecting and preserving within ourselves the means of national defense." Therefore, American iron, copper, hemp, wool, lead as "the grand materials of our national defense" deserved "adequate and fair protection."

In addition to the national defense argument, Jackson found the home market rationale appealing: we should "draw from agriculture the superabundant labor, employ it in . . . manufactures, thereby creating a home market. Take from agriculture . . . six hundred thousand men, women and children, and you at once give a home market for more breadstuffs than all Europe now furnishes us." [23] Consequently, on behalf of national defense and a home market Senator Jackson voted for the 1824 tariff bill. In the 1828 campaign, while not opposing the tariff of "Abominations" (which had been sponsored largely by his partisans in Congress), he reiterated his "judicious tariff" dodge leading Henry Clay to snort, "Well, by———, I am in favor of an injudicious tariff." [24]

In his 1829 message to Congress, Jackson praised the ideal of "free and friendly interchange" of products among nations but declared that since such an ideal was unrealizable we should follow the "principle of fair retaliation" by imposing duties on foreign manufactures to insure "equality between the labor of this and other countries." But such duties should operate within "proper safeguards" and "for the mutual benefit of the Whole United States." In 1830 he added that "While the chief object . . . should be revenue, they [tariff rates] may be so adjusted as to encourage manufactures," "essential to national defense." [25] Whatever the President meant by these bland generalities, he did in successive messages urge "a judicious reduction" of duties. The tariff act of 1832, though it made only minor adjustments, Jackson pronounced fair.

South Carolina's explosive reaction to the 1832 act surprised the President. But when Congress approved the 1833 compromise, Jackson, forgetting his earlier words, approved: "I have always thought that Congress should reduce the Tariff to the wants of the Government." But he labored under no illusion that the protective principle had been abandoned. Pointing to the high valuation on coarse woollens that would drop to only 35% by 1842, he remarked, "If this be not protection, I cannot understand." [26]

Calhoun's strong support for 1833's compromise tariff, as noted above, reflected his genuine desire to avoid an armed clash on Carolina's nullification and his belief that it was an equitable means of moving the country toward a tariff-for-revenue policy. Convinced that preservation of the compromise tariff was necessary for general harmony, he fought off during the 1830's subsequent efforts to nibble it away by piecemeal adjustments of individual rates.[27] He was reluctant to support outright distribution of the surplus for fear its elimination would bring renewed demands for increased tariff duties; hence, his move to make distribution a "loan-deposit" with the states and to extend it only to 1842, the year the compromise tariff rates would reach their minimum level.

When in 1842 a Whig-dominated Congress pushed through a tariff increase, Calhoun fought vigorously against it.[28] Four years later, the proposed Walker tariff, which largely moved away from the protection principle toward a tariff for revenue received Calhoun's hearty support. And even though some high rates got tacked on by amendment during Congressional action, its passage pleased Calhoun as moving well along on the way to the 20% uniform rates he had long urged.[29]

The 30-year tariff controversy had now concluded with enactment of a set of rates that would remain at the relatively low level of 1846 until the days of the Civil War, 15 years in the future.

The President: Popular Leader or Willful Tyrant?

In the endless tariff wrangling, Andrew Jackson played little part. But on most questions he gave new impact and force to the position of President. Running for office in 1828, he announced that if elected he wished to be "President of the nation, not of a party," the President of all the people, not of a faction or fraction. He maintained steadily that the Presidency was an office designed to serve the entire nation, that as the people's choice the President was accountable to all the people for his official acts.

During his eight years in office Jackson contributed to

developing the Presidential office in four principal ways: (1) the President serves as the direct and responsible representative of the people; (2) the President, as the responsible head of the Executive branch, must have full authority to direct his administration with power to appoint, direct, and dismiss his subordinates; (3) the President may veto legislation that he deems unwise and inexpedient and not only unconstitutional; (4) the President functions as leader of a political party based on mass participation.[30]

For some twenty years since the days of Washington and Jefferson, the office of President was in decline until Andrew Jackson revived and reinvigorated its prestige, power, independence, and influence. Injecting that "energy" advocated by Alexander Hamilton as vital to effective administration, Jackson, unconscious of any paradox, achieved the Hamilton end of a vigorous executive by resorting to Jeffersonian appeals.

First he insisted that the President must represent all the people, for the people were the source of his power. Many times Jackson reiterated that "the choice of President is a matter for the people."[31] The old method of nominating by Congressional caucus and the choice of Adams by the House following the 1824 contest, he believed, thwarted the people's will by "cabals" and sinister combinations of "demagogues." In his first annual message and almost every subsequent one, he urged a constitutional amendment to insure the people's "right of electing their Chief Magistrate." Direct election by the people should replace "all intermediate agency," i.e., the electoral college.[32] (See *Appendix* Doc. No. 3-A for fuller text.)

That the President has full power to control and direct his own administration seems today so self-evident as to need no discussion. But Jackson's immediate predecessors had allowed so much leeway to Cabinet officers and other subordinates that they produced divergent courses of action resulting in confusion, misdirection, and internal conflict. In the removal of the Bank deposits struggle, as noted above, the President at length fired his Secretary of the Treasury. When the Senate demanded that he give his reasons for the firing, he refused. "A secretary," the President bluntly asserted, "is merely an executive agent, a subordinate," an arm of the President. More formally, he replied to the Senate that by "the Constitution, the laws and . . . practice" it is unquestioned "that the entire executive power" is vested in the President, "and with it the right of appointing and removing those officers who . . . aid him in the execution of the laws." Since the President is charged with responsibility to execute the laws, he must have full "control" over his subordinates.[33] The principle laid down by Jackson that the President has complete control over his executive department heads has not been challenged since the Senate in 1837 erased its censure of Jackson.[34] (See *Appendix* Doc. No. 8 for fuller text.)

Jackson's appointments often ran into rough going in the Senate, which refused to confirm a large proportion. Fights over confirmations often ran on for months, President and Senate refusing to budge. Senator Webster observed that had it not been for Jackson's great personal popularity the Senate would have killed half of his appointments. But Jackson's stubborn persistence and loyalty to his nominees often paid off. Van Buren, rejected for minister of England, cropped up as Vice President. Roger Taney, refused confirmation by the Senate for the Treasury in 1834, and for associate Supreme Court justice in 1835, was approved one year later as Chief Justice of the United States, in which post he would serve to carry on Jacksonian traditions for the next twenty-eight years.[35]

It sounded almost like Jackson speaking when Taney, as Chief Justice, ruled in the *Charles River Bridge Company*

decision of 1837:   (1) that a charter granted by a state legislature conferred no implied powers on a private corporation
beyond those expressed in the charter; (2) that, since the
"object of all government is to promote the happiness and
prosperity of the community," the state's government retains
full police powers to insure that well being; (3) that, "while
the rights of private property" are carefully respected, "we
must not forget that the community also have rights" especially "in a country like ours, free, active and enterprizing,
continually advancing in numbers and wealth." Here was
constitutional sanction for the Jacksonian ideal of a competitive, unhampered economic system with opportunity open to
all, special privilege to none.

However "co-equal" the Executive might be in relation to
the other branches, Old Hickory recognized there were limits
to Presidential independence and discretion. He asserted that
Congress should make "definite appropriations," not loose,
discretionary ones, and for these the Executive should be held
to "a rigid adherence . . . in disposing of public moneys."
The President's tenure should be constitutionally limited,
Jackson recommending as Jefferson had earlier a single term
of no more than six years.[36]

The role of the President as leader of his political party
Jackson came to appreciate fully. His skillful distribution of
offices served to strengthen his own political support. Putting
it in general terms, he later expressed the realities of politics: "It is certain that whichever party makes the President
must give direction to his administration. . . . No one can
carry on this Government without support, and the Head of
it must rely on the party" that elected him. "I have labored
to reconstruct this great [Democratic] Party and bring the
popular power to bear with full influence upon the Government by securing its permanent ascendency. . . . It is as true
in politics as it is in morals, that those who are not for us
are against us." [37]

Understanding the need of party organization and support for a successful administration, Jackson did much to fashion the Democratic party out of diverse, often incongrous elements—Western farmers, Eastern workingmen, intellectuals and illiterates, conservative merchants and radical social reformers, political spoilsmen and pure idealists. In the Bank War he succeeded in combining and directing an effective political coalition that emerged as the Democratic Party. His skill as party leader in appealing to popular feeling in touching the emotions of the voters set a superbly impressive example of exercise of power through party politics.

As the public service came to be politicized under the impact of patronage distributed for political effect, the high tone of the public service, set in the Federalist age when a gentlemen served from a sense of duty and a desire to serve, deteriorated. On the more positive side the Jacksonian era introduced many citizens to their government for the first time, if not as office holders, at least as political party participants. The continuing democratic process of political education in self government was well begun. Jackson's colorful, driving personality captured the imagination of many who previously remained indifferent to politics and thrust them into the vortex of political action. But even political democracy might be pushed too far, Jackson came to concede.

After retirement Jackson viewed the Whigs' hoopla Harrison-hard cider campaign of 1840 as disgraceful, tending "to bring our republican institutions into perfect contempt by" telling the "world there are none fit to rule a representative Government but those who drink sour Cider and live in Log cabins." [38] The Whigs had shifted the shoe to the other foot. But Jackson could not shrug off his own responsibility for bringing American party politics to such a state.

Calhoun of course had no direct part in developing the office of President, since he never occupied it, much to his disappointment. But he did comment often and caustically upon Jackson's use of Presidential power during the 1830's. Already angry over having been rejected by Jackson and thereby losing any chance of succeeding and bitter over the nullification controversy, Calhoun was aroused to fury by the Presidents' proposed Force Bill in 1833. This "Bloody Bill," as Calhoun called it, would repeal the Constitution and "forever put down our beautiful federal system and rear on its ruins consolidated government." Liberty itself would be murdered if Congress acted to put "at the disposal of the President the army and navy, and . . . the entire militia which enables him to subject every man in the United States to martial law . . . and compel him to embrue his hand in his brother's blood." [19] To place such staggering power in the hands of the President would enthrone brutal despotism. To say, as Jackson said, that the law must be enforced, Calhoun characterized as the same as saying "The imperial edict must be executed." (See *Appendix* Doc. No. 14 for fuller text.) When Calhoun's ranting speech was reported to the White House, Jackson remarked, "Many people believe Calhoun to be demented." [40] Adams, observing him at close range, commented: "Calhoun looks like a man racked with furious passions and stung with disappointed ambition, as undoubtedly he is." [41]

The Force Bill's concentration of power in the hands of the Executive, especially a man as rash and impetuous as Jackson, was to invite catastrophe for the country, in Calhoun's opinion: "The spirit of liberty is dead . . . [under] the bloody act." [42] When the President fired Treasury Secretary Duane and ordered removal of deposits from the Bank, it was only further proof to Calhoun of the usurpation of power by King Andrew. Supporting the Senate resolution of censure he joined vigorously in denouncing the grab "on the part of the executive to seize on the power of congress, and to unite in the President the power of the sword and the purse." [43]

Alarmed over the growing use of Presidential patronage for political purposes, Calhoun got the Senate to establish a special Committee on the Executive Patronage to seek ways to reduce it.

As Chairman of this Committee, Calhoun reported extensively on the abuses and evils of the spoils systems and urged several corrective measures. At one point he declared that in his long years in government he had never "conceived that such rottenness, such corruption, such abominable violations of trust could ever exist in any of its departments. . . . It may exceed anything in the history of the rottenest ages of the Roman Empire." [44]

His report noted also a big increase of men holding office at the will of the President, serving as "corrupt sycophants and supple instruments of power" to perpetuate the President's domination. But the Senate failed to act on remedies proposed to reduce the patronage. [45]

When Jackson's diplomacy produced a rupture of relations with France and threatened war, Calhoun brooded that King Andrew in a fiendish "desire to retain power" was brewing "a French war." Jackson had earlier announced that nothing could induce him to accept a third term as President, except a war with France—and here now was proof of his tenacious desire for unchecked, perpetual power. [46] An attempt on Jackson's life by a deranged man in 1835 led to a further bitter exchange. Taken home "looking very ill and weak," Jackson was still strong enough to charge Calhoun and Poindexter with inciting the assault. It was their intemperate ravings in the Senate, charged the President, that had stirred this fanatic to believe that by murdering Jackson he would rid the country of a cruel tyrant. [47]

When it was learned that Jackson, giving up any third term notions, was planning to name Martin Van Buren as his hand-picked successor in the Presidency, Calhoun gloomily expressed his great "alarm" over "the attempt of the Chief Magistrate to appoint his successor. Should it succeed, resting [as it does] on the avowed subserviency of the nominee to the will of the President . . . it would afford conclusive proof of the consumation of Executive usurpation over the Government and the Constitution" and Presidential "power will forever silence the popular voice." [48]

Speaking to the Senate on Jackson's "Protest" of the censure resolution, Calhoun uncharacteristically shouted vituperation at the President: "Infatuated man! blinded by ambition . . . dark, lawless and insatiable ambition!" The old General had established not only one-man rule but a monarchy. On the federal payroll 60,000 employees, joined to 100,-000 pensioners dependent on the federal Treasury—surely King Andrew I was building a despotic dynasty. [49] His corrupt undermining of free, constitutional government must be resisted by all honest patriots by all means available.

Much of this was rhetoric for political effect, part was personal animosity born of jealousy and frustration. But there Calhoun was genuinely concerned over the twin evil trends toward an all-powerful, consolidated national government under the dominance of an omnipotent President. Whether Calhoun, had he made it to the Executive chair, would have conducted the office differently from Jackson, cannot be known. He desperately wanted to be President and sought the position time and again—though he had a fair chance in 1824, only to be disappointed; and again in 1832 to be disappointed because of the break with Jackson; and hopefully trying once more in 1843–44 when prospects appeared so favorable that he was induced to prepare his own campaign biography, only to have his expectations cruelly dashed a third time.

Early in 1837 during Senate debate of a land bill, Calhoun raised questions about "high officers of Government" using loans from pet banks to speculate in public lands, and was reported as saying, "Was it not notorious that the President . . . himself has been connected with the purchase of public lands." Reading these words in the *Congressional Globe*, Jackson fired off a brusque demand that Calhoun retract or lay charges before the House so that the President might formally respond. Calhoun had Jackson's letter read to the Senate followed by a reading of the more accurate report in the *National Intelligencer*, showing that Calhoun had not named the President, but only some executive officials. From this he launched into a fierce denunciation of Jackson's past despotic actions concluding that "I, as a legislator, . . . can condemn his acts freely." Here again was Calhoun seeking to protect the "purity" of the republic against the corroding corruption he was convinced was spreading under the Jacksonian "despotism." [50]

IX Manifest Destiny and Conflict

Expansion: Florida, Texas, War with Mexico

A FIRM BELIEVER in the virtue of the republic and an aggressive Westerner, Andrew Jackson sought to extend America's boundaries, where possible, by absorbing adjacent territory. "Manifest Destiny," he was certain, had fated the nation to expand westward to the Pacific shore. America's mission was clear—to spread liberty and the blessings of popular government to new areas and peoples. In his early years he cheered Jefferson's purchase of Louisiana, for possession of New Orleans assured the nation's spread in addition to opening an outlet to the sea for farmers of the Great Mississippi Valley. And west of the Great River trails beckoned Americans to occupy the vast land beyond. Southward, West Florida dropped into outstretched American hands. And Jackson's own military forays, as noted above, resulted in adding the entire Florida peninsula to the United States.

John Calhoun also was an aggressive expansionist during his early years in Congress, boasting that Canada could be swiftly grasped in the War of 1812. He did not, despite the imbroglio with Jackson, disapprove the General's invasion of Florida but only his exceeding orders of superiors in seizing the Spanish forts and executing two British subjects. He heartily welcomed acquisition of Florida in the 1819 treaty. Erasing that troublesome border eased Calhoun's task as Secretary of War to defend the United States. As Vice President 1825–1832 he had little opportunity to speak on expansionist questions.

When American pioneers under Stephen Austin's lead surged into Mexican-held Texas during the 1820's, Jackson was pleased that many Tennesseeans joined the migration. He was less than pleased, however, when the Adams administration concluded a treaty with Mexico in 1828, confirming the Sabine River, Texas's eastern border as the United States-Mexican boundary line.

In an effort to rectify this blunder, Jackson dispatched a free-wheeling operator, Anthony Butler, to Mexico City with authority to offer as much as $5,000,000 for Texas extending south to a line along the watershed between the Nueces and Rio Grande Rivers. Butler quickly succeeded in alienating the Mexican government with such a boastful, insolent campaign that Jackson exclaimed to his secretary, "A. Butler. What a Scamp!" [1] But the President kept Butler on in Mexico City with a virtual blank check to buy Texas and secure a transcontinental boundary from the Rio Grande north to and then west along the 37th parallel to the Pacific. Such a line would deliver San Francisco Bay into the possession of the United States. "The acquisition of Texas," Jackson instructed Butler in 1835, "is becoming every day an object of more importance to us." [2]

Meanwhile, Jackson's friend and early political backer, Sam Houston, having inexplicably resigned the governorship of Tennessee and suddenly parted from his bride of a few months, turned up living with the Cherokee tribe in the Indian country just north of Texas. After a few years there, he drifted across the line into Texas itself, where his previous military experience was soon put to use.

In 1836 Americans in Texas revolted against Mexico and declared independence. Jackson was disturbed by the news. Word reached Washington of two Tennesseeans he had known for years—old political foe, legendary Davy Crockett, killed at the Alamo, and Sam Houston now leading a Texas army. Hope for buying Texas was dashed. When Jackson ordered General Gaines to move American troops to the Texas border in an action reminiscent of the Florida exploit of eighteen years earlier, he was charged with aiding the Texans; some critics even alleged he had sent Houston to foment revolt. But Jackson maintained an impartial neutrality. When Austin sent a request for American help, Jackson noted on the back of the letter: "The writer does not reflect that we have a treaty with Mexico and our national faith is pledged to support it. The Texians [sic] before declaring themselves Independent, which has aroused and united all Mexico against them, ought to have pondered well; it was a rash and premature act; our neutrality must be faithfully maintained." [3]

After the Texans won a stunning victory at San Jacinto in April 1836, captured Mexican President Santa Ana and forced him to sign a treaty recognizing Texan independence, Jackson pursued an official course of "watchful waiting." To Santa Ana he wrote, "We cannot interfere . . . with the policy of other nations." [4] The President's official "hands off" policy was especially notable because his private feelings favored immediate diplomatic recognition and probably annexation. But publicly he gave no sign, keeping such views to himself, because of two considerations. First, sectional antagonism, already inflamed over the slavery question, especially abolitionist propaganda in the mails, would be further aroused over proposals to annex Texas as a slave state. Second, he wished to avoid rocking the political boat with his own hand-picked candidate Martin Van Buren running in the upcoming Presidential election of 1836. As the election neared, he warned Tennessee's Governor, we must "maintain a strict neutrality." [5] Therefore, Jackson announced he would be guided by Congress' decision in regard to Texas.

In the Senate, Calhoun declared there were "powerful reasons" not only for recognition of Texas but for her speedy admission to the Union. On July 1 he cast his vote for a resolution calling for recognition, which passed the Senate.[6] But the President uncharacteristically hesitated to act. Even after Van Buren's election, Jackson's message to Congress in December 1836 cautioned that recognition "could scarcely be regarded as consistent with that prudent reserve with which we have heretofore held ourselves bound to treat all similar questions. . . . we should stand aloof" until either Mexico or a "great foreign" power moves to recognize Texas' independence.[7]

Such strange procrastination in the usually decisive President stemmed from three factors: his desire to avoid increasing Northern hostility even more over the prospect of adding slaveholding Texas to the Union; his sensitivity to his successor Van Buren, who should be allowed to resolve the question in his own way; his wish for personal quiet during the few remaining months in office (his health was already weakening). At any rate, Jackson did nothing. Only when Congress appropriated funds to establish diplomatic relations did he on his last day in office appoint a diplomatic chargé to the Republic of Texas.[8] Van Buren, upon taking office, made no move for annexation, and in 1838 Texas withdrew her request, much to Calhoun's annoyance.

But the 1840's would see a different story. The Texas question became tangled in the web of Presidential politics and particularly in Calhoun's personal ambitions. Van Buren having lost 1840's election and the subsequent Tyler administration proving unpopular, Calhoun by 1843 came to believe that "now is the time . . . [for] my name to be presented for the next presidency." Thereupon he resigned his Senate seat. South Carolina's legislature formally nominated him for President. He visited political backers in Virginia, corresponded widely with Democratic supporters in other states suggesting campaign strategy, and prepared material for an anonymous autobiography published in 1843—a self-eulogy which defended his career from current charges of inconsistency. It even spoke in moderate tones concerning Jackson, now the retired patron saint of the Democratic party, whose nomination Calhoun coveted. A collection of Calhoun's speeches, omitting some early nationalist speeches that might now prove embarrassing, was published to accompany the autobiography.[9]

Prospects were bright. "It seems to me," wrote a supporter, "Calhoun must be the man unless he kicks over the pail of water, of which there is much danger." [10] Calhoun's optimism soared: New England, he was sure, and probably New York, along with a solid South, would put him in. Texas annexation would work heavily in his favor. But as 1843 advanced, his cause faltered as Calhoun men lost influence to Van Burenites in both Virginia and New York Democratic councils. Hope still persisted that even if he did not gain the Democratic nomination, he could run as an independent, produce a Democratic-Whig stalemate at the polls, and win the runoff in the House. A strong Texas and anti-tariff stand would make him a sure winner.

This strategy might possibly have worked, but Calhoun proceeded to muff his chance. In a letter to his South Carolina campaign committee he expressed reasons for withholding his name from the Democratic convention scheduled to meet in Baltimore in 1844. He did not intend the letter for public consumption. But the Charleston *Mercury's* editor, acting upon the letter, dropped Calhoun's name from its masthead where it had run for months as the *Mercury's* candidate. Virginia supporters, assuming that this signaled Calhoun's withdrawal from the race, now withdrew his name from the state convention and turned to Van Buren, much to the South Carolinian's dismay and irritation.[11] By this curious twist,

Calhoun "kicked over the pail," but, as a recent biographer notes, "the pail was empty," for it now appeared Van Buren would beat him for the nomination.[12]

When Van Buren shortly issued a public statement opposing annexation of Texas, Southern Democrats were stunned. From his Hermitage retirement, Jackson (who had already published a letter urging annexation) now endorsed Tennessee's James K. Polk. The Democrats nominated him, after Van Buren failed to capture the needed two-thirds convention majority. Their platform called for a low tariff, an Independent Treasury, "reoccupation of Oregon" and "reannexation of Texas." In the fall election Polk would oppose the Whigs' Clay.

Meanwhile Calhoun had accepted appointment as President Tyler's Secretary of State, when the previous Secretary was killed by a gun explosion on board the USS *Princeton.* He continued the negotiations already under way and swiftly concluded a treaty to annex Texas. His haste in making the treaty stemmed from apprehension over British moves regarding Texas. Britain, which eleven years earlier had abolished slavery in her colonies, wanted an independent Texas as a source of cheap raw cotton, a market from British manufactures and a buffer against further American expansion southwestward. But she also was seeking an end of slavery in Texas. Realizing the Texas treasury was empty, Britain offered needed funds if Texas would free its slaves. At the same time Britain urged Mexico to grant full recognition of Texas independence, which would be jointly guaranteed by Britain and France. Rumors circulated in Washington that Britain's real design was to annex Texas herself.

Calhoun's Texas treaty went to the Senate in mid-April 1844. Earlier the Secretary of State had argued for annexation on grounds of national security and markets it would afford Northern producers. Now, in diplomatic correspondence replying to the British Foreign Secretary's expressed desire for world-wide aboliton of slavery, Calhoun grounded the case for annexation of Texas on the necessity to defend slavery from British abolition, making it appear solely to the advantage of American slaveholders. The confidential letter leaked accidentally to the New York press, and an outraged cry of protest arose in the North. Clay and Van Buren followed with public statements repudiating annexation. A few days later, the Senate rejected the treaty 35–16.[13]

The Democrats, in nominating Polk and coupling Texas and Oregon annexation, thereby effected a Northwestern-Southern alliance (what Calhoun had sought for years) that produced victory at the polls, presumably indicating popular approval of Texas annexation. By February 1845 Congress passed a joint resolution to annex Texas, signed by Tyler on March 1. Calhoun supported the joint resolution, a move clearly inconsistent with his oft-stated strict constructionist views.

Thus, despite Calhoun's mishandling of the treaty presentation, Texas joined the United States under a constitutional dodge. By a curious twist of fate, it was Andrew Jackson's nephew, Andrew Jackson Donelson, whom Calhoun sent as American minister to Texas and to whom just before leaving the State Department he dispatched instructions for arranging the formal details of annexation.[14]

During his final days at the Hermitage, Andrew Jackson was cheered by news of Texas' entry into the Union. After leaving office, he had become fully convinced that "Texas [is] of the utmost importance to the safety of the U. States" in defending our southwest border from a "hostile power" (meaning England); the nation must obtain Texas "peaceably if we can, forcibly if we must," he wrote a friend.[15] Since it helped in "extending the area of freedom," he applauded the passage of the joint resolution.[16] He was pleased, too, when

Congress in 1844 adopted a bill reimbursing him the $1,000 fine (plus interest) he had paid for contempt of Judge Hall's court order in New Orleans back in 1815. He readily accepted the check for $2,732, which would enable him to meet some of the pressing debts that seemed ever present in his declining years.[17] About the same time Frank Blair extended him $10,-000 of credit, letting it be known repayment was not expected.

In regard to the Oregon country, Calhoun contended in the Senate as early as 1842 that the American title was clear at least to the 49th parallel but urged a policy of "wise and masterly inactivity." The 1817 joint occupation agreement could be continued with impunity, for increasing migration of Americans into the area would in time cement America's claim. As Secretary of State, he conducted negotiations with the British minister, developing a convincing case for American title to Oregon based on Grey's 1792 discovery of the Columbia River, the Lewis and Clark exploration, American settlement at the mouth of the Columbia in 1812, and American acquisiton by treaty of French and Spanish claims. Scoffing at a British offer to settle on the Columbia as a compromise line, Calhoun simply stalled, comfortable in the knowledge that time was on our side.[18]

Calhoun realized the importance of Oregon and California in establishing America's position on the Pacific, which he considered crucial, and in developing trade with the Orient. William M. Gwin (later a California Senator) said that it was Calhoun who interested him in California and prophesied that San Francisco would be to the Pacific coast what New York was to the Atlantic.[19]

Calhoun hoped to remain Secretary of State under the incoming President, but Polk offered him the mission to London instead. The South Carolinian declined and sadly handed the Department on to successor James Buchanan, who in time settled the Oregon dispute on the 49th parallel as earlier

proposed by Calhoun. Returning home, Calhoun was elected
again to a Senate seat, which he assumed in December 1845
and would hold until his death five years later.

In the 1846 Senate debate on Oregon, Calhoun urged moderation and conciliation rather than jingoistic insistence on
the extreme claim of 54° 40′. He succeeded in converting an
originally bellicose resolution into an authorization for the
President to compromise—the course ultimately adopted in
the subsequent British-American treaty fixing the 49th parallel boundary. At the same time Britain's repeal of her Corn
Law duties on American wheat paved the way for reduction
of American duties in the Walker tariff of 1846 and improved
relations.

Relieved that what he considered a serious threat of war
with England had been averted, he now broke with the Polk
administration over war with Mexico. Polk's negotiations
with Mexico to purchase New Mexico and California having
broken down in the spring of 1846, the President ordered
Zachary Taylor's troops to move into the disputed area lying
between the Nueces and Rio Grande Rivers. Here a clash
with Mexican forces occurred. When the news reached
Washington on May 9, Polk amended his already prepared
message asking Congress to declare war on Mexico changing
it to read that because "Mexico has passed the boundary of
the United States, invaded our territory and shed American
blood on American soil," there now existed a state of war,
which he demanded that Congress recognize.

Calhoun, who had deplored Polk's provocative orders to
Taylor, now labored in vain to forestall a war declaration.
Failing, he refused to vote on the final question. The President's action in provoking conflict Calhoun viewed as a naked
violation of the Constitution and (reminiscent of charges
against Jackson) executive usurpation of Congress' power to
declare war.[20] In the Senate Calhoun delivered heavy denun-

ciations of the war. In summary, his opposition rested on two grounds. One, war would as always breed rampant nationalism leading to extension of federal powers, centralization, and consolidation, which he had regularly resisted since Jackson's day. As he neatly phrased it, "Mexico is to us the forbidden fruit; the penalty of eating it would be to subject our institutions to political death." Secondly, he opposed the war because it would, he correctly predicted, lead to annexing new territory that would upset the delicate balance between free and slave states and tip the Senate scales against the South, which would be plunged thereby into the desperate position of a permanent minority.[21] He had already become convinced that any area that might be won from Mexico was unsuitable for slave labor, and hence future states carved from it would inevitably enter the Union as free states. The war was only a few months old when the Wilmot Proviso, seeking to bar slavery from any territory obtained from Mexico, injected a new, alarming note and aroused Calhoun to a renewed defense of the South's "peculiar institution" and of Southerners' rights. His fears were realized in 1848 when the Treaty of Guadalupe Hidalgo ending the war transferrred to the United States the huge area of land extending westward from Texas to California, a region roughly the equivalent of one-third of the United States.

"The Peculiar Institution": Slavery Attacked and Defended

As a Southern plantation slaveholder, Jackson gave no more thought to the moral aspects of slave-owning than did his neighbors, who merely accepted the "peculiar institution" as part of the natural order of things. In his early years he frequently bought and sold slaves, and his correspondence reveals frequent instructions to his agents in these transactions. He considered slavery a convenient, inexpensive labor

arrangement for getting done the work of large scale plantation agriculture, which afforded advantages of subdivision,
specialization, and close supervision of labor. Agitation
against slavery, especially by outsiders, he viewed as malicious, proposals to abolish slavery as downright dangerous.

During the first national airing of the question—Congress'
debate over admitting Missouri as a slave state in 1820—Old
Hickory commented to his nephew: "The Missouri question
. . . has agitated the public mind, and what I sincerely regret
and never expected . . . [is] the entering wedge to separate
the Union. It is even more wicked, it will excite the [slaves]
. . . to insurrection and massacre. It is a question of political
ascendancy and power, and Eastern interests are determined
to succeed regardless of the consequences. . . . They will find
the Southern and Western states equally resolved to support
their constitutional rights. I hope I may not live to see the
evils that must grow out of the wicked designs of demagogues. . . ." [22]

Later, as President, the Old Hero, who regarded slave
ownership as a property right guaranteed by the Constitution, instructed his Secretary of State to seek a British treaty
"whereby our citizens may reclaim their fugitive slaves from
Canady [sic]." [23]

During the nullification controversy of 1832–33 Jackson
came to believe (as did Calhoun, too) that the real, though
unspoken, issue was slavery, not the tariff. After the crisis
passed, he noted: "The nullifiers in the South intend to blow
up a storm on the slave question. . . . This ought to be met,
for . . . these men would do any act to destroy this Union
and form a southern confederacy bounded north by the Poto-
mac river." [24] Twenty-eight years later, his apprehension
would be tragically realized.

In January 1831 the first issues of William Lloyd Garrison's uncompromising abolitionist paper, *The Liberator*,

appeared. Seven months later Nat Turner's slave uprising killed 51 whites in southeastern Virginia. Southerners with an obsessive fear of a general slave revolt placed the blame for inciting Turner squarely on the abolitionists.

As abolitionists stepped up agitation against slavery, President Jackson reproached them as "monsters" seeking "to stir up amongst the South the horror of a servile war." He deplored the mailing of abolitionist tracts into the South and approved Postmaster Kendall's suggestion "verbally to the postmaster in [Charleston, S.C.] . . . *'to deliver to no person these inflamatory papers* but to those who are really subscribers' . . . ; and few men will be willing to acknowledge . . . subscribing for such . . . horrid and wicked" publications.[25] But the law must be upheld. He denounced a mob that broke into Charleston's post office and burned bundles of abolitionist mail. "The spirit of mob-law," he warned, would "ere long become as great an evil as servile war."

In his December 1835 message, Jackson condemned the "unconstitutional and wicked attempts" of "misguided persons" to circulate inflammatory appeals "calculated to produce all the horrors of a servile war." [26] His recommendation that Congress act to check such pamphlets from being mailed into Southern states was referred by the Senate to a special committee headed by John C. Calhoun. In February 1836 Calhoun returned to the Senate a report embodying an elaborate defense of slavery and recommending legislation. The South Carolinian stood in a position of curious contradiction. To allow Congress to legislate exclusion of materials from the mails was to employ a power that Calhoun denied had been granted under the Constitution—and which civil libertics spokesmen also contended would violate the Constitution's free speech guarantee. Calhoun's bill proposed a cagey straddle of the dilemma: no local postmaster in any state should receive or transmit any material relating to slavery which was addressed to a person residing in a state whose laws forbade delivery of such material (many Southern states had already adopted such legislation).

Thus, Calhoun's proposal, appearing to leave the matter in the states' hands, overlooked the fact that local postmasters were federal government officials and their decisions on what was mailable would constitute a clear interference with the mails (and freedom of expression). The result would be as many different interpretations of what could be mailed as there were different state laws on the subject. In the end, neither Calhoun's proposal nor Jackson's, which would have authorized the Post Master General to instruct local postmasters, was adopted.[27] Since no federal policy was set, the decision in fact remained with local postmasters as to what mail could be transmitted and delivered, which suited Calhoun well enough.

Upon bowing out of office, Jackson gave his fellow countrymen a fatherly warning against "systematic efforts" to "sow the seed of discord" and to "excite the *South* against the *North* and the *North* against the *South*" by forcing "into the controversy the most delicate and exciting topics." Continued agitation of the slavery question would lead to "mutual suspicions" and "fatal divisions."[28] Much as Jackson wished to submerge it, the irrepressible slavery issue was even then shouldering its way rudely into national politics —as Texas, use of the mails, and the Congressional "gag rule" all demonstrated.

During the Missouri compromise debates Calhoun had brushed aside the slavery controversy as a minor annoyance. By the 1830's he was fully roused to the threat posed by the abolitionist crusade to the South's security. He proceeded to the most contrived lengths to construct defenses for the "peculiar institution." In doing so, he aroused greater resentment in the North and unwittingly added more to the appeal and strength of the abolition drive than if he had left the question untouched. From 1830 on he grew increasingly rigid in slavery's defense.

During the tariff debate of 1832, Calhoun believed the tariff merely the occasion of the controversy; "the peculiar domestic institution of the Southern States" formed the root of the clash. Since slavery, joined with climate and soil, placed the South in a minority position vulnerable to the will of a Congressional majority, Southerners must resort to "the protective power in the reserved rights of the States" or "in the end be forced to rebel, or submit to have their permanent interests sacrificed, their domestic institutions subverted by Colonization and other schemes [abolition], and themselves and their children reduced to wretchedness." [29]

To defend slavery in a society stressing the Christian ethic and democratic principles of liberty, equality, and justice pushed Calhoun into an increasingly tight dilemma, tangling the "man of logic" in a snarl of illogical contradictions. In the 1820's moderate Southerners supported colonization, a scheme for compensated emancipation followed by voluntary Negro migration to Liberia, established on the west African coast by the American Colonization Society in 1827. Turner's insurrection of 1831, Virginia's rejecting gradual emancipation and the rising stridency of Northern abolitionists fueled a more rigid Southern defense in a new Congressional debate. In 1836 two disputes lighted the fire—abolitionist petitions flooding into Congress and mailing of abolitionist literature into the South.

On the first, as petitions calling for the end of slavery in the District of Columbia deluged Congress, the Senate, under Calhoun's urging, resorted to the parliamentary dodge of moving to refer such petitions to a committee and then tabling the motion to refer without permitting any discussion of the question. The House, taking a further step, adopted a "gag rule" that refused even to receive petitions relating to slavery. In adopting this course, Calhoun and his Southern colleague gave indirect aid to the abolitionists since many Northerners, previously indifferent to the slavery question, became aroused over this assault on free speech and listened now to abolition pleas.

On barring abolitionist literature from the mails Calhoun's repressive proposal has been discussed above. But his supporting speech was even more significant. In this speech, followed by many other speeches and writings, he developed his full-scale defense of slavery. In attempting to rationalize away the moral wrong of Negro bondage, Calhoun's defense shows the extremes of self deception and delusion the human mind (even a first-rate mind like Calhoun's) can resort to in justifying something it wants to believe. Calhoun argued: "I hold that in the present state of civilization where two races of different origin . . . color . . . physical differences, as well as intellectual, are brought together, the relation now existing in the slave-holding States between the two is, instead of an evil, a good—a positive good. . . . There has never yet existed a wealthy and civilized society in which one portion of the community did not . . . live on the labor of the other. . . . I fearlessly assert that the existing relation between the two races in the South, against which these blind fanatics [abolitionists] are waging war, forms the most solid and durable foundation on which to rear free and stable political institutions." [30]

The rest of the country must understand the South's absolute rejection of abolition: "It is to us a vital question," involving "not only our liberty, but . . . existence itself. The relation between the two races" in the South "has existed for two centuries . . . and has entered into and modified all our institutions. None other can be substituted. We will not permit it to be destroyed." [31]

The abolition crusade, directed by "ferocious zealots, blinded by fanaticism," and "organized throughout every section of the non-slaveholding States," commanding "almost unlimited funds, and . . . a powerful press" is "turned against the domestic institutions, and the peace and security of the South." If Congress should attempt abolition, the South must resist by force. "There would be to us one alternative—to triumph or perish as a people." [12] Continued agitation, as Calhoun saw it, would bring disunion and bloody civil war.

On this question no compromise was possible. He hoped moderate Northerners would restrain the abolitionists, but he did not expect it; therefore "it rests with ourselves [Southerners] to meet and repel them" with no aid from "this Government" or a "political party . . . If we do not defend ourselves, none will defend us. . . ." [13] (See *Appendix*, Doc. No. 17 for fuller text.)

Many Southern cohorts, who just as zealously defended slavery, believed Calhoun's tactics were mistaken, in fighting on the tangential mail and petition questions; they would reserve their fire until a more crucial issue arose. But Calhoun characteristically was certain that he was right, that aboliton attacks had to be met at the outset, "at the frontier" as he put it. In the case of the protective tariff, when he and his state had supported protection earlier in 1816, he had learned that it proved embarrassing and awkward to reverse position and to oppose it a dozen years later. Since slavery was more crucial to Southern security, abolition must be met immediately and opposed on the highest possible grounds.

In preparing the highest possible grounds, Calhoun presented to the Senate in December 1837 six resolutions on the status of slavery in the Union. The first four declared the main purpose of the constitutional "compact" was to provide domestic security among the states, that slavery was a domestic institution falling under the sole authority of the states where it existed and could not be interfered with by attacks from other states, which the general government as the agent of all the states was required to fend off. The other two denied that Congress had power to abolish slavery in the District of Columbia or in federal territories or to refuse to annex additional territory (meaning Texas) because of the slavery question. Calhoun won a smashing victory for his constitutional position and for his personal prestige when his resolutions (except the sixth relating to Texas) were adopted by large majorities.[34]

Calhoun's success here stemmed in part from his having reached an understanding with the Van Buren administration, thereby ending the Calhoun flirtation with the Whigs since 1833. Van Buren's Northern Democrats hence provided a sizable part of the majorities in support of Calhoun's Senate resolution. Calhoun delivered on his part of the agreement by speaking for the administration's plan for total separation of the government from private banking. This Independent Treasury plan, enacted by Congress in 1840, established branches of the federal Treasury in major cities where they handled tax receipts, custody of funds, paying of pensions and bills—performing in fact the public functions of the old Bank but not engaging in making loans or issuing paper money.

In a strong position by 1840, Calhoun devoted the remaining ten years of his public career to bolstering the South's position and defending slavery by every means he could command. For example, his labors, as noted above, helped add Texas to the Union as a slave-holding state to maintain the free-slave state balance. During the war with Mexico, introduction of the fateful Wilmot Proviso to ban slavery's extension into new territory obtained in the war roused Calhoun. The Provisio passed the House several times but met defeat regularly in the Senate.

Calhoun fought savagely against the Proviso, arguing that the federal government, as agent of the states, held western territories (before statehood) in the capacity of a trustee of common possessions of the states. Hence, Congress could not bar a citizen of a state from taking his constitutionally-sanctioned property (read, slaves) into such territories. And neither could the people of a territory, because a territory as the creation of Congress has no more power than its creator (Congress). By this reasoning Calhoun rejected the new popular sovereignty proposal, advanced in the late 1840's by Lewis Cass, to authorize the territorial residents to vote whether to allow or prohibit slavery. "Ours is a Federal Constitution, of which the States are parties, and they—the 'States United'—own jointly the territories." As "a Southern man and a slaveholder—a kind and merciful one I trust," "I would [not] . . . give up one inch of our equality." [35]

Although the Proviso was beaten, the question immediately cropped up again. On a bill to organize a government for Oregon Territory barring slavery, Calhoun fought vigorously but in vain against its passage in 1848. In his long, opposing speech he traced the trend toward consolidated government and the corresponding, increasing fanaticism of Northern abolitionism that accompanied it; denounced both trends as endangering the Union; and urged Northerners to halt aggressions upon the South,—excluding slavery from Oregon was only the latest in a long train of injuries to the South. [36]

When in December 1848 the House debated a resolution to end the slave trade in the District of Columbia, some 69 of the 121 Southerners in Congress caucused in protest and appointed a committee with Calhoun as chairman to prepare an address to the people. The "Southern Address," which Calhoun himself wrote, once again traced at length the long series of abolitionist-inspired Northern aggressions against slavery and the South—the Missouri Compromise, open flouting of the federal fugitive slave law, continued demands for emancipation, the recent Oregon bill, and now the proposed abolition of the District's slave trade. The South should take no more. All Southerners should now unite in their own defense to give the North "a pause" that hopefully "may lead to a change . . . of policy that may quietly and peacefully terminate this long conflict between the sections." [17] Adopted by a rump session of Southerners on January 22, 1849, it carried 48 signatures when published a week later. See *Appendix*, Doc. No. 18 for fuller text. Calhoun's exertions on the Address, in the Senate and Southern caucus, left him so exhausted that he collapsed suddenly on the Senate floor January 19. Laid up for a week, he never fully recovered from this heart seizure.

A year later he prodded himself into his final effort to protect his beloved South. Clay's 1850 compromise proposed to (1) admit California as a free state, (2) organize territorial governments in New Mexico and Utah without restriction on slavery, (3) tighten fugitive slave legislation, (4) end the slave trade (not slavery) in the District, (5) reduce Texas's size in return for federal payment of Texas's debt. Calhoun prepared an elaborate, forceful speech in opposition. But his physical condition had so deteriorated that he was too weak to deliver it personally. On March 4, 1850, he entered the Senate chamber holding the arm of a friend—weak, feeble, sunken cheeks and long white hair giving him a ghostly appearance. He struggled to his feet, asked the Senate's indulgence to have Senator James Mason read the speech, then sank into his seat, pulling his long cloak like a shroud about him, sitting lifeless —only his brilliant eyes still darting fire from his wasted shell.

"I have, Senators, believed from the first that the agitation of the subject of slavery would, it not prevented . . . end in disunion. . . . The agitation has" continued unchecked "until . . . it can no longer be denied that the Union is in danger." We face "the gravest question . . . how can the union be preserved?"

How had the crisis come about? Principally, as Calhoun saw it, because the original equilibrium between the slaveholding and nonslaveholding sections had not been fairly maintained. The North's rapid growth gave it control of the House and the electoral college. To admit California as a free state would further upset the balance by giving the North control of the Senate, and placing the South in a permanent minority position.

The South had been barred from great parts of the western territories—slavery bans in the Ordinance of 1787, the Missouri Compromise law and later legislation. The government's tariff policy had built the economic and political power of the North. The original confederation of states had been perverted into a consolidated government to the North's benefit. The abolition drive had already gone far toward dissolving the Union, which could survive only on the basis of "mutual trust and affection," by snapping many of "the cords which [bind] . . . together one common Union." The national religious denominations of Methodist and Baptist had already split; political parties were rapidly being sectionalized. Soon, the only means of holding the Union together would be force, but a Union by force would not be worth the name. The only fair solution then would be to "let the States we both represent agree to separate and part in peace." But the Union could yet be saved. How? Not by Clay's proposed compromise with its admission of California as a free state. But only by doing justice to the South by restoring that fair equilibrium between the sections. If the North persisted in her objects of "power and aggrandizement," the South would be forced "to act accordingly." [18]

Calhoun had spoken for an unrealistic turning back of

time, resurrection of an earlier day—as an apostle for the rural-agrarian order that was rapidly being shouldered aside by the new forces of economic and social progress. A paradoxical prophet of reaction, he had outlived his time. Less than four weeks later he was dead. Despite his efforts the Compromise of 1850 passed. The South accepted it. The Union was not ruptured then. But by the end of the decade that followed, Calhoun's prophecy would come true. In 1860–61 the Union split, Southern states withdrawing under the conviction that abolitionist control of Washington, that Calhoun forecast, menaced the South's security. Finally, after four years of bloody Civil War had ended, one soldier summed it up: the true monuments to Calhoun were the ravaged farms, shattered railroads, ruined ships, and gaunt chimneys strewn over the devastated South.

Bowing Out: Jackson and Calhoun Advise Americans

Upon departing the political scene both Jackson and Calhoun left a political testament to their fellow Americans. Typically, Jackson's was terse, colorful, and punch-packed; Calhoun's rambling, abstract, and obtuse.

During his last months in office it was clear that Jackson, much admired by his fellow Americans, had won an affection greater than for any predecessor. Gifts from admirers in all parts of the country flowed into the White House—hickory canes, pipes, hats, a small wooden wagon built entirely of hickory, an elegant phaeton carriage made of wood from the old naval frigate *USS Constitution,* and an enormous cheese (4 feet in diameter and weighing 1,400 pounds). Visitors to the White House found him not the snarling, angry tiger they expected but a courtly, dignified gentleman who treated all comers with deference and courtesy. But he still breathed fire; when asked if he had any regrets, he replied facetiously, yes, he should have had Henry Clay executed and John Calhoun hanged.

Following George Washington's example, Jackson issued a Farewell Address to his countrymen, cautioning "vigilance" in guarding "liberty." After ticking off the achievements of his administrations, he reminded Americans of the priceless value of the Union; the danger of sectional agitation; the advantage of a plain, republican regime over a gaudy, expensive establishment; the perils of too high a tariff, of surplus revenue, of unconstitutional federal road projects: the "curse" of paper money and the need for gold and silver money. "My own race is nearly run; advanced age and failing health warn me that before long I must pass beyond the reach of human events, and cease to feel the vicissitudes of human affairs. I thank God that my life has been spent in a land of liberty, and that he has given me a heart to love my country with the affection of a son. And filled with gratitude for your constant and unwavering kindness, I bid you a last and affectionate farewell." [39] (See *Appendix* No. 10, for fuller text.)

After returning to the Hermitage, the Old Hero looked back with satisfaction to his day in power when "opposed . . . by the . . . money power of the whole aristocracy, [I was] nobly supported by the Democratic republicans—the people . . . was now filling the summit of my gratification, and I can truly say, my ambition." [40] Now past 70, thin, infirm, with little money (he had only $90 in cash on reaching home in 1837), he supervised the affairs of his large plantation, borrowed heavily from Francis Blair to pay his son's debts, kept up a large correspondence and meditated on the state of public affairs. He began putting his own papers in order, authorized Amos Kendall to write a biography that the latter abandoned after seven installments had been published in *Harper's Magazine*. During his last years Jackson's health eroded rapidly—TB had ravaged one lung; he coughed steadily and suffered from dropsy and constant headaches. But even so, he cheerfully greeted hundreds of visitors who streamed to the Hermitage.

Following an operation in 1845, Jackson failed to recover his strength. On June 8, the household and friends, standing at his bedside, heard him whisper, "Be good children, . . . I hope to meet you all in heaven, white and black," just before he died. Some 10,000 people gathered as the Old Hero was buried in the garden beside his beloved Rachel. Sam Houston, who with his small son had ridden hundreds of miles to be present, said, "My son, try to remember that you have looked on the face of Andrew Jackson." [41] A less reverent observer, when asked if he thought General Jackson would go to Heaven, responded promptly, "If the General wants to go, he will." Supreme Court Justice John Catron wrote a day after the funeral that Jackson's "hardy industry, and a sleepless energy, [which] few could equal" were surpassed by "his awful *will*" that "stood alone, & was made the will of all he commanded"; "fierce, fearless, and unwavering" Jackson had commanded, sweeping over all opposition "terrible and clean as a prairie fire." And a free Negro shipwright in Washington noted in his diary: "the Hon. Maj. General Andrew Jackson is gone. . . . But his name still lives in the heart of the American people." [42] Three years later Calhoun gave his verdict in an interview with a young journalist: "General Jackson was a great man." [43]

In contrast Calhoun's testament came, perhaps characteristically, in two massive books composed in his last years and published shortly after his death. Bearing the imposing titles, *A Disquisition on Government* and *A Discourse on the Constitution and Government of the United States,* these works contain Calhoun's matured thought in the realm of political theory and particularly in relation to the nature of American government.[44]

The substance of Calhoun's theory in the *Disquisition* rests on these postulates: (1) Man is "a social being" impelled by "his inclinations and wants" to associate with his kind. Further, man's inherent, natural self-interest makes him "feel more intensely what affects him directly than what affects him through others." (2) This self-interest inevitably "leads to conflict between individuals" generating "suspicion, jealousy, anger, and revenge." Such conflict produces "universal discord and confusion destructive of society"; it must be prevented by a "controlling power" which "wherever vested or by whomsoever exercised is Government." Thus, man's "social feelings" compel him to live in society from being destroyed by man's "individual," selfish feelings. (3) Government itself tends to disorder and conflict, because government's powers "to repress violence and preserve order" are "administered by men" whose "individual [feelings] are stronger than the social feelings." Hence, government's powers, designed "to prevent injustice and oppression" will, if not restrained, be "converted into instruments to oppress the . . . community. That by which this is prevented . . . is what is called *constitution.* " Thus, "*constitution* stands to *government* as *government* stands to *society.* "

The crucial problem, as Calhoun saw it, was how to restrain government, holding sufficient power to prevent internal disorder and violence and "to repel assaults from abroad," from using its power for "aggrandizing" men who run government. Since "power can be resisted only by power," an effective "organism" must "furnish the ruled with the means of resisting successfully" the "tendency on the part of the rulers to oppression." The "primary principle" of "constitutional government" is the suffrage, whereby the ruled "choose their rulers at . . . intervals and hold them thereby responsible for their conduct."

But suffrage alone is not enough to restrain government

and its abuse of power. Society is subject to a continuous struggle between "various . . . interests of the community," which inevitably results in one interest gaining a numerical majority. In control of government, this majority naturally distributes favors, privileges, "honors and emoluments" to the few who control the majority; other parts of the community must pay for them through taxes imposed by the majority. Obviously, the numerical majority will tax the minority for revenues to go to benefit the majority. Such a policy, carried to extremes, must elevate one "class of portion of the community . . . to wealth and power" and depress the other "to abject poverty and dependence." Clearly Calhoun here was recalling what he conceived to be the protective tariff's effects in the Jackson era, enriching the North, impoverishing the South.

Since the suffrage alone did not restrain effectively a numerical majority, some additional device was needed to "counteract" government's "inherent" tendency "to oppression." Calhoun proposed such a device. He called it the "concurrent majority" which would "prevent any one interest or combination of interests from obtaining exclusive control of the government." This device would take "the sense of each interest or portion of the community . . . separately through its own majority." Thus, it would allow "each division or interest" to exercise "a concurrent voice in making and executing the laws or a veto on their execution." Hence, any proposed government policy would require "the concurrent consent of all" thereby protecting "the different interests, . . . classes or portions" of the community from "abuse, abasement or impoverishment" by hostile government action.

This concurrent majority device had the great advantage of truly reflecting "the sense of the entire community," since the "individuals composing each [interest or division] would be . . . truly represented by its own majority" in relation to all other interests. It was indispensable to constitutional government because a "negative power" was the essence of a constitution, and no effective "negative power" could operate without a concurrent majority. It would, moreover, insure liberty and security. Security by affording self protection "to each interest or portion" by blending "conflicting interests" into "one common attachment to the country"; liberty by leaving "each free to pursue the course he may deem best to promote his interest and happiness" and enjoy "the fruits of his exertions to better his condition." But liberty was not absolute, could not be used to undermine government's power to protect society against internal and external dangers, but rather was a reward earned by "the intelligent, patriotic, and virtuous." Further, equality was not a condition essential to liberty—indeed it might destroy liberty—but liberty, including liberty to become unequal, was essential as the spur to self-betterment and progress of society.

Calhoun dismissed the objection that the concurrent majority would be difficult to operate with the assertion that popular government itself was the most difficult of all governments to operate justly. Far outweighing its difficulties would stand its resulting benefits—"instead of faction, strife, and struggle for party ascendency" his device would engender "patriotism, nationality, harmony and common good of the whole." Obviously, Calhoun intended that the concurrent majority principle should be applied to the North-South sectional struggle within the United States. (See *Appendix,* Doc. No. 10, for fuller text of the *Disquisition.*)

Calhoun's political theory, expressed in general terms in the *Disquisition* he applied in particular terms to the United States in his *Discourse.* Contending that the concurrent principle had been originally incorporated in the Constitution (citing the Senate, executive, judicary and amending process as devices for restraining the numerical majority's will), he

traced developments, laws, and practices that had undermined the federal, concurrent principle in America. Since the
concurrent principle rested fundamentally upon a rough
equilibrium between the sections or interests, the undermining laws would have to be repealed, the subversive trends
reversed, in order that the states' original powers be restored
and the enlarged powers of the executive "be rigidly restricted." Beyond this, he proposed a dual executive. A president would be elected by each section and each president
endowed with veto power could prevent oppressive action by
numerical or sectional majority hostile to his home section's
interests. Such an arrangement would, Calhoun believed, restore balance and security to the Union and eliminate sectional hostility, continual conflict, and threat of disruption
of the Union. (For fuller text, see *Appendix*, Doc. No. 20.)

Here Calhoun had abandoned the doctrine of nullification
by a single state and moved to a device better calculated to
secure a minority section (the South) against the adverse
action by a more populous section (the North). In the
1832–33 tariff crisis, in the 1848 Oregon fight, in the 1850
California crisis, such a device would have negatived policy
adverse to the South—but would it not have generated
greater hostility in the North whose majority had been artifi-
cially thwarted? Whether government itself could operate
effectively under such a self-imposed strait-jacket of built-in
paralysis under two veto-wielding presidents was doubtful to
any practical mind.

X The Verdict of History

TO HIS CONTEMPORARIES Andrew Jackson was a hero and villain, a brave warrior and cruel murderer, hardy frontiersman and luxury loving aristocrat, hard-working planter and greedy speculator, forceful statesman and scheming politician, a people's President and willful tyrant.

At the same time John C. Calhoun appeared a selfless patriot and ambitious opportunist, champion of liberty and backer of slavery, constructive nation-builder and narrow sectionalist, lofty idealist and political blunderer, creative theorist and devious sophist.

Biographers and historians have wrestled with the contemporary evidence supporting these conflicting images of Jackson and Calhoun. In fact, the flood of biographical and historical writings on Jackson, Calhoun, and the "age of Jackson" has grown to such deluge proportions as to threaten to drown the unwary reader. Fortunately, several recent studies of Jacksonian historiography provide much needed guidance. Most helpful are Alfred A. Cave, *Jacksonian Democracy and the Historians* (Gainesville, 1964) and Charles G. Sellers, Jr., *Jacksonian Democracy*, a pamphlet published by the American Historical Association's Service Center for Teachers of History (Washington, 1958). In his *Jacksonian America* (Homewood, 1969) Edward Pessen provides in a "Bibliographical Essay" a thorough, critical survey of the historical and biographical literature dealing with the era. The chapter in the following pages here sketches how historians have viewed Jackson and Calhoun.

Jackson: How Historians See Him and His Era

To James Parton, writing a full-length biography in 1859, "Andrew Jackson . . . was a patriot and a traitor. He was one of the greatest of generals and wholly ignorant of the art of war. A writer brilliant, elegant and eloquent, and without being able to compose a correct sentence, or spell words of four syllables. The first of statesmen, he never framed a measure. He was the most candid of men, and yet capable of the profoundest dissimulation. A most law-defying, law-obeying citizen. A stickler for discipline, he never hesitated to disobey his superior. A democratic autocrat. An urbane savage. An atrocious saint." [1] Such a pack of contradictions would seem to defy explanation. Yet historians have tried.

Ever since Jackson's day historians and biographers have grappled with these paradoxes of his life, his actions and his significance. All agree that he left a large footprint on the landscape of America's history as the terms commonly used by historians indicate—"The Age of Jackson," "Jacksonian Democracy," "The Jacksonian Era," "Jacksonian America." But controversy persists over his significance and what kind of imprint he made. What is the meaning of Jackson's career and of "Jacksonian democracy"? To answer this question, writers for more than a century have poured out a torrent of Jackson books. Today the flood continues unabated.

The spotlights beamed on Jackson by biographers illuminate features of contrasting shadow and brilliance. Some focus on him as an inspiring leader who led egalitarian democracy to triumph over selfish, privileged aristocracy. Others view him as a self-seeking demagogue who cleverly exploited the credulity of the masses to satisfy ambition and gain advantage. Others picture him as a selfless, courageous champion of the common man; to others he appears an egotist manipulated by cunning subordinates. Some see him as a sturdy, unyielding nationalist; others as an advocate of state rights, strict construction, limited government. Some view him as fomentor of American progress into a new era; others as the spokesman for returning to the republican purity and simple Jeffersonian virtues of an earlier, agrarian day.

In 1817 when Jackson had just turned 50, his first biography was published, begun by his military aide of the Indian-British campaigns, John Reid, and completed by Tennessee lawyer John H. Eaton, upon Reid's death. It was only the beginning. By the time Jackson died in 1845, a half dozen more volumes had appeared. The most unusual of these was published in London in 1834. Its author, Irish reformer William Cobbett, pronounced Jackson "the bravest and greatest man now living in this world or that has ever lived in this world, as far as my knowledge extends." [2] A close associate of Jackson, Amos Kendall, was engaged to prepare a semi-official biography of the Old Hero and published seven chapters as installments in *Harper's Magazine* before giving up the project. Other early books repeated each other in reciting Jackson's career and in uncritically singing his praises. Critics would arise later.

As did Jackson, so did the movement, bearing his name—Jacksonian Democracy—generate widely divergent interpretations. Most historians agreed that the movement, so far as it could legitimately be called a movement, was far-reaching, complex and diverse: but many differed greatly in explaining its origins, nature, components, goals, and achievements. Some pictured it as arising from America's frontier environment; others as originating in the strivings of Eastern laboring men for equality of rights and opportunity. Some writers viewed it as strictly political in nature and aims; others as embracing economic, social, cultural elements and goals as well. Some saw it as a sectional contest ranging Western and Southern farmers against Eastern financial, industrial, busi-

ness promoters; others as a struggle of rising, would-be entrepreneurs to secure economic opportunities already enjoyed
by entrenched entrepreneurs; still others as a battle of urban
and rural workers against a privileged business community.
Some viewed it as foreshadowing a utopian future; others a
return to a purer past.

In general, writings of historians and biographers of Jackson and Jacksonian Democracy may be grouped loosely into
six categories of historical interpretation. For convenience,
these may be labeled: (1) early aristocratic or Whig school;
(2) democratic Progressive school; (3) revisionist, critical
school; (4) economic group conflict school; (5) entrepreneural
struggle school; (6) symbolic, psychological school. While
much overlapping and some agreement exist among these
interpretations, they differ in emphasis, degree, and substance, in many points reflecting the values of the eras in
which they were written as well as the philosophical view-
points of the individual writers.

Of the aristocratic interpretation, James Parton's three-
volume *Life of Andrew Jackson* (1859–60) was the earliest,
the most popular and influential and in many ways the best
work. Writing in a lively style and drawing on incidents
related to him by eye-witness participants, Parton believed
Jackson's "ignorance and passions" made "him, of all conceivable beings, the most unfit for office." While he had been
a good "fighting man," Jackson as President dangerously
stretched the powers of the office until "his will tyrannized
over friends . . . Congress and . . . country." Good government, formerly in the hands of men of talent and breeding,
degenerated under the Jacksonians' "pernicious" introduction of the "spoils system" which debauched the public service and corrupted honest, efficient administration, making
"pure, decent, orderly government impossible." A firm believer in the dominant *laissez faire* economic ideas prevailing

in his own time, Parton praised Jackson for fighting special economic privilege, resisting federal subsidy to road building companies and ending the Bank of the United States. But the "arrogant, ferocious" temper of the war on the Bank, the favoritism in placing government funds in pet banks and the corrupt extending of the federal patronage Parton found unpardonable. While conceding Jackson's strong character and recognizing his election as a "triumph of the people," Parton's general verdict was negative.

In the same tradition as Parton, William G. Sumner, eminent Yale economist in the late nineteenth century, produced a penetrating study of *Andrew Jackson as a Public Man* (1882). Jackson's elevation to the Presidency represented unfortunately, in Sumner's view, the rise of Western agrarian democracy and introduced the unrealistic, unnatural dogma of equality. Summer, as a devoted Social Darwinist who believed men of ability rose to the top of the economy and social under the operation of the "law of the survival of the fittest," denounced the notion of equality as intolerable. To contend that men are by nature "wise and good" and entitled to equality was fallacious nonsense in Sumner's view because "so long as men strive upwards and away from the original brutishness, the inequalities in their *being* and *doing* will inevitably produce inequalities in their *having* and *enjoying*." The triumph of the mob under the guise of majority rule and equality resulted in investing "an old Indian fighter" (Jackson) with "the power of the presidency."

Of Jackson's policies, too, Sumner is highly critical. He condemned the attack on the Bank and removal of government deposits from it. These actions stemmed from "ignorance of the realities of money and credit," as Jackson "unjustly, passionately, . . . and without regard to the truth assailed a great and valuable financial institution." The resulting chaos and collapse in the financial community were unavoidable consequences of such tampering, in Sumner's view in the late nineteenth century years when demands for radical monetary inflation were being heard and firmly resisted by classical economists like Sumner.

On the tariff issue, Sumner asserted Calhoun and South Carolina had a strong case against the policy of tariff protection, but regrettably they became diverted by the nullification delusion. The issue should have been fought out on strictly economic grounds. Sumner bitterly condemned Jackson for creating "personal government . . . in a Napoleonic fashion." Even so, he conceded, "It came in Andrew Jackson's way to do some good, to check some bad tendencies [e.g., nullification and high tariff] and to strengthen some good ones [non-interference in the economy]." But Jackson acted so much "from spite, pique, instinct, prejudice, emotion" that "he stumbled along through a magnificent career . . . leaving behind . . . turmoil and disaster in the future." Clearly Jackson's freewheeling operations did not fit the neat society functioning under the restraint of reason envisioned in Professor Sumner's orderly mind.

Quite remarkably, Sumner's treatment of the Jackson era carried seminal germs that would produce major interpretations of the twentieth century. The frontier influence, clash of sections, economic class conflicts, the amorphous nature of the Jackson political party—all are suggested in Sumner's writings.

Thus late nineteenth century biographers, joined by general historians James Schouler (1880) and Hermann E. Von Holst (1876), sharing their own age's devotion to *laissez faire,* Social Darwinism, Congressional supremacy, constitutional restraints and aversion to Presidential domination, popular sovereignty and equalitarian doctrines, rendered an unfavorable judgment on Jackson and his movement.

During the 1890's the upper-middle-class values and views

of American society, government and economy faced increasing challenge by new stirrings of a broad Progressive movement, emphasizing different goals and new approaches. Understandably, a shift in American historical writing occurred. In 1893 a new approach to Jackson and his era began when Frederick Jackson Turner presented his celebrated essay, "The Significance of the Frontier in American History." Calling for a new interpretation of America's past, Turner advanced the view that American democracy emerged "stark, strong and full of life from" the American experience on the western froniter where easily obtained land placed all men on essentially equal footing at the outset.

Turner presented Jackson as the champion of "democracy as an effective force," "the very personification" of frontier democracy, who with his followers "swept away the privacies and privileges of officialdom" substituting "a society free from the dominance of ancient forms." Jacksonian Democracy now appeared (not corrupt and degrading) as an invigorating force in the nation's development,—the political expression of frontier nationalism and egalitarianism, signaling the triumph of "new expansive democracy, emphasizing human rights and individualism" over "vested rights and corporate action." The Jackson era's political struggles Turner explained primarily as expressions of sectional clashes between agrarian West, manufacturing East and planting South.

Turner's views were soon echoed in the writings of such historians as Woodrow Wilson, John S. Bassett, William E. Dodd, Carl R. Fish, Frederick A. Ogg, Charles A. Beard, and Vernon L. Parrington—all of whom treated Jackson and his movement and influence in largely sympathetic terms. As Professor Charles G. Sellers has noted, nearly all these scholars came from "substantial middle-class families" with "rural or small-town backgrounds in the West or South" and shared with their contemporary allies in the rising Progressive reform movement a zeal "to preserve the traditional values of American society" from the threat posed by twentieth century America's urban-industrial complex. They injected a new viewpoint "into a field previously dominated by the urban Northeast." [1] Not surprising, then, that these historians anxious to revive faith in the capacity of the people and in the democratic process, responded warmly to Turner's view of Jacksonian Democracy as "strong in the faith of the intrinsic excellence of the common man . . . and in his capacity to share in government."

They found much to praise in the Jackson movement. For example, Wilson (1893) underscored Jackson's efforts "to nationalize the government" and to kill the Bank. Fish (1905) made a case for the spoils system, upholding it as needed to assure popular control over office holders and to make political parties function well in a democratic society. Dodd (1915) praised the "Old Hero" as the authentic leader of "small farmers" and "artisan classes," who restored control of the government to the people. Ogg (1919) pictured Jackson, despite his acknowledged faults, as a vigorous champion of "a mighty democratic uprising" that broke down oligarchy and liberalized American government. A few discordant voices rose: Ralph C. H. Catterall (1903) roundly condemned Jackson's destruction of the Bank, and William McDonald, (1907), while praising revival of democratic vigor, scored as demagogic and "dangerous" Jackson's "arbitrary, highhanded" dominance as President.

Of the Progressive era's Jackson biographies, the best was John S. Bassett's two-volume work (1911), the first substantial, scholarly appraisal since Sumner's. Critical but sympathetic, Bassett found "the secret of the Jacksonian movement" in the rise of democracy, typified by Jackson himself, and in sectional conflict with the democratic West playing an ascendant role. Praising Jackson's integrity, self-reliance, and vigorous leadership as President, Bassett also saw in Jackson's willfulness, narrowness, and stubborn provincialism the weaknesses (as well as the virtues) of his generation and particularly his section. Jackson's "crude judgments. . . ., occasional outbursts of passion, . . . habitual hatred of enemies . . . , and his crude ideas of some political policies—all lose some of their infelicity in the face of his brave, frank, masterly leadership of the democratic movement. . . . [He] lived up to the demands of the movement which brought . . . [him] to power."

Bassett's favorable appraisal extended the pro-democratic interpretation that continues its dominant influence on Jackson writings to the present. It grew stronger in the influential works of Parrington (1926) and Beard (1927). It is reflected in Marquis James's colorful, adulatory impressive, two-volume biography (1933, 1937) that won a Pulitzer prize; and in the strongly partisan work of Claude G. Bowers (1922). Political scientists Wilfred E. Binkley (1943) and Leonard D. White (1954) have incorporated it in their volumes, approving the Jacksonian development of the popularly based political party as well as Jackson's vigorous Presidential leadership as vital ingredients in democracy's successful functioning. This view is also shared in Glyndon Van Deusen's (1959) work. Even more tellingly, the pro-democratic interpretation has infused most general American histories and textbooks for the past sixty-five years.

True, the interpretation has been challenged at some points. Thomas P. Abernathy (1932) in the 1930's argued strongly that Jackson, far from being a democratic champion of the little people in his pre-Presidential years, was in fact a frontier aristocrat and large land speculator who fought democratic drives in Tennessee and emerged on the national scene as an ambitious opportunist, far from democracy's spokesman. Charles M. Wiltse in his comprehensive three-volume biography of Calhoun (1944, 1949, 1951) pictures Jackson as a scheming, vengeful politician seizing the main chance when it offered, but totally devoid of real comprehension of the democratic process, lacking any coherent political program of his own, capturing the tide of public feeling to his own gain, tending to personalize issues and acting too often from irrational, personal hatred of such enemies of his own creating as John Calhoun, Nicholas Biddle, and Henry Clay. Can the Abernathy-Wiltse Jackson be the same man as the Turner-Bassett Jackson?

In his 1945 Pulitzer prize winning book, Arthur M. Schlesinger, Jr., injected a major qualifying note into the prevailing view in *The Age of Jackson* (1945). The central fact of the Jacksonian movement, he contended, was a clash between economic-social groups or classes. It was not the West nor some vague embodiment of the "whole people" arising in concert to enthrone democracy in America of the 1820's and 30's. It was largely the East and Eastern working men and other underprivileged groups (not primarily Western farmers) who generated the driving force of the movement. Rather, the conflict of economic classes in Jackson's day, as Schlesinger saw it, was "a second phase of the enduring struggle between the business community and the rest of society." "More can be understood about Jacksonian democracy if it is regarded as a problem not of sections but of classes."

Seeing the central theme of American history as the struggle "on the part of other sections [i.e., groups] of society to restrain the power of the business community," Schlesinger analyzed the Jacksonian democratic drive as a movement "to control the power of the capitalistic groups, mainly Eastern, for the benefit of noncapitalist groups, farmers and laboring men, East, West and South." To the East and its working men and intellectuals Schlesinger assigned a dominant role in the Jacksonian crusade for reforms. The Jackson war on the Bank loomed in this view as the major Jacksonian democratic achievement in that it restrained the selfish, grasping drives of the business community. Despite Schlesinger's large emphasis on economic class antagonisms as the prime motivating force in the Jackson years, he devotes substantial attention to social, intellectual, and moral factors as important determinants also.

The Schlesinger book generated a brisk debate on the nature and significance of Jacksonian democracy that continues to the present. In 1947 Bray Hammond, a scholarly Federal Reserve officer, advanced his well-buttressed view that the Jacksonians were not essentially hostile to the business community itself, contrary to Schlesinger's interpretation, but rather were battling against the exclusion of new entrepreneurs from business opportunities already enjoyed by other entrepreneurs. A group of Columbia University scholars, including Richard Hofstadter (1948), Joseph Dorfman (1949), and Richard B. Morris (1949), joined the critics of Schlesinger's "labor" thesis in explaining the Jackson era. Noting that Jackson personally tended to be anti-labor and that laboring men more often than not opposed Jackson and his adherents at the polls or at best remained indifferent to Jacksonian appeals, the Columbians explained that Jacksonian democracy was fundamentally "a phase in the expansion of liberated capitalism" and remained "closely linked to the ambitions of the small capitalist." On this basis they rejected the Schlesinger "class conflict" or "labor" thesis. Agreeing largely with Hammond, they argued that if there was a major struggle it was a contest among contending entrepreneurs for free entry into the business community themselves by eliminating restrictions, artificial advantages, and special grants of privilege to favored entrepreneurs. Hofstadter (1948), with support from Louis Hartz (1955), Lee

Benson (1961), and other recent writers on Jacksonian developments, maintained that the Beard-Schlesinger view of class antagonism as the key to understanding the Jackson era was misleading. Rather, the reasoning went, while the party battles over specific issues were interesting and colorful, more essential to an understanding of the era was the existence of a "common climate of opinion" or "consensus" among virtually all Americans of the 1830's, including Andrew Jackson, John Calhoun, and Henry Clay. All of them, with slightly varying shades of emphasis, were practically unanimous in their acceptance of the values and virtues of both capitalism and democracy.

And so the debate continues. During the 1950's two other approaches, avoiding the tangle of labor-entrepreneur-consensus controversy, were suggested. John Ward (1953) presented the view that Jackson's influence in his time arose from his acquiring the mystique of a "symbolic figure" embodying the three symbolic concepts of Providence, Nature, and Will —representing those values that Americans of his generation held highest and reflecting those virtues most admired. Marvin Meyers (1957) finds the key to the Jacksonians in their desire "to preserve the virtues of a simple agrarian republic without sacrificing the rewards and conveniences of modern capitalism" with the "free pursuit of economic interest, just as the two were hopelessly splitting apart."

The paradoxical, complex nature of Jacksonian democracy and indeed of Jackson himself, as suggested by Meyers' book, goes far to explain why historians and biographers by focusing on different ingredients in the Jacksonian melange come up with such widely varying interpretations. So, more than a century and a quarter after his death, Andrew Jackson continues to unfold as a great American folk hero. As Robert V. Remini's fine biography (1966) explains his appeal, Jackson personified for his generation (and generations since) the promise of American life, the fulfillment of the American desire for improvement—improvement not only in wealth and economic status but in winning the good opinion of one's fellows.

Edward Pessen, in his *Jacksonian America: Society, Personality and Politics* (1969) is more skeptical and more critical of Jackson. Not strictly a biography, Pessen's volume notes as Jackson's strength "a blend of forthrightness, simplicity, stubbornness, self-righteousness, controlled anger, fearlessness, and more subtlety than meets the eye" but condemns his bellicose, overbearing manner and often inappropriate methods of enforcing his own will, and lack of any constructive approach for meeting the major issues of his day.

Calhoun in the Eyes of History

John C. Calhoun, in contrast to Jackson, has won only a small fraction of history's attention. Historical writings on Calhoun are much fewer and slimmer than those of Jackson. Before his death in 1850 only a few campaign biographies had appeared in newspapers and pamphlet form.

In 1843 Harper Brothers published a book entitled the *Life of John C. Calhoun.* The title page carried no author's name. Many contemporaries attributed it, as a campaign biography, to Calhoun's friend and supporter Robert M. T. Hunter. Three previous biographical sketches of Calhoun had appeared in newspapers, one as early as 1822 thought to be written by George M. Dallas of Pennsylvania, followed a year later by *Measures not Men*, essentially a recopy of the 1822 sketch and generally attributed to General Joseph B. Swift. Still another and longer biographical sketch by Calhoun's friend Virgil Maxcy was published in 1831 in Duff Green's *United States Telegraph.* All these works, written by close associates of Calhoun and bearing the marks of political campaign documents, appeared at times when Calhoun was actively seeking the Presidency. The 1843 *Life* expanded the previous sketches (which it follows closely) and brought the Calhoun story up to date. Much debate has developed over its authorship.

The evidence bearing on the point of authorship is scanty and inconclusive. One recent biographer suggests that New York journalist and Calhoun booster Joseph A. Scoville wrote the first part of it, that Calhoun's daughter Anna Clemson did the second part and Robert Hunter revised the whole. Other biographers have concluded that Calhoun himself wrote it. They cite, in support of this conclusion, a letter of October 25, 1854, from Calhoun's associate Robert Barnwell Rhett to Richard K. Crallé, a pro-Calhoun newspaper editor whom Calhoun authorized in his last days to prepare a posthumous edition of Calhoun's papers. Rhett wrote: "There is but one thing written by Calhoun that you [Crallé] ought not to publish as his—and that is 'his life'. He wished me to Father it—but I told him that it was impossible for me directly or indirectly to allow any one to understand that I was the author of something which I had not written. Hunter and I read it over together. . . . He inserted about a page and a half, and became the putative author; . . ." [4] Since Rhett was a close friend and political associate of Calhoun, as well as being a Charleston editor and in a position most likely to be consulted by Calhoun, his statement carries a ring of truth. Even those who contend for other authors concede that Calhoun supplied the material and read and approved the final work. In the light of all the evidence, Calhoun appears to have fathered the book. One is moved to agree with Gerald M. Capers that the *Life* of 1843 should be considered an *autobiography* (and it has been so treated in the present book).

In the year Calhoun died, a scissors and paste biography was published by hack writer John S. Jenkins (1950), who had already churned out biographical quickies on Jackson, Polk, and Silas Wright, all political contemporaries of Calhoun. Two years later, Mary Bates, friend and tutor to the Calhoun family, authored an intimate, personal picture, *The Private Life of John C. Calhoun* (1852). For another thirty years no biographer tackled Calhoun, primarily because the outbreak of the Civil War had blackened his name as the "great nullifier," "disunionist," and "father of secession."

In 1882 Professor Hermann E. Von Holst published the first major, scholarly study of Calhoun. Holding strong views on the inviolability of the Constitution and of the Union and on the immorality of slavery, the author attempted an evaluation of the "man of superior ability and intellect," who was "remembered [in 1882] more distinctly . . . than Webster or Clay." He was so clearly remembered, said Von Holst, because "he chained himself" to the "dying, evil institution" of slavery. Calhoun "may be called the very impersonation of the slavery question" that agitated American politics so disastrously for the 40 years preceding the Civil War.

Largely hostile to Calhoun, the volume neglects Calhoun's highly constructive, creative labors as Secretary of War, 1817–1825, at the same time conceding "considerable merit" to Calhoun's efforts in the 1830's and 40's to check national centralization, Presidential domination, and the drift toward war with England over the Oregon question in 1846. But on virtually all other questions after 1831, Calhoun became "blinded" by his zealous defense of slavery, which increasingly absorbed his energies into an irrational, dead-end channel. In "good faith" and under the mistaken impression that he was doing his "duty" (a favorite Calhoun word), he attempted the impossible: to espouse both government of law and the doctrine of nullification of law; to reconcile state supremacy with a general government sufficiently strong to govern a large, rapidly expanding country; to achieve equality of the states and consolidation of the South as a section by securing the artificial, contrived dominance of a numerical minority. To reconcile such incompatibles led Calhoun into such paths of sophistry as asserting that "slavery is the most solid basis of liberty." Von Holst's concluding verdict: Calhoun enabled the South for many years to force "the world's most democratic, progressive country to bend its knees" to slavery; therefore "blame for the ultimate outcome" in the catastrophe of Civil War "rests heavily on his shoulders," and Calhoun's career stands as "a great tragedy."

Twentieth century writers, in contrast, have produced biographies mainly favorable to Calhoun. Some volumes, written by avowed modern advocates of the state rights position, range from Gustavus M. Pinckney's superficial, rankly partisan *Life* (1903) that pictures Calhoun "as carrying on the torch of the true interpretation of the Constitution begun by Jefferson and Madison," to which his generation stubbornly refused to listen, through the more balanced Gaillard Hunt biography (1908) to the large, two-volume William M. Meigs *Life* (1917), which minutely details Calhoun's career and thought and in which the author concludes that "In my opinion neither Webster nor any one else ever approached an answer to Calhoun" in his state sovereignty interpretation of the Constitution and the Union.

The general rationale, which threads through the line of pro-Calhoun biographies from Meigs through the Arthur Styron (1935) to Margaret Coit's Pulitzer-prize-winning biography (1950) is that, assuming the correctness and desirability of Calhoun's premise that the rural-agricultural social order was the best form of society for the United States, then, in understandable Jeffersonan terms the coming of an urban, industrialized order had to be resisted. Calhoun resisted the coming of industrialism and developed a powerfully reasoned defense of the rural-agrarian order. Was he right or wrong?

The most comprehensive Calhoun biography is the monumental, solid, impressive work of Charles M. Wiltse, published in three volumes under the general title *John C. Calhoun,* each volume bearing a subtitle—Volume I, *John C. Calhoun, Nationalist, 1782–1828* (1944); II, *John C. Calhoun, Nullifier, 1829–1839* (1949); III, *John C. Calhoun, Sectionalist, 1840–1850* (1951). More than a biography in the ordinary sense, this impressive work offers such a remarkable and detailed coverage of the man, his life, his times and background developments (social and economic as well as political) as to constitute a virtual history of the United States during the first half of the nineteenth century.

Wiltse's sympathies lie almost completely and uncritically with Calhoun, whom he views as one of the "master statesmen" of his era. In Wiltse's pages Calhoun appears as a man of towering intellect, almost infallible thought, and unanswerable logic; Jackson as the man of emotional impulse, driving action, and relentless revenge. For example, in comparing the two men, Wiltse, after quoting approvingly Calhoun's comment that Jackson's disposition was to "use to its utmost every particle of power given to him. He has not sufficient regard for the genius of our institutions and popular opinion," raps Jackson for his "disregard" of "the opinion . . . of all those who had better heads and sounder judgments than his own." But correcting Calhoun's judgment, the author contends that Jackson "understood and followed" public feeling; "it was Calhoun rather than Jackson who lacked regard for the masses."

Jackson's following, which in Wiltse's analysis aligns largely with the economic class conflict interpretation noted above, "was not regional but stratified, coming from a section [of society] not bounded by state lines but by property and debt; since the dispossessed always outnumber those with means," Jackson polled "a decisive popular vote" in running for President.[6]

After becoming President, Jackson himself became the issue in American politics. As Wiltse sized up Jackson, "He was aggressive to the point of arrogance, never willing to count the cost, . . . slashing his way ahead. Often he went too far, often he was wrong, occasionally he was absurd; but he always had men around him who could mitigate or even capitalize his errors. . . . Jackson was a pocket-sized John Bunyan and a drawing-room Mike Fink rolled into one, with a dash of Davy Crockett and a large leaven of Scotch shrewdness. His enemies called him a frontier bully, and in many ways he was. What his enemies failed to appreciate in a growing, expanding, gambling . . . country like the United States of the 1820's and 30's, the frontier bully was a national hero." [7]

While Wiltse's interpretations are highly debatable, he marshalls impressive evidence to support them. He makes for Calhoun the best case that can be made—a calm, rational, thoughtful case, such as Calhoun himself would have made (often Wiltse simply reiterates approvingly Calhoun's arguments)—persuasive but not entirely convincing.

Wiltse, noting Calhoun's nationalism-to-nullification shift, sees nothing particularly inconsistent, arguing that Calhoun's goals remained the same—to protect the rights and interests of the numerical minority within the framework of the Union. So far as nullification and sectional tactics were a means to this end, they were justifiable and necessary, in Calhoun's and Wiltse's view. "Above all things," says the author, "Calhoun wanted to avoid a radical solution," meaning secession or armed clash, in the 1828–33 tariff dispute, in the 1842 tariff fight, in the battle over the Wilmot Proviso's limitation on slavery and in the 1850 crisis. "In developing and advocating the State Rights doctrine in 1828, Calhoun was not turning from nationalism to a narrow sectional point of view, and he was not acting from motives of personal ambition seeking to destroy the Union. He was . . . trying to save the Union in the only way it could be saved—by preserving the loyalty of its citizens." Consequently, "Calhoun fell back upon the sovereignty of the states, as the only hope of preserving the Union." [8] The paradox remains—is the nation's unity saved by building up the states?

Viewing Jackson's 1828 success as the victory "of the landless, the debt-ridden and those who worked with their hands," Wiltse lays stress on the clash of economic interests as determining the course of history in the Jackson-Calhoun era. Recognizing forces working for industrialization, Calhoun battled to preserve the rural-agrarian order that he knew at home and prized; that slavery was a part of that order in the South led him logically to an ardent defense of the "peculiar institution." To defend slavery, Calhoun developed his rationale for protecting the interests of the numerical minority (the South) against a power-wielding majority, seemingly bent on ruining the Old South, as Calhoun saw it. In so doing, he became convinced his protective devices (nullification, concurrent majority, dual presidency) would make preservation of the Union possible. But in attempting to stem the tide of industrialization, he made a hopeless stand against irresistible economic forces of the future—and although he seemed an immovable object, resistance was impossible and hence doomed to fail.

Margaret Coit's (1950) biography (a Pulitzer prize winner) offers much atmosphere surrounding an intimate, somewhat sentimentalized portrait of the South Carolinian. Here he stands as the farsighted champion of right and justice, seeking to stave off the wave of degrading industrialism and save the purer old order. Quite in contrast, Gerald M. Capers in his (1960) biography presents a radically different picture. Far from a fearless, selfless, high-minded theorist, seeking to save the old Union from ravages of centralization, Presidential tyranny and threats of disunion and secession, Calhoun appears here as strictly a political opportunist. Practically his every move, from his early nationalist speeches through his attacks on Jackson's "abuse" of the patronage to advocating Texas' annexation were deliberately calculated to advance his own political fortunes to ultimate elevation to the White House, as Capers sees it. His giant ego and massive self-conceit provide for Capers the key to understanding Calhoun's political career. Even his political theorizing in defense of minority interests, so widely acclaimed by other writers, receives scant praise here. Capers, while not entirely convincing, gives pause to writers like Coit, who class Calhoun among "the first rank of American statesmen."

Jackson Biographies and Histories

A Selective List of Books mentioned in Chapter X, listed chronologically

1817	John H. Eaton, *Life of Andrew Jackson*. Philadelphia.
1834	William Cobbett, *Life of Andrew Jackson*. London.
1859–60	James Parton, *Life of Andrew Jackson*. 3 vols. New York.
1882	William Graham Summer, *Andrew Jackson as a Public Man, What He Was, What Chances He Had, and What He Did With Them*. Boston.
1876–88	Hermann E. Von Holst, *Constitutional and Political History of the United States*. 8 vols. Chicago.

1880–89   James Schouler, *History of the United States under the Constitution.* 6 vols. New York.

1893   Frederick Jackson Turner, "The Significance of the Frontier in American History," paper delivered at American Historical Association meeting in Chicago, 1893.

1893   Woodrow Wilson, *Division and Reunion.* New York.

1903   Ralph C. H. Catterall, *The Second Bank of the United States.* Chicago.

1905   Carl R. Fish, *The Civil Service and the Patronage.* New York.

1907   William MacDonald, *Jacksonian Democracy, 1828–1837.* New York.

1911   John S. Bassett, *The Life of Andrew Jackson.* 2 vols. Garden City.

1915   William E. Dodd, *Expansion and Conflict.* Boston.

1919   Frederick A. Ogg, *The Reign of Andrew Jackson.* New Haven.

1922   Claude G. Bowers, *Party Battles of the Jackson Period.* New York.

1926   Vernon L. Parrington, *Main Currents of American Thought,* 3 vols. New York.

1927   Charles and Mary Beard, *The Rise of American Civilization.* New York.

1932   Thomas P. Abernathy, *From Frontier to Plantation in Tennessee.*

1933   Marquis James, Andrew Jackson, *The Border Captain.* Indianapolis.

1937   Marquis James, *Andrew Jackson, Portrait of a President.* Indianapolis.

1943   Wilfred E. Binkley, *American Political Parties: Their Natural History.* New York.

1945   Arthur M. Schlesinger, Jr., *The Age of Jackson*. Boston.

1947   Bray Hammond, "Jackson, Biddle, and the Bank of the United States," *Journal of Economic History,* VII, 1–23. Also his *Banks and Politics in America: From the Revolution to the Civil War* (1957).

1948   Richard Hofstadter, *The American Political Tradition and the Men Who Made It.* New York.

1949   Joseph Dorfman, "The Jackson Wage-Earner Thesis," *American Historical Review,* LIV (1949), 296–306.

1949   Richard B. Morris, "Andrew Jackson, Strikebreaker," *American Historical Review,* LV (1949), 54–68.

1953   John W. Ward, *Andrew Jackson: Symbol for An Age.* New York.

1954   Leonard D. White, *The Jacksonians: A Study in Administrative History, 1828–1861.* New York.

1955   Louis Hartz, *The Liberal Tradition in America.* New York.

1957   Marvin Meyers, *The Jacksonian Persuasion.* Stanford.

1959   Glyndon G. Van Deusen, *The Jacksonian Era, 1828–1848.* New York.

1961   Lee Benson, *The Concept of Jacksonian Democracy: New York as a Test Case.* Princeton.

1966   Robert V. Remini, *Andrew Jackson.* New York.

1969   Edward Pessen, *Jacksonian America: Society, Personality and Politics.* Homewood.

Calhoun Biographies

A Selective List of Books mentioned in Chapter X, listed chronologically

1843   (John C. Calhoun). *Life of John C. Calhoun.* New York, 1843.

1852   Mary Bates, *The Private Life of John C. Calhoun.* Charleston, 1852.

1882   Hermann E. Von Holst. *John C. Calhoun.* Boston, 1882.

1903   Gustavus M. Pinckney. *Life of John C. Calhoun.* Charleston, 1903.

1908   Gaillard Hunt. *John C. Calhoun.* Philadelphia, 1908.

1917   William M. Meigs. *Life of John C. Calhoun.* 2 vols. Philadelphia, 1917.

1935   Arthur Styron. *The Cast-Iron Man: John C. Calhoun and American Democracy.* New York. 1782–1828.

1944   Charles M. Wiltse. *John C. Calhoun, Nationalist, 1782–1828.* Indianapolis.

1949   Charles M. Wiltse. *John C. Calhoun, Nullifier, 1829–1839.* Indianapolis.

1950   Margaret L. Coit. *John C. Calhoun, An American Portrait.* Boston.

1951   Charles M. Wiltse. *John C. Calhoun, Sectionalist, 1840–1850.* Indianapolis.

1960   Gerald M. Capers. *John C. Calhoun, Opportunist: A Reappraisal.* Gainesville, Florida.

1968   John L. Thomas, ed. *John C. Calhoun: A Profile.* New York.

XI Conclusion

WHEN history's balance sheet is added up, how do Jackson and Calhoun stand? After all the fire and fury of their deeds and words, of their proclamations and expositions, what imprint did they leave on the history of their country?

Both men reinforced the American belief in the self-made man. Both Jackson and Calhoun early revealed remarkable talents and rapidly moved up the ladder of public recognition, without seeming effort and accepting advancement as their natural due. Jackson, for example, was a lawyer at 21, United States attorney at 23, Congressman at 29, Senator at 30, and Tennessee Supreme Court justice at 31. Calhoun became a lawyer at 25, South Carolina legislator at 26, Congressman at 28, Secretary of War and confident of President Monroe at 35. But sharp differences appeared—Jackson in his 30's seemed to have no strong political ambition, preferring an active military career, whereas Calhoun in his 30's, goaded by ambition, was devising well-made plans to elevate himself to the Presidency. By ironic twist, Calhoun for all his scheming missed, and Jackson scarcely raising a finger was propelled into the Executive chair.

In many ways Jackson and Calhoun resembled each other. In physical appearance, as Margaret Coit acutely observes in her Calhoun biography, each man carried his Scotch-Irish inheritance—"the thin, wiry bodies, the long heads, bristling with thick, unruly hair; the deep-set eyes, gaunt cheeks . . . grim lines of mouth and jaw." In their long striding gait, they seemed much alike, also in their "vigorous, accented speech of the Southern hill country, from which all Jackson's roamings and all Calhoun's years in New England and Washington could not smooth away the last traces of the Scotch-Irish brogue and burr."

Perhaps it was something in their Calvinist upbringing that , bred in each man a sense of duty, rock-like integrity, unshakeable courage, and a special feeling of self-righteousness and rectitude in their dealings with other men. Both saw in magnified size evils around them; both were subject to delusions of wicked plots against them—Jackson, for instance, obsessed with the thought that the "monster" Bank was out to destroy him, Calhoun that the "deluded" abolitionist "fiends" were bent on ruining him and the South.

Both men emerged from an underprivileged start in life, labored against odds, married into social status and acceptance, acquired substantial property. As landholder-planters, both were convinced they were—in true Jeffersonian style—pursuing the highest, noblest calling as husbandmen of the earth. Both felt, too, a certain *noblesse oblige* to serve their fellow men when called upon—even to volunteer—as Jackson did in defending his community against hostile Indian threat and Calhoun did in defending his community against British commercial imposition or abolitionist assault.

In both a streak of tenacity, spilling over into stubbornness, remained firm throughout their lives. But regardless of tenacious, fierce exteriors exhibited in public, both had private lives touched with gentility, affection, tenderness. In adopting two young sons, raising two other boys, welcoming into his home an endless array of Rachel's relatives, Jackson revealed a human warmth of feeling and devotion widely noted by contemporaries. Calhoun, too, showed a gentle sensitivity in dealing with his family of nine children that belied his severe exterior.

Along with self-righteous tenacity went suspiciousness. After their personal break in 1831, each grew increasingly suspicious of the other—Jackson convinced that Calhoun was plotting nullification in order to take the South out of the Union and establish himself as President of a Southern confederacy; Calhoun equally certain that Jackson through control of the army and Presidential patronage sought to consolidate his power as a military despot and perpetuate a Jacksonian dynasty.

If the two men did much resemble each other, in what ways did they differ? Clearly, in career and personality lay sharp differences. In his pre-Presidential years Jackson had experienced life to the full in a variety of roles—lawyer, prosecutor, judge, Senator, land speculator, fancier, raiser and racer of horses, bettor on horses and game cocks, merchant, debtor, duelist, Indian fighter, planter, military general, and civil governor. Into every situation he threw himself with full energy, enthusiasm, and enjoyment. He loved to be with people. He knew people, how to chat, how to appeal, how to sway, how to command. "General Jackson," said one Senator, "understands the people of the United States twenty times better than his antagonists. . . . [He] has a peculiar way of addressing himself to the feelings of every man with whom he comes in contact." Here lay the secret of his political success. People responded to him almost instinctively. His charisma surpassed that of all other nineteenth century Americans, save Lincoln. The flamboyant vigor of his personality projected him, while still living, into a genuine American folk hero—a legend that has grown since his time.

In contrast, Calhoun's career and personality were a single track. A few years as a lawyer, some time spent managing his plantation were his only non-political exposures. Outside his family he seems not to have enjoyed being with people nor to have found pleasure in the ordinary diversions of life. He was quite incongenial in company; he himself conceded that he was a stranger five miles from his home. "A cast-iron man," as Harriet Martineau saw him, "who looks as if he had never been born and could never be extinguished." A curious, perverse thing that such a man, with such handicaps of personality and limited human experience, should devote his lifetime to politics, to managing the affairs of men.

But politics became the all-absorbing passion, obsession of his life, his devotion to "his work," his unrelenting "duty," a word he used most often. From his first election to Congress in 1810 to his death 40 years later, he single-mindedly focused his mind and energies on American politics. A strange concentration for a man who impressed one friend "rather as a mental and moral abstraction than a politician" and others as "certainly the most unskillful leader of a party that ever wielded a truncheon." That a man whose mind in his last twenty years became so much consumed by his own abstract thoughts and intrigued with philosophical speculation should devote his time and talent to the "art of the possible" is one of the major paradoxes of American political history.

But what of the impact of these similar yet strikingly different leaders on American affairs? A case could be made for the proposition that American history would not have been radically different if all Jackson's pre-1831 activities and all Calhoun's post-1831 activities were totally erased from the record. With the exception of Indian land cessions and the Florida acquisition, little that Jackson did before his Presidency (even including New Orleans that served more to boost his own popularity than anything else) substantially changed the nation's course of evolution. With the exception of rousing the South's sectional conciousness, little Calhoun did after 1831 affected the country's history. The year 1831 forms the great divide, the watershed for the two men.

What credits accure to Calhoun in history's ledger? Prior to 1831 his credits are substantial and notable. His labors in Congress put the country well on the way to becoming a strong, unified nation. Demanding strong national defense, pushing for a tariff to encourage American manufacturing, a Bank to stabilize finances and roads to bind the country closer together—all were statesmanship at its best to make the young nation survive and flourish. As Secretary of War Calhoun's labors in planning defense, initiating a General Staff, creating the Surgeon General's office, tightening bureaucratic responsibility, striving for a nationwide transportation network formed constructive efforts of a high order. As an administrator, Calhoun demonstrated exceptional ability; and had he become President his administration would without doubt have been efficiently managed. Indeed, had he become President in 1832, as he fully and justifiably expected, all his later efforts at theorizing state rights, minority interest, concurrent majority and the rest would likely never have been undertaken.

But 1831 brought the final personal break with Jackson, doubtless a major emotional trauma for Calhoun, dashing his lifetime dream, destroying his Presidential prospects. Little wonder that he turned to repairing his fortunes at home. And thrust into a personal minority alone, his personal cause of self-defense expanded into a defense of his state and section as a minority in the larger affairs of the country. Attempting to develop a balance of sections at times—South-West alliance offsetting the Northeast's power—he moved beyond at times in an effort to develop a balance of classes—property holders of all kinds joined in self-defense. His active mind produced a penetrating analysis of the nature of man and of government and made a superb formulation of the problem of majority-minority relations. But in his minority defense, he became blinded to the realities of his own age. His last years became a throwback to early times—a philosopher-theoretician in a day that called for activists, a localist in an era of nationalism, a defender of slavery in an "age of advancing liberties," an agrarian in a rapidly industrializing economy. His tragedy lies in his having outlived his time, rigidly tying himself to the narrow defense of a dying, restricting order of human affairs.

Jackson, although firm, never allowed himself to be trapped in the rigid embrace of a self-made strait-jacket. Though he offered no broad constructive program and enunciated no special political philosophy of his own, he acted and impressed the force of his vigorous personality on everything he touched. In defeating the British at New Orleans, he became the symbol for all Americans (as John Ward so well shows) of the untutored man of nature exercising sheer force of will, under Divine blessing, to preserve the nation's destiny in upholding liberty. In directing the nation's affairs as President, Jackson asserted and built the strength and independence of the Executive as the direct spokesman, leader, and champion of the people. As a popular leader, Jackson insisted, the President must control and direct his administration of public business by exercising power to appoint, direct, and dismiss, if need be, his lieutenants in carrying out the popular will as he conceived it. To make government responsive and responsible to the people's wishes, he helped forge a new instrument—the democratic Democratic party, appealing in terms that all understood—farmer, working man, merchant, rising capitalist, tradesman. Whether he wished it or not, he became in the popular view the symbol of the individual's freedom to pursue his own interests and develop his own abilities and fortunes—the champion of equality of rights and opportunities in economic pursuits (in fighting down the Bank), untrammeled by special privilege and artificial advantage—the spokesman of government as the insurer of a fair measure of justice in human affairs. In fighting nullification and disunion, he spoke and battled to preserve the United States as a single nation, worth saving because it formed "the world's best hope" of an effective democratic government.

APPENDIX: DOCUMENTS,
including letters, proclamations, messages, and other writings

Part I. Andrew Jackson

DOCUMENT NO. 1. *General Jackson defends New Orleans, 1814–1815.*

When the British invading force threatened the city of New Orleans in the fall of 1814, General Jackson called upon local residents to rise in defense of their homes and join with the troops under Jackson's command to repel the invaders. In September, 1814, he issued the following appeals—No. 1-A to the citizens of Louisiana and No. 1-B to free Negroes of the state. Jackson, *Correspondence,* ed. by John S. Bassett (Washington: Carnegie Institution, 1926), II, 58–59, hereafter cited as Jackson, *Correspondence.*

DOCUMENT 1-A

Louisianians! The Government of your choice is engaged in a just and honorable contest, for the security of your individual, and her National rights. On you a part of America, the only Country on Earth where every Man enjoys freedom, where its blessings are alike extended to the poor, and Rich, calls on you to protect these rights from the invading usurpation of Britain, and she calls not in vain.

I well know that every Man whose Soul beats high at the proud title of freemen, that every Louisianian, either by birth or adoption will promtly obey the voice of his Country; will rally around the Eagle of Columbia, rescue it from impounding danger, or nobly die, in the last ditch in its defence. The Individual who refuses to defend his rights when called by his Government, deserves to be a slave, and must be punished as an enemy to his Country, and a friend to her foe. . . .

DOCUMENT 1-B To the Free Coloured Inhabitants of Louisiana.[1]

Through a mistaken policy, my brave fellow Citizens, you have heretofore been deprived of a participation in the Glorious struggle for National rights, in which our Country is engaged. This shall no longer exist, as sons of freedom, you are now called upon to defend our most estimable blessing: As Americans, your Country looks with confidence to her adopted Children, for a valorous support, as a partial return for the advantages enjoyed, under her mild and equitable government. As fathers, husbands, and Brothers, you are summoned to rally around the standard of the Eagle, to defend all which is dear in existance. Your intelligent minds are not to be led away by false representations. Your love of honor would cause you to despise the Man who should attempt to deceive you. I shall not attempt it. In the sincerity of a Soldier, and the language of truth I address you. Your Country, altho' calling for your exertions does not wish you to engage in her cause, without amply remunicating [*sic*] you, for the services rendered.

After his brilliant victory over the British on January 8, 1819, General Jackson made the following report to Secretary of War James Monroe (Jackson, *Correspondence,* II, 136–7):

DOCUMENT 1-C To Secretary Monroe.
Camp 4 Miles below New Orleans, January 9, 1815.

Sir: During the days of the 6th and 7th, the enemy had been actively employed in making preparations for an attack on my lines. With infinite labor they had succeeded on the night of the 7th in getting their boats across from the lake to the river, by widening and deepening the canal on which they had effected their disembarkation. It had not been in my power to impede these operations by a general attack: added to other reasons, the nature of the troops under my command, mostly militia, rendered it too hazardous to attempt extensive *offensive* movements in an open country, against a numerous and well disciplined army. Although my forces, as to number, had been increased by the arrival of the Kentucky division, my strength had received very little addition; a small portion only of that detachment being provided with arms. Compelled thus to wait the attack of the enemy, I took every measure to repel it when it should be made, and to defeat the object he had in view. General Morgan, with the New Orleans contingent, the Louisiana militia and a strong detachment of the Kentucky troops, occupied an entrenched camp on the opposite side of the river, protected by strong batteries on the bank, erected and superintended by commodore Patterson.

In *my* encampment everything was ready for action, when, early on the morning of the 8th, the enemy after throwing a heavy shower of bombs and Congreve rockets, advanced their columns on my right and left, to storm my entrenchments. I cannot speak sufficiently in praise of the firmness and deliberation with which my whole line received their approach—*more* could not have been expected from veterans inured to war. For an hour the fire of the small arms was an incessant and severe as can be imagined. The artillery, too, directed by officers who displayed equal skill and courage, did great execution. Yet the columns of the enemy continued to advance with a firmness which reflects upon them the greatest credit. Twice the column which approached me on my left, was repulsed by the troops of General Carroll, those of General Coffee, and a division of the Kentucky militia, and twice they formed again and renewed the assault. At length, however, cut to pieces, they fled in confusion from the field, leaving it covered with their dead and wounded. The loss which the enemy sustained on this occasion, cannot be estimated at less than 1500 in killed, wounded and prisoners. Upwards of three hundred have already been delivered over for burial; and my men are still engaged in picking them up within my lines and carrying them to the point where the enemy are to receive them. This is in addition to the dead and wounded whom the enemy have been enabled to carry from the field, during and since the action, and to those who have since died of the wounds they have received. We have taken about 500 prisoners, upwards of 300 of whom are wounded, and a great part of them mortally. My loss has not exceeded, and I believe has not amounted to ten killed and as many wounded.

After the British troops had been driven off from New Orleans and news that the war had ended reached Jackson, he issued on March 21, 1815 the following "Address" to his troops (Jackson, *Correspondence,* II, 196–6):

DOCUMENT 1-D

March 21, 1815.
On so interesting occassion the commanding General can neither suppress his feelings, nor give utterance to them as he ought.

In parting with those brave men whose destinies have been so long united with his own and in whose labours and glories it is his happiness and his boast to have participated, his bosom is penetrated with sentiments of the liveliest sensibility. But what suitable tribute can he render to their extraordinary merit—What adequate praise can he bestow on exertions that are without a parralele? Let him in one burst of joy, gratitude, and exultation exclaim "these are the saviours of their country—the patriot soldiers who triumphed over the Invinciples of Wellington and conquered the conquerors of Europe"! With what patience did you submit to privations, with what fortitude did you endure fatigue and toil—what valour did you display in the feild of battle!! Possessing those dispositions which equally adorn the citizen and the soldier, the expectations of your country will be met, in peace, as her hopes have been gratified in war. Go then to your homes, to those tender connexions and those blissful scecnes which render life so dear—go, full of honor and wreathed with Laurels whose leaves shall never wither. With what happiness will you not, when participating in the bosom of your families the enjoyment of peaceful life look back to the fatigues and toils which you have so honourably borne? How will all your past sufferings be converted into sources of inexpressible delight. Who that never experienced your troubles will be able to appreciate your joys! The man who slumbered ingloriously at home during your painful marches, your nights of watchfulness and your days of toil, will envy you the happiness which these recollections will afford—still more will he envy you, the gratitude of that country which you have saved! . . .

Again the commandg General, before pronouncing a painful farewell must present his acknowledgements and thanks to both officers and soldiers, for the Zealous aid and concert of the former and for the faithful services of the latter. Though the expression of these thanks be feeble they have the assurance that the gratitude of a nation of Freemen is theirs—the approbation of an admiring world.

DOCUMENT NO. 2

During the 1824 Presidential campaign L. H. Coleman of Warrenton, North Carolina, wrote to the then Senator Jackson asking the latter's view on the protective tariff bill then being considered by Congress. Since Jackson was also a candidate for President, he stated his views carefully in a reply to Coleman on April 26, 1824 (Jackson, *Correspondence,* II, 249–51), which runs in part:

To L. H. Coleman.
. . . . You ask my opinion on the Tariff. I answer, that I am in favor of a judicious examination and revision of it; and so far as the Tariff before us embraces the design of fostering, protecting, and preserving within

ourselves the means of national defense and independence, particularly in a state of war, I would advocate and support it. The experience of the late war ought to teach us a lesson; and one never to be forgotten. If our liberty and republican form of government, procured for us by our revolutionary fathers, are worth the blood and treasure at which they were obtained, it surely is our duty to protect and defend them. Can there be an American patriot who saw the privations, dangers, and difficulties experienced for the want of a proper means of defense during the last war, who would be willing again to hazard the safety of our country if embroiled; or rest it for defense on the precarious means of national resources to be derived from commerce, in a state of war with a maratime power which might destroy that commerce to prevent our obtaining the means of defense, and thereby subdue us? I hope there is not; and if there is, I am sure he does not deserve to enjoy the blessing of freedom. . . .

This Tariff—I mean a judicious one—possesses more fanciful than real dangers. I will ask what is the real situation of the agriculturalist? Where has the American farmer a market for his surplus products? Except for cotton he has neither a foreign nor a home market. Does not this clearly prove, when there is no market either at home or abroad, that there is too much labor employed in agriculture? and that the channels of labor should be multiplied? Common sense points out at once the remedy. Draw from agriculture the superabundant labor, employ it in mechanism and manufactures, thereby creating a home market for your breadstuffs, and distributing labor to a most profitable account, and benefits to the country will result. Take from agriculture in the United States six hundred thousand men, women, and children, and you at once give a home market for more bread stuffs than all Europe now furnishes us. In short, sir, we have been too long subject to the policy of the British merchants. It is time we should become a little more *Americanized,* and instead of feeding the paupers and laborers of Europe, feed our own, or else in a short time, by continuing our present policy, we shall all be paupers ourselves.

It is, therefore, my opinion that a careful Tariff is much wanted to pay our national debt, and afford us the means of that defense within ourselves on which the safety and liberty of the country depend; and last, though not least, give a proper distribution to our labor, which must prove beneficial to the happiness, independence, and wealth of the community. . . .

DOCUMENT NO. 3.   *Jackson's first annual message to Congress.*

After assuming the Presidency, Jackson labored with the aid of his advisors in preparing the first message that he sent to Congress on December 8, 1829 (J. D. Richardson, comp., *Messages and Papers of the Presidents,* 11 vols., New York: Bureau of National Literature, 1911, II, 442–461 hereafter cited as *Mess. Pres.*) Among other topics, President Jackson touched upon three important questions. The election and term of President, which had concerned Jackson ever since the unsatisfactory outcome of 1824's election, he dealt with in

DOCUMENT 3-A
. . . I consider it one of the most urgent of my duties to bring to your attention the propriety of amending that part of our Constitution which relates to the election of President and Vice-President. Our system of government was by its framers deemed an experiment, and they therefore consistently provided a mode of remedying its defects.

To the people belongs the right of electing their Chief Magistrate; it was never designed that their choice should in any case be defeated, either by the intervention of electoral colleges or by the agency confided, under certain contingencies, to the House of Representatives. Experience proves that in proportion as agents to execute the will of the people are multiplied there is danger of their wishes being frustrated. Some may be unfaithful;

all are liable to err. So far, therefore, as the people can with convenience speak, it is safer for them to express their own will.

The number of aspirants to the Presidency and the diversity of the interests which may influence their claims leave little reason to expect a choice in the first instance, and in that event the election must devolve on the House of Representatives, where it is obvious the will of the people may not be always ascertained, or, if ascertained, may not be regarded. From the mode of voting by States the choice is to be made by 24 votes, and it may often occur that one of these will be controlled by an individual Representative. Honors and offices are at the disposal of the successful candidate. Repeated ballotings may make it apparent that a single individual holds the cast in his hand. May he not be tempted to name his reward? But even without corruption, supposing the probity of the Representative to be proof against the powerful motives by which it may be assailed, the will of the people is still constantly liable to be misrepresented. One may err from ignorance of the wishes of his constituents; another from a conviction that it is his duty to be governed by his own judgment of the fitness of the candidates; finally, although all were inflexibly honest, all accurately informed of the wishes of their constituents, yet under the present mode of election a minority may often elect a President, and when this happens it may reasonably be expected that efforts will be made on the part of the majority to rectify this injurious operation of their institutions. But although no evil of this character should result from such a perversion of the first princple of our system—*that the majority is to govern*—it must be very certain that a President elected by a minority can not enjoy the confidence necessary to the successful discharge of his duties.

In this as in all other matters of public concern policy requires that as few impediments as possible should exist to the free operation of the public will. Let us, then, endeavor so to amend our system that the office of Chief Magistrate may not be conferred upon any citizen but in pursuance of a fair expression of the will of the majority.

I would therefore recommend such an amendment of the Constitution as may remove all intermediate agency in the election of the President and Vice-President. The mode may be so regulated as to preserve to each State its present relative weight in the election, and a failure in the first attempt may be provided for by confining the second to a choice between the two highest candidates. In connection with such an amendment it would seem advisable to limit the service of the Chief Magistrate to a single term of either four or six years. If, however, it should not be adopted, it is worthy of consideration whether a provision disqualifying for office the Representatives in Congress on whom such an election may have devolved would not be proper. . . .

In removing many hold-over appointees from previous administrations, Jackson filled the vacated places in the executive branch with his own partisans. In the face of a storm of criticism, Jackson explained his views of "rotation of office" in the message to Congress.

DOCUMENT 3-B

. . . There are, perhaps, few men who can for any great length of time enjoy office and power without being more or less under the influence of feelings unfavorable to the faithful discharge of their public duties. Their integrity may be proof against improper considerations immediately addressed to themselves, but they are apt to acquire a habit of looking with indifference upon the public interests and of tolerating conduct from which an unpracticed man would revolt. Office is considered as a species of property, and government rather as a means of promoting individual interests than as an instrument created solely for the service of the people. Corruption in some and in others a perversion of correct feelings and principles divert government from its legitimate ends and make it an engine for the support of the few at the expense of the many. The duties of all public officers are, or at least admit of being made, so plain and simple that men of intelligence may readily qualify themselves for their performance; and I can not but believe that more is lost by the long continuance of men in office than is generally to be gained by their experience. I submit, therefore, to your consideration whether the efficiency of the Government would not be promoted and official industry and integrity better secured by a general extension of the law which limits appointments to four years.

In a country where offices are created solely for the benefit of the people no one man has any more intrinsic right to official station than another. Offices were not established to give support to particular men at the public expense. No individual wrong is, therefore, done by removal, since neither appointment to nor continuance in office is matter of right. The incumbent became an officer with a view to public benefits, and when these require his removal they are not to be sacrificed to private interests. It is the people, and they alone, who have a right to complain when a bad officer is substituted for a good one. He who is removed has the same means of obtaining a living that are enjoyed by the millions who never held office. The proposed limitation would destroy the idea of property now so generally connected with official station, and although individual distress may be sometimes produced, it would, by promoting that rotation which constitutes a leading principle in the republican creed, give healthful action to the system. . . .

In his message Jackson included also the following statement and recommendation concerning the Indian tribes.

DOCUMENT 3-C

. . . I informed the Indians inhabiting parts of Georgia and Alabama that their attempt to establish an independent government would not be countenanced by the Executive of the United States, and advised them to emigrate beyond the Mississippi or submit to the laws of those States.

Our conduct toward these people is deeply interesting

to our national character. Their present condition, contrasted with what they once were, makes a most powerful appeal to our sympathies. Our ancestors found them the uncontrolled possessors of these vast regions. By persuasion and force they have been made to retire from river to river and from mountain to mountain, until some of the tribes have become extinct and others have left but remnants to preserve for awhile their once terrible names. Surrounded by the whites with their arts of civilization, which by destroying the resources of the savage doom him to weakness and decay, the fate of the Mohegan, the Narragansett, and the Delaware is fast overtaking the Choctaw, the Cherokee, and the Creek. That this fate surely awaits them if they remain within the limits of the States does not admit of a doubt. Humanity and national honor demand that every effort should be made to avert so great a calamity. It is too late to inquire whether it was just in the United States to include them and their territory within the bounds of new States, whose limits they could control. That step can not be retraced. A State can not be dismembered by Congress or restricted in the exercise of her constitutional power. But the people of those States and of every State, actuated by feelings of justice and a regard for our national honor, submit to you the interesting question whether something can not be done, consistently with the rights of the States, to preserve this much-injured race.

As a means of effecting this end I suggest for your consideration the propriety of setting apart an ample district west of the Mississippi, and without the limits of any State or Territory now formed, to be guaranteed to the Indian tribes as long as they shall occupy it, each tribe having a distinct control over the portion designated for its use. There they may be secured in the enjoyment of governments of their own choice, subject to no other control from the United States than such as may be necessary to preserve peace on the frontier and between the several tribes. There the benevolent may endeavor to teach them the arts of civilization, and, by promoting union and harmony among them, to raise up an interesting commonwealth, destined to perpetuate the race and to attest the humanity and justice of this Government.

This emigration should be voluntary, for it would be as cruel as unjust to compel the aborigines to abandon the graves of their fathers and seek a home in a distant land. But they should be distinctly informed that if they remain within the limits of the States they must be subject to their laws. In return for their obedience as individuals they will without doubt be protected in the enjoyment of those possessions which they have improved by their industry. But it seems to me visionary to suppose that in this state of things claims can be allowed on tracts of country on which they have neither dwelt nor made improvements, merely because they have seen them from the mountain or passed them in the chase. Submitting to the laws of the States, and receiving, like other citizens, protection in their persons and property, they will ere long become merged in the mass of our population. . . .

DOCUMENT NO. 4.   *Internal Improvements.*

Rejecting a bill passed by Congress authorizing the United States government to subscribe federal funds to the stock of a private corporation that would construct a road from Maysville to Lexington, Kentucky, Jackson sent to Congress the following Maysville Road Veto message (*Mess. Pres.* II, 483–93.):

May 27, 1830.

To the House of Representatives.

GENTLEMEN: I have maturely considered the bill proposing to authorize "a subscription of stock in the Maysville, Washington, Paris, and Lexington Turnpike Road Company," and now return the same to the House of Representatives, in which it originated, with my objections to its passage.

Sincerely friendly to the improvement of our country

by means of roads and canals, I regret that any difference of opinion in the mode of contributing to it should exist between us; and if in stating this difference I go beyond what the occasion may be deemed to call for, I hope to find an apology in the great importance of the subject, an unfeigned respect for the high source from which this branch of its has emanated, and an anxious wish to be correctly understood by my constituents in the discharge of all my duties. Diversity of sentiment among public functionaries actuated by the same general motives, on the character and tendency of particular measures, is an incident common to all Governments, and the more to be expected in one which, like ours, owes its existence to the freedom of opinion, and must be upheld by the same influence. Controlled as we thus are by a higher tribunal, before which our respective acts will be canvassed with the indulgence due to the imperfections of our nature, and with that intelligence and unbiased judgment which are the true correctives of error, all that our responsibility demands is that the public good should be the measure of our views, dictating alike their frank expression and honest maintenance. . . .

The constitutional power of the Federal Government to construct or promote works of internal improvement presents itself in two points of view—the first as bearing upon the sovereignty of the States within whose limits their execution is contemplated, if jurisdiction of the territory which they may occupy be claimed as necessary to their preservation and use; the second as asserting the simple right to appropriate money from the National Treasury in aid of such works when undertaken by State authority, surrendering the claim of jurisdiction. In the first view the question of power is an open one, and can be decided without the embarrassments attending the other, arising from the practice of the Government. Although frequently and strenuously attempted, the power to this extent has never been exercised by the Government in a single instance. It does not, in my opinion, possess it; and no bill, therefore, which admits it can receive my official sanction.

But in the other view of the power the question is differently situated. The ground taken at an early period of the Government was "that whenever money has been raised by the general authority and is to be applied to a particular measure, a question arises whether the particular measure be within the enumerated authorities vested in Congress. If it be, the money requisite for it may be applied to it; if not, no such application can be made." The document in which this principle was first advanced is of deservedly high authority, and should be held in grateful remembrance for its immediate agency in rescuing the country from much existing abuse and for its conservative effect upon some of the most valuable principles of the Constitution. The symmetry and purity of the Government would doubtless have been better preserved if this restriction of the power of appropriation could have been maintained without weakening its ability to fulfill the general objects of its institution, an effect so likely to attend its admission, notwithstanding its apparent fitness, that every subsequent Administration of the Government, embracing a period of thirty out of the forty-two years of its existence, has adopted a more enlarged construction of the power. It is not my purpose to detain you by a minute recital of the acts which sustain this assertion, but it is proper that I should notice some of the most prominent in order that the reflections which they suggest to my mind may be better understood. . . .

Independently of the sanction given to appropriations for the Cumberland and other roads and objects under this power, the Administration of Mr. Madison was characterized by an act which furnishes the strongest evidence of his opinion of its extent. A bill was passed through both Houses of Congress and presented for his approval, "setting apart and pledging certain funds for constructing roads and canals and improving the navigation of water courses, in order to facilitate, promote, and give security to internal commerce among the several States and to render more easy and less expensive the means and provisions for the common defense." Regarding the bill as asserting a power in the Federal Government to construct roads and canals within the limits of the States in which they were made, he objected to its passage on the ground of its unconstitutionality, declaring that the assent of the respective States in the mode provided by the bill could not confer the power in question; that the only cases in which the consent and cession of particular States can extend the power of Congress are those specified and provided for in the Constitution, and superadding to these avowals his opinion that "a restriction of the power 'to provide for the common defense and general welfare' to cases which are to be provided for by the expenditure of money would still leave within the legislative power of Congress all the great and most important measures of Government, money being the ordinary and necessary means of carrying them into execution." I have not been able to consider these declarations in any other point of view than as a concession that the right of appropriation is not limited by the power to carry into effect the measure for which the money is asked, as was formerly contended.

The views of Mr. Monroe upon this subject were not left to inference. During his Administration a bill was passed through both Houses of Congress conferring the jurisdiction and prescribing the mode by which the Federal Government should exercise it in the case of the Cumberland road. He returned it with objections to its passage, and in assigning them took occasion to say that in the early stages of the Government he had inclined to the construction that it had no right to expend money except in the performance of acts authorized by the other specific grants of power, according to a strict construction of them, but that on further reflection and observation his mind had undergone a change; that his opinion then was "that Congress have an unlimited power to raise money, and that in its appropriation they have a discretionary power, restricted only by the duty to appropriate it to purposes of common defense, and of general, not local, national, not State, benefit;" and this was avowed to be the governing principle through the residue of his Administration. The views of the last Administration are of such recent date as to render a particular reference to them unnecessary. It is well known that the appropriating power, to the utmost extent which had been claimed for it, in relation to internal improvements was fully recognized and exercised by it.

. . . What is properly *national* in its character or otherwise is an inquiry which is often extremely difficult of solution. The appropriations of one year for an object which is considered national may be rendered nugatory by the refusal of a succeeding Congress to continue the work on the ground that it is local. No aid can be derived from the intervention of corporations. The question regards the character of the work, not that of those by whom it is to be accomplished. Notwithstanding the union of the Government with the corporation by whose immediate agency any work of internal improvement is carried on, the inquiry will still remain, Is it national and conducive to the benefit of the whole, or local and operating only to the advantage of a portion of the Union?

But although I might not feel it to be my official duty to interpose the Executive veto to the passage of a bill appropriating money for the construction of such works as are authorized by the States and are national in their character, I do not wish to be understood as expressing an opinion that it is expedient at this time for the General Government to embark in a system of this kind; and anxious that my constituents should be possessed of my views on this as well as on all other subjects which they have committed to my discretion, I shall state them frankly and briefly. Besides many minor considerations, there are two prominent views of the subject which have made a deep impression upon my mind, which, I think, are well entitled to your serious attention, and will, I hope, be maturely weighed by the people. . . .

Although many of the States, with laudable zeal and under the influence of an enlightened policy, are successfully applying their separate efforts to works of this character, the desire to enlist the aid of the General Government in the construction of such as from their nature ought to devolve upon it, and to which the means of the individual States are inadequate, is both rational and patriotic, and if that desire is not gratified now it does not follow that it never will be. The general intelligence and public spirit of the American people furnish a sure guaranty that at the proper time this policy will be made to prevail under circumstances more auspicious to its successful prosecution than those which now exist. But great as this object undoubtedly is, it is not the only one which demands the fostering care of the Government. The preservation and success of the republican principle rest with us. To elevate its character and extend its influence rank among our most important duties, and the best means to accomplish this desirable end are those which will rivet the attachment of our citizens to the Government of their choice by the comparative lightness of their public burthens and by the attraction which the superior success of its operations will present to the admiration and respect of the world. Through the favor of an overruling and indulgent Providence our country is blessed with general prosperity and our citizens exempted from the pressure of taxation, which other less favored portions of the human family are obliged to bear; yet it is true that many of the taxes collected from our citizens through the medium of imposts have for a considerable period been onerous. In many particulars these taxes have borne severely upon the laboring and less prosperous classes of the community, being imposed on the necessaries of life, and this, too, in cases where the burthen was not relieved by the consciousness that it would ultimately contribute to make us independent of foreign nations for articles of prime necessity by the encouragement of their growth and manufacture at home. They have been cheerfully borne because they were thought to be necessary to the support of Government and the payment of the debts unavoidably incurred in the acquisition and maintenance of our national rights and liberties. But have we a right to calculate on the same cheerful acquiescence when it is known that the necessity for their continuance would cease were it not for irregular, improvident, and unequal appropriations of the public funds? Will not the people demand, as they have a right to do, such a prudent system of expenditure as will pay the debts of the Union and authorize the reduction of every tax to as low a point as the wise observance of the necessity to protect that portion of our manufactures and labor whose prosperity is essential to our national safety and independence will allow? When the national debt is paid, the duties upon those articles which we do not raise may be repealed with safety, and still leave, I trust, without oppression to any section of the country, an accumulating surplus fund, which may be beneficially applied to some well-digested system of improvement. . . .

How gratifying the effect of presenting to the world the sublime spectacle of a Republic of more than 12,000,000 happy people, in the fifty-fourth year of her existence, after having passed through two protracted wars—the one for the acquisition and the other for the maintenance of liberty—free from debt and with all her immense resources unfettered! What a salutary influence would not such an exhibition exercise upon the cause of liberal principles and free government throughout the world! Would we not ourselves find in its effect an additional guaranty that our political institutions will be transmitted to the most remote posterity without decay? A course of policy destined to witness events like these can not be benefited by a legislation which tolerates a scramble for appropriations that have no relation to any general system of improvement, and whose good effects must of necessity be very limited. In the best view of these appropriations, the abuses to which they lead far exceed the good which they are capable of promoting. They may be resorted to as artful expedients to shift upon the Government the losses of unsuccessful private speculation, and thus, by ministering to personal ambition and self-aggrandizement, tend to sap the foundations of public virtue and taint the administration of the Government with a demoralizing influence.

In the other view of the subject, and the only remaining one which it is my intention to present at this time, is involved the expediency of embarking in a system of internal improvement without a previous amendment of the Constitution explaining and defining the precise powers of the Federal Government over it. Assuming the right to appropriate money to aid in the construction of national works to be warranted by the cotemporaneous and continued exposition of the Constitution, its insufficiency for the successful prosecution of them must be admitted by all candid minds. If we look to usage to define the extent of the right, that will be found so variant and embracing so much that has been overruled as to involve the whole subject in great uncertainty and to render the execution of our respective duties in relation to it replete with difficulty and embarrassment. It is in regard to such works and the acquisition of additional territory that the practice obtained its first footing. In most, if not all, other disputed questions of appropriation the construction of the Constitution may be regarded as unsettled if the right to apply money in the enumerated cases is placed on the ground of usage.

This subject has been one of much, and, I may add, painful, reflection to me. It has bearings that are well calculated to exert a powerful influence upon our hitherto prosperous system of government, and which, on some accounts, may even excite despondency in the breast of an American citizen. I will not detain you with professions of zeal in the cause of internal improvements. If to be their friend is a virtue which deserves commendation, our country is blessed with an abundance of it, for I do not suppose there is an intelligent citizen who does not wish to see them flourish. But though all are their friends, but few, I trust, are unmindful of the means by which they should be promoted; none certainly are so degenerate as to desire their success at the cost of that sacred instrument with the preservation of which is indissolubly bound our country's hopes. If different impressions are entertained in any quarter; if it is expected that the people of this country, reckless of their constitutional obligations, will prefer their local interest to the principles of the Union, such expectations will in the end be disappointed; or if it be not so, then indeed has the world but little to hope from the example of free government. When an honest observance of constitutional compacts can not be obtained from communities like ours, it need not be anticipated elsewhere, and the cause in which there has been so much martyrdom, and from which so much was expected by the friends of liberty, may be abandoned, and the degrading truth that man is unfit for self-government admitted. And this will be the case if *expediency* be made a rule of construction in interpreting the Constitution. Power in no government could desire a better shield for the insidious advances which it is ever ready to make upon the checks that are designed to restrain its action.

But I do not entertain such gloomy apprehensions. If it be the wish of the people that the construction of roads and canals should be conducted by the Federal Government, it is not only highly expedient, but indispensably necessary, that a previous amendment of the Constitution, delegating the necessary power and defining and restricting its exercise with reference to the sovereignty of the States, should be made. Without it nothing extensively useful can be effected. The right to exercise as much jurisdiction as is necessary to preserve the works and to raise funds by the collection of tolls to keep them in repair can not be dispensed with. The Cumberland road should be an instructive admonition of the consequences of acting without this right. Year after year contests are witnessed, growing out of efforts to obtain the necessary appropriations for completing and repairing this useful work. Whilst one Congress may claim and exercise the power, a succeeding one may deny it; and this fluctuation of opinion must be unavoidably fatal to any scheme which from its extent would promote the interests and elevate the character of the country. The experience of the past has shown that the opinion of Congress is subject to such fluctuations.

If it be the desire of the people that the agency of the Federal Government should be confined to the appropriation of money in aid of such undertakings, in virtue of State authorities, then the occasion, the manner, and the extent of the appropriations should be made the subject of constitutional regulation. This is the more necessary in order that they may be equitable among the several States, promote harmony between different sections of the Union and their representatives, preserve other parts of the Constitution from being undermined by the exercise of doubtful powers or the too great extension of those which are not so, and protect the whole subject against the deleterious influence of combinations to carry by concert measures which, considered by themselves, might meet but little countenance.

That a constitutional adjustment of this power upon equitable principles is in the highest degree desirable can scarcely be doubted, nor can it fail to be promoted by every sincere friend to the success of our political institutions. In no government are appeals to the source of power in cases of real doubt more suitable than in ours. No good motive can be assigned for the exercise of power by the constituted authorities, while those for whose benefit it is to be exercised have not conferred it and may not be willing to confer it. It would seem to me that an honest application of the conceded powers of the General Government to the advancement of the common weal present a sufficient scope to satisfy a reasonable ambition. The difficulty and supposed impracticability of obtaining an amendment of the Constitution in this respect is, I firmly believe, in a great degree unfounded. The time has never yet been when the patriotism and intelligence of the American people were not fully equal to the greatest exigency, and it never will when the subject calling forth their interposition is plainly presented to them. To do so with the questions involved in this bill, and to urge them to an early, zealous, and full consideration of their deep importance, is, in my estimation, among the highest of our duties.

A supposed connection between appropriations for internal improvement and the system of protecting duties, growing out of the anxieties of those more immediately interested in their success, has given rise to suggestions which it is proper I should notice on this occasion. My opinions on these subjects have never been concealed from those who had a right to know them. Those which I have entertained on the latter have frequently placed me in opposition to individuals as well as communities whose claims upon my friendship and gratitude are of the strongest character, but I trust there has been nothing in my public life which has exposed me to the suspicion of being thought capable of sacrificing my views of duty to private considerations, however strong they may have been or deep the regrets which they are capable of exciting.

As long as the encouragement of domestic manufactures is directed to national ends it shall receive from me a temperate but steady support. There is no necessary connection between it and the system of appropriations. On the contrary, it appears to me that the supposition of their dependence upon each other is calculated to excite the prejudices of the public against both. The former is sustained on the grounds of its consistency with the letter and spirit of the Constitution, of its origin being traced to the assent of all the parties to the original compact, and of its having the support and approbation of a majority of the people, on which account it is at least entitled to a fair experiment. The suggestions to which I have alluded refer to a forced continuance of the national debt by means of large appropriations as a substitute for the security which the system derives from the principles on which it has hitherto been sustained. Such a course would certainly indicate either an unreasonable distrust of the people or a consciousness that the system does not possess sufficient soundness for its support if left to their voluntary choice and its own merits. Those who suppose that any policy thus founded can be long upheld in this country have looked upon its history with eyes very different from mine. This policy, like every other, must abide the will of the people, who will not be likely to allow any device, however specious, to conceal its character and tendency.

In presenting these opinions I have spoken with the freedom and candor which I thought the occasion for their expression called for, and now respectfully return the bill which has been under consideration for your further deliberation and judgment.

DOCUMENT NO. 5.   *Veto of Bank of United States Recharter Bill.*

During the first half of 1832, amid conflicting pressures and demands, Congress fashioned a bill to recharter the Bank of the United States, extending the Bank's authority to operate for another 20 years after its current charter would expire in 1836. The move to pass a bill to recharter the Bank in 1832, four years before it would become necessary, was dictated by Presidential politics, the Henry Clay opposition seeking to embarrass President Jackson on the Bank issue with a Presidential election coming up in November. Jackson refused his assent to the bill and explained his disapproval in one of the great state papers of American history, the Bank veto message, sent to Congress, July 10, 1832, (*Mess. Pres.,* II, 576–591):

To the Senate:
    The bill "to modify and continue" the act entitled "An act to incorporate the subscribers to the Bank of the United States" was presented to me on the 4th July instant. Having considered it with that solemn regard to the principles of the Constitution which the day was calculated to inspire, and come to the conclusion that it ought not to become a law, I herewith return it to the Senate, in which it originated, with my objections.
    A bank of the United States is in many respects convenient for the Government and useful to the people. Entertaining this opinion, and deeply impressed with the belief that some of the powers and privileges possessed by the existing bank are unauthorized by the Constitution, subversive of the rights of the States, and dangerous to the liberties of the people, I felt it my duty at an early

period of my Administration to call the attention of
Congress to the practicability of organizing an institution combining all its advantages and obviating these
objections. I sincerely regret that in the act before me
I can perceive none of those modifications of the bank
charter which are necessary, in my opinion, to make it
compatible with justice, with sound policy, or with the
Constitution of our country.

The present corporate body, denominated the president, directors, and company of the Bank of the United
States, will have existed at the time this act is intended
to take effect twenty years. It enjoys an exclusive privilege of banking under the authority of the General Government, a monopoly of its favor and support, and, as
a necessary consequence, almost a monopoly of the foreign and domestic exchange. The powers, privileges, and
favors bestowed upon it in the original charter, by increasing the value of the stock far above its par value,
operated as a gratuity of many millions to the stockholders.

An apology may be found for the failure to guard
against this result in the consideration that the effect of
the original act of incorporation could not be certainly
foreseen at the time of its passage. The act before me
proposes another gratuity to the holders of the same
stock, and in many cases to the same men, of at least
seven millions more. This donation finds no apology in
any uncertainty as to the effect of the act. On all hands
it is conceded that its passage will increase at least 20
or 30 per cent more the market price of the stock, subject
to the payment of the annuity of $200,000 per year
secured by the act, thus adding in a moment one-fourth
its par value. It is not our own citizens only who are to
receive the bounty of our Government. More than eight
millions of the stock of this bank are held by foreigners.
By this act the American Republic proposes virtually to
make them a present of some millions of dollars. For
these gratuities to foreigners and to some of our own
opulent citizens the act secures no equivalent whatever.
They are the certain gains of the present stockholders

under the operation of this act, after making full allowance for the payment of the bonus.

Every monopoly and all exclusive privileges are granted at the expense of the public, which ought to receive a fair equivalent. The many millions which this act proposes to bestow on the stockholders of the existing bank must come directly or indirectly out of the earnings of the American people. It is due to them, therefore, if their Government sell monopolies and exclusive privileges, that they should at least exact for them as much as they are worth in open market. The value of the monopoly in this case may be correctly ascertained. The twenty-eight millions of stock would probably be at an advance of 50 per cent, and command in market at least $42,000,000, subject to the payment of the present bonus. The present value of the monopoly, therefore, is $17,000,000, and this the act proposes to sell for three millions, payable in fifteen annual installments of $200,000 each.

It is not conceivable how the present stockholders can have any claim to the special favor of the Government. The present corporation has enjoyed its monopoly during the period stipulated in the original contract. If we must have such a corporation, why should not the Government sell out the whole stock and thus secure to the people the full market value of the privileges granted? Why should not Congress create and sell twenty-eight millions of stock, incorporating the purchasers with all the powers and privileges secured in this act and putting the premium upon the sales into the Treasury?

But this act does not permit competition in the purchase of this monopoly. It seems to be predicated on the erroneous idea that the present stockholders have a prescriptive right not only to the favor but to the bounty of Government. It appears that more than a fourth part of the stock is held by foreigners and the residue is held by a few hundred of our own citizens, chiefly of the richest class. For their benefit does this act exclude the whole American people from competition in the purchase of this monopoly and dispose of it for many millions less than it is worth. This seems the less excusable because some of our citizens not now stockholders petitioned that the door of competition might be opened, and offered to take a charter on terms much more favorable to the Government and country.

. . . The modifications of the existing charter proposed by this act are not such, in my view, as make it consistent with the rights of the States or the liberties of the people. The qualification of the right of the bank to hold real estate, the limitation of its power to establish branches, and the power reserved to Congress to forbid the circulation of small notes are restrictions comparatively of little value or importance. All the objectionable principles of the existing corporation, and most of its odious features, are retained without alleviation.

The fourth section provides "that the notes or bills of the said corporation, although the same be, on the faces thereof, respectively made payable at one place only, shall nevertheless be received by the said corporation at the bank or at any of the offices of discount and deposit thereof if tendered in liquidation or payment of any balance or balances due to said corporation or to such office of discount and deposit from any other incorporated bank." This provision secures to the State banks a legal privilege in the Bank of the United States which is withheld from all private citizens. If a State bank in Philadelphia owe the Bank of the United States and have notes issued by the St. Louis branch, it can pay the debt with those notes, but if a merchant, mechanic, or other private citizen be in like circumstances he can not by law pay his debt with those notes, but must sell them at a discount or send them to St. Louis to be cashed. This boon conceded to the State banks, though not unjust in itself, is most odious because it does not measure out equal justice to the high and the low, the rich and the poor. To the extent of its practical effect it is a bond of union among the banking establishments of the nation, erecting them into an interest separate from that of the people, and its necessary tendency is to unite the Bank of the United States and the State banks in any measure which may be thought conducive to their common interest. . . .

Of the twenty-five directors of this bank five are chosen by the Government and twenty by the citizen stockholders. From all voice in these elections the foreign stockholders are excluded by the charter. In proportion, therefore, as the stock is transferred to foreign holders the extent of suffrage in the choice of directors is curtailed. Already is almost a third of the stock in foreign hands and not represented in elections. It is constantly passing out of the country, and this act will accelerate its departure. The entire control of the institution would necessarily fall into the hands of a few citizen stockholders, and the ease with which the object would be accomplished would be a temptation to designing men to secure that control in their own hands by monopolizing the remaining stock. There is danger that a president and directors would then be able to elect themselves from year to year, and without responsibility or control manage the whole concerns of the bank during the existence of its charter. It is easy to conceive that great evils to our country and its institutions might flow from such a concentration of power in the hands of a few men irresponsible to the people.

Is there no danger to our liberty and independence in a bank that in its nature has so little to bind it to our country? The president of the bank has told us that most of the State banks exist by its forbearance. Should its influence become concentered, as it may under the operation of such an act as this, in the hands of a self-elected directory whose interests are identified with those of the foreign stockholders, will there not be cause to tremble for the purity of our elections in peace and for the independence of our country in war? Their power would be great whenever they might choose to exert it; but if this monopoly were regularly renewed every fifteen or twenty years on terms proposed by themselves, they might seldom in peace put forth their strength to influence elections or control the affairs of the nation. But if any private citizen or public functionary should interpose to curtail its powers or prevent a renewal of its privileges, it can not be doubted that he would be made to feel its influence.

Should the stock of the bank principally pass into the hands of the subjects of a foreign country, and we should unfortunately become involved in a war with that country, what would be our condition? Of the course which would be pursued by a bank almost wholly owned by the subjects of a foreign power, and managed by those whose interests, if not affections, would run in the same direction there can be no doubt. All its operations within would be in aid of the hostile fleets and armies without. Controlling our currency, receiving our public moneys, and holding thousands of our citizens in dependence, it would be more formidable and dangerous than the naval and military power of the enemy.

If we must have a bank with private stockholders, every consideration of sound policy and every impulse of American feeling admonishes that it should be *purely American.* . . .

It is maintained by the advocates of the bank that its constitutionality in all its features ought to be considered as settled by precedent and by the decision of the Supreme Court. To this conclusion I can not assent. Mere precedent is a dangerous source of authority, and should not be regarded as deciding questions of constitutional power except where the acquiescence of the people and the States can be considered as well settled. So far from this being the case on this subject, an argument against the bank might be based on precedent. One Congress, in 1791, decided in favor of a bank; another, in 1811, decided against it. One Congress, in 1815, decided against a bank; another, in 1816, decided in its favor. Prior to the present Congress, therefore, the precedents drawn from that source were equal. If we resort to the States, the expressions of legislative, judicial, and executive opinions against the bank have been probably to those in its favor as 4 to 1. There is nothing in precedent, therefore, which, if its authority were admitted, ought to weigh in favor of the act before me.

If the opinion of the Supreme Court covered the whole ground of this act, it ought not to control the coordinate authorities of this Government. The Congress, the Executive, and the Court must each for itself be guided by its own opinion of the Constitution swears that he will support it as he understands it, and not as it is understood by others. It is as much the duty of the House of Representatives, of the Senate, and of the President to decide upon the constitutionality of any bill or resolution which may be presented to them for passage or approval as it is of the supreme judges when it may be brought before them for judicial decision. The opinion of the judges has no more authority over Congress than the opinion of Congress has over the judges, and on that point the President is independent of both. The authority of the Supreme Court must not, therefore, be permitted to control the Congress or the Executive when acting in their legislative capacities, but to have only such influence as the force of their reasoning may deserve.

But in the case relied upon the Supreme Court have not decided that all the features of this corporation are compatible with the Constitution. It is true that the court have said that the law incorporating the bank is a constitutional exercise of power by Congress; but taking into view the whole opinion of the court and the reasoning by which they have come to that conclusion, I understand them to have decided that inasmuch as a bank is an appropriate means for carrying into effect the enumerated powers of the General Government, therefore the law incorporating it is in accordance with that provision of the Constitution which declares that Congress shall have power "to make all laws which shall be necessary and proper for carrying those powers into execution." Having satisfied themselves that the word *"necessary"* in the Constitution means *"needful,"* *"requisite,"* *"essential,"* *"conducive to,"* and that "a bank" is a convenient, a useful, and essential instrument in the prosecution of the Government's "fiscal operations," they conclude that to "use one must be within the discretion of Congress" and that "the act to incorporate the Bank of the United States is a law made in pursuance of the Constitution;" "but," say they, *"where the law is not prohibited and is really calculated to effect any of the objects intrusted to the Government, to undertake here to inquire into the degree of its necessity would be to pass the line which circumscribes the judical department and to tread on legislative ground."*

The principle here affirmed is that the "degree of its necessity," involving all the details of a banking institution, is a question exclusively for legislative consideration. A bank is constitutional, but it is the province of the Legislature to determine whether this or that particular power, privilege, or exemption is "necessary and proper" to enable the bank to discharge its duties to the Government, and from their decision there is no appeal to the courts of justice. Under the decision of the Supreme Court, therefore, it is the exclusive province of Congress and the President to decide whether the particular features of this act are *necessary* and *proper* in order to enable the bank to perform conveniently and efficiently the public duties assigned to it as a fiscal agent, and therefore constitutional, or *unnecessary* and *improper,* and therefore unconstitutional.

Without commenting on the general principle affirmed by the Supreme Court, let us examine the details of this act in accordance with the rule of legislative action which they have laid down. It will be found that many of the powers and privileges conferred on it can not be supposed necessary for the purpose for which it is proposed to be created, and are not, therefore, means necessary to attain the end in view, and consequently not justified by the Constitution. . . .

If Congress possessed the power to establish one bank, they had power to establish more than one if in their opinion two or more banks had been "necessary" to facilitate the execution of the powers delegated to them in the Constitution. If they possessed the power to establish a second bank, it was a power derived from the Constitution to be exercised from time to time, and at any time when the interests of the country or the emergencies of the Government might make it expedient. It was possessed by one Congress as well as another, and by all Congresses alike, and alike at every session But the Congress of 1816 have taken it away from their successors for twenty years, and the Congress of 1832 proposes to abolish it for fifteen years more. It can not be *"necessary"* or *"proper"* for Congress to barter away or divest themselves of any of the powers vested in them by the Constitution to be exercised for the public good. It is not *"necessary"* to the efficiency of the bank, nor is it *"proper"* in relation to themselves and their successors. They may *properly* use the discretion vested in them, but they may not limit the discretion of their successors. This restriction on themselves and grant of a monopoly to the bank is therefore unconstitutional.

In another point of view this provision is a palpable attempt to amend the Constitution by an act of legislation. The Constitution declares that "the Congress shall have power to exercise exclusive legislation in all cases whatsoever" over the District of Columbia. Its constitutional power, therefore, to establish banks in the District of Columbia and increase their capital at will is unlimited and uncontrollable by any other power than that which gave authority to the Constitution. Yet this act declares that Congress shall *not* increase the capital of existing banks, nor create other banks with capitals exceeding in the whole $6,000,000. The Constitution declares that Congress *shall* have power to exercise exclusive legislation over this District *"in all cases whatsoever,"* and this act declares they shall not. Which is the supreme law of the land? This provision can not be *"necessary"* or *"proper"* or *constitutional* unless the absurdity be admitted that whenever it be "necessary and proper" in the opinion of Congress they have a right to barter away one portion of the powers vested in them by the Constitution as a means of executing the rest. . . .

The Government is the only *"proper"* judge where its agents should reside and keep their offices, because it best knows where their presence will be *"necessary."* It can not, therefore, be *"necessary"* or *"proper"* to authorize the bank to locate branches where it pleases to perform the public service, without consulting the Government, and contrary to its will. . . .

It is maintained by some that the bank is a means of executing the constitutional power "to coin money and regulate the value thereof." Congress have established a mint to coin money and passed laws to regulate the value thereof. The money so coined, with its value so regulated, and such foreign coins as Congress may adopt are the only currency known to the Constitution. But if they have other power to regulate the currency, it was conferred to be exercised by themselves, and not to be transferred to a corporation. If the bank be established for that purpose, with a charter unalterable without its consent, Congress have parted with their power for a term of years, during which the Constitution is a dead letter. It is neither necessary nor proper to transfer its legislative power to such a bank, and therefore unconstitutional.

By its silence, considered in connection with the decision of the Supreme Court in the case of McCulloch against the State of Maryland, this act takes from the States the power to tax a portion of the banking business carried on within their limits, in subversion of one of the strongest barriers which secured them against Federal encroachments. . . .

It can not be *necessary* to the character of the bank as a fiscal agent of the Government that its private business should be exempted from that taxation to which all the State banks are liable, nor can I conceive it *"proper"* that the substantive and most essential powers reserved by the States shall be thus attacked and annihilated as a means of executing the powers delegated to the General Government. It may be safely assumed that none of those sages who had an agency in forming or adopting our Constitution ever imagined that any portion of the taxing power of the States not prohibited to them nor delegated to Congress was to be swept away and annihilated as a means of executing certain powers delegated to Congress.

The bank is professedly established as an agent of the executive branch of the Government, and its constitutionality is maintained on that ground. Neither upon the propriety of present action nor upon the provisions of this act was the Executive consulted. It has had no opportunity to say that it neither needs nor wants an agent clothed with such powers and favored by such exemptions. There is nothing in its legitimate functions which makes it necessary or proper. Whatever interest or influence, whether public or private, has given birth to this act, it can not be found either in the wishes or necessities of the executive department, by which present action is deemed premature, and the powers conferred upon its agent not only unnecessary, but dangerous to the Government and country.

It is to be regretted that the rich and powerful too often bend the acts of government to their selfish purposes. Distinctions in society will always exist under every just government. Equality of talents, of education, or of wealth can not be produced by human institutions. In the full enjoyment of the gifts of Heaven and the fruits of superior industry, economy, and virtue, every man is equally entitled to protection by law; but when the laws undertake to add to these natural and just advantages artificial distinctions, to grant titles, gratuities, and exclusive privileges, to make the rich richer and the potent more powerful, the humble members of society—the farmers, mechanics, and laborers—who have neither the time nor the means of securing like favors to themselves, have a right to complain of the injustice of their Government. There are no necessary evils in government. It evils exist only in its abuses. If it would confine itself to equal protection, and, as Heaven does its rains, shower its favors alike on the high and the low, the rich and the poor, it would be an unqualified blessing. In the act before me there seems to be a wide and unnecessary departure from these just principles.

Nor is our Government to be maintained or our Union

preserved by invasions of the rights and powers of the several States. In thus attempting to make our General Government strong we make it weak. Its true strength consists in leaving individuals and States as much as possible to themselves—in making itself felt, not in its power, but in its beneficence; not in its control, but in its protection; not in binding the States more closely to the center, but leaving each to move unobstructed in its proper orbit.

Experience should teach us wisdom. Most of the difficulties our Government now encounters and most of the dangers which impend over our Union have sprung from an abandonment of the legitimate objects of Government by our national legislation, and the adoption of such principles as are embodied in this act. Many of our rich men have not been content with equal protection and equal benefits, but have besought us to make them richer by act of Congress. By attempting to gratify their desires we have in the results of our legislation arrayed section against section, interest against interest, and man against man, in a fearful commotion which threatens to shake the foundations of our Union. It is time to pause in our career to review our principles, and if possible revive that devoted patriotism and spirit of compromise which distinguished the sages of the Revolution and the fathers of our Union. If we can not at once, in justice to interests vested under improvident legislation, make our Government what it ought to be, we can at least take a stand against all new grants of monopolies and exclusive privileges, against any prostitution of our Government to the advancement of the few at the expense of the many, and in favor of compromise and gradual reform in our code of laws and system of political economy.

I have now done my duty to my country. If sustained by my fellowcitizens, I shall be grateful and happy; if not, I shall find in the motives which impel me ample grounds for contentment and peace. In the difficulties which surround us and the dangers which threaten our institutions there is cause for neither dismay nor alarm.

For relief and deliverance let us firmly rely on that kind
Providence which I am sure watches with peculiar care
over the destinies of our Republic, and on the intelligence and wisdom of our countrymen. Through *His*
abundant goodness and *their* patriotic devotion our liberty and Union will be preserved.

ANDREW JACKSON

DOCUMENT NO. 6.   *Nullification Crisis of 1832–33.*

After Congress adopted a new tariff act in 1832, the state of
South Carolina held a specially-elected convention, which
announced the state's nullification of the federal tariff act.
South Carolinians were forbidden by state law to obey the
federal tariff law. The state also made preparations to resist
any attempt to enforce the law. In response to the state's
proposed defiance, President Jackson determined to enforce
the federal law in South Carolina. To a South Carolina Un-
ionist supporter, Joel R. Poinsett, Jackson sent his views in
a letter of December 2, 1832, (Jackson, *Correspondence,* IV,
493–4), Document No. 6-A. He followed this with a ringing
statement in defense of the Union and in rejection of nullification in his powerful Proclamation of December 10, 1832,
(*Mess. Pres.,* II, 640–56), Document No. 6-B.

DOCUMENT 6-A
To JOEL R. POINSETT.
WASHINGTON, December 2, 1832.
. . . I fully concur with you in your views of Nullification. It leads directly to civil war and bloodshed and
deserves the execration of every friend of the
country. . . .
    The Union must be preserved; and its laws duly ex-
ecuted, but by proper means. With calmness and firmness such as becomes those who are conscious of being
right and are assured of the support of public opinion,
we must perform our duties without suspecting that
there are those around us desiring to tempt us into the
wrong. We must act as the instruments of the law and

if force is offered to us in that capacity then we shall repel it with the certainty, even should we fall as individuals, that the friends of liberty and union will still be strong enough to prostrate their enemies. . . .

Nullification therefore means insurrection and war; and the other states have a right to put it down: and you also and all other peaceable citizens have a right to aid in the same patriotic object when summoned by the violated laws of the land. Should an emergency occur for the arms before the order of the Secretary of war to the commanding officer to deliver them to your order, shew this to him and he will yield a compliance . . .

DOCUMENT 6-B

Whereas a convention assembled in the State of South Carolina have passed an ordinance by which they declare "that the several acts and parts of acts of the Congress of the United States purporting to be laws for the imposing of duties and imposts on the importation of foreign commodities, and now having actual operation and effect within the United States, and more especially" two acts for the same purposes passed on the 29th of May, 1828, and on the 14th of July, 1832, "are unauthorized by the Constitution of the United States, and violate the true meaning and intent thereof, and are null and void and no law," nor binding on the citizens of that State or its officers; and by the said ordinance it is further declared to be unlawful for any of the constituted authorities of the State or of the United States to enforce the payment of the duties imposed by the said acts within the same State, and that it is the duty of the legislature to pass such laws as may be necessary to give full effect to the said ordinance. . . .

Whereas the said ordinance prescribes to the people of South Carolina a course of conduct in direct violation of their duty as citizens of the United States, contrary to the laws of their country, subversive of its Constitution, and having for its object the destruction of the Union—that Union which, coeval with our political existence, led our fathers, without any other ties to unite them than those of patriotism and a common cause, through a sanguinary struggle to a glorious independence; that sacred Union, hitherto inviolate, which, perfected by our happy Constitution, has brought us, by the favor of Heaven, to a state of prosperity at home and high consideration abroad rarely, if ever, equaled in the history of nations:

To preserve this bond of our political existence from destruction, to maintain inviolate this state of national honor and prosperity, and to justify the confidence my fellow-citizens have reposed in me, I, Andrew Jackson, President of the United States, have thought proper to issue this my proclamation, stating my views of the Constitution and laws applicable to the measures adopted by the convention of South Carolina and to the reasons they have put forth to sustain them, declaring the course which duty will require me to pursue, and, appealing to the understanding and patriotism of the people, warn them of the consequences that must inevitably result from an observance of the dictates of the convention. . . .

The ordinance is founded, not on the indefeasible right of resisting acts which are plainly unconstitutional and too oppressive to be endured, but on the strange position that any one State may not only declare an act of Congress void, but prohibit its execution; that they may do this consistently with the Constitution; that the true construction of that instrument permits a State to retain its place in the Union and yet be bound by no other of its laws than those it may choose to consider as constitutional. It is true, they add, that to justify this abrogation of a law it must be palpably contrary to the Constitution; but it is evident that to give the right of resisting laws of that description, coupled with the uncontrolled right to decide what laws deserve that character, is to give the power of resisting all laws; for as by the theory there is no appeal, the reasons alleged by the State, good or bad, must prevail. If it should be said that public opinion is a sufficient check against the abuse of this power, it may be asked why it is not deemed a sufficient guard against the passage of an unconstitutional act by Congress? There is, however, a restraint in this last case which makes the assumed power of a State more indefensible, and which does not exist in the other. There are two appeals from an unconstitutional act passed by Congress —one to the judiciary, the other to the people and the States. There is no appeal from the State decision in theory, and the practical illustration shows that the courts are closed against an application to review it, both judges and jurors being sworn to decide in its favor. But reasoning on this subject is superfluous when our social compact, in express terms, declares that the laws of the United States, its Constitution, and treaties made under it are the supreme law of the land, and, for greater caution, adds "that the judges in every State shall be bound thereby, anything in the constitution or laws of any State to the contrary notwithstanding." And it may be asserted without fear of refutation that no federative government could exist without a similar provision. . . .

If the doctrine of a State veto upon the laws of the Union carries with it internal evidence of its impracticable absurdity, our constitutional history will also afford abundant proof that it would have been repudiated with indignation had it been proposed to form a feature in our Government. . . .

We declare ourselves a nation by a joint, not by several acts, and when the terms of our Confederation were reduced to form it was in that of a solemn league of several States, by which they agreed that they would collectively form one nation for the purpose of conducting some certain domestic concerns and all foreign relations. In the instrument forming that Union is found an article which declares that "every State shall abide by the determinations of Congress on all questions which by that Confederation should be submitted to them."

Under the Confederation, then, no State could legally annul a decision of the Congress or refuse to submit to its execution; but no provision was made to enforce these decisions. Congress made requisitions, but they were not complied with. The Government could not operate on individuals. They had no judiciary, no means of collecting revenue.

But the defects of the Confederation need not be detailed. Under its operation we could scarcely be called a nation. We had neither prosperity at home nor consideration abroad. This state of things could not be endured, and our present happy Constitution was formed, but formed in vain if this fatal doctrine prevails. It was formed for important objects that are announced in the preamble, made in the name and by the authority of the people of the United States, whose delegates framed and whose conventions approved it. The most important among these objects—that which is placed first in rank, on which all the others rest—is "*to form a more perfect union.*" Now, is it possible that even if there were no express provision giving supremacy to the Constitution and laws of the United States over those of the States, can it be conceived that an instrument made for the purpose of "*forming a more perfect union*" than that of the Confederation could be so constructed by the assembled wisdom of our country as to substitute for that Confederation a form of government dependent for its existence on the local interest, the party spirit, of a State, or of a prevailing faction in a State? Every man of plain, unsophisticated understanding who hears the question will give such an answer as will preserve the Union. Metaphysical subtlety, in pursuit of an impracticable theory, could alone have devised one that is calculated to destroy it.

I consider, then, the power to annul a law of the United States, assumed by one State, *incompatible with the existence of the Union, contradicted expressly by the letter of the Constitution, unauthorized by its spirit, inconsistent with every principle on which it was founded, and destructive of the great object for which it was formed.* . . .

Here is a law of the United States, not even pretended to be unconstitutional, repealed by the authority of a small majority of the voters of a single State. Here is a provision of the Constitution which is solemnly abrogated by the same authority.

On such expositions and reasonings the ordinance grounds not only an assertion of the right to annul the laws of which it complains, but to enforce it by a threat of seceding from the Union if any attempt is made to execute them. . . .

The Constitution of the United States, then, forms a *government,* not a league; and whether it be formed by compact between the States or in any other manner, its character is the same. It is a Government in which all the people are represented, which operates directly on the people individually, not upon the States; they retained all the power they did not grant. But each State, having expressly parted with so many powers as to constitute, jointly with the other States, a single nation, can not, from that period, possess any right to secede, because such secession does not break a league, but destroys the unity of a nation; and any injury to that unity is not only a breach which would result from the contravention of a compact, but it is an offense against the whole Union. To say that any State may at pleasure secede from the Union is to say that the United States are not a nation, because it would be a solecism to contend that any part of a nation might dissolve its connection with the other parts, to their injury or ruin, without committing any offense. Secession, like any other revolutionary act, may be morally justified by the extremity of oppression; but to call it a constitutional right is confounding the meaning of terms, and can only be done through gross error or to deceive those who are willing to assert a right, but would pause before they made a revolution or incur the penalties consequent on a failure. . . .

This, then, is the position in which we stand: A small majority of the citizens of one State in the Union have elected delegates to a State convention; that convention has ordained that all the revenue laws of the United States must be repealed, or that they are no longer a member of the Union. The governor of that State has recommended to the legislature the raising of an army to carry the secession into effect, and that he may be empowered to give clearances to vessels in the name of the State. No act of violent opposition to the laws has yet been committed, but such a state of things is hourly apprehended. And it is the intent of this instrument to *proclaim,* not only that the duty imposed on me by the Constitution "to take care that the laws be faithfully executed" shall be performed to the extent of the powers already vested in me by law, or of such others as the wisdom of Congress shall devise and intrust to me for that purpose, but to warn the citizens of South Carolina who have been deluded into an opposition to the laws of the danger they will incur by obedience to the illegal and disorganizing ordinance of the convention; to exhort those who have refused to support it to persevere in their determination to uphold the Constitution and laws of their country; and to point out to all the perilous situation into which the good people of that State have been led, and that the course they are urged to pursue is one of ruin and disgrace to the very State whose rights they affect to support.

Fellow-citizens of my native State, let me not only admonish you, as the First Magistrate of our common country, not to incur the penalty of its laws, but use the influence that a father would over his children whom he saw rushing to certain ruin. In that paternal language, with that paternal feeling, let me tell you, my countrymen, that you are deluded by men who are either deceived themselves or wish to deceive you. Mark under what pretenses you have been led on to the brink of insurrection and treason on which you stand. First, a diminution of the value of your staple commodity, lowered by overproduction in other quarters, and the consequent diminution in the value of your lands were the sole effect of the tariff laws. The effect of those laws was confessedly injurious, but the evil was greatly exaggerated by the unfounded theory you were taught to believe—that its burthens were in proportion to your exports, not to your consumption of imported articles.

Your pride was roused by the assertion that a submission to those laws was a state of vassalage and that resistance to them was equal in patriotic merit to the opposition our fathers offered to the oppressive laws of Great Britain. You were told that this opposition might be peaceably, might be constitutionally, made; that you might enjoy all the advantages of the Union and bear none of its burthens. Eloquent appeals to your passions, to your State pride, to your native courage, to your sense of real injury, were used to prepare you for the period when the mask which concealed the hideous features of *disunion* should be taken off. It fell, and you were made to look with complacency on objects which not long since you would have regarded with horror. Look back to the arts which have brought you to this state; look forward to the consequences to which it must inevitably lead! Look back to what was first told you as an inducement to enter into this dangerous course. The great political truth was repeated to you that you had the revolutionary right of resisting all laws that were palpably unconstitutional and intolerably oppressive. It was added that the right to nullify a law rested on the same principle, but that it was a peaceable remedy. This character which was given to it made you receive with too much confidence the assertions that were made of the unconstitutionality of the law and its oppressive effects. Mark, my fellow-citizens, that by the admission of your leaders the unconstitutionality must be *palpable,* or it will not justify either resistance or nullification. What is the meaning of the word *palpable* in the sense in which it is here used? That which is apparent to everyone; that which no man of ordinary intellect will fail to perceive. Is the unconstitutionality of these laws of that description? Let those among your leaders who once approved and advocated the principle of protective duties answer the question; and let them choose whether they will be considered as incapable then of perceiving that which must have been apparent to every man of common understanding, or as imposing upon your confidence and endeavoring to mislead you now. In either case they are unsafe guides in the perilous path they urge you to tread. Ponder well on this circumstance, and you will know how to appreciate the exaggerated language they address to you. They are not champions of liberty, emulating the fame of our Revolutionary fathers, nor are you an oppressed people, contending, as they repeat to you, against worse than colonial vassalage. You are free members of a flourishing and happy Union. There is no settled design to oppress you. You have indeed felt the unequal operation of laws which may have been unwisely, not unconstitutionally, passed; but that inequality must necessarily be removed. At the very moment when you were madly urged on to the unfortunate course you have begun a change in public opinion had commenced. The nearly approaching payment of the public debt and the consequent necessity of a diminution of duties had already produced a considerable reduction, and that, too, on some articles of general consumption in your State. The importance of this change was underrated, and you were authoritatively told that no further alleviation of your burthens was to be expected at the very time when the condition of the country imperiously demanded such a modification of the duties as should reduce them to a just and equitable scale. But, as if apprehensive of the effect of this change in allaying your discontents, you were precipitated into the fearful state in which you now find yourselves.

I have urged you to look back to the means that were used to hurry you on to the position you have now assumed and forward to the consequences it will produce. Something more is necessary. Contemplate the condition of that country of which you still form an important part. Consider its Government, uniting in one bond of common interest and general protection so many different States, giving to all their inhabitants the proud title of *American citizen,* protecting their commerce, securing their literature and their arts, facilitating their intercommunication, defending their frontiers, and making their name respected in the remotest parts of the earth. Consider the extent of its territory, its increasing and happy population, its advance in arts which render life agreeable, and the sciences which elevate the mind! See education spreading the lights of religion, morality, and general information into every cottage in this wide extent of our Territories and States. Behold it as the asylum where the wretched and the oppressed find a refuge and support. Look on this picture of happiness and honor and say, *We too are citizens of America.* Carolina is one of these proud States; her arms have defended, her best blood has cemented, this happy Union. And then add, if you can, without horror and remorse, This happy Union we will dissolve; this picture of peace and prosperity we will deface; this free intercourse we will interrupt; these fertile fields we will deluge with blood; the protection of that glorious flag we renounce; the very name of Americans we discard. And for what, mistaken men? For what do you throw away these inestimable blessings? For what would you exchange your share in the advantages and honor of the Union? For the dream of a separate independence—a dream interrupted by bloody conflicts with your neighbors and a vile dependence on a foreign power. If your leaders could succeed in establishing a separation, what would be your situation? Are you united at home? Are you free from the apprehension of civil discord, with all its fearful consequences? Do our neighboring republics, every day suffering some new revolution or contending with some new insurrection, do they excite your envy? But the dictates of a high duty oblige me solemnly to announce that you can not succeed. The laws of the United States must be executed. I have no discretionary power on the subject; my duty is emphatically pronounced in the Constitution. Those who told you that you might peaceably prevent their execution deceived you; they could not have been deceived themselves. They know that a forcible opposition could alone prevent the execution of the laws, and they know that such opposition must be repelled. Their object is disunion. But be not deceived by names. Disunion by armed force is *treason.* Are you really ready to incur its guilt? If you are, on the heads of the instigators of the act be the dreadful consequences; on their heads be the dishonor, but on yours may fall the punishment. On your unhappy State will inevitably fall all the evils of the conflict you force upon the Government of your country. It can not accede to the mad project of disunion, of which you would be the first victims. Its First Magistrate can not, if he would, avoid the performance of his duty. The consequence must be fearful for you, distressing to your fellow-citizens here and to the friends of good government throughout the world. Its enemies have beheld our prosperity with a vexation they could not conceal; it was a standing refutation of their slavish doctrines, and they will point to our discord with the triumph of malignant joy. It is yet in your power to disappoint them. There is yet time to show that the descendants of the Pinckneys, the Sumpters, the Rutledges, and of the thousand other names which adorn the pages of your Revolutionary history will not abandon that Union to support which so many of them fought and bled and died. I adjure you, as you honor their memory, as you love the cause of freedom, to which they dedicated their lives, as you prize the peace of your country, the lives of its best citizens, and your own fair fame, to retrace your steps. Snatch from the archives of your State the disorganizing edict of its convention; bid its members to reassemble and promulgate the decided expressions of your will to remain in the path which alone can conduct you to safety, prosperity, and honor. Tell them that compared to disunion all other evils are light, because that brings with it an accumulation of all. Declare that you will never take the field unless the star-spangled banner of your country shall float over you; that you will not be stigmatized when dead, and dishonored and scorned while you live, as the authors of the first attack on the Constitution of your country. Its destroyers you can not be. You may disturb its peace, you may interrupt the course of its prosperity, you may cloud its reputation for stability; but its tranquillity will be restored, its prosperity will return, and the stain upon its national character will be transferred and remain an eternal blot on the memory of those who caused the disorder.

Fellow-citizens of the United States, the threat of unhallowed disunion, the names of those once respected by whom it is uttered, the array of military force to support it, denote the approach of a crisis in our affairs on which the continuance of our unexampled prosperity, our political existence, and perhaps that of all free governments may depend. The conjuncture demanded a free, a full, and explicit enunciation, not only of my intentions, but of my principles of action; and as the claim was asserted of a right by a State to annul the laws of the Union, and even to secede from it at pleasure, a frank exposition of my opinions in relation to the origin and form of our Government and the construction I give to the instrument by which it was created seemed to be proper. Having the fullest confidence in the justness of the legal and constitutional opinion of my duties which has been expressed, I rely with equal confidence on your undivided support in my determination to execute the laws, to preserve the Union by all constitutional means, to arrest, if possible, by moderate and firm measures the necessity of a recourse to force; and if it be the will of Heaven that the recurrence of its primeval curse on man for the shedding of a brother's blood should fall upon our land, that it be not called down by any offensive act on the part of the United States.

Fellow-citizens, the momentous case is before you. On your undivided support of your Government depends the decision of the great question it involves—whether your sacred Union will be preserved and the blessing it secures to us as one people shall be perpetuated. No one can doubt that the unanimity with which that decision will be expressed will be such as to inspire new confidence in republican institutions, and that the prudence, the wisdom, and the courage which it will bring to their defense will transmit them unimpaired and invigorated to our children.

May the Great Ruler of Nations grant that the signal blessings with which He has favored ours may not, by the madness of party or personal ambition, be disregarded and lost; and may His wise providence bring those who have produced this crisis to see the folly before they feel the misery of civil strife, and inspire a returning veneration for that Union which, if we may dare to penetrate His designs, He has chosen as the only means of attaining the high destinies to which we may reasonably aspire.

In testimony whereof I have caused the seal of the United States to be hereunto affixed, having signed the same with my hand.

Done at the city of Washington, this 10th day of December, A.D. 1832, and of the Independence of the United States the fifty-seventh.

ANDREW JACKSON.

DOCUMENT NO. 7.   *Removal of the Deposits.*

Having vetoed recharter of the Bank in 1832, Jackson renewed the Bank war the following year, by seeking to remove the federal government's deposits from the Bank. When two successive Secretaries of the Treasury failed to order removal, Jackson appointed as Secretary Roger B. Taney, who issued the removal order. On December 3, 1833, in his annual message, Jackson explained the action to Congress (*Mess. Pres.,* III, 30–31):

. . . Since the last adjournment of Congress the Secretary of the Treasury has directed the money of the United States to be deposited in certain State banks designated by him, and he will immediately lay before you his reasons for this direction. I concur with him entirely in the view he has taken of the subject, and some months before the removal I urged upon the Department the propriety of taking that step. The near approach of the day on which the charter will expire, as well as the conduct of the bank, appeared to me to call for this measure upon the high considerations of public interest and public duty. The extent of its misconduct, however, although known to be great, was not at that time fully developed by proof. It was not until late in the month of August that I received from the Government directors an official report establishing beyond question that this great and powerful institution had been actively engaged in attempting to influence the elections of the public officers by means of its money, and that, in violation of the express provisions of its charter, it had by a formal resolution placed its funds at the disposition of its president to be employed in sustaining the political power of the bank. A copy of this resolution is contained in the report of the Government directors before referred to, and however the object may be disguised by cautious language, no one can doubt that this money was in truth intended for electioneering purposes, and the particular uses to which it was proved to have been applied abundantly show that it was so understood. Not only was the evidence complete as to the past application of the money and power of the bank to electioneering purposes, but that the resolution of the board of directors authorized the same course to be pursued in future.

It being thus established by unquestionable proof that the Bank of the United States was converted into a permanent electioneering engine, it appeared to me that the path of duty which the executive department of the Government ought to pursue was not doubtful. As by the terms of the bank charter no officer but the Secretary of the Treasury could remove the deposits, it seemed to me that this authority ought to be at once exerted to deprive that great corporation of the support and countenance of the Government in such an use of its funds and such an exertion of its power. In this point of the case the question is distinctly presented whether the people of the United States are to govern through representatives chosen by their unbiased suffrages or whether the money and power of a great corporation are to be secretly exerted to influence their judgment and control their decisions. It must now be determined whether the bank is to have its candidates for all offices in the country, from the highest to the lowest, or whether candidates on both sides of political questions shall be brought forward as heretofore and supported by the usual means.

At this time the efforts of the bank to control public opinion, through the distresses of some and the fears of others, are equally apparent, and, if possible, more objectionable. By a curtailment of its accommodations more rapid than any emergency requires, and even while it retains specie to an almost unprecedented amount in its vaults, it is attempting to produce great embarrassment in one portion of the community, while through presses known to have been sustained by its money it attempts by unfounded alarms to create a panic in all.

These are the means by which it seems to expect that it can force a restoration of the deposits, and as a necessary consequence extort from Congress a renewal of its charter. I am happy to know that through the good sense of our people the effort to get up a panic has hitherto failed, and that through the increased accommodations which the State banks have been enabled to afford, no public distress has followed the exertions of the bank, and it can not be doubted that the exercise of its power and the expenditure of its money, as well as its efforts to spread groundless alarm, will be met and rebuked as they deserve. . . .

DOCUMENT NO. 8.   *Protest to the United States Senate.*

Jackson's course in removing federal deposits from the Bank encountered disapproval in Congress. On March 28, 1834, the Senate passed a "Resolution of Censure," condemning Jackson for acting in derogation of both the Constitution and laws of the United States. On April 15, 1834 Jackson shot back a sharp assertion of the independence of the Executive in his Protest to the Senate (*Mess. Pres.,* III, 69–93).

To the Senate of the United States:
It appears by the published Journal of the Senate that on the 26th of December last a resolution was offered by a member of the Senate, which after a protracted

debate was on the 28th day of March last modified by the mover and passed by the votes of twenty-six Senators out of forty-six who were present and voted, in the following words, viz:

Resolved, That the President, in the late Executive proceedings in relation to the public revenue, has assumed upon himself authority and power not conferred by the Constitution and laws, but in derogation of both.

Having had the honor, through the voluntary suffrages of the American people, to fill the office of President of the United States during the period which may be presumed to have been referred to in this resolution, it is sufficiently evident that the censure it inflicts was intended for myself. Without notice, unheard and untried, I thus find myself charged on the records of the Senate, and in a form hitherto unknown in our history, with the high crime of violating the laws and Constitution of my country.

It can seldom be necessary for any department of the Government, when assailed in conversation or debate or by the strictures of the press or of popular assemblies, to step out of its ordinary path for the purpose of vindicating its conduct or of pointing out any irregularity or injustice in the manner of the attack; but when the Chief Executive Magistrate is, by one of the most important branches of the Government in its official capacity, in a public manner, and by its recorded sentence, but without precedent, competent authority, or just cause, declared guilty of a breach of the laws and Constitution, it is due to his station, to public opinion, and to a proper self-respect that the officer thus denounced should promptly expose the wrong which has been done.

In the present case, moreover, there is even a stronger necessity for such a vindication. By an express provision of the Constitution, before the President of the United States can enter on the execution of his office he is required to take an oath or affirmation in the following words:

I do solemnly swear (or affirm) that I will faithfully execute the office of President of the United States and will to the best of my ability preserve, protect, and defend the Constitution of the United States.

The duty of defending so far as in him lies the integrity of the Constitution would indeed have resulted from the very nature of his office, but by thus expressing it in the official oath or affirmation, which in this respect differs from that of any other functionary, the founders of our Republic have attested their sense of its importance and have given to it a peculiar solemnity and force. Bound to the performance of this duty by the oath I have taken, by the strongest obligations of gratitude to the American people, and by the ties which unite my every earthly interest with the welfare and glory of my country, and perfectly convinced that the discussion and passage of the above-mentioned resolution were not only unauthorized by the Constitution, but in many respects repugnant to its provisions and subversive of the rights secured by it to other coordinate departments, I deem it an imperative duty to maintain the supremacy of that sacred instrument and the immunities of the department intrusted to my care by all means consistent with my own lawful powers, with the rights of others, and with the genius of our civil institutions. To this end I have caused this my *solemn protest* against the aforesaid proceedings to be placed on the files of the executive department and to be transmitted to the Senate.

It is alike due to the subject, the Senate, and the people that the views which I have taken of the proceedings referred to, and which compel me to regard them in the light that has been mentioned, should be exhibited at length, and with the freedom and firmness which are required by an occasion so unprecedented and peculiar.

Under the Constitution of the United States the powers and functions of the various departments of the Federal Government and their responsibilities for violation or neglect of duty are clearly defined or result by necessary inference. The legislative power is, subject to the qualified negative of the President, vested in the Congress of the United States, composed of the Senate and House of Representatives; the executive power is vested exclusively in the President, except that in the conclusion of treaties and in certain appointments to office he is to act with the advice and consent of the Senate; the judicial power is vested exclusively in the Supreme and other courts of the United States, except in cases of impeachment, for which purpose the accusatory power is vested in the House of Representatives and that of hearing and determining in the Senate. But although for the special purposes which have been mentioned there is an occasional intermixture of the powers of the different departments, yet with these exceptions each of the three great departments is independent of the others in its sphere of action, and when it deviates from that sphere is not responsible to the others further than it is expressly made so in the Constitution. In every other respect each of them is the coequal of the other two, and all are the servants of the American people, without power or right to control or censure each other in the service of their common superior, save only in the manner and to the degree which that superior has prescribed.

The responsibilities of the President are numerous and weighty. He is liable to impeachment for high crimes and misdemeanors, and on due conviction to removal from office and perpetual disqualification; and notwithstanding such conviction, he may also be indicted and punished according to law. He is also liable to the private action of any party who may have been injured by his illegal mandates or instructions in the same manner and to the same extent as the humblest functionary. In addition to the responsibilities which may thus be enforced by impeachment, criminal prosecution, or suit at law, he is also accountable at the bar of public opinion for every act of his Administration. Subject only to the restraints of truth and justice, the free people of the United States have the undoubted right, as individuals or collectively, orally or in writing, at such times and in such language and form as they may think proper, to discuss his official conduct and to express and promulgate their opinions concerning it. Indirectly also his conduct may come under review in either branch of the Legislature, or in the Senate when acting in its executive capacity, and so far as the executive or legislative proceedings of these bodies may require it, it may be exercised by them. These are believed to be the proper and only modes in which the President of the United States is to be held accountable for his official conduct.

Tested by these principles, the resolution of the Senate is wholly unauthorized by the Constitution, and in derogation of its entire spirit. It assumes that a single branch of the legislative department may for the purposes of a public censure, and without any view to legislation or impeachment, take up, consider, and decide upon the official acts of the Executive. But in no part of the Constitution is the President subjected to any such responsibility, and in no part of that instrument is any such power conferred on either branch of the Legislature.

The high functions assigned by the Constitution to the Senate are in their nature either legislative, executive, or judicial. It is only in the exercise of its judicial powers, when sitting as a court for the trial of impeachments, that the Senate is expressly authorized and necessarily required to consider and decide upon the conduct of the President or any other public officer. Indirectly, however, as has already been suggested, it may frequently be called on to perform that office. Cases may occur in the course of its legislative or executive proceedings in which it may be indispensable to the proper exercise of its powers that it should inquire into and decide upon the conduct of the President or other public officers, and in every such case its constitutional right to do so is cheerfully conceded. But to authorize the Senate to enter on such a task in its legislative or executive capacity the inquiry must actually grow out of and tend to some legislative or executive action, and the decision, when expressed, must take the form of some appropriate legislative or executive act.

The resolution in question was introduced, discussed, and passed not as a joint but as a separate resolution. It asserts no legislative power, proposes no legislative action, and neither possesses the form nor any of the attributes of a legislative measure. It does not appear to have been entertained or passed with any view or expectation of its issuing in a law or joint resolution, or in the repeal of any law or joint resolution, or in any other legislative action.

Whilst wanting both the form and substance of a legislative measure, it is equally manifest that the resolution was not justified by any of the executive powers conferred on the Senate. These powers relate exclusively to the consideration of treaties and nominations to office, and they are exercised in secret session and with closed doors. This resolution does not apply to any treaty or nomination, and was passed in a public session. . . .

The whole executive power being vested in the President, who is responsible for its exercise, it is a necessary consequence that he should have a right to employ agents of his own choice to aid him in the performance of his duties, and to discharge them when he is no longer willing to be responsible for their acts. In strict accordance with this principle, the power of removal, which, like that of appointment, is an original executive power, is left unchecked by the Constitution in relation to all executive officers, for whose conduct the President is responsible, while it is taken from him in relation to judicial officers, for whose acts he is not responsible. In the Government from which many of the fundamental principles of our system are derived the head of the executive department originally had power to appoint and remove at will all officers, executive and judicial. It was to take the judges out of this general power of removal, and thus make them independent of the Executive, that the tenure of their offices was changed to good behavior. Nor is it conceivable why they are placed in our Constitution upon a tenure different from that of all other officers appointed by the Executive unless it be for the same purpose. . . .

The dangerous tendency of the doctrine which denies to the President the power of supervising, directing, and controlling the Secretary of the Treasury in like manner with the other executive officers would soon be manifest in practice were the doctrine to be established. The President is the direct representative of the American people, but the Secretaries are not. If the Secretary of the Treasury be independent of the President in the execution of the laws, then is there no direct responsibility to the people in that important branch of this Government to which is committed the care of the national finances. And it is in the power of the Bank of the United States, or any other corporation, body of men, or individuals, if a Secretary shall be found to accord with them in opinion or can be induced in practice to promote their views, to control through him the whole action of the Government (so far as it is exercised by his Department) in defiance of the Chief Magistrate elected by the people and responsible to them.

. . . It is due to the high trust with which I have been charged, to those who may be called to succeed me in it, to the representatives of the people whose constitutional prerogative has been unlawfully assumed, to the people and to the States, and to the Constitution they have established that I should not permit its provisions to be broken down by such an attack on the executive department without at least some effort "to preserve, protect, and defend" them. With this view, and for the reasons which have been stated, I do hereby *solemnly protest* against the aforementioned proceedings of the Senate as unauthorized by the Constitution, contrary to its spirit and to several of its express provisions, subversive of that distribution of the powers of government which it has ordained and established, destructive of the checks and safeguards by which those powers were intended on the one hand to be controlled and on the other to be protected, and calculated by their immediate and collateral effects, by their character and tendency, to concentrate in the hands of a body not directly amenable to the people a degree of influence and power dangerous to their liberties and fatal to the Constitution of their choice.

The resolution of the Senate contains an imputation

upon my private as well as upon my public character, and as it must stand forever on their journals, I can not close this substitute for that defense which I have not been allowed to present in the ordinary form without remarking that I have lived in vain if it be necessary to enter into a formal vindication of my character and purposes from such an imputation. In vain do I bear upon my person enduring memorials of that contest in which American liberty was purchased; in vain have I since periled property, fame, and life in defense of the rights and privileges so dearly bought; in vain am I now, without a personal aspiration or the hope of individual advantage, encountering responsibilities and dangers from which by mere inactivity in relation to a single point I might have been exempt, if any serious doubts can be entertained as to the purity of my purposes and motives. If I had been ambitious, I should have sought an alliance with that powerful institution which even now aspires to no divided empire. If I had been venal, I should have sold myself to its designs. Had I preferred personal comfort and official ease to the performance of my arduous duty, I should have ceased to molest it. In the history of conquerors and usurpers, never in the fire of youth nor in the vigor of manhood could I find an attraction to lure me from the path of duty, and now I shall scarcely find an inducement to commence their career of ambition when gray hairs and a decaying frame, instead of inviting to toil and battle, call me to the contemplation of other worlds, where conquerors cease to be honored and usurpers expiate their crimes. The only ambition I can feel is to acquit myself to Him to whom I must soon render an account of my stewardship, to serve my fellowmen, and live respected and honored in the history of my country. No; the ambition which leads me on is an anxious desire and a fixed determination to return to the people unimpaired the sacred trust they have confided to my charge; to heal the wounds of the Constitution and preserve it from further violation; to persuade my countrymen, so far as I may, that it is not in a splendid government supported by powerful monopolies and aristocratical establishments that they will find happiness or their liberties protection, but in a plain system, void of pomp, protecting all and granting favors to none, dispensing its blessings, like the dews of Heaven, unseen and unfelt save in the freshness and beauty they contribute to produce. It is such a government that the genius of our people requires; such an one only under which our States may remain for ages to come united, prosperous, and free. If the Almighty Being who has hitherto sustained and protected me will but vouchsafe to make my feeble powers instrumental to such a result, I shall anticipate with pleasure the place to be assigned me in the history of my country, and die contented with the belief that I have contributed in some small degree to increase the value and prolong the duration of American liberty.

To the end that the resolution of the Senate may not be hereafter drawn into precedent with the authority of silent acquiescence on the part of the executive department, and to the end also that my motives and views in the Executive proceedings denounced in that resolution may be known to my fellow-citizens, to the world, and to all posterity, I respectfully request that this message and protest may be entered at length on the journals of the Senate.

ANDREW JACKSON.

DOCUMENT NO. 9. *An Appeal for Hard Money Currency.*

Harboring a lifelong distrust of paper bank notes and paper currency, Jackson frequently urged adoption of a hard money currency. One such appeal he included in his December 1836 message to Congress (Mess. Pres., III, 246–49) in the following terms:

It is apparent from the whole context of the Constitution, as well as the history of the times which gave birth to it, that it was the purpose of the Convention to establish a currency consisting of the precious metals. These, from their peculiar properties which rendered them the standard of value in all other countries, were adopted in this as well to establish its commercial standard in reference to foreign countries by a permanent rule as to exclude the use of a mutable medium of exchange, such as of certain agricultural commodities recognized by the statutes of some States as a tender for debts, or the still more pernicious expedient of a paper currency. The last, from the experience of the evils of the issues of paper during the Revolution, had become so justly obnoxious as not only to suggest the clause in the Constitution forbidding the emission of bills of credit by the States, but also to produce that vote in the Convention which negatived the proposition to grant power to Congress to charter corporations—a proposition well understood at the time as intended to authorize the establishment of a national bank, which was to issue a currency of bank notes on a capital to be created to some extent out of Government stocks. Although this proposition was refused by a direct vote of the Convention, the object was afterwards in effect obtained by its ingenious advocates through a strained construction of the Constitution. The debts of the Revolution were funded at prices which formed no equivalent compared with the nominal amount of the stock, and under circumstances which exposed the motives of some of those who participated in the passage of the act to distrust.

The facts that the value of the stock was greatly enhanced by the creation of the bank, that it was well understood that such would be the case, and that some of the advocates of the measure were largely benefited by it belong to the history of the times, and are well calculated to diminish the respect which might otherwise have been due to the action of the Congress which created the institution.

On the establishment of a national bank it became the interest of its creditors that gold should be superseded by the paper of the bank as a general currency. A value was soon attached to the gold coins which made their exportation to foreign countries as a mercantile commodity more profitable than their retention and use at home as money. It followed as a matter of course, if not designed by those who established the bank, that the bank became in effect a substitute for the Mint of the United States.

Such was the origin of a national-bank currency, and such the beginning of those difficulties which now appear in the excessive issues of the banks incorporated by the various States.

Although it may not be possible by any legislative means within our power to change at once the system which has thus been introduced, and has received the acquiescence of all portions of the country, it is certainly our duty to do all that is consistent with our constitutional obligations in preventing the mischiefs which are threatened by its undue extension. That the efforts of the fathers of our Government to guard against it by a constitutional provision were founded on an intimate knowledge of the subject has been frequently attested by the bitter experience of the country. The same causes which led them to refuse their sanction to a power authorizing the establishment of incorporations for banking purposes now exist in a much stronger degree to urge us to exert the utmost vigilance in calling into action the means necessary to correct the evils resulting from the unfortunate exercise of the power, and it is to be hoped that the opportunity for effecting this great good will be improved before the country witnesses new scenes of embarrassment and distress.

Variableness must never be the characteristic of a currency of which the precious metals are not the chief ingredient, or which can be expanded or contracted without regard to the principles that regulate the value of those metals as a standard in the general trade of the world. With us bank issues constitute such a currency, and must ever do so until they are made dependent on those just proportions of gold and silver as a circulating medium which experience has proved to be necessary not only in this but in all other commercial countries. Where those proportions are not infused into the circulation and do not control it, it is manifest that prices must vary according to the tide of bank issues, and the value and stability of property must stand exposed to all the uncertainty which attends the administration of institutions that are constantly liable to the temptation of an interest distinct from that of the community in which they are established.

The progress of an expansion, or rather a depreciation, of the currency by excessive bank issues is always attended by a loss to the laboring classes. This portion of the community have neither time nor opportunity to watch the ebbs and flows of the money market. Engaged from day to day in their useful toils, they do not perceive that although their wages are nominally the same, or even somewhat higher, they are greatly reduced in fact by the rapid increase of a spurious currency, which, as it appears to make money abound, they are at first inclined to consider a blessing. It is not so with the speculator, by whom this operation is better understood, and is made to contribute to his advantage. It is not until the prices of the necessaries of life become so dear that the laboring classes can not supply their wants out of their wages that the wages rise and gradually reach a justly proportioned rate to that of the products of their labor. When thus, by the depreciation in consequence of the quantity of paper in circulation, wages as well as prices become exorbitant, it is soon found that the whole effect of the adulteration is a tariff on our home industry for the benefit of the countries where gold and silver circulate and maintain uniformity and moderation in prices. It is then perceived that the enhancement of the price of land and labor produces a corresponding increase in the price of products until these products do not sustain a competition with similar ones in other countries, and thus both manufactured and agricultural productions cease to bear exportation from the country of the spurious currency, because they can not be sold for cost. This is the process by which specie is banished by the paper of the banks. Their vaults are soon exhausted to pay for foreign commodities. The next step is a stoppage of specie payment—a total degradation of paper as a currency—unusual depression of prices, the ruin of debtors, and the accumulation of property in the hands of creditors and cautious capitalists.

It was in view of these evils, together with the dangerous power wielded by the Bank of the United States and its repugnance to our Constitution, that I was induced to exert the power conferred upon me by the American people to prevent the continuance of that institution. But although various dangers to our republican institutions have been obviated by the failure of that bank to extort from the Government a renewal of its charter, it is obvious that little has been accomplished except a salutary change of public opinion toward restoring to the country the sound currency provided for in the Constitution. In the acts of several of the States prohibiting the circulation of small notes, and the auxiliary enactments of Congress at the last session forbidding their reception or payment on public account, the true policy of the country has been advanced and a larger portion of the precious metals infused into our circulating medium. These measures will probably be followed up in due time by the enactment of State laws banishing from circulation bank notes of still higher denominations, and the object may be materially promoted by further acts of Congress forbidding the employment as fiscal agents of such banks as continue to issue notes of low denominations and throw impediments in the way of the circulation of gold and silver.

The effects of an extension of bank credits and overissues of bank paper have been strikingly illustrated in the sales of the public lands. From the returns made by the various registers and receivers in the early part of last summer it was perceived that the receipts arising from the sales of the public lands were increasing to an unprecedented amount. In effect, however, these receipts amounted to nothing more than credits in bank. The banks lent out their notes to speculators. They were paid to the receivers and immediately returned to the banks, to be lent out again and again, being mere instruments to transfer to speculators the most valuable public land and pay the Government by a credit on the books of the banks. Those credits on the books of some of the Western banks, usually called deposits, were already greatly beyond their immediate means of payment, and were rapidly increasing. Indeed, each speculation furnished means for another; for no sooner had one individual or company paid in the notes than they were immediately lent to another for a like purpose, and the banks were extending their business and their issues so largely as to alarm considerate men and render it doubtful whether these bank credits if permitted to accumulate would ultimately be of the least value to the Government. The spirit of expansion and speculation was not confined to the deposit banks, but pervaded the whole multitude of banks throughout the Union and was giving rise to new institutions to aggravate the evil.

The safety of the public funds and the interest of the people generally required that these operations should be checked; and it became the duty of every branch of the General and State Governments to adopt all legitimate and proper means to produce that salutary effect. Under this view of my duty I directed the issuing of the order which will be laid before you by the Secretary of the Treasury, requiring payment for the public lands sold to be made in specie, with an exception until the 15th of the present month in favor of actual settlers. This measure has produced many salutary consequences. It checked the career of the Western banks and gave them additional strength in anticipation of the pressure which has since pervaded our Eastern as well as the European commercial cities. By preventing the extension of the credit system it measurably cut off the means of speculation and retarded its progress . . .

DOCUMENT NO. 10.   *Farewell Address.*

Having spent almost eight years in the Presidential office, Jackson decided to follow the example of predecessor George

Washington. In his final weeks as President, he gathered
together his thoughts and offered them as advice to his fellow
Americans in his Farewell Address, issued on his last day in
office, March 4, 1837 (*Mess. Pres.*, III, 292–308).

FELLOW-CITIZENS: Being about to retire finally from
public life, I beg leave to offer you my grateful thanks
for the many proofs of kindness and confidence which
I have received at your hands. It has been my fortune
in the discharge of public duties, civil and military, frequently to have found myself in difficult and trying situa-
tions, where prompt decision and energetic action were
necessary, and where the interest of the country required
that high responsibilities should be fearlessly encountered; and it is with the deepest emotions of gratitude
that I acknowledge the continued and unbroken confidence with which you have sustained me in every trial.
My public life has been a long one, and I can not hope
that it has at all times been free from errors; but I have
the consolation of knowing that if mistakes have been
committed they have not seriously injured the country
I so anxiously endeavored to serve, and at the moment
when I surrender my last public trust I leave this great
people prosperous and happy, in the full enjoyment of
liberty and peace, and honored and respected by every
nation of the world.

If my humble efforts have in any degree contributed
to preserve to you these blessings, I have been more than
rewarded by the honors you have heaped upon me, and,
above all, by the generous confidence with which you
have supported me in every peril, and with which you
have continued to animate and cheer my path to the
closing hour of my political life. The time has now come
when advanced age and a broken frame warn me to
retire from public concerns, but the recollection of the
many favors you have bestowed upon me is engraven
upon my heart, and I have felt that I could not part from
your service without making this public acknowledgment of the gratitude I owe you. And if I use the occasion to offer to you the counsels of age and experience,

you will, I trust, receive them with the same indulgent kindness which you have so often extended to me, and will at least see in them an earnest desire to perpetuate in this favored land the blessings of liberty and equal law.

We have now lived almost fifty years under the Constitution framed by the sages and patriots of the Revolution. The conflicts in which the nations of Europe were engaged during a great part of this period, the spirit in which they waged war against each other, and our intimate commercial connections with every part of the civilized world rendered it a time of much difficulty for the Government of the United States. We have had our seasons of peace and of war, with all the evils which precede or follow a state of hostility with powerful nations. We encountered these trials with our Constitution yet in its infancy, and under the disadvantages which a new and untried government must always feel when it is called upon to put forth its whole strength without the lights of experience to guide it or the weight of precedents to justify its measures. But we have passed triumphantly through all these difficulties. Our Constitution is no longer a doubtful experiment, and at the end of nearly half a century we find that it has preserved unimpaired the liberties of the people, secured the rights of property, and that our country has improved and is flourishing beyond any former example in the history of nations. . . .

If the Union is once severed, the line of separation will grow wider and wider, and the controversies which are now debated and settled in the halls of legislation will then be tried in fields of battle and determined by the sword. Neither should you deceive yourselves with the hope that the first line of separation would be the permanent one, and that nothing but harmony and concord would be found in the new associations formed upon the dissolution of this Union. Local interests would still be found there, and unchastened ambition. And if the recollection of common dangers, in which the people of these United States stood side by side against the common foe, the memory of victories won by their united valor, the prosperity and happiness they have enjoyed under the present Constitution, the proud name they bear as citizens of this great Republic—if all these recollections and proofs of common interest are not strong enough to bind us together as one people, what tie will hold united the new divisions of empire when these bonds have been broken and this Union dissevered? The first line of separation would not last for a single generation; new fragments would be torn off, new leaders would spring up, and this great and glorious Republic would soon be broken into a multitude of petty States, without commerce, without credit, jealous of one another, armed for mutual aggression, loaded with taxes to pay armies and leaders, seeking aid against each other from foreign powers, insulted and trampled upon by the nations of Europe, until, harassed with conflicts and humbled and debased in spirit, they would be ready to submit to the absolute dominion of any military adventurer and to surrender their liberty for the sake of repose. It is impossible to look on the consequences that would inevitably follow the destruction of this Government and not feel indignant when we hear cold calculations about the value of the Union and have so constantly before us a line of conduct so well calculated to weaken its ties. . . .

But in order to maintain the Union unimpaired it is absolutely necessary that the laws passed by the constituted authorities should be faithfully executed in every part of the country, and that every good citizen should at all times stand ready to put down, with the combined force of the nation, every attempt at unlawful resistance, under whatever pretext it may be made or whatever shape it may assume. Unconstitutional or oppressive laws may no doubt be passed by Congress, either from erroneous views or the want of due consideration; if they are within the reach of judicial authority, the remedy is easy and peaceful; and if, from the character of the law, it is an abuse of power not within the control of the judiciary, then free discussion and calm appeals to reason and to the justice of the people will not fail to redress the wrong. But until the law shall be declared void by

the courts or repealed by Congress no individual or combination of individuals can be justified in forcibly resisting its execution. It is impossible that any government
can continue to exist upon any other principles. It would
cease to be a government and be unworthy of the name
if it had not the power to enforce the execution of its
own laws within its own sphere of action.

It is true that cases may be imagined disclosing such
a settled purpose of usurpation and oppression on the
part of the Government as would justify an appeal to
arms. These, however, are extreme cases, which we have
no reason to apprehend in a government where the
power is in the hands of a patriotic people. And no
citizen who loves his country would in any case whatever
resort to forcible resistance unless he clearly saw that the
time had come when a freeman should prefer death to
submission; for if such a struggle is once begun, and the
citizens of one section of the country arrayed in arms
against those of another in doubtful conflict, let the battle result as it may, there will be an end of the Union
and with it an end to the hopes of freedom. The victory
of the injured would not secure to them the blessings of
liberty; it would avenge their wrongs, but they would
themselves share in the common ruin.

But the Constitution can not be maintained nor the
Union preserved, in opposition to public feeling, by the
mere exertion of the coercive powers confided to the
General Government. The foundations must be laid in
the affections of the people, in the security it gives to life,
liberty, character, and property in every quarter of the
country, and in the fraternal attachment which the citizens of the several States bear to one another as members
of one political family, mutually contributing to promote
the happiness of each other. Hence the citizens of every
State should studiously avoid everything calculated to
wound the sensibility or offend the just pride of the
people of other States, and they should frown upon any
proceedings within their own borders likely to disturb
the tranquillity of their political brethren in other portions of the Union. . . .

In the legislation of Congress also, and in every measure of the General Government, justice to every portion of the United States should be faithfully observed. No free government can stand without virtue in the people and a lofty spirit of patriotism, and if the sordid feelings of mere selfishness shall usurp the place which ought to be filled by public spirit, the legislation of Congress will soon be converted into a scramble for personal and sectional advantages. Under our free institutions the citizens of every quarter of our country are capable of attaining a high degree of prosperity and happiness without seeking to profit themselves at the expense of others; and every such attempt must in the end fail to succeed, for the people in every part of the United States are too enlightened not to understand their own rights and interests and to detect and defeat every effort to gain undue advantages over them; and when such designs are discovered it naturally provokes resentments which can not always be easily allayed. Justice—full and ample justice—to every portion of the United States should be the ruling principle of every freeman, and should guide the deliberations of every public body, whether it be State or national. . . .

There is, perhaps, no one of the powers conferred on the Federal Government so liable to abuse as the taxing power. The most productive and convenient sources of revenue were necessarily given to it, that it might be able to perform the important duties imposed upon it; and the taxes which it lays upon commerce being concealed from the real payer in the price of the article, they do not so readily attract the attention of the people as smaller sums demanded from them directly by the tax-gatherer. But the tax imposed on goods enhances by so much the price of the commodity to the consumer, and as many of these duties are imposed on articles of necessity which are daily used by the great body of the people, the money raised by these imposts is drawn from their pockets. Congress has no right under the Constitution to take money from the people unless it is required to execute some one of the specific powers intrusted to the

Government; and if they raise more than is necessary for such purposes, it is an abuse of the power of taxation, and unjust and oppressive. It may indeed happen that the revenue will sometimes exceed the amount anticipated when the taxes were laid. When, however, this is ascertained, it is easy to reduce them, and in such a case it is unquestionably the duty of the Government to reduce them, for no circumstances can justify it in assuming a power not given to it by the Constitution nor in taking away the money of the people when it is not needed for the legitimate wants of the Government.

Plain as these principles appear to be, you will yet find there is a constant effort to induce the General Government to go beyond the limits of its taxing power and to impose unnecessary burdens upon the people. Many powerful interests are continually at work to procure heavy duties on commerce and to swell the revenue beyond the real necessities of the public service, and the country has already felt the injurious effects of their combined influence. They succeeded in obtaining a tariff of duties bearing most oppressively on the agricultural and laboring classes of society and producing a revenue that could not be usefully employed within the range of the powers conferred upon Congress, and in order to fasten upon the people this unjust and unequal system of taxation extravagant schemes of internal improvement were got up in various quarters to squander the money and to purchase support. Thus one unconstitutional measure was intended to be upheld by another, and the abuse of the power of taxation was to be maintained by usurping the power of expending the money in internal improvements. You can not have forgotten the severe and doubtful struggle through which we passed when the executive department of the Government by its veto endeavored to arrest this prodigal scheme of injustice and to bring back the legislation of Congress to the boundaries prescribed by the Constitution. The good sense and practical judgment of the people when the subject was brought before them sustained the course of the Executive, and this plan of unconstitutional expenditures for the purposes of corrupt influence is, I trust, finally overthrown.

The result of this decision has been felt in the rapid extinguishment of the public debt and the large accumulation of a surplus in the Treasury, notwithstanding the tariff was reduced and is now very far below the amount originally contemplated by its advocates. But, rely upon it, the design to collect an extravagant revenue and to burden you with taxes beyond the economical wants of the Government is not yet abandoned. The various interests which have combined together to impose a heavy tariff and to produce an overflowing Treasury are too strong and have too much at stake to surrender the contest. The corporations and wealthy individuals who are engaged in large manufacturing establishments desire a high tariff to increase their gains. Designing politicians will support it to conciliate their favor and to obtain the means of profuse expenditure for the purpose of purchasing influence in other quarters; and since the people have decided that the Federal Government can not be permitted to employ its income in internal improvements, efforts will be made to seduce and mislead the citizens of the several States by holding out to them the deceitful prospect of benefits to be derived from a surplus revenue collected by the General Government and annually divided among the States; and if, encouraged by these fallacious hopes, the States should disregard the principles of economy which ought to characterize every republican government, and should indulge in lavish expenditures exceeding their resources, they will before long find themselves oppressed with debts which they are unable to pay, and the temptation will become irresistible to support a high tariff in order to obtain a surplus for distribution. Do not allow yourselves, my fellow-citizens, to be misled on this subject. . . . The Constitution of the United States unquestionably intended to secure to the people a circulating medium of gold and silver. But the establishment of a national bank by Congress, with the privilege of issuing paper money receivable in the payment of the public dues, and the unfortunate course of legislation in the several States upon the same subject, drove from general circulation the constitutional currency and substituted one of paper in its place.

It was not easy for men engaged in the ordinary pursuits of business, whose attention had not been particularly drawn to the subject, to foresee all the consequences of a currency exclusively of paper, and we ought not on that account to be surprised at the facility with which laws were obtained to carry into effect the paper system. Honest and even enlightened men are sometimes misled by the specious and plausible statements of the designing. But experience has now proved the mischiefs and dangers of a paper currency, and it rests with you to determine whether the proper remedy shall be applied.

The paper system being founded on public confidence and having of itself no intrinsic value, it is liable to great and sudden fluctuations, thereby rendering property insecure and the wages of labor unsteady and uncertain. The corporations which create the paper money can not be relied upon to keep the circulating medium uniform in amount. . . . These ebbs and flows in the currency and these indiscreet extensions of credit naturally engender a spirit of speculation injurious to the habits and character of the people. . . . It is the duty of every government so to regulate its currency as to protect this numerous class, as far as practicable, from the impositions of avarice and fraud. It is more especially the duty of the United States, where the Government is emphatically the Government of the people, and where this respectable portion of our citizens are so proudly distinguished from the laboring classes of all other nations by their independent spirit, their love of liberty, their intelligence, and their high tone of moral character. Their industry in peace is the source of our wealth and their bravery in war has covered us with glory; and the Government of the United States will but ill discharge its duties if it leaves them a prey to such dishonest impositions. Yet it is evident that their interests can not be effectually protected unless silver and gold are restored to circulation.

Recent events have proved that the paper-money system of this country may be used as an engine to undermine your free institutions, and that those who desire to engross all power in the hands of the few and to govern by corruption or force are aware of its power and prepared to employ it. Your banks now furnish your only circulating medium, and money is plenty or scarce according to the quantity of notes issued by them. While they have capitals not greatly disproportioned to each other, they are competitors in business, and no one of them can exercise dominion over the rest; and although in the present state of the currency these banks may and do operate injuriously upon the habits of business, the pecuniary concerns, and the moral tone of society, yet, from their number and dispersed situation, they can not combine for the purposes of political influence, and whatever may be the dispositions of some of them their power of mischief must mecessarily be confined to a narrow space and felt only in their immediate neighborhoods. . . .

The distress and sufferings inflicted on the people by the bank are some of the fruits of that system of policy which is continually striving to enlarge the authority of the Federal Government beyond the limits fixed by the Constitution. The powers enumerated in that instrument do not confer on Congress the right to establish such a corporation as the Bank of the United States, and the evil consequences which followed may warn us of the danger of departing from the true rule of construction and of permitting temporary circumstances or the hope of better promoting the public welfare to influence in any degree our decisions upon the extent of the authority of the General Government. Let us abide by the Constitution as it is written, or amend it in the constitutional mode if it is found to be defective.

The severe lessons of experience will, I doubt not, be sufficient to prevent Congress from again chartering such a monopoly, even if the Constitution did not present an insuperable objection to it. But you must remember, my fellow citizens, that eternal vigilance by the people is the price of liberty, and that you must pay the price if you wish to secure the blessing. It behooves you, therefore, to be watchful in your States as well as in the Federal Government. The power which the moneyed interest can exercise, when concentrated under a single head and with our present system of currency, was sufficiently demonstrated in the struggle made by the Bank of the United States. . . .

It is one of the serious evils of our present system of banking that it enables one class of society—and that by no means a numerous one—by its control over the currency, to act injuriously upon the interests of all the others and to exercise more than its just proportion of influence in political affairs. The agricultural, the mechanical, and the laboring classes have little or no share in the direction of the great moneyed corporations, and from their habits and the nature of their pursuits they are incapable of forming extensive combinations to act together with united force. Such concert of action may sometimes be produced in a single city or in a small district of country by means of personal communications with each other, but they have no regular or active correspondence with those who are engaged in similar pursuits in distant places; they have but little patronage to give to the press, and exercise but a small share of influence over it; they have no crowd of dependents about them who hope to grow rich without labor by their countenance and favor, and who are therefore always ready to execute their wishes. The planter, the farmer, the mechanic, and the laborer all know that their success depends upon their own industry and economy, and that they must not expect to become suddenly rich by the fruits of their toil. Yet these classes of society form the great body of the people of the United States; they are the bone and sinew of the country—men who love liberty and desire nothing but equal rights and equal laws, and who, moreover, hold the great mass of our national wealth, although it is distributed in moderate amounts among the millions of freemen who possess it. But with overwhelming numbers and wealth on their side they are in constant danger of losing their fair influence in the Government, and with difficulty maintain their just rights against the incessant efforts daily made to encroach upon them. The mischief springs from the power which the moneyed interest derives from a paper currency which they are able to control, from the multitude of corporations with exclusive privileges which they have succeeded in obtaining in the different States, and which are employed altogether for their benefit; and unless you become more watchful in your States and check this spirit of monopoly and thirst for exclusive privileges you will in the end find that the most important powers of Government have been given or bartered away, and the control over your dearest interests has passed into the hands of these corporations.

The paper-money system and its natural associations—monopoly and exclusive privileges—have already struck their roots too deep in the soil, and it will require all your efforts to check its further growth and to eradicate the evil. . . .

But it will require steady and persevering exertions on your part to rid yourselves of the iniquities and mischiefs of the paper system and to check the spirit of monopoly and other abuses which have sprung up with it, and of which it is the main support. . . .

While I am thus endeavoring to press upon your attention the principles which I deem of vital importance in the domestic concerns of the country, I ought not to pass over without notice the important considerations which should govern your policy toward foreign powers. It is unquestionably our true interest to cultivate the most friendly understanding with every nation and to avoid by every honorable means the calamities of war, and we shall best attain this object by frankness and sincerity in our foreign intercourse, by the prompt and faithful execution of treaties, and by justice and impartiality in our conduct to all. But no nation, however desirous of peace, can hope to escape occasional collisions with other powers, and the soundest dictates of policy require that we should place ourselves in a condition to assert our rights if a resort to force should ever become necessary. Our local situation, our long line of seacoast, indented by numerous bays, with deep rivers opening into the interior, as well as our extended and still increasing commerce, point to the Navy as our natural means of defense. It will in the end be found to be the cheapest and most effectual, and now is the time, in a season of peace and with an overflowing revenue, that we can year after year add to its strength without increasing the burdens of the people. It is your true policy, for your Navy will not only protect your rich and flourishing commerce in distant seas, but will enable you to reach and annoy the enemy and will give to defense its greatest efficiency by meeting danger at a distance from home. It is impossible by any line of fortifications to guard every point from attack against a hostile force advancing from the ocean and selecting its object, but they are indispensable to protect cities from bombardment, dockyards and naval arsenals from destruction, to give shelter to merchant vessels in time of war and to single ships or weaker squadrons when pressed by superior force. Fortifications of this description can not be too soon completed and armed and placed in a condition of the most perfect preparation. The abundant means we now possess can not be applied in any manner more useful to the country, and when this is done and our naval force sufficiently strengthened and our militia armed we need not fear that any nation will wantonly insult us or needlessly provoke hostilities. We shall more certainly preserve peace when it is well understood that we are prepared for war.

In presenting to you, my fellow-citizens, these parting counsels, I have brought before you the leading principles upon which I endeavored to administer the Government in the high office with which you twice honored me. Knowing that the path of freedom is continually beset by enemies who often assume the disguise of friends, I have devoted the last hours of my public life to warn you of the dangers. The progress of the United States under our free and happy institutions has surpassed the most sanguine hopes of the founders of the Republic. Our growth has been rapid beyond all former example in numbers, in wealth, in knowledge, and all the useful arts which contribute to the comforts and convenience of man, and from the earliest ages of history to the present day there never have been thirteen millions of people associated in one political body who enjoyed so much freedom and happiness as the people of these United States. You have no longer any cause to fear danger from abroad; your strength and power are well known throughout the civilized world, as well as the high and gallant bearing of your sons. It is from within, among yourselves—from cupidity, from corruption, from disappointed ambition and inordinate thirst for power—that factions will be formed and liberty endangered. It is against such designs, whatever disguise the actors may assume, that you have especially to guard yourselves. You have the highest of human trusts committed to your care. Providence has showered on this favored land blessings without number, and has chosen you as the guardians of freedom, to preserve it for the benefit of the human race. May He who holds in His hands the destinies of nations make you worthy of the favors He has bestowed and enable you, with pure hearts and pure hands and sleepless vigilance, to guard and defend to the end of time the great charge He has committed to your keeping.

My own race is nearly run; advanced age and failing health warn me that before long I must pass beyond the reach of human events and cease to feel the vicissitudes of human affairs. I thank God that my life has been spent in a land of liberty and that He has given me a heart to love my country with the affection of a son. And filled with gratitude for your constant and unwavering kindness, I bid you a last and affectionate farewell.

ANDREW JACKSON.

Part II. John C. Calhoun

DOCUMENT NO. 11. *Tariff of 1816.*

Joining in the nationalist spirit that swept the United States
in the days immediately following the end of the war of 1812,
Calhoun supported and proposed measures by which the
government would actively stimulate the economy in order
to develop a self-sufficient, self-reliant nation. A year after the
war, as British goods were flooding the American market,
Congress considered a protective tariff bill. On April 4, 1816,
Congressman Calhoun expressed his views on the tariff in the
House of Representatives (John C. Calhoun, *Works,* 6 vols.,
ed. Richard K. Cralle, New York, 1854–1857, hereafter cited
as Calhoun, *Works;* the following passage is found in II,
163–73):

SPEECH ON THE TARIFF BILL
April 4, 1816 [*Mr. Calhoun, replying to Mr. Randolph,
said:*]

He had asserted, that the subject before them was
conncctcd with the security of the country. It would,
doubtless, by some be considered a rash assertion; but
he conceived it to be susceptible of the clearest proof;
and he hoped, with due attention, to establish it to the
satisfaction of the House.

The security of a country mainly depends on its spirit
and its means; and the latter principally on its monied
resources. Modified as the industry of this country now
is, combined with our peculiar situation and want of a
naval ascendancy; whenever we have the misfortune to
be involved in a war with a nation dominant on the
ocean, and it is almost only with such we can at present
be, the monied resources of the country, to a great extent, must fail. He took it for granted, that it was the
duty of this body to adopt those measures of prudent
foresight, which the event of war made necessary. . . .
Our commerce neither is or can be protected, by the
present means of the country. What, then, are the effects

of a war with a maritime power—with England? Our commerce annihilated, spreading individual misery, and producing national poverty; our agriculture cut off from its accustomed markets, the surplus product of the farmer perishes on his hands; and he ceases to produce, because he cannot sell. His resources are dried up, while his expences are greatly increased; as all manufactured articles, the necessaries, as well as the conveniences of life, rise to an extravagant price. The recent war fell with peculiar pressure on the growers of cotton and tobacco, and other great staples of the country; and the same state of things will recur in the event of another, unless prevented by the foresight of this body.

If the mere statement of facts did not carry conviction to any mind, as he conceives it is calculated to do, additional arguments might be drawn from the general nature of wealth. Neither agriculture, manufactures or commerce, taken separately, is the cause of wealth; it flows from the three combined; and cannot exist without each. The wealth of any single nation or an individual, it is true, may not *immediately* depend on the three, but such wealth always presupposes their existence. He viewed the words in the most enlarged sense. Without commerce, industry would have no stimulus; without manufactures, it would be without the means of production; and without agriculture, neither of the others can subsist. When separated entirely and permanently, they perish. War in this country produces, to a great extent, that effect; and hence, the great embarrassment which follows in its train. The failure of the wealth and resources of the nation necessarily involved the ruin of its finances and its currency. It is admitted by the most strenuous advocates, on the other side, that no country ought to be dependent on another for its means of defence; that, at least, our musket and bayonet, our cannon and ball, ought to be of domestic manufacture. But what, he asked, is more necessary to the defence of a country than its currency and finance? Circumstanced as our country is, can these stand the shock of war? Behold the effect of the late war on them. When our manufactures are grown to a certain perfection, as they soon will under the fostering care of government, we will no longer experience these evils. The farmer will find a ready market for his surplus produce; and what is almost of equal consequence, a certain and cheap supply of all his wants. His prosperity will diffuse itself to every class in the community; and instead of that languor of industry and individual distress now incident to a state of war, and suspended commerce, the wealth and vigor of the community will not be materially impaired. The arm of government will be nerved, and taxes in the hour of danger, when essential to the independence of the nation, may be greatly increased; loans, so uncertain and hazardous, may be less relied on; thus situated, the storm may beat without, but within all will be quiet and safe. . . . The result of a war in the present state of our naval power is the blockade of our coast, and consequent destruction of our trade. The wants and habits of the country, founded on the use of foreign articles, must be gratified; importation to a certain extent continues, through the policy of the enemy, or unlawful traffic; the exportation of our bulky articles is prevented too, the specie of the country is drawn to pay the balance perpetually accumulating against us; and the final result is a total derangement of our currency.

To this distressing state of things there are two remedies, and only two; one in our power immediately, the other requiring much time and exertion; but both constituting, in his opinion, the essential policy of this country; he meant the navy, and domestic manufactures. . . . he firmly believed that the country is prepared, even to maturity, for the introduction of manufactures. We have abundance of resources, and things naturally tend at this moment in that direction. A prosperous commerce has poured an immense amount of commerical capital into this country. This capital has, till lately, found occupation in commerce; but that state of the world which transferred it to this country, and gave it active employment, has passed away, never to return. Where shall we now find full employmemt for our prodigious amount of tonnage; where markets for the numerous and abundant products of our country? This great body of active capital, which for *the moment* has found sufficient employment in supplying our markets, exhausted by the war, and measures preceding it, must find a new direction; it will not be idle. What channel can it take, but that of manufactures? This, if things continue as they are, will be its direction. It will introduce a new era in our affairs, in many respects highly advantageous, and ought to be countenanced by the government.

Besides, we have already surmounted the greatest difficulty that has ever been found in undertakings of this kind. The cotton and woollen manufactures are not to be *introduced*—they are *already* introduced to a great extent; freeing us entirely from the hazards, and, in a great measure the sacrifices experienced in giving the capital of the country a new direction. The restrictive measures and the war, though not intended for that purpose, have, by the necessary operation of things, turned a large amount of capital to this new branch of industry.

It has been objected to this bill, that it will injure our marine, and consequently impair our naval strength. How far it is fairly liable to this charge, he was not prepared to say. He hoped and believed, it would not, at least to any alarming extent, have that effect immediately; and he firmly believed, that its lasting operation would be highly beneficial to our commerce.

. . . Other objections of a political character were made to the encouragement of manufactures. It is said they destroy the moral and physical power of the people. This might formerly have been true to a considerable extent, before the perfection of machinery, and when the success of the manufactures depended on the minute subdivision of labor. At that time it required a large portion of the population of a country to be engaged in them; and every minute sub-division of labor is undoubtedly unfavorable to the intellect; but the great perfection of machinery has in a considerable degree obviated these objections. In fact it has been stated that the manufacturing districts in England furnish the greatest number of recruits to her army, and that, as soldiers, they are not materially inferior to the rest of her population. It has been further asserted that manufactures are the fruitful cause of pauperism; and England has been referred to as furnishing conclusive evidence of its truth. For his part, he could perceive no such tendency in them, but the exact contrary, as they furnished new stimulus and means of subsistence to the laboring classes of the community. We ought not to look to the cotton and woollen establishments of Great Britain for the prodigious numbers of poor with which her population was disgraced. Causes much more efficient exist. Her poor laws and statutes regulating the price of labor with heavy taxes, were the real causes. But if it must be so, if the mere fact that England manufactured more than any other country, explained the cause of her having more beggars, it is just as reasonable to refer her courage, spirit, and all her masculine virtues, in which she excels all other nations, with a single exception; he meant our own; in which we might without vanity challenge a pre-eminence.

Another objection had been made, which he must acknowledge was better founded, that capital employed in manufacturing produced a greater dependance on the part of the employed, than in commerce, navigation or agriculture. It is certainly an evil and to be regretted; but he did not think it a decisive objection to the system; especially when it had incidental political advantages which in his opinion more than counterpoised it. It produced an interest strictly American, as much so as agriculture; in which it had the decided advantage of commerce or navigation. The country will from this derive much advantage. Again, it is calculated to bind together more closely our widely-spread Republic. It will greatly increase our mutual dependence and intercourse; and will as a necessary consequence, excite an increased attention to internal improvement, a subject every way so intimately connected with the ultimate attainment of national strength and the perfection of our

political institutions. He regarded the fact that it would
make the parts adhere more closely, that it would form
a new and most powerful cement, far out-weighing any
political objections that might be urged against the system. In his opinion the *liberty* and the *union* of this
country were inseparably [3] united! That as the destruction of the latter would most certainly involve the
former; so its maintenance will with equal certainty preserve it. He did not speak lightly. He had often and long
revolved it in his mind; and he had critically examined
into the causes that destroyed the liberty of other states.
There are none that apply to us, or apply with a force
to alarm. The basis of our Republic is too broad and its
structure too strong to be shaken by them. Its extension
and organization will be found to afford effectual
security against their operation; but let it be deeply impressed on the heart of this House and country, that
while they guarded against the old they exposed us to
a new and terrible danger, disunion. This single word
comprehended almost the sum of our political dangers;
and against it we ought to be perpetually guarded. . . .

DOCUMENT NO. 12. *Building a Transportation
System.*

As part of the program to strengthen the United States and
to bind the nation more closely together, Congressman Calhoun proposed a vast scheme of internal improvements,
mainly roads and canals, to be built by the federal government. On February 4, 1817, he made his proposal in a speech
to the House of Representatives (Calhoun, *Works,* 186–96).

DOCUMENT 12-A
4 February 1817   *On Internal Improvements*
                                          February 4, 1817
Mr. Calhoun rose and observed, . . . it seemed to him,
when he reflected how favorable was the present moment, and how confessedly important a good system of
roads and canals was to our country, he might reasona-

bly be very sanguine of success. At peace with all the world; abounding in pecuniary means; and, what was of the most importance, and at what he rejoiced, as most favorable to the country, party and sectional feelings immerged in a liberal and enlightened regard to the general concerns of the nation. Such, said he, are the favorable circumstances under which we are now deliberating. Thus situated, to what can we direct our resources and attention more important than internal improvements? What can add more to the wealth, the strength, and the political prosperity of our country? The manner in which facility and cheapness of intercourse, added to the wealth of a nation, had been so often and ably discussed by writers on political economy, that he presumed the House to be perfectly acquainted with the subject. It was sufficient to observe, that every branch of national industry, Agricultural, Manufacturing, and Commercial, was greatly stimulated and rendered by it more productive. The result is, said he, that it tends to diffuse universal opulence. It gives to the interior the advantages possessed by the parts most eligibly situated for trade. It makes the country price, whether in the sale of the raw product, or in the purchase of the articles for consumption, approximate to that of the commercial towns. In fact, if we look into the nature of wealth we will find, that nothing can be more favorable to its growth than good roads and canals. An article, to command a price, must not only be useful, but must be the subject of demand; and the better the means of commercial intercourse, the larger is the sphere of demand. . . . Let it not be said that internal improvements may be wholly left to the enterprize of the states and of individuals. He knew, he said, that much might justly be expected to be done by them; but in a country so new, and so extensive as ours, there is room enough, said he, for all the general and state governments and individuals, in which to exert their resources. But many of the improvements contemplated, said Mr. C. are on too great a scale for the resources of the states or individuals; and many of such a nature, that the rival jealousy of the states, if left alone, might prevent. They required the resources and the general superintendence of this government to effect and complete them.

But, said Mr. C. there are higher and more powerful considerations why Congress ought to take charge of this subject. If we were only to consider the pecuniary advantages of a good system of roads and canals, it might indeed admit of some doubt whether they ought not to be left wholly to individual exertions; but when we come to consider how intimately the strength and political prosperity of the Republic are connected with this subject, we find the most urgent reasons why we should apply our resources to them. In many respects, no country of equal population and wealth, possesses equal materials of power with ours. The people, in muscular power, in hardy and enterprizing habits, and in a lofty and gallant courage, are surpassed by none. In one respect, and in my opinion, in one only, are we materially weak. We occupy a surface prodigiously great in proportion to our numbers. The common strength is brought to bear with great difficulty on the point that may be menaced by an enemy. It is our duty, then, as far as in the nature of things it can be effected, to counteract this weakness. Good roads and canals judiciously laid out, are the proper remedy. In the recent war, how much did we suffer for the want of them! Besides the tardiness and the consequential inefficacy of our military movements, to what an increased expence was the country put for the article of transportation alone! In the event of another war, the saving in this particular would go far towards indemnifying us for the expense of constructing the means of transportation. . . .

But on this subject of national power, what, said Mr. C. can be more important than a perfect unity in every part, in feelings and sentiments? And what can tend more powerfully to produce it, than overcoming the effects of distance? No country, enjoying freedom, ever occupied any thing like as great an extent of country as this Republic. Let it not however be forgotten; let it, said he, be forever kept in mind, that it exposes us to the greatest of all calamities, next to the loss of liberty, and even to that in its consequence—*disunion*.[1] We are great, and rapidly, he was about to say fearfully, growing. This, said he, is our pride and danger—our weakness and our strength. Little, said Mr. C. does he deserve to be entrusted with the liberties of this people, who does not raise his mind to these truths. We are under the most imperious obligation to counteract every tendency to disunion. The strongest of all cements is, undoubtedly, the wisdom, justice, and, above all, the moderation of this House; yet the great subject on which we are now deliberating, in this respect, deserves the most serious consideration. Whatever, said Mr. C. impedes the intercourse of the extremes with this, the centre of the Republic, weakens the union. The more enlarged the sphere of commercial circulation, the more extended that of social intercourse; the more strongly are we bound together; the more inseparable are our destinies. Those who understand the human heart best, know how powerfully distance tends to break the sympathies of our nature. Nothing, not even dissimilarity of language, tends more to estrange man from man. Let us then, said Mr. C. bind the Republic together with a perfect system of roads and canals. Let us conquer space. It is thus the most distant parts of the republic will be brought within a few days travel of the centre; it is thus that a citizen of the West will read the news of Boston still moist from the press. The mail and the press, said he, are the nerves of the body politic. By them, the slightest impression made on the most remote parts, is communicated to the whole system; and the more perfect the means of transportation, the more rapid and true the vibration. To aid us in this great work, to maintain the integrity of this Republic, we inhabit a country presenting the most admirable advantages. Belted around, as it is, by lakes and oceans, intersected in every direction by bays and rivers, the hand of industry and art is tempted to improvement. So situated, said he, blessed with a form of government at once combining liberty and strength, we may reasonably raise our eyes to a most splendid future, if we only act in a manner worthy of our advantages. If, however, neglecting them, we permit a low, sordid, selfish, and sectional spirit to take possession of this House, this happy scene will vanish. We will divide, and in its consequences will follow misery and despotism.

To legislate for our country, said Mr. C. requires not only the most enlarged views, but a species of self-devotion, not exacted in any other. In a country so extensive, and so various in its interests, what is necessary for the common good, may apparently be opposed to the interest of particular sections. . . . He understood there were, with some members, constitutional objections. The power of Congress is objected to; first, that they have none to cut a road or canal through a state without its consent—and next, that the public monies can only be appropriated to effect the particular powers enumerated in the Constitution. The first of these objections, said Mr. C. it is plain does not apply to this bill. No particular road or canal is proposed to be cut through any state. The bill simply appropriates money to the general purpose of improving the means of communication. When a bill is introduced to apply the money to a particular object in any state, then, and not till then, will the question be fairly before us. Mr. C. gave no opinion on this point. In fact, he scarcely thought it worth the discussion, since the good sense of the states might be relied on. They will in all cases readily yield their assent. The fear is in a different direction: in a too great a solicitude to obtain an undue share to be expended within their respective limits. In fact, he said he understood that this was not the objection insisted on. It was mainly urged that the Congress can only apply the public money in execution of the enumerated powers. He was no advocate for refined arguments on the Constitution.[2] The instrument was not intended as a thesis for the logician to exercise his ingenuity on. It ought to be construed with plain, good sense; and what can be more express than the Constitution on this very point? The first power delegated to Congress, is comprized in these words: "to lay and collect taxes, duties, imposts and excises; to pay the debts, and provide for the common defence and general welfare of the United States; but all duties, imposts and excises shall be uniform throughout the United States." First—the power is given to lay taxes; next, the objects are enumerated to which the money accruing from the exercise of this power, may be applied—to pay the debts, provide for the defence, and promote the general welfare; and last, the rule for laying the taxes is prescribed—that all duties, imposts and excises shall be uniform. If the framers had intended to limit the use of the money to the powers afterwards enumerated and defined, nothing could be more easy than to have expressed it plainly. . . .

The Constitution, said he, gives to Congress the power to establish post offices and post-roads. He knew the interpretation which was usually given to these words confined our power to that of designating only the post roads; but it seemed to him that the word "establish" comprehended something more. . . .

He believed that the passage of the bill would not be much endangered by a doubt of the power; as he conceived on that point there were not many who were opposed. The mode is principally objected to. A system it is contended ought to be presented before the money is appropriated. He thought differently. To set apart the fund appeared to him to be naturally the first act; at least he took it to be the only practicable course. A bill filled with details would have but a faint prospect of passing. The enemies to any possible system in detail and those who are opposed in principle, would unite and defeat it. Though he was unwilling to incorporate details in the bill, yet he was not adverse to presenting his views on that point. The first great object was to perfect the communication from Maine to Louisiana. This might be fairly considered as the principal artery of the whole system. The next was the connection of the Lakes with the Hudson River. In a political, commercial and military point of view, few objects could be more important. The next object of chief importance was to connect all the great commercial points on the Atlantic, Philadelphia, Baltimore, Washington, Richmond, Charleston and Savannah, with the Western States; and finally, to perfect the intercourse between the West and New Orleans. These seem to him to be the great objects. There were others no doubt of great importance which would receive the aid of government. The fund proposed to be set apart in this bill was about 650,000 dollars a year, which was doubtless, too small to effect such great objects of itself; but it would be a good beginning; and he had no doubt when it was once begun, the great work will be finished.

As Secretary of War, charged with the defense of the nation, Calhoun developed a broad plan for federally-built roads and canal. On January 7, 1819, he sent his proposal to Congress accompanied by this message addressed to House Speaker Henry Clay (Calhoun, *Works*, V, 40–54):

DOCUMENT 12-B   *To Speaker Henry Clay*
                                Department of War, January 7, 1819
A judicious system of roads and canals, constructed for the convenience of commerce, and the transportation of the mail only, without any reference to military operations, is itself among the most efficient means for "the more complete defence of the United States." Without adverting to the fact that the roads and canals which such a system would require are, with few exceptions, precisely those which would be required for the operations of war, such a system, by consolidating our Union, and increasing our wealth and fiscal capacity, would add greatly to our resources in war. It is in a state of war, when a nation is compelled to put all of its resources in men, money, skill, and devotion to country into requisition, that its Government realizes in its security the beneficial effects from a people made prosperous and happy by a wise direction of its resources in peace. But I forbear to pursue this subject, though so interesting, and which, the further it is pursued, will the more clearly establish the intimate connexion between the defence and safety of the country and its improvement and pros-

perity, as I do not conceive that it constitutes the immediate object of this report.

There is no country to which a good system of military roads and canals is more indispensable than to the United States. As great as our military capacity is, when compared with the number of our people, yet, when considered in relation to the vast extent of our country, it is very small; and if so great an extent of territory renders it very difficult to conquer us, as has frequently been observed, it ought not to be forgotten that it renders it no less difficult for the Government to afford protection to every portion of the community. In the very nature of things, the difficulty of protecting every part, so long as our population bears so small a proportion to the extent of the country, cannot be entirely overcome, but it may be very greatly diminished, by a good system of military roads and canals. The necessity of such a system is still more apparent, if we take into consideration the character of our political maxims and institutions. Opposed in principle to a large standing army, our main reliance for defence must be on the militia, to be called out frequently from a great distance, and under the pressure of an actual invasion. The experience of the late war amply proves, in the present state of our internal improvements, the delay, the uncertainty, the anxiety, and exhausting effects of such calls. . . .

Should Congress think proper to commence a system of roads and canals for the "more complete defence of the United States," the disbursement of the sums appropriated for the purpose might be made by the Department of War, under the direction of the President. Where incorporated companies are already formed, or the road or canal commenced under the superintendence of a State, it perhaps would be advisable to direct a subscription on the part of the United States, on such terms and conditions as might be thought proper. In other cases, and where the army cannot be made to execute it, the work ought to be done by contract, under the superintendence and inspection of officers of the engineer corps. . . .

DOCUMENT NO. 13.   *State Rights and Nullification.*

When Congress adopted an increase in the protective tariff in 1828, South Carolina's legislature was furious. Convinced that the tariff for protective purpose was not only unconstitutional but worked an economic hardship on the state, the legislature appointed a committee to draft a statement on the tariff. The committee approached John C. Calhoun, then Vice President, for assistance. In the fall of 1828 Calhoun, who insisted that his authorship not be made public, prepared the statement, which was presented on December 2, 1832 to South Carolina's legislature which ordered it printed under the title the *Exposition* (Calhoun, *Works*, VI, 1–57):

EXPOSITION.

. . . the act of Congress of the last session, with the whole system of legislation imposing duties on imports, —not for revenue, but the protection of one branch of industry at the expense of others,—is unconstitutional, unequal, and oppressive, and calculated to corrupt the public virtue and destroy the liberty of the country . . .

The Constitution grants to Congress the power of imposing a duty on imports for revenue, which power is abused by being converted into an instrument of rearing up the industry of one section of the country on the ruins of another. The violation, then, consists in using a power granted for one object to advance another, and that by the sacrifice of the original object. It is, in a word, a violation by perversion,—the most dangerous of all because the most insidious and difficult to resist. . . .

So partial are the effects of the system, that its burdens are exclusively on one side and its benefits on the other. It imposes on the agricultural interest of the South, including the South-west, and that portion of the country particularly engaged in commerce and navigation, the burden not only of sustaining the system itself, but that also of the Government. . . .

It has already been proved that our contribution, through the Custom-House, to the Treasury of the Union, amounts annually to $16,650,000, which leads to the inquiry,—What becomes of so large an amount of the products of our labor, placed, by the operation of the system, at the disposal of Congress? One point is certain,—a very small share returns to us, out of whose labor it is extracted. It would require much investigation to state, with precision, the proportion of the public revenue disbursed annually in the Southern, and other States respectively; but the committee feel a thorough conviction, on examination of the annual appropriation acts, that a sum much less than two millions of dollars falls to our share of the disbursements; and that it would be a moderate estimate to place our contribution, above what we receive back, through all of the appropriations, at $15,000,000; constituting, to that great amount, an annual, continued, and uncompensated draft on the industry of the Southern States, through the Custom-House alone. . . .

The committee having presented its views on the partial and oppressive operation of the system, will proceed to discuss the next position which they proposed,—its tendency to corrupt the Government, and to destroy the liberty of the country.

If there be a political proposition universally true, —one which springs directly from the nature of man, and is independent of circumstances,—it is, that irresponsible power is inconsistent with liberty, and must corrupt those who exercise it. On this great principle our political system rests. We consider all powers as delegated by the people, and to be controlled by them, who are interested in their just and proper exercise; and our Governments, both State and General, are but a system of judicious contrivances to bring this fundamental principle into fair, practical operation. Among the most prominent of these is the responsibility of representatives to their constituents, through frequent periodical elections, in order to enforce a faithful performance of their delegated trust. Without such a check on their powers, however clearly they may be defined and distinctly prescribed, our liberty would be but a mockery. The Government, instead of being directed to the general good, would speedily become but the instrument to aggrandize those who might be intrusted with its administration. On the other hand, if laws were uniform in their operation, —if that which imposed a burden on one, imposed it likewise on all—or that which acted beneficially for one, acted also, in the same manner, for all—the responsibility of representatives to their constituents would alone be sufficient to guard against abuse and tyranny—provided the people be sufficiently intelligent to understand their interest, and the motives and conduct of their public agents.

If it be conceded, as it must be by every one who is the least conversant with out institutions, that the sovereign powers delegated are divided between the General and State Governments, and that the latter hold their portion by the same tenure as the former, it would seem impossible to deny to the States the right of deciding on the infractions of their powers, and the proper remedy to be applied for their correction. The right of judging, in such cases, is an essential attribute of sovereignty,—of which the States cannot be divested without losing their sovereignty itself,—and being reduced to a subordinate corporate condition. . . . In this inquiry a question may be made,—whether a State can interpose its sovereignty through the ordinary Legislature, but which the committee do not deem it necessary to investigate. It is sufficient that plausible reasons may be assigned against this mode of action, if there be one (and there is one) free from all objections. Whatever doubts may be raised as to the question,—whether the respective Legislatures fully represent the sovereignty of the States for this high purpose, there can be none as to the fact that a Convention fully represents them for all purposes whatever. Its authority, therefore, must remove every objection as to form, and leave the question on the single point of the right of the States to interpose at all. When convened, it will belong to the Convention itself to determine, authoritatively, whether the acts of which we complain be unconstitutional; and, if so, whether they constitute a violation so deliberate, palpable, and dangerous, as to justify the interposition of the State to protect its rights. . . . if the present usurpations and the professed doctrines of the existing system be persevered in,—after due forbearance on the part of the State,—that it will be her sacred duty to interpose;—a duty to herself,—to the Union,—to the present, and to future generations,—and to the cause of liberty over the world, to arrest the progress of a usurpation which, if not arrested, must, in its consequences, corrupt the public morals and destroy the liberty of the country.

DOCUMENT NO. 14. *The Union and Presidential Power.*

During the nullification crisis of 1832–33, President Jackson asked Congress for authority to use the armed forces of the United States and to call upon state militias, if it became necessary, to enforce the tariff laws within South Carolina, which was threatening to refuse to allow collection of federal tariff duties within its borders. Calhoun protested against the President's reaching for such extreme power in the following speech delivered in the Senate on February 15 and 16, 1833 (Calhoun, *Works,* II, 197–262):

SPEECH

On the Revenue Collection Bill (commonly called the Force Bill), in reference to the Ordinance of the South Carolina Convention, delivered in the Senate, February 15th and 16th, 1833. . . .

The decision of this question involves an inquiry into the provisions of the bill. What are they? It puts at the disposal of the President the army and navy, and the entire militia of the country; it enables him, at his pleasure, to subject every man in the United States, not exempt from militia duty, to martial law; to call him from his ordinary occupation to the field, and under the penalty of fine and imprisonment, inflicted by a court martial, to imbrue his hand in his brother's blood. There is no limitation on the power of the sword;—and that over the purse is equally without restraint; for among the extraordinary features of the bill, it contains no appropriation, which, under existing circumstances, is tantamount to an unlimited appropriation. The President may, under its authority, incur any expenditure, and pledge the national faith to meet it. He may create a new national debt, at the very moment of the termination of the former—a debt of millions, to be paid out of the proceeds of the labor of that section of the country whose dearest constititional rights this bill prostrates! Thus exhibiting the extraordinary spectacle, that the very section of the country which is urging this measure, and carrying the sword of devastation against us, is, at the same time, incurring a new debt, to be paid by those whose rights are violated; while those who violate them are to receive the benefits, in the shape of bounties and expenditures.

And for what purpose is the unlimited control of the purse and of the sword thus placed at the disposition of the Executive? To make war against one of the free and sovereign members of this confederation, which the bill proposes to deal with, not as a State, but as a collection of banditti or outlaws. Thus exhibiting the impious spectacle of this Government, the creature of the States, making war against the power to which it owes its existence.

The bill violates the constitution, plainly and palpably, in many of its provisions, by authorizing the President at his pleasure, to place the different ports of this Union on an unequal footing, contrary to that provision of the constitution which declares that no preference shall be given to one port over another. It also violates the constitution by authorizing him, at his discretion, to impose cash duties on one port, while credit is allowed in others; by enabling the President to regulate commerce, a power vested in Congress alone; and by drawing within the jurisdiction of the United States Courts, powers never intended to be conferred on them. As great as these objections are, they become insignificant in the provisions of a bill which, by a single blow—by treating the States as a mere lawless mass of individuals—prostrates all the barriers of the constitution. I will pass over the minor considerations, and proceed directly to the great point. This bill proceeds on the ground that the entire sovereignty of this country belongs to the American people, as forming one great community, and regards the States as mere fractions or counties, and not as integral parts of the Union; having no more right to resist the encroachments of the Government than a county has to resist the authority of a State; and treating such resistance as the lawless acts of so many individuals, without possessing sovereignty or political rights. It has been said that the bill declares war against South Carolina. No. It decrees a massacre of her citizens! . . . the great question at issue: Is this a federal union? a union of States, as distinct from that of individuals? Is the sovereignty in the several States, or in the American people in the aggregate? The very language which we are compelled to use when speaking of our political institutions, affords proof conclusive as to its real character. The terms union, federal, united, all imply a combination of sovereignties, a confederation of States. They are never applied to an association of individuals. Who ever heard of the United State of New-York, of Massachusetts, or of Virginia? Who ever heard the term federal or union applied to the aggregation of individuals into one community? Nor is the other point less clear—that the sovereignty is in the several States, and that our system is a union of twenty-four sovereign powers, under a constitutional compact. . . .

I have thus presented all possible modes in which a government founded upon the will of an absolute majority will be modified; and have demonstrated that, in all its forms, whether in a majority of the people, as in a mere Democracy, or in a majority of their representatives, without a constitution or with a constitution, to be interpreted as the will of the majority, the result will be the same: two hostile interests will inevitably be created by the action of the government, to be followed by hostile legislation, and that by faction, corruption, anarchy, and despotism.

The great and solemn question here presents itself, Is there any remedy for these evils? on the decision of which depends the question, whether the people can govern themselves, which has been so often asked with so much skepticism and doubt. There is a remedy, and but one,—the effect of which, whatever may be the form, is to organize society in reference to this conflict of interests, which springs out of the action of government; and which can only be done by giving to each part the right of self-protection. . . .

But, to return to the General Government. We have now sufficient experience to ascertain that the tendency to conflict in its action is between the southern and other sections. The latter having a decided majority, must habitually be possessed of the powers of the Government, both in this and in the other House; and, being governed by that instinctive love of power so natural to the human breast, they must become the advocates of the power of Government, and in the same degree opposed to the limitations; while the other and weaker section is as necessarily thrown on the side of the limitations. One section is the natural guardian of the delegated powers, and the other of the reserved; and the struggle on the side of the former will be to enlarge the powers, while that on the opposite side will be to restrain them within their constitutional limits. The contest will, in fact, be a contest between power and liberty, and such I consider the present—a contest in which the weaker section, with its peculiar labor, productions, and institutions, has at stake all that can be dear to freemen. Should we be able to maintain in their full vigor our reserved rights, liberty and prosperity will be our portion; . . . Nor do I repine that the duty, so difficult to be discharged, of defending the reserved powers against apparently such fearful odds, has been assigned to us. To discharge it successfully requires the highest qualities, moral and intellectual; and should we perform it with a zeal and ability proportioned to its magnitude, instead of mere planters, our section will become distinguished for its patriots and statesmen. But, on the other hand, if we prove unworthy of the trust—if we yield to the steady encroachments of power, the severest calamity and most debasing corruption will overspread the land. Every Southern man, true to the interests of his section, and faithful to the duties which Providence has allotted him, will be for ever excluded from the honors and emoluments of this Government, which will be reserved for those only who have qualified themselves, by political prostitution, for admission into the *Magdalen* Asylum.

DOCUMENT NO. 15.   *A New Bank of the United States.*

After Jackson refused to approve a recharter for the Bank of the United States, Congress deliberated on what action to take in regard to the banking question. Calhoun presented his views in a speech to the Senate on March 21, 1834 (Calhoun, *Works*, II, 344–376):

SPEECH

On the proposition of Mr. Webster to recharter the Bank of the United States, delivered in the Senate, March 21st, 1834. . . .

Let, then, the Bank charter be renewed for twelve years after the expiration of the present term, with such modifications and limitations as may be judged proper; and that after that period it shall issue no notes under ten dollars—that Government shall not receive in its dues any sum less than ten dollars, except in the legal coins of the notes of any bank that issues notes of a denomination less than five dollars; and that the United States Bank shall not receive in payment, or on deposit, the notes of any bank whose notes are not receivable in the dues of the Government, nor the notes of any bank which may receive those of any other whose notes are not receivable by the Government. At the expiration of six years from the commencement of the renewed charter, let the Bank be prohibited from issuing any note under twenty dollars, and let no sum under that amount be received in dues of the Government, except in specie; and let the value of gold be raised at least equal to that of silver, to take effect immediately; so that the country may be replenished with the coin, the lightest and the most portable in proportion to its value, to take the place of the receding bank-notes. It is unnecessary for me to state, that at present the standard value of gold is less than that of silver; the necessary effect of which has been to expel gold entirely from circulation, and to deprive us of a coin so well calculated for the circulation of a country so great in extent, and having so vast an intercourse, commercial, social, and political, between all its parts, as ours. As an additional recommendation to raise its relative value, gold has, of late, become an important product of three considerable States of the Union—Virginia, North Carolina, and Georgia—to the industry of which the measure proposed would give a strong impulse, and which, in turn, would greatly increase the quantity produced.

And it may be hoped, that if, on experience, it should be found that neither these provisions, nor any other in the power of Congress, are fully adequate to effect the important reform of Congress, are fully adequate to effect the important reform which I have proposed, the co-operation of the States may be secured, at least to the extent of suppressing the circulation of notes under five dollars, where such are permitted to be issued under their authority.

Such are the means which have occurred to me. There are members of this body far more competent to judge of their practical operation than myself; and as my object is simply to suggest them for their reflection, and for that of others who are more familiar with this part of the subject, I will not at present enter into an inquiry as to their efficiency, with a view of determining whether they are fully adequate to effect the object in view or not. There are, doubtless, others of a similar description, and perhaps more efficacious, that may occur to the experienced, which I would freely embrace, as my object is to adopt the best and most efficient.

I omitted, in the proper place, to state my reason for suggesting twelve years as the term for the renewal of the charter of the Bank. It appears to me that it is long enough to permit the agitation and distraction which now disturbs the country to subside, while it is sufficiently short to enable us to avail ourselves of the full benefit of the light of experience, which may be expected to be derived from the operation of the system under its new provisions.

DOCUMENT NO. 16. *Danger of Unchecked Executive Power.*

After the Senate "Resolution of Censure" for President Jackson's action in removing federal deposits from the Bank of the United States, the President sent a "Protest" to the Senate (see Document No. 8). When the Senate debated whether to receive the "Protest," Calhoun offered his views on Jackson's action in a speech given on May 6, 1834 (Calhoun, *Works,* II, 405–25):

SPEECH

On the Protest of the President of the United States, delivered in the Senate, May 6th, 1834.

. . . It is this resolution, thus forced upon us, and thus cautiously expressed, which has so deeply offended the President, and called forth his Protest, in which he has undertaken to judge of the powers of the Senate; to assign limits in their exercise to which they may, and beyond which they shall not go; to deny their right to pass the resolution; to charge them with usurpation and the violation of law and of the constitution in adopting it; and, finally, to interpose between the Senate and their constituents, and virtually to pronounce upon the validity of the votes of some of its members on the ground that they do not conform with the will of their constituents.

This is a brief statement of the controversy, which presents for consideration the question, What is the real nature of the issue between the parties?—a question of the utmost magnitude, and on the just and full comprehension of which the wisdom and propriety of our course must mainly depend.

It would be a great mistake to suppose that the issue involves the question, whether the Senate had a right to pass the resolution or not; . . . It is whether *the President has a right to question our decision?* This is the real question at issue—a question which goes in its consequences to all the powers of the Senate, and which involves in its decision the fact, whether it is a separate and independent branch of the Government, or a mere appendix of the executive department. . . . I deny the right of the President to question the *proceedings* of the Senate—utterly deny it; and I call upon his advocates and supporters on this floor to exhibit his authority; to point out the article, the section, and the clause of the constitution which contains it; to show, in a word, the *express* grant of the power. None other can fulfil the requirements of the constitution. I proclaim it as a truth —as an unquestionable truth of the highest import, and heretofore not sufficiently understood, that the President has no right to exercise any implied or constructive power. I speak upon the authority of the constitution itself, which, by an express grant, has vested all the implied and constructive powers in Congress, and in Congress alone. Hear what the constitution says: Congress shall have power "to make all laws which shall be necessary and proper for carrying into execution the foregoing powers (those granted to Congress), and all other power vested by this constitution in the Government of the United States, or in any department or officer thereof."

DOCUMENT NO. 17.   *Slavery Defended.*

When citizens' petitions calling for the abolition of slavery in the District of Columbia poured into the Senate, Calhoun was roused to defend the South's "peculiar institution. He would continue until the day of his death the line of rationalization in defense of slavery that he presented to the Senate on Feburary 6, 1837 (Calhoun, *Works*, II, 625–633):-

SPEECH

On the reception of Abolition Petitions, delivered in the Senate, February 6th, 1837.

. . . The peculiar institution of the South—that, on the maintenance of which the very existence of the slave-holding States depends, is pronounced to be sinful and odious, in the sight of God and man; and this with a systematic design of rendering us hateful in the eyes of the world—with a view to a general crusade against us and our institutions. This, too, in the legislative halls of the Union; created by these confederated States, for the better protection of their peace, their safety, and their respective institutions;—and yet, we, the representatives of twelve of these sovereign States against whom this deadly war is waged, are expected to sit here in silence, hearing ourselves and our constituents day after day denounced, without uttering a word; for if we but open our lips, the charge of agitation is resounded on all sides, and we are held up as seeking to aggravate the evil which we resist. Every reflecting mind must see in all this a state of things deeply and dangerously diseased.

I do not belong, said Mr. C., to the school which holds that aggression is to be met by concession. Mine is the opposite creed, which teaches that encroachments must be met at the beginning, and that those who act on the opposite principle are prepared to become slaves. In this case, in particular, I hold concession or compromise to be fatal. If we concede an inch, concession would follow concession—compromise would follow compromise, until our ranks would be so broken that effectual resistance would be impossible. We must meet the enemy on the frontier, with a fixed determination of maintaining our position at every hazard. Consent to receive these insulting petitions, and the next demand will be that they be referred to a committee in order that they may be deliberated and acted upon. At the last session we were modestly asked to receive them, simply to lay them on the table, without any view to ulterior action. I then told the Senator from Pennsylvania (Mr. Buchanan), who so strongly urged that course in the Senate, that it was a position that could not be maintained; as the argument in favor of acting on the petitions if we were bound to receive, could not be resisted. I then said, that the next step would be to refer the petition to a committee, and I already see indications that such is now the intention. If we yield, that will be followed by another, and we will thus proceed, step by step, to the final consummation of the object of these petitions. We are now told that the most effectual mode of arresting the progress of abolition is, to reason it down; and with this view it is urged that the petitions ought to be referred to a committee. That is the very ground which was taken at the last session in the other House, but instead of arresting its progress it has since advanced more rapidly than ever. The most unquestionable right may be rendered doubtful, if once admitted to be a subject of controversy, and that would be the case in the present instance. The subject is beyond the jurisdiction of Congress—they have no right to touch it in any shape or form, or to make it the subject of deliberation or discussion. . . .

As widely as this incendiary spirit has spread, it has not yet infected this body, or the great mass of the intelligent and business portion of the North; but unless it be speedily stopped, it will spread and work upwards till it brings the two great sections of the Union into deadly conflict. . . .

Standing at the point of time which we have now arrived, it will not be more difficult to trace the course of future events now than it was then. They who imagine that the spirit now abroad in the North, will die away of itself without a shock or convulsion, have formed a very inadequate conception of its real character; it will continue to rise and spread, unless prompt and efficient measures to stay its progress be adopted. Already it has taken possession of the pulpit, of the schools, and, to a considerable extent, of the press; those great instruments by which the mind of the rising generation will be formed. . . .

Abolition and the Union cannot co-exist. As the friend of the Union I openly proclaim it,—and the sooner it is known the better. The former may now be controlled, but in a short time it will be beyond the power of man to arrest the course of events. We of the South will not, cannot surrender our institutions. To maintain the existing relations between the two races, inhabiting that section of the Union, is indispensable to the peace and happiness of both. It cannot be subverted without drenching the country in blood, and extirpating one or the other of the races. Be it good or bad, it has grown up with our society and institutions, and is so interwoven with them, that to destroy it would be to destroy us as a people. . . .

But I take higher ground. I hold that in the present state of civilization, where two races of different origin, and distinguished by color, and other physical differences, as well as intellectual, are brought together, the relation now existing in the slaveholding States between the two, is, instead of an evil, a good—a positive good. I feel myself called upon to speak freely upon the subject where the honor and interests of those I represent are involved. I hold then, that there never has yet existed a wealthy and civilized society in which one portion of the community did not, in point of fact, live on the labor of the other. Broad and general as is this assertion, it is fully borne out by history. . . .

I fearlessly assert that the existing relation between the two races in the South, against which these blind fanatics are waging war, forms the most solid and durable foundation on which to rear free and stable political institutions. It is useless to disguise the fact. There is and always has been in an advanced stage of wealth and civilization, a conflict between labor and capital. The condition of society in the South exempts us from the disorders and dangers resulting from this conflict; and which explains why it is that the political condition of the slaveholding States has been so much more stable and quiet than that of the North. The advantages of the former, in this respect, will become more and more manifest if left undisturbed by interference from without, as the country advances in wealth and numbers. We have, in fact, but just entered that condition of society where the strength and durability of our political institutions are to be tested; and I venture nothing in predicting that the experience of the next generation will fully test how vastly more favorable our condition of society is to that of other sections for free and stable institutions, provided we are not disturbed by the interference of others, or shall have sufficient intelligence and spirit to resist promptly and successfully such interference. It rests with ourselves to meet and repel them. . . .

If we do not defend ourselves none will defend us; if we yield we will be more and more pressed as we recede; and if we submit we will be trampled under foot. . . .

Surrounded as the slaveholding States are with such imminent perils, I rejoice to think that our means of defence are ample, if we shall prove to have the intelligence and spirit to see and apply them before it is too late. All we want is concert, to lay aside all party differences, and unite with zeal and energy in repelling approaching dangers. Let there be concert of action, and we shall find ample means of security without resorting to secession or disunion.

DOCUMENT NO. 18.   *Repelling Northern Aggressions on the Rights of the South.*

Following the war with Mexico, the country became aroused over the question of extending slavery into the new area obtained as a result of the war. The Wilmot Proviso proposed to prohibit slavery from the whole area; Southerners protested that such a move would deny them their rights. Other moves, organizing Oregon as a free territory and proposing to abolish slavery in the District of Columbia, stirred Southern members of Congress to join in issuing on January 23,

1849 an "Address of the Southern Delegates in Congress to their Constitutents," which was written by Senator John C. Calhoun (Calhoun, *Works*, VI, 285–313):

THE ADDRESS

Of the Southern Delegates in Congress, to their Constituents.

We, whose names are hereunto annexed, address you in discharge of what we believe to be a solemn duty, on the most important subject ever presented for your consideration. We allude to the conflict between the two great sections of the Union, growing out of a difference of feeling and opinion in reference to the relation existing between the two races, the European and African, which inhabit the southern section, and the acts of aggression and encroachment to which it has led.

The conflict commenced not long after the acknowledgment of our independence, and has gradually increased until it has arrayed the great body of the North against the South on this most vital subject. In the progress of this conflict, aggression has followed aggression, and encroachment encroachment, until they have reached a point when a regard for your peace and safety will not permit us to remain longer silent. The object of this address is to give you a clear, correct, but brief account of the whole series of aggression and encroachments on your rights, with a statement of the dangers to which they expose you. Our object in making it is not to cause excitement, but to put you in full possession of all the facts and circumstances necessary to a full and just conception of a deep-seated disease, which threatens great danger to you and the whole body politic. We act on the impression, that in a popular government like ours, a true conception of the actual character and state of a disease is indispensable to effecting a cure. . . .

With few exceptions of no great importance, the South had no cause to complain prior to the year 1819—a year, it is to be feared, destined to mark a train of events, bringing with them many, and great, and fatal disasters, on the country and its institutions. With it commenced the agitating debate on the question of the admission of Missouri into the Union. . . .

There remains to be noticed another class of aggressive acts of a kindred character, but which instead of striking at an express and specific provision of the Constitution, aims directly at destroying the relation between the two races at the South, by means subversive in their tendency of one of the ends for which the Constitution was established. We refer to the systematic agitation of the question by the Abolitionists, which, commencing about 1835, is still continued in all possible forms. Their avowed intention is to bring about a state of things that will force emancipation on the South. To unite the North in fixed hostility to slavery in the South, and to excite discontent among the slaves with their condition, are among the means employed to effect it. . . .

The war with Mexico soon followed, and that terminated in the acquisition of New Mexico and Upper California, embracing an area equal to about one half of the entire valley of the Mississippi. If to this we add the portion of Oregon acknowledged to be ours by the recent treaty with England, our whole territory on the Pacific and west of the Rocky Mountains will be found to be in extent but little less than that vast valley. The near prospect of so great an addition rekindled the excitement between the North and South in reference to slavery in its connection with the territories, which has become, since those on the Pacific were acquired, more universal and intense than ever.

The effects have been to widen the difference between the two sections, and to give a more determined and hostile character to their conflict. The North no longer respects the Missouri compromise line, although adopted by their almost unanimous vote. Instead of compromise, they avow that their determination is to exclude slavery from all the territories of the United States, acquired, or to be acquired; and, of course, to prevent the citizens of the Southern States from emigrating with their property in slaves into any of them. Their object, they allege, is to prevent the extension of slavery, and ours to extend it, thus making the issue between them and us to be the naked question, shall slavery be extended or not? We do not deem it necessary, looking to the object of this address, to examine the question so fully discussed at the last session, whether Congress has the right to exclude the citizens of the South from immigrating with their property into territories belonging to the confederated States of the Union. . . . Entertaining these opinions, we ask not, as the North alleges we do, for the extension of slavery. That would make a discrimination in our favor, as unjust and unconstitutional as the discrimination they ask against us in their favor. It is not for them, nor for the Federal Government to determine, whether our domestic institution is good or bad; or whether it should be repressed or preserved. It belongs to us, and us only, to decide such questions. What then we do insist on, is, not to extend slavery, but that we shall not be prohibited from immigrating with our property, into the Territories of the United States, because we are slaveholders; or, in other words, that we shall not on that account be disfranchised of a privilege possessed by all others, citizens and foreigners, without discrimination as to character, profession, or color. All, whether savage, barbarian, or civilized, may freely enter and remain, we only being excluded.

We rest our claim, not only on the high grounds above stated, but also on the solid foundation of right, justice, and equality. The territories immediately in controversy—New Mexico and California—were acquired by the common sacrifice and efforts of all the States, towards which the South contributed far more than her full share of men,* to say nothing of money, and is, of course, on every principle of right, justice, fairness, and equality, entitled to participate fully in the benefits to be derived from their acquisition.

Very different would be the circumstances under which emancipation would take place with us. If it ever should be effected, it will be through the agency of the Federal Government, controlled by the dominant power of the Northern States of the Confederacy, against the resistance and struggle of the Southern. It can then only be effected by the prostration of the white race; and that would necessarily engender the bitterest feelings of hostility between them and the North. But the reverse would be the case between the blacks of the South and the people of the North. Owing their emancipation to them, they would regard them as friends, guardians, and patrons, and centre, accordingly, all their sympathy in them. The people of the North would not fail to reciprocate and to favor them, instead of the whites. Under the influence of such feelings, and impelled by fanaticism and love of power, they would not stop at emancipation. Another step would be taken—to raise them to a political and social equality with their former owners, by giving them the right of voting and holding public offices under the Federal Government. We see the first step toward it in the bill already alluded to—to vest the free blacks and slaves with the right to vote on the question of emancipation in this District. But when once raised to an equality, they would become the fast political associates of the North, acting and voting with them on all questions, and by this political union between them, holding the white race at the South in complete subjection. The blacks, and the profligate whites that might unite with them, would become the principal recipients of federal offices and patronage, and would, in consequence, be raised above the whites of the South in the political and social scale. We would, in a word, change conditions with them—a degradation greater than has ever yet fallen to the lot of a free and enlightened people, and one from which we could not escape, should emancipation take place (which it certainly will if not prevented), but by fleeing the homes of ourselves and ancestors, and by abandoning our country to our former slaves, to become the permanent abode of disorder, anarchy, poverty, misery, and wretchedness.

With such a prospect before us, the gravest and most solemn question that ever claimed the attention of a people is presented for your consideration: What is to be done to prevent it? It is a question belonging to you to decide. All we propose is, to give you our opinion.

We, then, are of the opinion that the first and indispensable step, without which nothing can be done, and with which every thing may be, is to be united among yourselves, on this great and most vital question. The want of union and concert in reference to it has brought the South, the Union, and our system of government to their present perilous condition. Instead of placing it above all others, it has been made subordinate, not only to mere questions of policy, but to the preservation of party ties and ensuring of party success. As high as we hold a due respect for these, we hold them subordinate to that and other questions involving our safety and happiness. Until they are so held by the South, the North will not believe that you are in earnest in opposition to their encroachments, and they will continue to follow, one after another, until the work of abolition is finished. To convince them that you are, you must prove by your acts that you hold all other questions subordinate to it. If you become united, and prove yourselves in earnest, the North will be brought to a pause, and to a calculation of consequences; and that may lead to a change of measures, and the adoption of a course of policy that may quietly and peaceably terminate this long conflict between the two sections. If it should not, nothing would remain for you but to stand up immovably in defence of rights, involving your all—your property, prosperity, equality, liberty, and safety. . . .

DOCUMENT No. 19. *Defending a "Conscious Minority."*

In the 1830's Calhoun had contended for state rights and nullification of unconstitutional federal acts by a single state. By the 1840's he moved away from those positions, viewing them as essentially inadequate. Rather, in his private thinking, in his speeches in Congress and private correspondence, he developed the doctrine of the "concurrent majority" as a defense for a numerical minority within the framework of constitutional government. In his last years he brought together in systematic form his general ideas on this subject and incorporated them in a lengthy work entitled *A Disquisition on Government*, which was published shortly after his death (Calhoun, *Works*, I, 1–109) from which the following selections are taken:

A DISQUISITION ON GOVERNMENT

[THE NATURE OF MAN AND THE ORIGIN OF GOVERNMENT]

In order to have a clear and just conception of the nature and object of government, it is indispensable to understand correctly what that constitution or law of our nature is in which government originates, or to express it more fully and accurately—that law without which government would not and with which it must necessarily exist. Without this, it is as impossible to lay any solid foundation for the science of government as it would be to lay one for that of astronomy without a like understanding of that constitution or law of the material world according to which the several bodies composing the solar system mutually act on each other and by which they are kept in their respective spheres. The first question, accordingly, to be considered, What is that constitution or law of our nature without which government would not exist and with which its existence is necessary?

In considering this, I assume as an incontestable fact that man is so constituted as to be a social being. His inclinations and wants, physical and moral, irresistibly impel him to associate with his kind; and he has, accordingly, never been found, in any age or country, in any state other than the social. In no other, indeed, could he exist, and in no other—were it possible for him to exist—could he attain to a full development of his moral and intellectual faculties or raise himself, in the scale of being, much above the level of the brute creation.

I next assume also as a fact not less incontestable that,

while man is so constituted as to make the social state necessary to his existence and the full development of his faculties, this state itself cannot exist without government. The assumption rests on universal experience. In no age or country has any society or community ever been found, whether enlightened or savage, without government of some description.

Having assumed these as unquestionable phenomena of our nature, I shall, without further remark, proceed to the investigation of the primary and important question, What is that constitution of our nature which, while it impels man to associate with his kind, renders it impossible for society to exist without government?

The answer will be found in the fact (not less incontestable than either of the others) that, while man is created for the social state and is accordingly so formed as to feel what affects others as well as what affects himself, he is, at the same time, so constituted as to feel more intensely what affects him directly than what affects him indirectly through others, or, to express it differently, he is so constituted that his direct or individual affections are stronger than his sympathetic or social feelings. I intentionally avoid the expression "*selfish* feelings" as applicable to the former, because, as commonly used, it implies an unusual excess of the individual over the social feelings in the person to whom it is applied and, consequently, something depraved and vicious. My object is to exclude such inference and to restrict the inquiry exclusively to facts in their bearings on the subject under consideration, viewed as mere phenomena appertaining to our nature—constituted as it is; and which are as unquestionable as is that of gravitation or any other phenomenon of the material world.

In asserting that our individual are stronger than our social feelings, it is not intended to deny that there are instances, growing out of peculiar relations—as that of a mother and her infant—or resulting from the force of education and habit over peculiar constitutions, in which the latter have overpowered the former; but these instances are few and always regarded as something extraordinary. The deep impression they make, whenever they occur, is the strongest proof that they are regarded as exceptions to some general and well-understood law of our nature, just as some of the minor powers of the material world are apparently to gravitation.

I might go farther and assert this to be a phenomenon not of our nature only, but of all animated existence throughout its entire range, so far as our knowledge extends. It would, indeed, seem to be essentially connected with the great law of self-preservation which pervades all that feels, from man down to the lowest and most insignificant reptile or insect. In none is it stronger than in man. His social feelings may, indeed, in a state of safety and abundance, combined with high intellectual and moral culture, acquire great expansion and force, but not so great as to overpower this all-pervading and essential law of animated existence.

But that constitution of our nature which makes us feel more intensely what affects us directly than what affects us indirectly through others necessarily leads to conflict between individuals. Each, in consequence, has a greater regard for his own safety or happiness than for the safety or happiness of others, and, where these come in opposition, is ready to sacrifice the interests of others to his own. And hence the tendency to a universal state of conflict between individual and individual, accompanied by the connected passions of suspicion, jealousy, anger, and revenge—followed by insolence, fraud, and cruelty—and, if not prevented by some controlling power, ending in a state of universal discord and confusion destructive of the social state and the ends for which it is ordained. This controlling power, wherever vested or by whomsoever exercised, is *Government.*

It follows, then, that man is so constituted that government is necessary to the existence of society, and society to his existence and the perfection of his faculties. It follows also that government has its origin in this twofold constitution of his nature: the sympathetic or social feelings constituting the remote, and the individual or direct the proximate, cause . . .

[Protection Against the Abuse of Power by Government]

But government, although intended to protect and preserve society, has itself a strong tendency to disorder and abuse of its powers, as all experience and almost every page of history testify. The cause is to be found in the same constitution of our nature which makes government indispensable. The powers which it is necessary for government to possess in order to repress violence and preserve order cannot execute themselves. They must be administered by men in whom, like others, the individual are stronger than the social feelings. And hence the powers vested in them to prevent injustice and oppression on the part of others will, if left unguarded, be by them converted into instruments to oppress the rest of the community. That by which this is prevented, by whatever name called, is what is meant by *constitution,* in its most comprehensive sense, when applied to *government.* . . .

How government, then, must be constructed in order to counteract, through its organism, this tendency on the part of those who make and execute the laws to oppress those subject to their operation is the next question which claims attention.

How government, then, must be constructed in order to counteract, through its organism, this tendency on the part of those who make and execute the laws to oppress those subject to their operation is the next question which claims attention.

There is but one way in which this can possibly be done, and that is by such an organism as will furnish the ruled with the means of resisting successfully this tendency on the part of the rulers to oppression and abuse. Power can only be resisted by power—and tendency by tendency. Those who exercise power and those subject to its exercise—the rulers and the ruled—stand in antagonistic relations to each other. The same constitution of our nature which leads rulers to oppress the ruled —regardless of the object for which government is ordained—will, with equal strength, lead the ruled to resist when possessed of the means of making peaceable and effective resistance. Such an organism, then, as will furnish the means by which resistance may be systematically and peaceably made on the part of the ruled to oppression and abuse of power on the part of the rulers is the first and indispensable step toward *forming* a constitutional government. And as this can only be effected by or through the right of suffrage—the right on the part of the ruled to choose their rulers at proper intervals and to hold them thereby responsible for their conduct—the responsibility of the rulers to the ruled, through the right of suffrage, is the indispensable and primary principle in the *foundation* of a constitutional government. When this right is properly guarded, and the people sufficiently enlightened to understand their own rights and the interests of the community and duly to appreciate the motives and conduct of those appointed to make and execute laws, it is all-sufficient to give to those who elect effective control over those they have elected. . . .

[THE CONCURRENT MAJORITY]

As, then, the right of suffrage, without some other provision, cannot counteract this tendency of government, the next question for consideration is, What is that other provision? This demands the most serious consideration, for of all the questions embraced in the science of government it involves a principle, the most important and the least understood, and when understood, the most difficult of application in practice. It is, indeed, emphatically that principle which *makes* the constitution, in its strict and limited sense.

From what has been said, it is manifest that this provision must be of a character calculated to prevent any one interest or combination of interests from using the powers of government to aggrandize itself at the expense of the others. Here lies the evil: and just in proportion as it shall prevent, or fail to prevent it, in the same degree it will effect, or fail to effect, the end intended to be accomplished. There is but one certain mode in which this result can be secured, and that is by the adoption of some restriction or limitation which shall so effectually prevent any one interest or combination of interests from obtaining the exclusive control of the government as to render hopeless all attempts directed to that end. There is, again, but one mode in which this can be effected, and that is by taking the sense of each interest or portion of the community which may be unequally and injuriously affected by the action of the government separately, through its own majority or in some other way by which its voice may be fairly expressed, and to require the consent of each interest either to put or to keep the government in action. This, too, can be accomplished only in one way, and that is by such an organism of the government—and, if necessary for the purpose, of the community also—as will, by dividing and distributing the powers of government, give to each division or interest, through its appropriate organ, either a concurrent voice in making and executing the laws or a veto on their execution. It is only by such an organism that the assent of each can be made necessary to put the government in motion, or the power made effectual to arrest its action when put in motion; and it is only by the one or the other that the different interests, orders, classes, or portions into which the community may be divided can be protected, and all conflict and struggle between them prevented—by rendering it impossible to put or to keep it in action without the concurrent consent of all.

Such an organism as this, combined with the right of suffrage, constitutes, in fact, the elements of constitutional government. The one, by rendering those who make and execute the laws responsible to those on whom they operate, prevents the rulers from oppressing the ruled; and the other, by making it impossible for any one interest or combination of interests, or class, or order, or portion of the community to obtain exclusive control, prevents any one of them from oppressing the other. It is clear that oppression and abuse of power must come, if at all, from the one or the other quarter. From no other can they come. It follows that the two, suffrage and proper organism combined, are sufficient to counteract the tendency of government to oppression and abuse of power and to restrict it to the fulfillment of the great ends for which it is ordained. . . .

[THE NUMERICAL VERSUS THE CONCURRENT MAJORITY]

It results, from what has been said, that there are two different modes in which the sense of the community may be taken: one, simply by the right of suffrage, unaided; the other, by the right through a proper organism. Each collects the sense of the majority. But one regards numbers only and considers the whole community as a unit having but one common interest throughout, and collects the sense of the greater number of the whole as that of the community. The other, on the contrary, regards interests as well as numbers—considering the community as made up of different and conflicting interests, as far as the action of the government is concerned—and takes the sense of each through its majority or appropriate organ, and the united sense of all as the sense of the entire community. The former of these I shall call the numerical or absolute majority, and the latter, the concurrent or constitutional majority. I call it the constitutional majority because it is an essential element in every constitutional government, be its form what it may. So great is the difference, politically speaking, between the two majorities that they cannot be confounded without leading to great and fatal errors; and yet the distinction between them has been so entirely overlooked that when the term "majority" is used in political discussions, it is applied exclusively to designate the numerical—as if there were no other. Until this distinction is recognized and better understood, there will continue to be great liability to error in properly constructing constitutional governments, especially of the popular form, and of preserving them when properly constructed. Until then, the latter will have a strong tendency to slide, first, into the government of the

numerical majority, and, finally, into absolute government of some other form. To show that such must be
the case, and at the same time to mark more strongly
the difference between the two in order to guard against
the danger of overlooking it, I propose to consider the
subject more at length. . . .

[CONCURRENT MAJORITY ESSENTIAL TO CONSTITU-
TIONAL GOVERNMENT]

Having now explained the reasons why it is so difficult
to form and preserve popular constitutional government
so long as the distinction between the two majorities is
overlooked and the opinion prevails that a written
constitution, with suitable restrictions and a proper division of its powers, is sufficient to counteract the tendency
of the numerical majority to the abuse of its power—I
shall next proceed to explain, more fully, why the concurrent majority is an indispensable element in forming
constitutional governments and why the numerical
majority, of itself, must, in all cases, make governments
absolute.

The necessary consequence of taking the sense of the
community by the concurrent majority is, as has been
explained, to give to each interest or portion of the community a negative on the others. It is this mutual negative among its various conflicting interests which invests
each with the power of protecting itself, and places the
rights and safety of each where only they can be securely
placed, under its own guardianship. Without this there
can be no systematic, peaceful, or effective resistance to
the natural tendency of each to come into conflict with
the others; and without this there can be no constitution.
It is this negative power—the power of preventing or
arresting the action of the government, be it called by
what term it may, veto, interposition, nullification,
check, or balance of power—which in fact forms the
constitution. They are all but different names for the
negative power. In all its forms, and under all its names,
it results from the concurrent majority. Without this
there can be no negative, and without a negative, no

constitution. The assertion is true in reference to all constitutional governments, be their forms what they may. It is, indeed, the *negative* power which makes the constitution, and the *positive* which makes the government. The one is the power of acting, and the other the power of preventing or arresting action. The two, combined, make constitutional governments.

But as there can be no constitution without the negative power, and no negative power without the concurrent majority, it follows necessarily that, where the numerical majority has the sole control of the government, there can be no constitution, as constitution implies limitation or restriction—and, of course, is inconsistent with the idea of sole or exclusive power. And hence the numerical, unmixed with the concurrent, majority necessarily forms, in all cases, absolute government.

It is, indeed, the single or *one power* which excludes the negative and constitutes absolute government, and not the *number* in whom the power is vested. The numerical majority is as truly a *single power*—and excludes the negative as completely as the absolute government of one or of the few. The former is as much the absolute government of the democratic or popular form as the latter of the monarchical or aristocratical. It has, accordingly, in common with them the same tendency to oppression and abuse of power. . . .

[CONCURRENT MAJORITY TENDS TO UNITE THE COMMUNITY]

In another particular, governments of the concurrent majority have greatly the advantage. I allude to the difference in their respective tendency in reference to dividing or uniting the community. That of the concurrent, as has been shown, is to unite the community, let its interests be ever so diversified or opposed, while that of the numerical is to divide it into two conflicting portions, let its interests be naturally ever so united and identified.

That the numerical majority will divide the community, let it be ever so homogeneous, into two great parties which will be engaged in perpetual struggles to obtain the control of the government has already been established. The great importance of the object at stake must necessarily form strong party attachments and party antipathies—attachments on the part of the members of each to their respective parties through whose efforts they hope to accomplish an object dear to all; and antipathies to the opposite party, as presenting the only obstacle to success.

In order to have a just conception of their force it must be taken into consideration that the object to be won or lost appeals to the strongest passions of the human heart—avarice, ambition, and rivalry. It is not then wonderful that a form of government which periodically stakes all its honors and emoluments as prizes to be contended for should divide the community into two great hostile parties; or that party attachments, in the progress of the strife, should become so strong among the members of each respectively as to absorb almost every feeling of our nature, both social and individual; or that their mutual antipathies should be carried to such an excess as to destroy, almost entirely, all sympathy between them and to substitute in its place the strongest aversion. Nor is it surprising that under their joint influence the community should cease to be the common center of attachment or that each party should find that center only in itself. It is thus that in such governments devotion to party becomes stronger than devotion to country—the promotion of the interests of party more important than the promotion of the common good of the whole, and its triumph and ascendency objects of far greater solicitude than the safety and prosperity of the community. It is thus also that the numerical majority, by regarding the community as a unit and having, as such, the same interests throughout all its parts, must, by its necessary operation, divide it into two hostile parts waging, under the forms of law, incessant hostilities against each other.

The concurrent majority, on the other hand, tends to

unite the most opposite and conflicting interests and to blend the whole in one common attachment to the country. By giving to each interest, or portion, the power of self-protection, all strife and struggle between them for ascendency is prevented, and thereby not only every feeling calculated to weaken the attachment to the whole is suppressed, but the individual and the social feelings are made to unite in one common devotion to country. Each sees and feels that it can best promote its own prosperity by conciliating the good will and promoting the prosperity of the others. And hence there will be diffused throughout the whole community kind feelings between its different portions and, instead of antipathy, a rivalry amongst them to promote the interests of each other, as far as this can be done consistently with the interest of all. Under the combined influence of these causes, the interests of each would be merged in the common interests of the whole; and thus the community would become a unit by becoming the common center of attachment of all its parts. And hence, instead of faction, strife, and struggle for party ascendency, there would be patriotism, nationality, harmony, and a struggle only for supremacy in promoting the common good of the whole. . . .

[LIBERTY AND POWER THE OBJECTIVES OF GOOD GOVERNMENT]

If the two be compared in reference to the ends for which government is ordained, the superiority of the government of the concurrent majority will not be less striking. These, as has been stated, are twofold: to protect and to perfect society. But to preserve society, it is necessary to guard the community against injustice, violence, and anarchy within, and against attacks from without. If it fail in either, it would fail in the primary end of government and would not deserve the name.

To perfect society, it is necessary to develop the faculties, intellectual and moral, with which man is endowed. But the mainspring to their development and, through this, to progress, improvement, and civilization, with all their blessings, is the desire of individuals to better their condition. For this purpose liberty and security are indispensable. Liberty leaves each free to pursue the course he may deem best to promote his interest and happiness, as far as it may be compatible with the primary end for which government is ordained, while security gives assurance to each that he shall not be deprived of the fruits of his exertions to better his condition. These combined give to this desire the strongest impulse of which it is susceptible. For to extend liberty beyond the limits assigned would be to weaken the government and to render it incompetent to fulfill its primary end—the protection of society against dangers, internal and external. The effect of this would be insecurity; and of insecurity, to weaken the impulse of individuals to better their condition and thereby retard progress and improvement. On the other hand, to extend the powers of the government so as to contract the sphere assigned to liberty would have the same effect, by disabling individuals in their efforts to better their condition.

Herein is to be found the principle which assigns to power and liberty their proper spheres and reconciles each to the other under all circumstances. For if power be necessary to secure to liberty the fruits of its exertions, liberty, in turn, repays power with interest—by increased population, wealth, and other advantages which progress and improvement bestow on the community. By thus assigning to each its appropriate sphere, all conflicts between them cease, and each is made to cooperate with and assist the other in fulfilling the great ends for which government is ordained.

But the principle, applied to different communities, will assign to them different limits. It will assign a larger sphere to power and a more contracted one to liberty, or the reverse, according to circumstances. To the former, there must ever be allotted, under all circumstances, a sphere sufficiently large to protect the community against danger from without and violence and anarchy within. The residuum belongs to liberty. More cannot be safely or rightly allotted to it.

[LIBERTY AND EQUALITY]

There is another error, not less great and dangerous, usually associated with the one which has just been considered. I refer to the opinion that liberty and equality are so intimately united that liberty cannot be perfect without perfect equality.

That they are united to a certain extent, and that equality of citizens, in the eyes of the law, is essential to liberty in a popular government is conceded. But to go further and make equality of *condition* essential to liberty would be to destroy both liberty and progress. The reason is that inequality of condition, while it is a necessary consequence of liberty, is at the same time indispensable to progress. In order to understand why this is so, it is necessary to bear in mind that the mainspring to progress is the desire of individuals to better their condition, and that the strongest impulse which can be given to it is to leave individuals free to exert themselves in the manner they may deem best for that purpose, as far at least as it can be done consistently with the ends for which government is ordained, and to secure to all the fruits of their exertions. Now, as individuals differ greatly from each other in intelligence, sagacity, energy, perseverance, skill, habits of industry and economy, physical power, position and opportunity—the necessary effect of leaving all free to exert themselves to better their condition must be a corresponding inequality between those who may possess these qualities and advantages in a high degree and those who may be deficient in them. The only means by which this result can be prevented are either to impose such restrictions on the exertions of those who may possess them in a high degree as will place them on a level with those who do not, or to deprive them of the fruits of their exertions. But to impose such restrictions on them would be destructive of liberty, while to deprive them of the fruits of their exertions would be to destroy the desire of betting their condition. It is, indeed, this inequality of condition between the front and rear ranks, in the march of progress, which gives so strong an impulse to the former to maintain their position, and to the latter to press forward into their files. This gives to progress its greatest impulse. To force the front rank back to the rear or attempt to push forward the rear into line with the front, by the interposition of the government, would put an end to the impulse and effectually arrest the march of progress. . . .

I have now finished the brief sketch I proposed of the origin and character of these two renowned governments and shall next proceed to consider the character, origin, and structure of the Government of the United States. It differs from the Roman and British more than they differ from each other; and although an existing government of recent origin, its character and structure are perhaps less understood than those of either.

DOCUMENT NO. 20. *Safeguarding a Numerical Minority in the United States.*

Those ideas that he had developed in general terms in the *Disquistion*, Calhoun went on to refine and apply in more specific terms to the American situation in his *Discourse of the Constitution and Government of the United States*, also published shortly after his death (Calhoun, *Works*, I, 111–406).

A DISCOURSE
ON THE
CONSTITUTION AND GOVERNMENT
OF THE
UNITED STATES.

Ours is a system of governments, compounded of the separate governments of the several States composing the Union, and of one common government of all its members, called the Government of the United States. The former preceded the latter, which was created by their agency. Each was framed by written constitutions; those of the several States by the people of each, acting separately, and in their sovereign character; and that of the United States by the same, acting in the same character,—but jointly instead of separately. All were formed on the same model. They all divide the powers of government into legislative, executive, and judicial; and are founded on the great principle of the responsibility of the rulers to the ruled. The entire powers of government are divided between the two; those of a more general character being specifically delegated to the United States; and all others not delegated, being reserved to the several States in their separate character. Each, within its appropriate sphere, possesses all the attributes, and performs all the functions of government. . . .

The Government of the United States was formed by the Constitution of the United States;—and ours is a democratic, federal republic.

It is democratic, in contradistinction to aristocracy and monarchy. It excludes classes, orders, and all artificial distinctions. To guard against their introduction, the constitution prohibits the granting of any title of nobility by the United States, or by any State.* The whole system is, indeed, democratic throughout. It has for its fundamental principle, the great cardinal maxim, that the people are the source of all power; that the governments of the several States and of the United States were created by them, and for them; that the powers conferred on them are not surrendered, but delegated; and, as such, are held in trust, and not absolutely; and can be rightfully exercised only in furtherance of the objects for which they were delegated.

It is federal as well as democratic. *Federal*, on the one hand, in contradistinction to *national*, and on the other, to a *confederacy*. In showing this, I shall begin with the former.

It is federal, because it is the government of States united in a political union, in contrdistinction to a government of individuals socially united; that is, by what is usually called, a social compact. To express it more concisely, it is federal and not national, because it is the government of a community of States, and not the government of a single State or nation.

That it is federal and not national, we have the high authority of the convention which framed it. . . .

Such, and so convincing are the arguments going to show, that the government of the United States has no more right to enforce its decisions against those of the separate governments of the several States, where they disagree as to the extent of their respective powers, than the latter have of enforcing their decisions in like cases. They both stand on equal grounds, in this respect. But as convincing as are these arguments, there are many, who entertain a different opinion;—and still affirm that the government the United States possesses the right, fully, absolutely, and exclusively. . . .

The introduction of, what are well known as, the Alien and Sedition laws, was the immediate cause of systematic and determined resistance. . . .

The passage of these acts, especially the latter, —caused deep and general excitement and opposition throughout the Union; being intended, as was supposed, to protect the government in its encroachment on the reserved powers.

Virginia, seconded by Kentucky, took the lead in opposition to these measures. . . .

The Kentucky resolutions, which are now known to have emanated from the pen of Mr. Jefferson,—then the Vice-President, and the acknowledged head of the party, —are similar in objects and substance with those of Virginia; but as they are differently expressed, and, in some respects, fuller than the latter, it is proper to give the two corresponding resolutions. The former is in the following words: "That the several States, composing the United States of America, are not united on the principle of unlimited submission to the general government; but that, by a compact under the style and title of a constitution of the United States, and of amendments thereto, they constituted a general government for special purposes;—delegated to that government, certain definite powers; reserving, each State to itself, the residuary mass of right to their own self-government; that whensoever the general government assumes undelegated powers, its acts are unauthoritative, void, and of no force; that to this compact each State acceded as a State, and is an integral party,—its co-States forming, as to itself, the other party; that the government created by this compact, was not made the exclusive or final judge of the extent of the powers delegated to it—since that would have made its discretion, and not the constitution, the measure of its powers; but that, as in all other cases of compact among parties, having no common judge, each party has an equal right to judge for itself, as well of infractions as of the mode and measure of redress.". . . it is indispensable that the government of the United States should be restored to its federal character. Nothing short of a perfect restoration, as it came from the hands of its framers, can avert them. It is folly to suppose that any popular government, except one strictly federal, in *practice*, as well as in *theory*, can last, over a country of such vast extent and diversity of interests and institutions. It would not be more irrational to suppose, that it could last, without the responsibility of the rulers to the ruled. The tendency of the former to oppress the latter, is not stronger than is the tendency of the more powerful section, to oppress the weaker. Nor is the right of suffrage more indispensable to enforce the responsibility of the rulers to the ruled, than a *federal organization*, to compel the parts to respect the rights of each other. . . .

But still more must be done to complete the work of restoration. The executive department must be rigidly restricted within its assigned limits, by divesting the President of all discretionary powers, and confining him strictly to those expressly conferred on him by the constitution and the acts of Congress. According to the express provisions of the former, he cannot rightfully exercise any other. Nor can he be permitted to go beyond, and to assume the exercise of whatever power he may deem necessary to carry those vested in him into execution, without finally absorbing all the powers vested in the other departments and making himself absolute. Having the disposal of the patronage of the government, and the command of all its forces, and standing at the head of the dominant party for the time, he will be able, in the event of a contest between him and either of the other departments, as to the extent of their respective powers, to make good his own, against its construction. . . .

Indeed, it may be doubted, whether the framers of the constitution did not commit a great mistake, in constituting a single, instead of a plural executive. Nay, it may even be doubted whether a single chief magistrate, —invested with all the powers properly appertaining to the executive department of the government, as is the President,—is compatible with the permanence of a popular government; especially in a wealthy and populous community, with a large revenue and a numerous body of officers and employees. Certain it is, that there is no instance of a popular government so constituted, which has long endured. Even ours, thus far, furnished no evidence in its favor, and not a little against it; for, to it, the present disturbed and dangerous state of things, which threatens the country with monarchy, or disunion, may be justly attributed. On the other hand, the two most distinguished constitutional governments of antiquity, both in respect to permanence and power, had a dual executive. I refer to those of Sparta and of Rome. The former had two hereditary, and the latter two elective chief magistrates. . . .

But it is objected that a plural executive necessarily leads to intrigue and discord among its members; and that it is inconsistent with prompt and efficient action. This may be true, when they are all elected by the same constituency; and may be a good reason, where this is the case, for preferring a single executive, with all its objections, to a plural executive. But the case is very different where they are elected by different constituencies,—having conflicting and hostile interests; as would be the fact in the case under consideration. Here the two would have to act, concurringly, in approving the acts of Congress,—and, separately, in the sphere of their respective departments. The effect, in the latter case, would be, to retain all the advantages of a single executive, as far as the administration of the laws were concerned; and, in the former, to insure harmony and concord between the two sections, and, through them, in the government. For as no act of Congress could become a law without the assent of the chief magistrates representing both sections, each, in the elections, would choose the candidate, who, in addition to being faithful to its interests, would best command the esteem and confidence of the other section. And thus, the presidential election, instead of dividing the Union into hostile geographical parties, the stronger struggling to enlarge its powers, and the weaker to defend its rights,—as is now the case,—would become the means of restoring harmony and concord to the country and the government. It would make the Union a union in truth,—a bond of mutual affection and brotherhood;—and not a mere connection used by the stronger as the instrument of dominion and aggrandizement,—and submitted to by the weaker only from the lingering remains of former attachment, and the fading hope of being able to restore the government to what it was originally intended to be, a blessing to all. . . .

Such are the happy fruits of a wisely constituted Republic;—and such are some of the means by which it may be organized and established. Ours, like all other well constituted constitutional governments, is the offspring of a conflict, timely and wisely compromised. May its success, as an example, lead to its imitation by others;—until our whole system,—the united government of all the States, as well as the individual governments of each—shall settle down in like concord and harmony.

FOOTNOTES

I Jackson: "Hero of New Orleans" in the Making

1 Marquis James, *Andrew Jackson, The Border Captain* (Vol. I of 2 vols., Indianapolis, 1933), 13–17; hereafter cited as James, I. The following account relies most heavily on the standard Jackson biographies by James, Bassett, Remini and Parton as noted in the Bibliography, and on Jackson's correspondence.
2 Robert V. Remini, *Andrew Jackson* (New York, 1966), 18, hereafter cited as Remini, *Jackson.*
3 James, I, 29–33.
4 *Ibid.,* 33–40.
5 *Ibid.,* 47–49.
6 Remini, *Jackson,* 27–29.
7 *Ibid.,* 30.
8 James, I, 64.
9 Remini, *Jackson,* 31.
10 James, I. 69.
11 *Ibid ,* 70
12 Gerald W. Johnson, *Andrew Jackson* (New York, 1927), 71.
13 Quoted in Remini, *Jackson,* 39.
14 James, I, 95–97; Remini, *Jackson,* 39.
15 James, I, 97–100.
16 *Ibid.,* 122–25.
17 *Ibid.,* 161–63.
18 Remini, *Jackson,* 57.
19 James, I, 169, 183–84.
20 Remini, *Jackson,* 67–72.
21 Johnson, *Jackson,* 141–42.
22 John W. Ward, *Andrew Jackson: Symbol for an Age* (New York, 1955), 4–6.
23 Ward, *Jackson,* 7–10.

II Calhoun: "Young Hercules" Emerges, 1782–1815

1 Gerald M. Capers, *John C. Calhoun, Opportunist: A Reappraisal* (Gainesville, 1960), p. 7; hereafter cited as Capers, *Calhoun.* The standard biographies of Calhoun are discussed in Chapter X. The account here leans heavily on the best recent biographies by Charles M. Wiltse, Margaret Coit and Capers.

2 *Life of John C. Calhoun* (New York, 1843), 6–7; hereafter cited as *Life Calhoun;* this volume appears to be largely autobiographical since Calhoun supplied the material for it.

3 *Ibid.*, 6; Charles M. Wiltse, *John C. Calhoun, Nationalist, 1782–1828* (Vol. I of 3 vols., Indianapolis, 1944), 32–33, hereafter cited as Wiltse, I.

4 Capers, *Calhoun,* 15.

5 Wiltse, I, 38.

6 *Ibid.,* 41.

7 *Ibid.,* 43.

8 Capers, *Calhoun,* 19.

9 *Ibid.,* 20–21.

10 Wiltse, I, 46–48.

11 Quoted in Capers, *Calhoun,* 29.

12 *Works of John C. Calhoun,* ed. by Richard K. Crallé (6 vols., New York, 1854–1857), II, 5–7, hereafter cited as Calhoun, *Works.*

13 Quoted in Wiltse, I, 59.

14 Wiltse, I, 70–72.

15 Quoted in article on Calhoun in *Dictionary of American Biography* (26 vols., New York, 1929), III, 412.

16 *Memoirs of John Quincy Adams,* ed. by Charles F. Adams (12 vols., Philadelphia, 1874–1877), V, 361, hereafter cited as Adams, *Memoirs.*

17 John W. Ward, *Andrew Jackson: Symbol for an Age* (New York, 1953).

III Jackson: Military Chieftain to President

1 Robert V. Remini, Andrew Jackson (New York, 1966), 76–77.

2 James, I, 295.

3 Andrew Jackson, *The Correspondence of Andrew Jackson,* ed. by John S. Bassett (7 vols., Washington, 1926–35), II, 342; hereafter cited as Jackson, *Corresp.*

4 *Ibid.,* 343.

5 James, I, 307.

6 James Parton, *The Presidency of Andrew Jackson,* ed. by Robert V. Remini (New York, 1967), 144; a reprint of parts of Parton's Vol. III of *Life of Jackson* (New York, 1860), hereafter cited as Parton, *Presidency.*

7 John S. Bassett, *The Life of Andrew Jackson* (2 vols., New York, 1928 ed.), I, 283, hereafter cited as Bassett, *Jackson.*

8 Jackson, *Corresp.,* II, 439.

9 *Ibid.,* II, 447; III, 2, 12.

10 Adams, *Memoirs,* IV, 76.

11 James, II, 18.

12 Parton, *Life*, II, 354.
13 James, II, 20.
14 James, II, 34.
15 Jackson, *Corresp.*, III, 140.
16 *Ibid.*
17 Bassett, *Jackson*, I, 328.
18 Jackson, *Corresp.*, III, 174.
19 *Ibid.*, 189.
20 James, I, 55.
21 Jackson, *Corresp.*, III, 210.
22 *Ibid.*, III, 216–217.
23 James, II, 68, 77; Adams, *Memoirs*, VI, 333.
24 Jackson, *Corresp.*, III, 218; James, II, 70–71.
25 James, II, 75.
26 Jackson, *Corresp.*, III, 294.
27 *Ibid.*, 355.
28 James, II, 107.
29 Jackson, *Corresp.*, III, 270.
30 Martin Van Buren, *Autobiography*, quoted in James, II, 125–127.
31 Quoted in Wiltse, I, 307–308.
32 James, II 128.
33 Jackson, *Corresp.*, III, 276.
34 *Ibid.*, 278.
35 Jackson, *Corresp.*, III, 307–308.
36 Remini, *Jackson*, 101–102.
37 Jackson, *Corresp.*, III, 396.
38 Parton, *Life*, II, 153.
39 Quoted in James, II, 169.
40 James, II, 171, 174–175; Jackson, *Corresp.*, IV, 2.

IV Calhoun: From Congress to Vice President

1 Wiltse, I. 105.
2 Calhoun, *Works*, II, 135–153.
3 *Ibid.*, 153–162.
4 *Ibid.*, 163–172.
5 *Ibid.*, 173–184.
6 *Ibid.*, 186–196.
7 *Ibid.*, 136–142.
8 *Ibid.*, 191.
9 *Ibid.*, 152.
10 *Ibid.*, 173.
11 Jackson, *Corresp.*, II, 264–72.
12 Quoted in *Dictionary of American Biography*, II, 413.
13 Calhoun, *Life*, 24–25.

14 Capers, *Calhoun,* 61–63; Leonard D. White, *The Jeffersonians: A Study in Administrative History, 1801–1829* (New York, 1951), 81–82.

15 White, *Jeffersonians,* 236–248.

16 John C. Calhoun, *Correspondence of John C. Calhoun,* ed. by J. Franklin Jameson, Annual Rept., Am. Hist. Assn. (Washington, 1900), II, 194.

17 White, *Jeffersonians,* 274.

18 Jackson, *Corresp.,* II, 281–282.

19 *Ibid.,* 291, 319, 329–331.

20 *Ibid.,* 332–3, 343, n.l.

21 Calhoun, *Corresp.,* 160–162.

22 White, *Jeffersonians,* 257.

23 *Ibid.,* 246–50.

24 Adams, *Memoirs,* IV, 36.

25 Wiltse, I, 214.

26 Adams, *Memoirs,* V, 5–12.

27 Wiltse, I, 219.

28 Margaret L. Coit, *John C. Calhoun, American Portrait* (Boston, 1950), 136.

29 William M. Meigs, *Life of John C. Calhoun* (2 vols., New York, 1917), II, 102.

30 Capers, *Calhoun,* 76.

31 Wiltse, I, 240–42.

32 Capers, *Calhoun,* 81.

33 Coit, *Calhoun,* 138.

34 Capers, *Calhoun,* 85–87.

35 Wiltse, I, 247; Capers, 81.

36 Wiltse, I, 248; Coit, 141.

37 Coit, 148; Adams, *Memoirs,* V, 315, 515.

38 Wiltse, I, 309–310.

39 Calhoun, *Life,* 30.

V   Jackson and Calhoun in Collision

1 Leonard D. White, *The Jacksonians: A Study in Administrative History, 1829–1861* (New York, 1954), 1.

2 Van Buren, *Autobiography,* 267.

3 Adams, *Memoirs,* VII, 546.

4 Henry Clay, *Works of Henry Clay,* ed. by Calvin Colton (6 vols., New York, 1857), IV, 368.

5 Jackson, *Corresp.,* III, 256.

6 Quoted in White, *Jacksonians,* 2.

7 Frederick A. Ogg, *The Reign of Andrew Jackson* (New Haven, 1919), 119.

8 Marvin Meyers, *The Jacksonian Persuasion* (New York, 1960), *passim.*

9 Wiltse, II, 11–12.

10 Parton, *Life,* III, 1–4.

11 Ogg, *Reign,* 121.

12 Jackson, *Corresp.,* III, 247, V, 338.

13 *Ibid.,* IV, 39.

14 Bassett, *Jackson,* II, 447.

15 James D. Richardson, ed., *Messages and Papers of the Presidents* (11 vs., New York, 1911), III, 1011–12, hereafter cited as *Pres. Mess.*

16 Jackson, *Corresp.* VI, 36.

17 Jackson, *Corresp.,* III, 59; Bassett, *Jackson,* II, 498.

18 James, II, 70.

19 Parton, III, 185.

20 Quoted in James, II, 203.

21 Quoted in Wiltse, II, 26.

22 *Ibid.,* II, 28–29.

23 Quoted in James, II, 205.

24 Quoted in Wiltse, II, 33.

25 Calhoun, *Corresp.,* 794.

26 Parton, *Life,* III, 187–88, 202–5.

27 Adams, *Memoirs,* VIII, 185.

28 Jackson, *Corresp.,* IV, 124, 163, 195.

29 William G. Brown, *Andrew Jackson* (New York, 1900), 127.

30 Quoted in Wiltse, II, 49.

31 *Pres. Mess.,* III, 450–62.

32 Parton, *Life,* III, 282.

33 *Pres. Mess.,* III, 1015.

34 James, II, 234–235.

35 Quoted in Ogg, *Reign,* 164–5.

36 James, II, 236; Calhoun, *Corresp.,* 271.

37 Jackson, *Corresp.,* IV, 151–55.

38 Calhoun, *Works,* VI, 362.

39 Jackson, *Corresp.,* IV, 141.

40 *Ibid.,* IV, 176–77, 202, 208.

41 Wiltse, II, 81.

42 Calhoun, *Corresp.,* 279–80.

43 Bassett, Jackson, II, 512.

44 Van Buren, *Autobiography,* 407.

45 Jackson, *Corresp.,* IV, 400.

46 Thomas Hart Benton, *Thirty Years View* (2 vols., New York, 1854–56), I, 219.

47 Wiltse, II, 130–131.

VI Nation and State in Collision

1 Frederick Jackson Turner, *The Rise of the New West* (New York, 1906), 159–160.
2 Capers, *Calhoun,* 102–104.
3 Calhoun, *Corresp.,* 249–51; Wiltse, *Calhoun,* I, 357.
4 Wiltse, *Calhoun,* I, 370–382.
5 Calhoun, *Works,* III, 52–53; *Correspondence,* 266–267.
6 Wiltse, *Calhoun,* I, 355–6, 382–3.
7 Calhoun, *Works,* VI, 1–57.
8 Capers, *Calhoun,* 117–119.
9 *Ibid.,* 120.
10 James, II, 306.
11 Jackson, *Corresp.,* IV, 430.
12 *Ibid.,* 316.
13 Calhoun, *Works,* VI, 59–123.
14 Quoted in Capers, 132, fn.
15 Wiltse, *Calhoun,* II, 114–115.
16 Jackson, *Corresp.,* IV, 462–3.
17 *Ibid.,* 429.
18 *Ibid.,* 470, 483.
19 Wiltse, II, 149–151.
20 Remini, *Jackson,* 133.
21 Jackson, *Corresp.,* IV, 241–2.
22 Remini, *Jackson,* 134; Adams, *Memoirs,* VIII, 503.
23 Bassett, *Jackson,* II, 564–5.
24 Jackson, *Corresp.,* IV, 494, 498.
25 Parton, *Presidency,* 298; Jackson, *Corresp.,* IV, 495.
26 Richardson, *Pres. Mess.,* II, 640–56.
27 James, II, 314; Ogg, *Reign,* 176.
28 James, II, 316; Parton, *Presidency,* 294.
29 Ogg, *Reign,* 176; Wiltse, II, 174; James, II, 314.
30 Jackson, *Corresp.* IV, 506.
31 Capers, *Calhoun,* 156–7.
32 Remini, *Jackson,* 135.
33 Jackson, *Corresp.,* V, 11.
34 Capers, *Calhoun,* 159; Wiltse, II, 175.
35 Wiltse, II, 178.
36 *Ibid.,* 179.
37 *Ibid.,* 184–5.
38 *Ibid.,* 185.

VII   Jackson and the Bank War

1 Glyndon G. Van Deusen, *The Jacksonian Era, 1828–1848* (New York, 1959), 63.
2 James, II, 253–55.
3 *Pres. Mess.*, II, 1025.
4 Quoted in Remini, *Jackson*, 144.
5 Jackson, *Corresp.*, V, 236.
6 Arthur M. Schlesinger, Jr., *The Age of Jackson* (Boston, 1945), 79.
7 Robert V. Remini, *Andrew Jackson and the Bank War* (New York, 1967), 69.
8 *Pres. Mess.*, II, 1091–92.
9 *Ibid.*, 1121.
10 Shlesinger, *Age*, 81 fn.
11 White, *Jacksonians*, 465–69.
12 Benton, *Thirty Years*, I, 187–205.
13 Schlesinger, *Age*, 86.
14 James, II, 291.
15 Remini, *Bank War*, 77.
16 Remini, *Bank War*, 80.
17 Jackson, *Corresp.*, IV, 449.
18 *Pres. Mess.*, II, 590.
19 Schlesinger, *Age*, 90.
20 *Pres. Mess.*, II, 1141–53.
21 Schlesinger, *Age*, 91.
22 Remini, *Jackson*, 152.
23 Remini, *Bank War*, 50.
24 *Ibid.*, 106–7.
25 Jackson, *Corresp.*, V, 109.
26 Schlesinger, *Age*, 99.
27 James, II, 348–49.
28 Adams, *Memoirs*, VIII, 346.
29 James, II, 347.
30 Schlesinger, *Age*, 101.
31 Remini, *Jackson*, 151.
32 Jackson, *Corresp.*, V, 149.
33 Schlesinger, *Age*, 106.
34 Calhoun, *Works*, II, 302–43.
35 Schlesinger, *Age*, 109.
36 Parton, *Life*, II, 549–50.
37 Schlesinger, *Age*, 109.
38 Remini, *Jackson*, 158.
39 *Ibid.*, 138–9.
40 *Ibid.*, 140.

41 Jackson, *Corresp.* V, 249.
42 Calhoun, *Life,* 53–55; Wiltse, II, 226–28.
43 *Pres. Mess.* II, 1295–1309
44 Remini, *Jackson,* 146
45 Parton, *Presidency,* 452.
46 Wiltse, II, 354–55.
47 *Ibid.,* 408.
48 White, *Jacksonians,* 38–42, 49.
49 Remini, *Jackson,* 168.

VIII Battles over Issues

1 Jackson, *Corresp.,* II, 280.
2 Calhoun, *Works,* V, 80–87.
3 Wiltse, I, 186, 250–51.
4 Remini, *Jackson,* 128.
5 Ogg, *Reign,* 214–15.
6 Schlesinger, *Age,* 184, 348.
7 *Pres. Mess.,* III, 1057, 1164.
8 *Ibid.,* IV, 1459, 1463.
9 William G. Sumner, *Andrew Jackson as a Public Man* (Boston, 1882), 380–83.
10 Calhoun, *Life,* 56.
11 Calhoun, *Corresp.,* 361–62.
12 Calhoun, Works, III, 360–75.
13 *Pres. Mess.,* III, 1032–54.
14 Jackson, *Corresp.,* IV, 138.
15 *Pres. Mess.,* III, 1052–54.
16 *Ibid.,* 1165.
17 Wiltse, II, 101–102.
18 *Ibid.,* 324–41.
19 *Ibid.,* III, 234–35.
20 *Ibid.,* 235–46.
21 Calhoun, *Works,* VI, 41.
22 *Ibid.,* I, 57.
23 Jackson, *Corresp.,* III, 249–50.
24 James, II, 79.
25 *Pres. Mess.,* III, 1087.
26 Jackson, *Corresp.,* V, 28, 72.
27 Wiltse, II, 302, 400–01.
28 *Ibid.,* III, 82–87.
29 *Ibid.,* III, 266–72.
30 White, *Jacksonians,* 21.
31 Jackson, *Corresp.,* III, 268–69.
32 *Ibid.,* 431; *Pres. Mess.,* III, 1011, 1082, 1120.
33 *Pres. Mess.,* III, 69–93.

34 White, *Jacksonians,* 38.
35 *Ibid.,* 106–110.
36 *Pres. Mess.,* III, 1011, 1035.
37 Jackson, *Corresp.,* V, 338–339.
38 *Ibid.,* VI, 63.
39 Calhoun, *Works,* II, 197–262.
40 Jackson, *Corresp.,* V, 18.
41 Herman E. Von Holst, *John C. Calhoun* (Boston, 1882), 162.
42 Calhoun, *Corresp.,* 343.
43 Calhoun, *Works,* II, 335–37.
44 Capers, *Calhoun,* 173.
45 Wiltse, II, 255–60.
46 Meigs, *Calhoun,* II, 218.
47 Coit, *Calhoun,* 270.
48 Calhoun, *Corresp.,* 347–48.
49 Calhoun, *Works,* II, 418–25, 446–65.
50 Wiltse, II, 303, 467.

IX Manifest Destiny and Conflict

1 James, II, 407.
2 Jackson, *Corresp.,* IV, 80.
3 *Ibid.,* V, 398.
4 *Ibid.,* V, 425–6.
5 *Ibid.,* V, 417.
6 Wiltse, II, 291.
7 *Pres. Mess.,* IV, 1487–88.
8 James, II, 423–27.
9 Capers, *Calhoun,* 205.
10 *Ibid.,* 206.
11 Calhoun, *Works,* VI, 239–54.
12 Capers, *Calhoun,* 208.
13 Capers, *Calhoun,* 220.
14 St. George L. Sioussat, "John Caldwell Calhoun," in *American Secretaries of State,* ed. Samuel F. Bemis (New York, 1928), V, 173.
15 Jackson, *Corresp.,* VI, 278.
16 *Ibid.,* VI, 201.
17 Remini, *Jackson,* 186.
18 Wiltse, II, 204–06.
19 Sioussat, "Calhoun," 201.
20 Calhoun, *Works,* IV, 338, 378.
21 *Ibid.,* IV, 304–425.
22 Jackson, *Corresp.,* III, 21.
23 *Ibid.,* IV, 385.
24 *Ibid.,* V, 56.

25 *Ibid.*, V, 360.
26 *Pres. Mess.*, III, 175–6.
27 White, *Jacksonians*, 519–22.
28 *Pres. Mess.*, IV, 1514–16.
29 Capers, *Calhoun*, 120.
30 Meigs, *Calhoun*, II, 201.
31 Calhoun, *Works*, III, 244, 279.
32 Calhoun, *Works*, III, 274.
33 Quoted in Capers, *Calhoun*, 184.
34 Wiltse, II, 370–73.
35 Calhoun, *Works*, IV, 339–45.
36 Wiltse, III, 353–57.
37 Calhoun, *Works*, VI, 290–313.
38 *Ibid.*, IV, 542–73.
39 *Pres. Mess.*, III, 292–308.
40 Remini, *Jackson*, 184.
41 Jackson, *Corresp.*, VI, 415.
42 Schlesinger, *Age*, 448–9.
43 Oliver Dyer, *Great Statesmen of Forty Years Ago* (New York, 1889), 171.
44 The *Disquisition* is in Calhoun, *Works*, I, 1–109; the *Discourse* in *Ibid.*, I, 111–406.

X The Verdict of History

1 James Parton, *Life of Andrew Jackson* (New York, 1859, 3 vols.), I, vii.
2 William Cobbett, *The Life of Andrew Jackson, President of the United States of America* (London, 1834), iii–vii.
3 Charles G. Sellers, Jr., "Andrew Jackson and the Historians," *Mississippi Valley Historical Review*, XLIV (March, 1958), 615–34.
4 Gerald M. Capers, *John C. Calhoun, Opportunist: A Reappraisal* (Gainesville, Fla., 1960), 255; Charles M. Wiltse, *John C. Calhoun, Nationalist, 1782–1828* (1st of a 3 vol. series, Indianapolis, 1944), 401.
5 Wiltse, I, 234–5.
6 *Ibid.*, 301.
7 Charles M. Wiltse, *John C. Calhoun, Nullifier, 1829–1839* (Indianapolis, 1949), 234–5.
8 Wiltse, I, 396–7.

CHRONOLOGY

	prosecution; Jackson campaigns against Indians in Southeast.
1813	Jackson gains name Old Hickory in campaign march, fights tavern brawl with Benton brothers in Nashville.
1815	Jackson defeats British in Battle of New Orleans Jan. 8, wins national fame as "Hero of New Orleans."
1816–17	Calhoun pushes nationalist program in Congress: Bank, protective tariff, internal improvement, national defense.
1817–25	Calhoun is Secretary of War.
1818	Jackson leads Seminole invasion of Florida, created international incident that leads to internal debate in Monroe's cabinet and to drafting of.
1819	Adams-Onis Treaty transferring Florida to U.S.
1820	Missouri Compromise legislation bars slavery in federal territories north of 36°30′ latitude.
1821	Jackson Governor of Florida, resigns after few months.
1821	Calhoun announces candidacy for President.
1822	Jackson nominated for President by Tennessee legislature.
1823	Jackson elected to U.S. Senate; Monroe Doctrine announced stating Europe no longer to colonize or interfere in domestic politics of west hemisphere nations.
1824	Calhoun withdraws from Presidential race, leaving 4-way contest of Adams, Clay, Crawford, Jackson.
1825	Adams chosen President by House over Jackson, leading to "corrupt bargain" charge by Jackson men; Calhoun in as Vice President, takes oath from Senator Jackson. Jackson resigns from U.S. Senate.
1826	Calhoun moves to support Jackson for President.
1827	Calhoun casts tie-breaking vote, defeats high tariff.
1828	Jackson elected President, Calhoun reelected Vice President. Congress adopts high "tariff of abominations"; Calhoun writes South Carolina's "Exposition and Protest" against tariff.
1829	Jackson inaugurated President; Peggy Eaton affair splits his cabinet.
1830	Webster delivers in Senate his reply to Hayne on state rights. Jackson delivers toast to "Our Federal Union", April 13.
1830	Jackson vetoes Maysville Road bill, approves Indian removal.
1831	Jackson enraged by Crawford letter, demands explanation from Calhoun, cuts off relations with Calhoun.

1832   Calhoun resigns as Vice President; South Carolina issues ordinance of nullification of federal tariff; Jackson issues Proclamation Dec. 10 denouncing nullification. Jackson vetoes Bank recharter bill.

1833   Calhoun as Senator defends South Carolina's course, opposes Force Bill but supports compromise tariff law. Jackson orders Secretary of Treasury to remove deposits from Bank.

1834   Senate censures Jackson for removal of deposits. Jackson sends "Protest" on Senate's censure. Jackson announces final payment of U.S. national debt.

1835   Jackson escapes assassination attempt on his life.

1836   Abolition drives raise questions on use of mails and petitions to Congress; Jackson and Calhoun would restrict mails for abolitionist propaganda. Jackson issues Specie Circular on land purchases.

1837   Calhoun gets Senate adoption of his resolutions on nature of the Union and protection of slavery in states. Jackson leaving office, issues "Farewell Address" Panic of 1837; Calhoun supports Van Buren's Independent Treasury plan to separate government from banks.

1843   Calhoun seeks support to win Democratic nomination for President.

1844–45   Calhoun as Tyler's Secretary of State drafts treaty to annex Texas, defeated in Senate; supports annexation by joint resolution of Congress.

1845   Calhoun opposes war with Mexico, aroused by Wilmot Proviso to renewed defense of slavery and South's rights in Western territories. Jackson dies at Hermitage in June.

1849   Calhoun writes "Address of Southern Delegates in Congress" calling for united South to defend its rights.

1850   Calhoun makes final speech in Senate opposing compromise measures, dies in March.

A Selective Bibliography

Adams, John Quincy. *Memoirs, Comprising Portions of His Diary from 1795 to 1848.* 12 vols. Ed. by Charles Francis Adams. Philadelphia: Lippincott, 1875–77.

Bassett, John S. *The Life of Andrew Jackson.* 2 vols. Garden City: Doubleday, 1928.

Bates, Mary. *The Private Life of John C. Calhoun.* Charleston: Walker, Richards, 1852.

Benson, Lee. *The Concept of Jacksonian Democracy: New York as a Test.* Princeton: University Press, 1961.

Benton, Thomas Hart. *Thirty Years View . . . from 1820 to 1850.* 2 vols. New York: Appleton, 1854–56.

Black, Jeremiah S. *Eulogy on the Life of Jackson.* Chambersburg, Pa.: (n.p.), 1845.

Blau, Joseph L., ed. *Social Theories of Jacksonian Democracy.* New York: Liberal Arts Press, 1947.

Bowers, Claude G. *Party Battles of the Jackson Period.* Boston: Houghton Mifflin, 1922.

Brown, William G. *Andrew Jackson.* Boston: Houghton Mifflin, 1900.

Buell, Augustus C. *A History of Andrew Jackson.* 2 vols. New York: Scribners, 1904.

Calhoun, John C. "Correspondence of John C. Calhoun" in *Annual Report,* American Historical Association. Washington: American Historical Association, 1900.

——— *Life of John C. Calhoun.* New York: Harper, 1843.

——— *Correspondence between Andrew Jackson and John C. Calhoun . . . on the Subject . . . of the Seminole War.* Washington: Green, 1831.

——— *Papers of John C. Calhoun.* Ed. by Robert L. Merriwether, et al. 6 vols. to date. Columbia: University of South Carolina Press, 1959—.

——— *Works of John C. Calhoun.* Ed by Richard K. Cralle. 6 vols. New York: (n.p.), 1854–57.

———— "Correspondence . . . John C. Calhoun," in *Annual Report,* American Historical Association. Washington: American Historical Association, 1929.

Capers, Gerald M. *John C. Calhoun, Opportunist: A Reappraisal.* Gainesville: University of Florida Press, 1964.

Catterall, Ralph C. H. *The Second Bank of the United States.* Chicago: University of Chicago Press, 1903.

Cave, Alfred A., *Jacksonian Democracy and the Historians.* Gainesville: University of Florida Press, 1964.

Clay, Henry. *The Life, Correspondence and Speeches of Henry Clay.* 6 vols. Ed. by Calvin Colton. New York: A. S. Barnes, 1857.

Cobbett, William. *Life of Andrew Jackson.* London: Mills, Jewett, 1834.

Coit, Margaret L. *John C. Calhoun: American Portrait.* Boston: Houghton Mifflin, 1950.

Dyer, Oliver. *Great Senators of Forty Years Ago.* New York: Bonner, 1889.

Eaton, John H. *Life of Andrew Jackson.* New York: Bonner, 1824.

Fish, Carl R. *The Civil Service and the Patronage.* New York: Longmans, Green, 1905.

Goodwin, Philo A. *Andrew Jackson.* Hartford: (n.p.), 1832.

Grund, Francis J. *Aristocracy in America.* London: Bentley, 1839.

Hammond, Bray. *Banks and Politics in America From the Revolution to the Civil War.* Princeton: Princeton University Press, 1957.

Hollis, M. C. *The American Heresy.* London: Sheed & Ward, 1927.

Hugins, Walter. *Jacksonian Democracy and the Working Class.* Stanford: Stanford University Press, 1967.

Hunt, Gaillard. *John C. Calhoun.* Philadelphia: Jacobs, 1908.

Jackson, Andrew. *Correspondence of Andrew Jackson.* 7 vols. Ed. by John S. Bassett. Washington: Carnegie Institution, 1926–35.

James, Marquis. *Andrew Jackson, the Border Captain.* Indianapolis: Bobbs-Merrill, 1933.

———— *Andrew Jackson, Portrait of a President.* Indianapolis: Bobbs-Merrill, 1937.

Jenkins, John S. *Life of John C. Calhoun*. Auburn, N.Y.: Alden, 1850.

———— *Life of Andrew Jackson*. Auburn, N.Y.: Derby, 1847.

Johnson, Gerald W. *Andrew Jackson*. New York: Minton, Balch, 1927.

Lindsey, David. *Andrew Jackson and Henry Clay: Democracy and Enterprise in America*. Cleveland: Allen, 1962.

MacCormick, Richard P. *The Second American Party System: Party Formation in the Jackson Era*. Chapel Hill: University of North Carolina Press, 1966.

MacDonald, William. *Jacksonian Democracy*. New York: Harper, 1906.

Meigs, William M. *The Life of John Caldwell Calhoun*. 2 vols. New York: Neale, 1917.

Meyers, Marvin. *The Jacksonian Persuasion*. Stanford: Stanford University Press, 1957.

Ogg, Frederick A. *The Reign of Andrew Jackson*. New Haven: Yale University Press, 1919.

Parton, James. *Life of Andrew Jackson*. 3 vols. New York: Mason, 1860.

Peck, Charles H. *The Jacksonian Epoch*. New York: Harper, 1899.

Pessen, Edward. *Jacksonian America: Society, Personality and Politics*. Homewood, Ill.: Dorsey Press, 1969.

Pinckney, Gustavus M. *Life of John C. Calhoun*. Charleston: Walker, Evans, 1903.

Remini, Robert V., ed., *The Age of Jackson*. New York: Harper, 1972.

———— *Andrew Jackson*. New York: Twayne, 1966.

———— *Andrew Jackson and the Bank War*. New York: Norton, 1967.

Richardson, James D., ed. *Messages and Papers of the Presidents, 1789–1910*. New York: Bureau of National Literature, 1911.

Rozwenc, Edwin C., ed. *Ideology and Power in the Age of Jackson*. Garden City: Doubleday, 1964.

———— ed. *The Meaning of Jacksonian Democracy*. Boston: Heath, 1963.

Schlesinger, Arthur M., Jr., *The Age of Jackson*. Boston: Little, Brown, 1945.

Sellers, Charles G., Jr. "Andrew Jackson versus the Historians," *Mississippi Valley Historical Review,* XLIV (March, 1958), 615–634.

—— *Jacksonian Democracy.* Washington: American Historical Association, 1958.

Sioussat, St. George L. "John C. Calhoun," in Vol. V, *American Secretaries of State.* Ed. by Samuel F. Bemis. New York: Knopf, 1928.

Styron, Arthur. *The Cast-Iron Man: John C. Calhoun and American Democracy.* New York: Longmans, Green, 1935.

Sumner, William G. *Andrew Jackson as a Public Man.* Boston: Houghton, Mifflin, 1882.

Temin, Peter. *The Jacksonian Economy.* New York, Norton, 1969.

Thomas, John L., ed. *John C. Calhoun: A Profile.* New York: Hill and Wang, 1968.

Turner, Frederick Jackson. *The Rise of the New West.* New York: Harper, 1906.

Van Buren, Martin. "Autobiography of Martin VanBuren," ed. by John C. Fitzpatrick, in *Annual Report,* American Historical Association, vol. 2. Washington: American Historical Association, 1918.

Van Deusen, Glyndon G. *The Jacksonian Era.* New York: Harper, 1959.

Von Holst, Hermann E. *John C. Calhoun.* Boston: Houghton Mifflin, 1882.

Ward, John W. *Andrew Jackson, Symbol for an Age.* New York: Oxford, 1953.

Wiltse, Charles M. *John C. Calhoun, Nationalist, 1782–1828.* Indianapolis: Bobbs-Merrill, 1944.

—— *John C. Calhoun, Nullifier, 1829–1839.* Indianapolis: Bobbs-Merrill, 1949.

—— *John C. Calhoun, Sectionalist, 1839–1850.* Indianapolis: Bobbs-Merrill, 1951.

White, Leonard D., *The Jacksonians: A Study in Administrative History.* New York: Macmillan, 1954.

Index